D1232220

# 2 YEARS,

# 2 SHELLBACKS

*Paula Sellens*

PAULA SELLENS

&

CHARLES SELLENS

*Glad to
meet you!*

*Charlie Sellens*

# Contents

# *Family And Friends'* FOREWORDS

**We met Paula and Charlie** Sellens when they first came to Auki. Their book, *2 Years, 2 Shellbacks,* merges their unique lives with Solomon Islands' history and culture. They are not always politically correct when documenting their exchanges among Solomon Islanders, other expatriates, and themselves. We are happy that the Sellens got to live in Japan for thirteen years after their Peace Corps Service. **Yasuo and Masako Isozaki, Yokohama, Japan**

**Peace Corps took eight** very different volunteers and placed them in five very different locations in the Solomon Islands. All of us made it through our entire two years of service. Due to our common struggles, we remained extremely close and respectful of the others' strengths, weaknesses, and completely different experiences throughout our tours. We will always have that bond. *2 Years, 2 Shellbacks* accurately records those friendships. **Matthew Ottinger, Middlebury, Vermont**

**I kept up on my parents'** Peace Corps adventures with letters and phone calls. Their book: *2 Years, 2 Shellbacks* provides concise details that I would not have learned had they had not made this record. I have been in ninety-five countries in my career as Army Ranger, Iraqi Private Contractor, Head of Security for the President of the World Bank, and Senior Security Advisor for Global Guardian. Their unique experiences are equal to mine in every way. **Charlie Sellens, Woodbridge, Virginia**

**We met Paula and Charlie** Sellens during our Peace Corps training in Ugheli, Western Province. Their book, *2 Years, 2 Shellbacks,* accurately conveys the rich and diverse cultures, languages, and customs that characterized the Solomon villages. The volume provides insightful, new perspectives about Peace Corps lives in developing countries. The book brought back a lot of memories. We enjoyed reading it. **Monique Incitti Hartman and Paul Hartman, Colorado Springs, Colorado**

**When my sister, Paula** Sellens, and I were saying goodbye, we pledged to not get haircuts until we met again. We kept our promises. I enjoyed learning facts and details about Paula's and Charlie's exciting Peace Corps service. My husband, Mike, and I are now living own own adventures. We have lived in the Caribbean for eleven years. Many sights, adventures and difficulties that Paula and Charlie endured are similar to what Mike and I experience. **Mary Eddy, Providenciales, Turks and Caicos**

**I was very young** when Paula and Charles Sellens started coming to Buma Village. I didn't know why they were there, but I knew Grandfather Simon Buarafi was happy when them came. Their book, *2 Years, 2 Shellbacks,* taught me to understand what they were doing to help my people. Their unique volume explains how they adapted to, and accepted, Solomon Islands' rich history and culture. **Patricia Maelado, Honiara, Solomon Islands**

**My parents** left the U.S. 1990. I didn't see them again for over two years. We exchanged telephone calls and letters, so I had some idea of what they were doing. Their book provided details about their exciting lives. I'm glad that I got to live in Japan for two years during the thirteen years they were there. I'm sure I'll be an active character in an upcoming book about legal issues confronting them while they were overseas. **Jason Sellens, Russell, Kansas**

**A full account** of a Peace Corps mission in the Solomon Islands in the early 1990s. Written with candour, warmth, and humour, the richness of all Charlie and Paula's relationships shines through from negotiating with local administrators, teaching English to Japanese nurses, advising on gardening techniques in villages, to canasta with the clergy, and a haircutting service for expats. **Dr. Paul and Dr. Teresa van den Bosch, Freetown, Sierra Leone**

**Paula's and Charlie's book** brought back long forgotten memories of our time in the Solomons. In a country where distractions like media, nightlife, and shopping were not available, socializing was the most important part of the society. Paula and Charlie reached out to the local people and clans to document their remembered history and genealogy. The Sellens came visiting regularly. We would snorkel on the reef outside my house and talk story. Charlie told about the incredibly detailed clan lineage he was documenting. The people we worked with, and the people of the Solomons, were the best people I have spent time with. **Tom Shearer, Rockport, Texas**

**My earliest memories** of my grandparents are when they vacationed from Japan to Kansas. I knew they had interesting lives in the Peace Corps, but I didn't know any details until I read their book. They tell about their lives in an easily read, humorous way. I appreciate the effort they made to make a record of those unique years of their lives. **Jacob Sellens, Russell, Kansas**

# *Paula Sellens'*
# FOREWORD

When I was a child and on into the years when I was a young adult, I imagined what it would be like to live on an exotic island. My imagined sunsets were always deep, passionate, and rich. My days were filled with the sweet-smelling aroma of island spices hanging in the air. In 1990, my dreams came to fruition. Charles and I had talked about joining the Peace Corps for twenty-three years. Our sons were grown and living on their own, so it was time to walk the talk.

We were initially assigned to an African country teaching in an Agricultural college. Charles had a degree in agriculture, and we had spent eighteen years farming in Russell County, Kansas. One summer day, we received a phone call from Peace Corp with "good" and "bad" news. The good news was that we were being assigned to the Solomon Islands as Community Development Workers. The bad news was we had to leave in only four weeks.

What a stroke of luck! I was finally going to have the opportunity to live the island life I had always dreamed about! We gave our employers two weeks' notice, sold our belongings at an auction, packed, said our goodbyes, and left for Hawaii.

Staging in Hawaii was a good transition to my dreams of a romantic, island life. But when we arrived in the Solomon Islands, the scene was suddenly warped. We would be living on a beautiful island, but the disadvantages were overwhelming. The realities of life were harsh. For the next two years, we would be encircled by poverty, flying cockroaches the size of small birds, squat toilets, standpipe showers, and shark worshippers. Our Solomon Islands' hosts were only one or two generations away from head hunting and cannibalism.

Our "walkabout" to our assignment island, Malaita, was a shock. Although we had reservations at the "hotel", our room had been given to the tax collector who had shown up unexpectedly. Our only option was to spend the night on the dining room floor of the hotel. We had to share our sleeping arrangements with a couple from Italy who had the same misfortune. Two chairs with a sheet hung over it separated us from our roommates. I was afraid to go to sleep for fear I would wake our neighbors with my snoring! I was disillusioned and wanted to go home.

Over time, I settled into the realities of our new island life. I quickly and happily adjusted to living on Malaita. The unique customs, strange food, new friends, and living without money all began to seem normal. I accepted the Solomon Islands' people and their way of doing things. They accepted me and understood that my goals for changes in their lives were driven by a sincere desire to help them.

Two years on the Island of Malaita in the Solomon Islands were two of the best years of my life. I matured in unimaginable ways. Charlie and I achieved goals against all odds and became one with the "Islanders" during that time. I realized that life is what you make it. It takes more than dreaming to sculpt a life worth living no matter where you are and no matter the circumstances. Thank you, Charlie, for sharing my two years of learning, excitement, and happiness.

# *Charles Sellens'*
# FOREWORD

*2 Years, 2 Shellbacks* is a description of events during the time Paula and I served as Peace Corps Volunteers in the Solomon Islands. The accounts of facts and happenings are arranged in chronological order. Equal weight is given to historical events, important events, not so important events, international events, national events, and local events.

When Paula and I were in Hawaii for staging, we were encouraged to keep diaries. We were advised that we might want to write books sometime in the future and our diaries would be useful. I didn't keep a diary. Fortunately, Paula did. Paula and I discussed each writing a book seen from our individual perspective. In the end, we decided to combine our individual writings into one book, coauthored by both. My goal became documenting the events that occurred, seen from my perspective, while incorporating Paula's perspectives as described in her diary.

Paula's diary included the details that are prevalent throughout the book. What we had for dinner, who came to a party, who won canasta games are details she recorded and details that are included. Many quotes attributed to her were taken directly from diary entries. In addition, I had the letters I wrote to my mother and letters Paula wrote to her parents.

Most of the conversations recorded in our book with Solomon Islanders were in Pisin. When a Solomon Islander spoke English, I noted that and wrote in grammatically correct sentences. When a Solomon Islander spoke Pisin, I wrote in an abbreviated style. When I record my own conversations, even though spoken in Pisin, I used grammatically correct sentences to make it easier to understand.

The chapters on Laulasi shark callers, pagan Begau, pagan Kwara'ae, and Kafo'elia Village were rewritten from articles that I produced at the times of their occurrence. I submitted each of them for publication in Kansas newspapers. Many were reprinted in other newspapers. In addition to Paula's diary, our letters, and my articles, we had scores of pictures.

Other parts of our book come from our memories, our Peace Corps descriptions of service, and Larry Christiansen's report on his V.O.C.A. assignment. I also relied on notes that I took and copies that I made during my preparation for service, study in the Solomon Islands National Library, and study in Turnbull National Library in New Zealand.

A positive issue that I had to deal with was having too much information. There are incidents that I write about once or twice that happened many times. I had many discussions about the U.S. putting a man on the moon. I had discussions with many young Solomon men about the U.S. Army. There were several times when village men joked about their grandfathers killing and eating me. I saw young men chewing betel nut and giving it to old men or children several times.

I used my assumed sociological lenses to record the rich and diverse cultures, languages, and customs that characterised Solomon people. I recognize that many of my contributions to the book are not politically correct. I made little effort to vet what I was told. What I heard, is what I repeated. What I saw, felt, and believed is what I wrote.

Some names of some people and villages may not be spelled correctly. Unfortunately, I forgot the last names of some people I write about. Paula and I often remembered things differently. Our memory differences were always trumped by her diary entries. Her diary was law.

Many people provided corrections and additions to our book. Foremost among them are: Dr. Paul and Dr. Teresa van den Bosch, Dr. Graham and Sheila MacBride-Stewart, Bill Wise, Colin and Alison Cameron, Paul Hartman, Monique Incitti Hartman, Rick Treleaven, Matt Ottinger, Haruko "Sunny" Nishikawa, Father Jon Volkers, and Patricia Maelado.

Kelley Marshall provided valuable editing services. To all of these contributors, Paula and I extend our grateful thanks. For errors and omissions, I take full responsibility. I am happy that I made many friends. If some people whom I met might think of me as less than a friend, I take solace in Winston Churchill's dismissal of enemies made. "You have enemies?" He asked. "Good. That means you've stood up for something, sometime in your life."

# CHAPTER 1

# *Application*

"I am Tamiyasu," a young man said, as he greeted us at the wide, double doors of Komagane Training Institute (K.T.I.). "Welcome to Komagane."

My wife, Paula, and I introduced ourselves. We followed Mr. Tamiyasu down a wide hall past uniformed guards. He opened the door to a spacious room that contained computers, a television, and several comfortable chairs and sofas. "Sit here, the director will come soon," Mr. Tamiyasu said, as he politely pointed to a comfortable appearing couch. "I'll be right back."

He smiled as he left the room, closing the door behind him. Mr. Tamiyasu was young, tall, and had an athletic appearance. He was dressed in a dark-blue suit, white shirt, and conservative red tie. Paula and I seated ourselves on a new leather couch. We were in the instructors' room at K.T.I. in Komagane, Japan. I was there for an interview with expectations of being hired as an English as a Second Language Instructor.

Japan Overseas Cooperation Volunteers (J.O.C.V.) Solomon Islands Director Yasuo Kasai had interviewed me while I was a Peace Corps Volunteer (P.C.V.) in the Solomon Islands. Not only had I been tentatively accepted, but I had been asked for my preference for teaching in either Komagane or Tokyo. I was the first English instructor to be hired outside Japan and I was ecstatic. My decade's long hopes and dreams were being fulfilled. I pinched myself forcefully. It hurt, but it assured me that I was not dreaming.

Paula and I exchanged satisfied looks. We glanced around the room and admired a calendar featuring Japanese art. I couldn't read the kanji, but it was August 12, 1992. Paula and I had just completed two years of Peace Corps service in the Solomon Islands.

Mr. Tamiyasu soon returned, escorting a middle-aged man who was obviously the director. The director was dressed in a dark-brown suit, white shirt, and striped tie. Our trip from the Solomon Islands to Japan included a stop in Hawaii. I felt gratified that I had bought a new suit, white shirt, and tie while in Hawaii. I would have been embarrassed had I been wearing the simple clothes that I had worn for two years in the Solomon Islands.

We stood, but the customary Japanese bows were not exchanged. Instead, the American custom of shaking hands was observed. "This is Mr. Nagakura, Takashi," Mr. Tamiyasu said. "Nagakura San is the K.T.I. director."

Nagakura San smiled and motioned for us to sit. He lowered himself into an overstuffed, leather covered chair that was placed directly across from us. Tamiyasu San sat in another overstuffed chair in an observation position. Nagakura San didn't have my resume' or a file of any sort. He conducted my interview in a conversational tone. "How did you like the Solomon Islands?" he asked, in excellent English.

"It's primitive, but it was very interesting," I replied. "We made many friends there. We would like to go back someday."

"I heard that you met some Japanese there."

"Oh yes. There were six J.O.C.V.s in Auki. We also had a joint nutrition project with some J.O.C.V. nurses. We were very happy to get to work with them. There were also some J.O.C.V.s that came to our house to study English. They taught us to speak a little Japanese. We were also good friends with Yasuo and Masako Isozaki."

"And how did you meet Mr. Kasai?"

"Paula and I wanted to find jobs in Japan when we finished our Peace Corps service. When we asked Yasuo and Masako to help us, they introduced us to Mr. Kasai. Mr. Kasai was really enthusiastic about making friends for Japan."

I went on to tell Nagakura San that Paula and I met Mr. Kasai again when he came to Malaita Island. He had come to see the sawmill/reforestation project that we had in Buma Village. I told Nagakura San that I met Mr. Kasai again when there was a group meeting with J.O.C.V.s and P.C.V.s.

Staff members were having discussions about organizing a joint project with J.O.C.V.s and P.C.V.s. The project being considered was teaching math in Auki Primary School. The last time I saw Mr. Kasai was at the Honiara Hotel when he interviewed me for a possible position at K.T.I.

Nagakura San asked us about our lives and families in the United States. He told us that the J.O.C.V.s that we knew in Auki had been trained at K.T.I. At an appropriate time, he paused, stood, and smiled. Paula and I also stood. We waited quietly and expectantly. "You can have a job here," Nagakura San said. "Tamiyasu San will get some paperwork started tomorrow."

It was late in the afternoon. Tamiyasu San escorted us to a guest house on the training complex where we were to spend the night. When we were alone, we reminisced on how we came to be in Komagane, Japan.

Four years. It was four years earlier. Paula and I had been married for twenty-one years. Our two sons, Charles Shane and Jason Daniel, had left Kansas for jobs in California. We were ready for changes in our lives. Perhaps we were simultaneously experiencing mid-life crises. We had dreamed of joining the Peace Corps for years. Ah, but it could only be when our children were grown. Now, our sons were adults and had left home to live in California.

We requested Peace Corps applications and packets soon arrived by mail. There was information included on Peace Corps history. The Sunday after the information arrived, I sat at our kitchen table in Augusta, Kansas and began reading. I learned that more than 150,000 volunteers had served in 130 countries since its founding. Applicants had to be at least eighteen years old. There were no upper age limits. Teaching and agriculture were the fields to which most volunteers were assigned.

Because of the substantial number of applicants for each opening, only one applicant out of seven was accepted. Forty percent of accepted volunteers didn't complete their two-year commitment. The average waiting period before acceptance and training was eight months. My mind drifted away. I day-dreamed about living on an exotic island in the Caribbean or South Pacific. "Are you ready to start working on your application?" Paula asked, snapping me back to reality.

"Yes," I answered. "I'm doing research. I'll start filling out the application forms tomorrow."

"Well, I've already started mine. You look like you are just sitting there dreaming about being in Lala Land."

The very next Sunday, I did begin the process of completing my own application. Name, Date of Birth, Place of Birth, all questions that are typically on applications. Height. I smiled. Discussions of height always amuse me. American men seem to feel obligated to be six feet tall. I am personally five feet, eleven and three-fourths inches tall. I have often met men who are at least two inches shorter than me claiming to be six feet tall.

Unfortunately, the space where I had to record my height was rather small. Perhaps too tiny to write 5'-11 ¾". I was perplexed. What should I do? I certainly wasn't going to write 5'-11" in that space. I was much taller! Suddenly, I had a stroke of genius and checked my Kansas driver's license. A neat 6' was recorded, likely via alteration by a state employee after I had reported my true height. I scribed a neat 6' in the Peace Corps application space for height.

Now, the next question. Weight. I smiled again. Height is to men as weight is to women. Men are consistently truthful about their weight and women are consistently truthful about their height. Conversely, men usually lie about their height and women usually lie about their weight. I thought that I weighed about 250 pounds, but I worried that I might get writer's cramp when I began to make the entry.

Two hundred, fifty pounds is one-eight ton, but it's mostly because I have big bones and a lot of muscles. I thought deeply about how to solve this dilemma. This was good training as I knew that I would be confronted with problems in the Peace Corps that would be nearly as difficult to solve. Suddenly, I had an inspiration! I checked my driver's licenses again and learned that I weighed only 215. Two hundred, fifteen pounds it was then. I made the entry.

Now, for the next question. "Why do you want to join the Peace Corps?"

That was a thought-provoking question. There was a big space for the answer. I had thought about joining the corps ever since newly elected President John Kennedy had challenged young Americans to serve their own country by living and working in developing countries. But when I graduated from high school, I joined the Army and was soon assigned to a post in Oberammergau, Germany.

When I had completed my three-year army commitment, I was reluctant to commit to two more years of service. Then came marriage and two sons. Peace Corps service was out of the question. Regardless, Paula and I had often talked about joining the Peace Corps when our children were grown. We had talked the talk. It was time to walk the walk.

Images of young, beautiful, scantily clad maidens, dancing gracefully in the moonlight popped into my mind. I quickly rejected identifying these images as a reason for wanting to join. I considered writing that I wanted to join knowing that I would be assigned to a country far from the United States, thus our sons couldn't move back home. After careful reflection, I rejected documenting that as a reason. I was concerned that some stuffy, childless reviewer wouldn't appreciate, or even understand, my advanced parenting skills.

It was obvious that it wasn't for financial reasons because I would be a volunteer. The truth was that I didn't really want to join the Peace Corps. I wanted a high-paying, prestigious, international position. Unfortunately, I couldn't get one. I had applied for several international positions on previous occasions, but I was never hired. I knew when

I applied that I wasn't likely to be accepted because the qualifications always demanded three or four-years overseas experience.

However, there were many quite valid reasons that prompted me to want to join. Peace Corps service might provide an opportunity to travel south of the equator, so I could claim shellback status and feel superior to pollywogs. I still might get to see young, beautiful, scantily clad maidens dancing in the moonlight. If I were south of the equator, I would personally learn if water draining from a sink or bath-tub whirled counter clock-wise or clock-wise.

Perhaps I could find some previously unknown tribal medicines and bring them back for the benefit of humanity and make millions of dollars for myself. I could have exciting adventures and write a book about them that would be made into a movie making me more millions. Peace Corps service might lead to exciting, overseas positions. Jobs in the U.S. State Department or U.S. Foreign Service would be a goal. I might even be able to get an international job where I did little work for high pay.

Upon deep reflection, I became concerned that these reasons might provide justification for reviewers to think that I was driven by trivial pursuits. I finally wrote that my motivation was tri-faceted. "I want to join the Peace Corps for humanistic reasons," I wrote. "I want to help deserving people in developing countries who are not as fortunate as I am. I want to join to serve the U.S., driven by a patriotic sense of duty to country. Finally, I want to join for adventure, to fill my life with excitement."

More questions about job experience, health, current involvement in litigation, education, and more. There is more vetting for Peace Corps applicants than there is for candidates for president of the United States. Health? Yes, I was very healthy! Six feet tall! Two hundred, fifteen pounds of solid muscle! And I had my driver's license and Peace Crops application to prove it!

Our application processes required us to each have twelve people send letters of recommendation directly to Peace Corps in Chicago for review. We contacted our people and asked them to mail the recommendations. We mailed our applications and went into waiting mode with expectations of not hearing anything for months.

Surprisingly, it was only four weeks when we received a telephone call from the Peace Corps office in Kansas City. "Sellens residence," I said, when I answered the phone.

"Hello," a male voice said. "I'm a Peace Corps recruiter calling from Kansas City. I have reviewed your applications and letters of recommendation. I would like to continue the selection process with an initial interview. Could you and Paula come in sometime soon for interviews?"

"I'm sure we can. When would you like us to come?"

Our conversation continued until a date and time were agreed upon. We were in the Kansas City Peace Corps office at the appointed time. Our recruiter was honest and frank. He didn't attempt to glorify Peace Corps service. He told us about the hardships we could expect. He told us that we would likely be confronted with poor food, strange diseases, and unknown customs that we would be expected to observe.

He showed us a short movie clip that had been taken by a Peace Corps Volunteer in an African village. As our recruiter prepared the clip, I thought he would likely show us young, beautiful, scantily clad maidens dancing gracefully in the moonlight. I expected this because he needed to make up for his honest and frank description of the difficult conditions expected in the Peace Corps.

In the movie clip, several scenes in a primitive African village were shown. Finally, there was a scene in which a young, African man was running toward the camera that was positioned behind a small, stagnant pool of water. The man was thin, almost emaciated. He needed a good bath. He was totally naked.

His long, slender arms and legs were covered with open sores and scabs. He ran in an awkward, side-to-side, loping gait. His large penis swung powerfully, pendulum like, as he neared his goal. When he reached the pool of dirty water, he threw himself to the ground and drank deeply from the filthy liquid.

Images of young, beautiful, scantily clad maidens dancing gracefully in the moon-light, fled my mind. Well, unknown customs that we would be expected to observe be damned! If I were assigned to a like village, I wouldn't be running around naked and partaking in foul water! I felt confident that Paula was neither overly impressed with young, naked, black men with large penises nor shocked to learn of their existence.

"You might be assigned to a really primitive village like the one in the movie clip," our recruiter advised us.

"We knew that was a possibility when we applied," Paula answered.

"Living in a village like that would give us an opportunity to share our own good fortune," I said, adding the accepted Peace Corps platitudes. "I'm sure that we'll learn much more than we'll ever be able to teach them."

"I'm certainly going to recommend your selection," our recruiter continued. "You have real work experience and recognizable maturity. So many of the applicants that I interview are young. They often bring credentials limited to a college degree and a Red Cross first aid certificate."

The next step was waiting for the results of the second screening in Chicago. If we were acceptable to the reviewers in the Chicago office, our applications would be sent on to Washington D.C. for final consideration. We waited patiently for two months then we waited impatiently for two more months. I eventually decided that the best course of action was to call the Chicago office. "Peace Corps, Chicago," was the cheerful answer.

"Hello, I'm Charlie Sellens from Augusta, Kansas," I said. "My wife, Paula, and I applied to be volunteers several months ago. I'm calling to learn of our status."

"Thank you, Charles," was the reply, still cheerful. "I'll transfer you to records."

I waited some minutes, then a new cheerful voice came. "Hello, this is Ashley," a young woman said. "How may I help you?"

"Hello, I'm Charlie Sellens from Augusta, Kansas," I answered. "My wife and I applied to be volunteers several months ago. We passed our initial screening in Kansas City about four months ago. I'm calling to learn of our status."

"I'll check," Ashley said. "Can you hold?"

"Of course," I answered.

I waited patiently for what seemed like an hour. I'm confident that it was over a minute. I then waited impatiently for another minute. I was rewarded with the privilege of talking to a new screener. "Hello," a man said. "I'm Bruce. How may I help you?"

"Hello, Bruce. I'm Charlie Sellens from Augusta, Kansas," I said. "My wife, Paula, and I applied to be volunteers several months ago. We passed our initial screening in Kansas City about four or five months ago. Our recruiter told us that he would forward our applications to Chicago for a second screening. We haven't heard anything. I'm call-ing to see what is happening."

"How do you spell your last name?"

5

"S E L L E N S."

"And that's Charles and Paula, right?" Bruce asked.

"Yes, Charles and Paula Sellens," I answered.

"I'll check. Can you hold?"

"Yes, certainly."

I waited for what was an annoying amount of time. However, I was rewarded with Bruce returning with news and a pertinent question. "Your applications are in the inactive file," he informed me. "Why are they in the inactive file?"

I bit my tongue until it hurt. I bit it a little bit more. It hurt a lot, but it did give me time to understand the situation. The Peace Corps deliberately creates frustrating situations for applicants as part of the screening process. They only pretend to be incompetent to learn who is motivated enough to keep their applications moving through the system. Screeners cleverly know that P.C.V.s would live in less developed countries where they would be constantly confronted with exasperating, cultural inefficiencies.

I bit my tongue again, hoping my voice wouldn't quiver when I spoke. That made my tongue hurt even more. "I really can't understand why our applications are in the inactive file," I said, over my quivering voice. "We're well qualified and willing to serve. I would appreciate it if you would take them out of the inactive file and give them fair consideration."


That was nearly three years before. We were eventually accepted by the Peace Corps. That was the beginning of the odyssey that resulted in us being in Japan. We sold all our property then spent a week in Hawaii for orientation. We spent two months in training then completed two years' service in the Solomon Islands as community development workers.

I thought back to the goals that had prompted me to apply. I had achieved most of these goals. I traveled south of the equator, so I could claim shellback status and feel superior to pollywogs. I saw many scantily clad women in primitive villages. Some of the women danced and some of them were young and beautiful.

I personally saw water whirling clock-wise as it drained from a sink. Importantly, I learned that that water can whirl clock-wise and counter-clock-wise in both the northern and southern hemispheres. In both hemispheres, the Coriolis force is simply too weak to affect small qualities of water. My patriotic sense of duty to country had been fulfilled. I am as proud of my Peace Corps services as I am of my military service.

Surprisingly, I understood that learning more than I taught was not a platitude. I certainly enjoyed adventure, excitement, and more than my share of danger. My new job with the Japanese Foreign Service exceeded my goal of obtaining international employment. And finally, I'm writing the book about my Peace Corps service. I have given up on the idea that it might be made into a movie, making me wealthy. However, I feel compelled to write it to make a record of our adventures.

Oh, yes. I had substantial excitement and many adventures in the Solomon Islands. Paula and I made many life-long friends with Solomon Islanders and expatriates. We participated in filming a documentary about shark callers in Laulasi. We achieved a better understanding of Solomon Islands' tribal medicines. We learned of Melanesian customs and had a memorable trip to Ngongosila Island. We were successful in instigating several community development projects in portable sawmills, health and nutrition, tourism, reforestation, and others.

I accepted an invitation to observe a unique ancestor worship ceremony in a pagan Begau village. Paula and I traveled to Australia, New Zealand, and many islands in the Solomons. We visited Kennedy Island in Western Province. We received an invitation from three Kwaio chiefs to live the rest of our lives with the fierce tribe. I'll now share these adventures, and many more, with you via this publication.

# CHAPTER 2

# *Invitation, Research, Preparation*

Paula received a call from Peace Corps, Washington D.C. informing us that we had been selected for assignments in Africa. We would begin training in about five or six months. Our assignments would be teaching agriculture in a college. Well, it wasn't an exotic island in the South Pacific, but it wasn't going to be in a village where young men ran around naked and drank filthy water. "What country are we going to?" Paula asked.

"I don't know yet," our caller said. "You won't go for several months. We'll contact you when we know something more."

Three weeks later we received a surprise telephone call. "Sellens' residence," I said, when I answered the phone.

"Do I have the residence of Paula and Charles Sellens?" I was asked.

"Yes, you do," I answered. "How can I help you?"

"My name is John," he said. "I'm calling from Peace Corps Washington with good news and bad news. Which do you want first?"

"Let's start with the good news, John. Then, I'll be ready for the bad news."

"The good news is that the Peace Corps wants to change your assignment from Africa to the South Pacific. You and Paula are being offered positions in the Solomon Islands as community development workers. The bad news is that we want you to be ready to go in a month."

"One month?" I asked in disbelief. "Only one month? It would be hard to get ready to go in only one month. I'll talk to Paula and see what she thinks. What is the number where we can call you with our decision?"

He gave me his number and I gave Paula the import of the call. We had serious discussions about what we would have to do to get ready. We eventually decided we could manage it. We called John and told him we would accept the assignment. We started selling our cars, furniture, and other things that would have been too difficult to store while we were overseas.

Peace Corps sent instructions that we were to get "Peace Corps passports." If we currently had valid passports, we were to surrender them with our applications for Peace Corps passports. Our Peace Corps passports would be good for a few months more than the time we would serve in the Peace Corps. We were told that when we arrived in the Solomons, we would leave our Peace Corps passports at the office in Honiara. The reason given was that if we had to evacuate, Peace Corps would have our passports.

I didn't like the idea of surrendering passports that didn't expire for five years to get Peace Corps passports that would expire in a little more than two years. Nor, did I like the idea of leaving my passport in the custody of some unknown person at the Peace Corps office in Honiara. Paula and I did apply for Peace Corps passports and explained that our current passports had been lost. We wrote that we needed new ones for our scheduled departure date in three weeks. Our Peace Corps passports arrived promptly.

Our Peace Corps passports were ordinary passports that had "Peace Corps" affixed to the outside using that cheesy, plastic strip method that was common in 1990. We owned one of the hand-held tools used to make the plastic strips. It had cost us about $5.00. There were no special rights or privileges attached to the passports. They did expire in a little over two years. We took our Peace Corps passports and our regular passports with us. One set for us and one set for the Peace Corps. Rules are rules!

Paula and I were both working for the Kansas Social and Rehabilitation Services when we accepted our invitations to go to the Solomons. Paula was a social services supervisor and I was an income maintenance worker. Richard Kimberly was my supervisor. Richard had retired from the navy after serving twenty years. He had been stationed in the South Pacific. "How long is a Peace Corps assignment?" Richard asked.

"Over two years," I answered. "We have two months training then two years actually on the job."

"Two years? You can do that. The humidity is very high in the South Pacific. Everything gets moldy. The humidity can ruin everything. If you have electricity where you live, you can rig a light bulb in a closet. Let if run twenty-four hours a day. Keep your camera and other things in the closet so they don't mold."

"Thanks Richard. I'll remember that."

"The Solomon Islands will have very strange customs. There was a lot of headhunting and cannibalism years ago. You can find books and read about the history."

I took Richard's advice and started learning about the Solomon Islands. In addition to instructions for obtaining passports, Peace Corps officials had sent us a Solomon Islands' tourist book. I also found considerable information about the Solomon Islands from other sources.

Every source reported that the Solomons are an archipelago of over 900 islands. Solomon Islands lie east of Papua New Guinea and northeast of Australia. There are some low-lying coral atolls, but most islands were created by volcanic eruptions. The major islands were: Guadalcanal, Malaita, New Georgia, San Cristobal, Santa Isabel, Choiseul, and Santa Cruz.

Sources differed widely, but one reported that humans first occupied the Solomon Islands 30,000 years ago when Papuans from New Guinea made settlements. Austronesian-language speakers brought agricultural and maritime technology around 4,000 B.C. Most Solomon Islands' languages derive from the Austronesian languages, but some thirty Papuans derived languages survive.

Paula found a reference book at the Augusta Public Library that provided information about surviving shrines that existed before Europeans came. Western Province has the Bao megalithic shrine complex that dates from the 13th century A.D. The Nusa Roviana fortress and shrines date from the 14th to the 19th centuries. The Nusa Roviana skull shrines were described as legionary. Vonavona Skull island was yet another Western Provence cultural monument I read about.

The Nusa Roviana fortress complex served as the center of regional trade networks from the 17th to the 19th centuries. A better-known shrine was the Tiola shrine. This complex of archaeological monuments typified development of local Roviana culture through trade and headhunting expeditions.

One source said that Spaniard Álvaro de Mendana de Neira was the first European to document seeing the Solomon Islands. He found traces of gold on Guadalcanal in 1568 and believed he had discovered the source of King Solomon's wealth. As a result, he named the islands: "The Islands of Solomon."

In 1595, and again in 1605, Spain sent several expeditions to relocate the islands. The expeditions were organized and conducted with intentions of establishing Spanish colonies. Both of the expeditions were unsuccessful resulting in the Spanish abandoning their efforts.

British naval officer and explorer Captain Philip Carteret rediscovered the Santa Cruz Islands and Malaita in 1767. Carteret was leading the second British Royal Navy's circumnavigation expedition at the time. French, Dutch, and more British navigators visited the islands after Carteret's sightings.

When I learned that we were going to the Solomon Islands, images of headhunters and cannibals popped into my head. My research revealed that the practices did exist. Western Provence's Roviana area developed headhunting traditions over 500 years. Heads were taken when Roviana war parties attacked tribes on distant islands of Choiseul, Russell, Isabel, Malaita, and Guadalcanal.

Chiefs sometimes paid raiders to kill powerful rival warriors or to destroy entire villages. Throughout the 19th century, headhunting raids provided Roviana chiefs and warriors political legitimacy. Severed heads were processed, and the skulls were displayed as status symbols.

Children were sometimes captured on the raids. Girls were kidnapped and used for slaves and ritualized sex. Girls were sometimes adopted and married into the tribe. Boys were kidnapped for slaves and sacrifices that included purification rituals intended to maintain the perceived natural order.

Many heads were sometimes taken in single raids. In the 1840s, Andrew Cheyne participated in four trading voyages to the South Pacific. Cheyne wrote that during a stop in the Solomon Islands in 1844, he counted ninety-three heads taken in a raid on Simbo Island in Western Province.

Charles Woodford was a British naturalist who did early work in the Solomons. Woodford wrote that he counted thirty-one heads taken in a raid from Roviana in 1880. Missionaries began visiting the Solomon Islands in the mid-1800s. This was the time "blackbirding" was common in the Solomons.

Blackbirding was a system in which men, and sometimes women, were forcefully recruited for labor on sugar and cotton plantations in Australia and Fiji. The United Kingdom declared a protectorate over the southern Solomons in 1893 to quash blackbirding and headhunting.

More outlying islands were added to the protectorate in 1898 and 1899. In 1900, the area under German jurisdiction was transferred to British administration. Missionaries used the protection granted by the protectorate to begin converting Solomon Islanders to Christianity. Several British and Australian companies began large-scale coconut production. Economic benefits from coconut production were limited and the islanders themselves received little economic benefits.

Solomon Islands historically operated under unique governmental systems. Many tribes on Malaita developed leadership triumvirates of priest, feast giver, and ramo. Sometimes, one man filled more than one position. Ramos assumed primary roles in wars and blood feuding. Aggrieved parties also paid ramos to enforce custom laws by revenge assassinations.

Ramos' reputations were enhanced because common men believed ramos had the support of powerful, ancestor spirts. Ramos could fulfill assassination contract obligations by killing a relative of the named victim. I read an account where a common man pledged valuables for someone to kill a named ramo. The ramo learned of the contract and killed his own sister. He then confronted the man who had offered the bounty and demanded the valuables pledged for his personal death.

Malitian ramos' power increased during the decades of blackbirding when they acquired rifles brought back from Australia. When the British Solomon Islands Protectorate was initially established, one of the primary methods to curb headhunting and cannibalism on Malaita was to limit ramos' power and authority. This goal was sometimes accomplished by publicly hanging offenders.

When Britain declared Solomon Islands a protectorate in 1893, no funding was provided to establish a government. Naturalist Charles Woodford was appointed resident commissioner in 1896 and served until 1915. Woodford believed that native contact with labor recruiters contributed to increased lawlessness.

In his book *A Naturalist Among the Head-Hunters*, he noted that cannibalism and killing had become common. "I know no place where firm and paternal government would sooner produce beneficial results than the Solomons," he wrote. "..... I believe that the natives themselves would not be slow to recognize the advantages of increased security to life and property. Here is an object worthy indeed of the devotion of one's life."

The high commissioner of the British Western Pacific Territories reported that a proper government could not be established because there was no way to raise necessary revenue. The colonial office insisted that Woodford devise a system to compel the Solomon Islands to pay for any government that he could establish. The colonial office didn't offer suggestions how Woodford might accomplish his mandate.

Woodford's first report to the colonial office was sufficiently impressive that he was granted a small amount of money. With this start, he founded the colonial capital of Tulagi on the island of Nggela Sule.

Woodford urged Britain to assume possession of all unclaimed land to prevent large-scale land purchases for coconut plantations. The colonial office supported his position and gave him £1,200 to build a residency. One year later, he reported that headhunting and cannibalism were declining.

By that time Woodford left the Solomons in 1914, the islands were largely pacified. New Georgia and Malaita remained troubled areas, but a district office had been established at Auki, Malaita in 1909. Unfortunately, after Woodford left, much of the progress he had made was undone. The protectorate government never regained the status that it had during his leadership.

Kwaio tribesmen reportedly attacked the *Borealis* in 1880 in retaliation for blackbirding atrocities. They killed the crewmembers and looted the ship. The Kwaio repeated their revenge attacks with killings and looting of the *Janet Steward* in 1880, the *Young Dick* in 1886, and the *Ruby* in 1911.

American author and adventurer Jack London travelled to the Solomon Islands in 1905. He wrote that when he was near Malaita, he entered the Langa Langa Lagoon. He abandoned his plan to visit the mainland when headhunters from Laulasi attacked his ship. Martin Johnson, a young man from Lincoln, Kansas, was a crewman on London's ship, the Snark.

Martin Johnson later performed stage shows portraying his adventures with London. He performed in Chanute, Kansas where he met and married Osa Leighty. The Johnsons lived adventuresome lives. Martin and Osa Johnson visited Laulasi in the early 1920s. They had traveled to Malaita with a goal of taking photos of cannibals in the act of eating human flesh. The Johnsons stayed for some time in Auki with District Officer William R. Bell.

A few years later, District Officer Bell, Cadet Kenneth Lillies, and several native policemen were massacred by tribesmen from the fierce Kwaio tribe. The Solomon Islands was a British protectorate at that time. British officials had mandated a head tax to offset some the expenses incurred in governing the islands. Bell had led the group to a Kwaio stronghold to collect taxes demanded by the British.

The Kwaio resented the British and the dramatic changes that were demanded. The Kwaio were led by the war chief Basiana. Basiana paid the demanded tax then killed Bell by smashing in his skull. Cadet Lillies and the native policemen were also killed.

Christian Kwaio were eventually allowed to collect the remains of the deceased. They took them to Ngongosila Island off Malaita and buried them in two common graves. A punitive raid was organized to punish the Kwaio. Many Kwaio were killed and 200 were arrested.

Basiana and five others were tried for the murders and hung. Other Kwaio received trials and prison sentences. Kwaio descendants still held animosity over the incident. They discouraged outside visitors and continued their lives by traditional customs.

World War II came to the Solomon Islands in 1942 when Japanese forces invaded. The United States countered with a Marine attack on Guadalcanal and Tulagi. At that time, Tulagi, Nggela Sule was still the headquarters of the British administration. It was destroyed in the heavy fighting that followed.

With the outbreak of W.W. II, most expatriates were evacuated to Australia and most coconut plantations were abandoned. Western Province gained international fame after John F. Kennedy's patrol torpedo boat was destroyed by a Japanese cruiser. Lieutenant, junior grade Kennedy commanded *PT 109* during World War II. Kennedy's prompt actions are credited with saving the lives of many sailors after *PT-109* sunk,

The Battle of the Coral Sea was fought off Savo Island, near Guadalcanal, in May 1942. The battle is recognized as one of the most furious sea battles ever fought. Before the Japanese withdrew from Guadalcanal in February 1943, over 7,000 Americans and 31,000 Japanese had died. By December 1943, the Allies were in command of the entire Solomon chain.

Many Solomon Islanders worked for the Americans as laborers, coast watchers, and a few participated in combat. Until the Japanese evacuated in December 1943, there was constant combat in the Solomons. Although U.S. forces landed on Guadalcanal virtually unopposed in August 1942, they were soon engaged in a bloody fight for control of the island's airstrip. United States' forces named the airfield Henderson Field after winning control.

The town of Honiara developed close to Henderson Field as the U.S. logistics center. The war's profound impact on the islanders continued after cessation of hostilities. The Solomon Islands didn't receive any war reparations to rebuild. The plantations that had been the backbone of the economy had been destroyed.

The introduction of modern machinery and western culture transformed traditional ways of life. Following the end of W.W. II, the British colonial government returned. The capital was moved from Tulagi to Honiara to take advantage of the infrastructure left behind by the U.S. military.

Several natives began organizing Maasina Ruru to seek independence. Maasina Ruru followers created havoc for the British by revolting against colonial rule. Malitian Nori Nono'oohimae was a primary founder of the Maasina Ruru movement.

British authorities regained control by jailing several of the leaders. Throughout the 1950s, other dissident groups formed and disbanded. A legislative council and an executive council were created as the protectorate's policymaking body in 1960. The councils initially had little authority, but they were granted more authority over the years.

As late as 1970, the British did not envisage independence for Solomon Islands in the foreseeable future. However, supporting the protectorate financially became increasingly difficult as the world economy was hit by the oil price shock of 1973. A new constitution was adopted in 1974. It established a parliamentary democracy and ministerial governmental system. On July 7, 1978, Britain granted the Solomon Islands independence.

About 92% of Solomon Islanders identified themselves as Christians. The main Christian denominations were: The Anglican Church of Melanesia 35%, Roman Catholic 19%, South Seas Evangelical Church 17%, United Church in Papua New Guinea and the Solomon Islands 11%, and Seventh-day Adventist 10%. The Roman Catholic Church supported the Diocese of Auki, the Archdiocese of Honiara, and the Diocese of Gizo.

Before the beginning of the protectorate era in 1893, people had strong beliefs in custom rituals and magic. Solomon Islanders believed that sorcerers were the cause of serious problems. In their view, nothing happened by chance. Whatever happened occurred because someone had the ability to channel power from the ancestor spirits.

The primary way of gaining access to the spirits was through sorcery. The sorcerer used rituals to call ancestral spirits who possessed great powers. The spirits could be summoned for good or evil purposes. Despite decades of missionaries working in the Solomons, practicing Christians held parallel belief systems. They saw no conflict in depending on their Christian God to hold their ancestors' spirits at bay.

Sorcery magic was an example of belief systems that were still strong and alive in Solomon Islands society while Paula and I were there. Common examples in Solomon Islands sorcery included *piro, kibokibo*, and *vele*. Accusations of sorcery were made for various reasons. Jealousy due to social and economic advancement of others, customary land disputes, criminal activities, and friendship breakdowns were often reasons for sorcery accusations.

Laulasi Islands natives in Malaita believed that the spirts of their deceased ancestors lived in sharks and could be summoned by a special pagan priest (*Fata'abu*) to do his bidding. Laulasi is also the location where Solomon Islands' traditional shell money was made. Shell money was often demanded as bride-price payments.

I read that an anthropologist, Dr. Roger Keesing, had lived with the Kwaio for several years. Dr. Keesing learned Kwaio language and customs. He authored several books and papers on Kwaio religion, history, and politics.

During my research, I learned that there was an ongoing civil war near the Solomons. It was known as the Bougainville Conflict and had begun in 1988. The war was between Papua New Guinea (P.N.G.) and the secessionist forces of the Bougainville Revolutionary Army (B.R.A.). The B.R.A. simultaneously clashed with other armed groups on Bougainville.

The precipitating issues included unfair distribution of mineral wealth. Gold was discovered on Bougainville in 1930. Vast copper ore deposits were discovered in the Crown Prince Range on Bougainville Island during the 1960s. An Australian company, Conzinc Rio Tinto, established the Bougainville Copper Mine in 1972.

The Bougainville Copper Mine made the P.N.G. government a 20 % shareholder. At the time, the mine was the largest open cut mine in the world. It earned more than 45% of P.N.G.'s national export revenue. At 45% of export revenue, the mine was vitally important to P.N.G.'s economy.

Bougainville Copper had recruited thousands of workers for the project. Most were Papua New Guineans whom Bougainvilleans called "red-skins." The Australian nationals who came to work at the mine were identified as "white-skins." By contrast, Bougainville natives identified themselves as black.

Conflict began to emerge with the beginning of mining operations. Local landowners resented the foreign workers and their foreign cultures. They were outraged by the adverse environmental effects and most of the mine's profits leaving the island. By late 1988, disagreements among the parties had led to violence.

The P.N.G. government deployed police and military forces to enforce its positions. Fighting was initially limited to the mine site area, but quickly spread into the Solomon Islands. Both sides reported abuses against the native population during fighting. The conflict evolved into a general separatist insurgency.

Bougainville Copper closed the mine and most foreigners left the island. Fighting continued for a year, during which widespread human rights violations occurred. People were killed, women raped, and villages burned.

I was satisfied with what I had learned about the history of the Solomon Islands. Paula was ready to go. I was ready to go. We had sold most of what we owned. We had given our dog, Chamois, to Paula's sister, Mary Eddy. We had opened a checking account at the Kearny County Bank in Lakin. Paula's mother, Zelma Coyne, agreed to become an owner of the checking account, so she could send us some of our money if we needed it.

Richard Kimberly and S.R.S. Co-workers Mary Ann, Judy, Sherrie, Norma, and Don Slimmer gave me a going-away party. We had a lot of fun. They gave me what they considered gag gifts including fly-swatters to fend off cannibals, a sewing kit to reattach our heads when severed, coconuts, sun-tan lotion, and insect repellent. Paula and I selected many of them, including the fly-swatters, sewing kit, sun-tan lotion, and insect repellent, to take to the Solomons.

I had learned a lot about the Solomon Islands. We had packed our suitcases and were ready to leave the next day. I thought we was ready to begin our odyssey. We went to bed to dream of our upcoming adventures. That night was to be the last time we would sleep in Kansas for over two years. That we expected. What we did not expect was that we would live outside the U.S. for the next fifteen years.

# CHAPTER 3

# *Orientation*

Our friends, Bob and Desiree Renner, gave us a ride to Wichita for our flight to Los Angeles. Our younger son, Jason, met us at the airport and took us to his apartment. We spent two days with him and Chuck. Chuck and Jason had a party to introduce us to some of their friends.

Wade Etcher, originally from Russell County, came to the party. We said our good-byes and the next day, Jason gave us a ride to the airport for our flight to Hawaii.

We arrived in Honolulu on July 12, 1990. We transferred to the University of Hawaii to begin the staging process. We took a tour of Waikiki the next day. Our training started on July 14, so didn't have much time to adjust to the time change.

There were about fifty potential volunteers assembled in Hawaii for

Chuck and Jason in Los Angeles

staging. We were all being assigned to islands in the South Pacific. Most were young, cheerful, and very lively. There was a function in which we met citizens from several of the island countries where various volunteers would be assigned. No one was present from the Solomon Islands.

There was one volunteer who I remember well. He was probably in his late thirties and single. He approached me during a break. "Can I ask you a personal question?" he asked.

"Of course," I answered. "What would you like to know?"

"Do you have a college degree?"

"I have two degrees. I have a Bachelor of Science in Agriculture from Ft. Hays State in Hays, Kansas and a Master of Public Administration from Kansas State University in Manhattan, Kansas."

"You know, I've asked nearly everyone here. I think I'm the only one that doesn't have a college education. I know that college isn't a requirement for Peace Corps Volunteers, but it seems everyone except me has a college degree."

"Where are you going to be assigned?"

"Fiji."

"What's your job going to be?"

"Agriculture advisor. I'll live in a nice apartment in a modern city. I'll have a driver to take me around to where I need to go. It's a much better assignment than I expected."

"Lucky you! What agriculture experience do you have?"

"I homesteaded for a year and raised my own food."

I felt a small pang of jealously. It sounded like he was going to have a much better assignment than Paula and me. I talked to him some more to understand what he was doing that he identified as homesteading. He told me that he had moved onto land that was owned by someone else. Once established, he raised vegetables for his personal use. What he called homesteading, I was confident the landowner would call squatting.

We were introduced to six other people who were going to the Solomons. Rick Treleaven and Carrie Hooton were a married couple. Rick was a psychologist with a master's degree. Carrie also had a master's degree and taught in an Oregon high school. Rick and Carrie wore walking sandals that I thought were cool. Paula also liked the sandals, so she wrote her mother and asked her to buy two pairs and send them to us. Peace Corps Volunteers need to look cool in addition to being cool.

Bill Wise was in his early thirties and the youngest in the group. He was a single man with a degree in accounting. He didn't have walking sandals, but I thought he was cool. Matt and Margaret Ottinger were another married couple. Matt had a bachelor's degree and had owned and managed a restaurant. Margaret had a bachelor's degree and was a primary school teacher. Matt told us that he was a former Peace Corps Volunteer in Africa.

Matt's service had to be terminated due to a medical problem. "I rode in the back of a truck for several hours," he told us. "I got a boil on my butt that wouldn't heal. They had to ship me home to get cured. Many volunteers don't complete their two-year assignment. Some of us that are here today won't be here at the end. I just hope I'm not one that has to go back."

Tom Scherer was single and had a bachelor's degree. After obtaining his bachelor's degree, Tom returned to college and earned an associate degree in computer science. He had served in the Navy for four years. Tom was going to work outside Honiara on a giant clam farm. Paula had a bachelor's degree in elementary education and had been a social worker for eighteen years. We eight were a small training group.

We met Peter Corsey the first day we arrived in Hawaii. Peter was the Solomon Islands' Peace Corps administration officer. He was there to escort us to the Solomons. "There's a big problem with malaria in the Solomons," Peter said. "I'm going to give all of you a supply of paludrine and chloroquine. Take two paludrine and two chloroquine tablets now."

"How long will we have to take them?" Carrie asked.

"You'll take them all the time you're in the Solomons," Peter answered. "You'll take two paludrine pills each day and two chloroquine tablets on Sunday. Chloroquine Sunday is how you can remember when to take them."

"Are there any side effects?" Tom wanted to know.

"There might be, but you'll learn more about them in training," Peter answered. "Peace Corps has a full-time nurse who will explain more about malaria. You'll want to learn how to avoid getting it and what to do if you do get it."

We were scheduled to fly to Sydney, Australia leaving at 9:00 p.m. on July 18, 1990. We were to have a four-hour lay-over in Sydney then fly on to Honiara. We expected the flight to Sydney to last from fourteen to sixteen hours. Our flight was delayed. We waited patiently for our flight to materialize. Bill Wise frequently checked the flight scheduling board.

In due time, Bill returned to our group and spoke to Peter Corsey. "I've been checking the flight schedule," Bill said. "Our scheduled flight is now so late that if we leave on it, we'll miss our transfer from Sydney to Honiara. That means we'll be stranded in Australia for at least two days without visas."

"Are you sure?" Peter asked.

"I'm sure. Let's check it together."

Peter and Bill moved to the flight scheduling board. Peter soon departed, and Bill returned to our group. "Peter agrees with me," he said. "Our flight is so late that if we go to Australia tonight, we might be stranded in Sydney for several days without visas. Peter is trying to make changes."

I was very impressed with our group. Bill had just proven that he was a sound thinker. Peter did get changes made, obligating us to stay in Hawaii extra time. We didn't suffer. We had two days of lounging on Waikiki Beach with the airline picking up the tab for food and accommodations.

We took the opportunity to visit the U.S.S. Arizona Memorial in Pearl Harbor. The memorial commemorates the December 7, 1941 Japanese attack. The memorial straddles the sunken hull of the battleship where most of the 1,177 sailors and marines that were killed are interned. The memorial was constructed in 1962 and was accessible only by boat. The battleship's sunken remains were declared a national historic landmark in 1989.

The airline must have been anxious to move us on. We were first flown to Auckland, New Zealand then on to Sydney, Australia. After a short lay-over in Sydney, we departed for the Solomons and arrived on July 23, 1990. As we were approaching Honiara International Airport, I looked out the window. My immediate reaction was that it didn't deserve designation as an international airport. I expected something more from the airstrip that thousands of Japanese and American died fighting over in 1943.

When we left the plane, we were met by other Peace Corps Volunteers. They put leis around our necks and gave us coconut water served in coconut shells. I felt like a heavy, wet blanket had been laid on me. I couldn't get my breath.

We were four degrees south of the equator, but it wasn't the heat that made me uncomfortable. The humidity was likely near 100%. I had endured many Kansas summers when the temperature was much hotter than what I was then experiencing in Honiara.

There were several small monuments at the airport honoring Americans who had been awarded medals of honor. Most of them had been awarded posthumously including Major Lofton Henderson. Henderson was killed during the Battle of Midway while leading his flight squadron against Japanese carrier forces.

Welcome in Honiara

We traveled to the Peace Corps office and, among other things, turned over our Peace Corps passports. Rules are rules. We soon met our trainers. Jimmie Wilkerson was the training officer. She was a former Peace Corps Volunteer who had served in Jamaica. Jim and Chris were a married Peace Corps couple currently serving in the Solomon Islands. Their volunteer service would end after our training.

Charles and Ephraim were Solomon Islands' language instructors. Joseph was the logistics coordinator. Soon after we began our training, Charles and Ephraim organized a field trip for us at the open-air market in Honiara. We followed a foot path that paralleled a paved road to get to the market area. We waited at a stop light for it to turn green rather than attempt to jay walk.

Ephraim told us that the stop light was the only one in the Solomon Islands. We learned later that an aid donor had funded the stop light. The donor had originally proposed an overhead walkway crossing the road, so vehicle traffic would not be interrupted. Honiara officials were outraged. An overhead walkway would ensure grave violations of Solomon culture. Women using the walkway would be higher than men who would be passing underneath in vehicles. Men were always to be higher than women, both literally and figuratively.

Vendors had set fruit, vegetables, root crops, coconuts, and other items on banana leaves on the ground. Charles pointed out betel nut and leaf for sale and told us of its use. "Most Solomon men chew betel nut," he said, in English. "It makes them alert and happy. They can walk and work without getting tired. A Solomon man will give you betel nut when you visit his village."

"Do you chew betel nut?" I asked.

"Don't chew betel nut," he said, with a wide smile. "Church don't like betel nut."

His white teeth and healthy gums contrasted with the mouths of the betel nut vendors. Most of them had missing teeth. The teeth that were intact were stained a dark, reddish-black. The men's beards and naked chests were spotted red from betel nut juice that slobbered out of their mouths as they talked to Charles in their native language.

I leisurely sauntered around enjoying the variety of items for sale. Two locations included small items salvaged from W.W. II debris. Badly rusted helmets, bayonets, and canteens were displayed. One even included an American "dog tag" with a rusted chain.

Market in Honiara

I was surprised to see a vendor selling what I thought were dog turds. Why would anyone buy dog turds? What use could anyone have for three to four-inch, dark-brown, canine feces? Well, this was an educational tour and I wanted to know. I found Charles and Ephraim explaining stages of coconut ripening to Margaret and Paula. "Ephraim, can you come with me and answer a question?" I asked.

Ephraim didn't answer, but he smiled and quickly raised his brow to indicate he would accompany me. When we arrived at the dog turd vendor, I pointed to the items. "Why do Solomon people buy dog turds?" I asked.

"That's tobacco," Ephraim informed me. "Grown in Guadalcanal."

I thanked him and looked a little closer. I could then recognize that it was tobacco leaf that had been wrapped into small, tight rolls. Ephraim explained that the rolls would be sliced into shreds to make recognizable tobacco. The tobacco would be rolled into useable cigarettes using exercise paper manufactured to be used by children for school work.

Peace Corps officials scheduled our first week of training at Tambea Resort. Tambea was chosen to help us assimilate into Solomon Islands' life. After our first week, we were to move to a traditional village for training in a total immersion environment. Our Tambea Resort accommodations were imitations of small Solomon Islands' huts. Each hut could hold up to four people.

Tambea Resort had a welcoming feast then we received our hut assignments. Jimmie had a hut by herself, Jim and Chris had a hut. Tom and Bill were assigned a hut. Matt, Rick, and I were given a hut to share. Margaret, Carrie, and Paula were assigned a hut. When we turned in for the night, Matt, Rick, and I formed a group opinion that this was not the best arrangement. Great minds think alike. "I wonder who thought of this arrangement," Matt mused. "Maybe they're trying to save money."

"Well, if money is the issue, Paula and I will pay for our own hut," I offered. "That would allow we married men to be with our wives. I made no pledge of celibacy in my application."

"I think we could split the cost of another room three ways," Rick proposed. "It wouldn't cost any of us very much. These rooms can't be very expensive."

We all thought that was the best plan. We agreed to discuss the situation with Jimmie the next morning. When morning arrived, we approached Jimmie, but our offer was not necessary. She informed us that she had decided to rent another hut, so those of us who were married could spend the nights with our spouses.

We began our training focusing on Pisin language lessons and Solomon Islands' culture. Jim and Chris had lived in the Solomon Islands for several months. They provided valuable information on life in the Solomons.

"Houses in the villages are very simple," Jim told us. "But you should never call them huts. People will get mad if you say they live in huts. They might even demand compensation."

"What do you mean by compensation?" Bill asked.

"Demanding and paying compensation is an accepted Solomon Islands' way to resolve disputes," Jim answered. "Many conflicts are settled when an offending party gives money or valuables to someone that claims damages."

Carrie, Rick, Bill, Margaret, Paula, Matt, Tom and Charlie at Tambea Resort

"Have you ever been asked to pay compensation?" Tom asked.

"I've never paid compensation, but I received it once. A man got mad over a soccer match and went into a rage. His rant went on for several minutes. The next time we had a soccer match, he gave all of us compensation in the form of tobacco."

Chris showed the ladies how to wear lava lavas. A lava lava was a large, square piece of colorful cloth. Woman wrapped the lava lavas around their lower bodies. They were held in place by tucking the final wrap into the existing wraps. Solomon men wore the same garb, but when worn by men, the garments were called lap laps. Some of us began wearing lava lavas and lap laps at Tambea Resort.

Tambea Resort's owner and manager liked to listen to B.B.C.'s radio broadcasts in the evening. I joined him on August 2, 1990 to hear the international news while my fellow trainees visited about the day's training.

The broadcast began with a startling report that Iraq had invaded Kuwait. I returned to my group and informed them of what I had just heard. The invasion became the topic of conversation until we went to bed.

We listened to the news each night for the remainder of our stay at Tambea. It only took two days for the Iraqi Republican Guard to overrun most Kuwait's forces. The rest of Kuwait's forces retreated to neighboring Saudi Arabia and Bahrain. Saddam Hussein quickly announced that Iraq had annexed Kuwait and that it was Iraq's nineteenth province.

Charlie and Paula wearing lava lavas and lap laps.

We completed our first week of training at Tambea Resort and moved to the city of Honiara. During our free time, we visited Chinese shops, restaurants, and modern stores owned by expatriates. Milk was available in powdered and long-life forms. Chicken and beef were available in the expatriate owned stores, but it was expensive. Expensive being relative to income, but each volunteer was paid only US$165 per month. Oh yes, we also got US$26 per month for travel.

Solomon Islands is four degrees south of the equator, thus residents are subjected to a hot climate. The extensive rain and humidity are moderated by trade winds during much of the day. Cool, mountain breezes make evenings and night much more comfortable. The trade winds are also responsible for the "wet" season and the "dry" season.

What is wet and dry to a Solomon Islander is much different from what wet and dry means to Kansans. Western Kansas commonly gets from twenty-four to thirty inches of moisture during wet years. It often varies, but Solomon Islands is blessed with from five to eight inches per month during the dry season.

Pre-service training included medical issues and interviews, shots, Pisin lessons, Solomon Islands taboos, culture shock issues, site assignments information, walkabout preparation, and volunteers in development. We went to Peace Corps Director John Mark's home for a traditional Solomon Islands' meal. "Some Peace Corps directors feel their jobs are limited," he told us. "They provide money, mail, and medicine. I want you to know you can depend on me for more than that."

John Mark was tall, slender and neatly dressed. He was an African American who was highly respected by Solomon Islanders. They often referred to John Mark as a "black, white man." We community development workers were soon informed what province we were assigned to. We were told to prepare to travel to our work assignment for a familiarization visit. Matt and Margaret Ottinger were to go to the Shortland Islands in Western Province. Rick and Carrie were assigned to work and live in Honiara. Paula and I were assigned to Malaita.

Paula hadn't voiced an opinion, but had I been allowed to choose, Malaita would have been my choice. While Honiara was not a modern city by my standards, I thought I wanted a more exotic assignment. I was also confident that since Honiara was the capital, we would spend considerable time there.

The Shortlands seemed too exotic, isolated, and dangerous for Paula and me. The western islands of the Solomons were close to the Bougainville group that was part of Papua New Guinea (P.N.G.). The division was originally the border between the colonial British Solomons and colonial German New Guinea.

I knew from my prior research that Bougainville was seeking independence from P.N.G. The driving issue was over an operating copper mine in Bougainville from which the citizens were not receiving any economic benefits. An armed conflict began in 1988 and sometimes spilled over into Western Province. Matt and Margaret would join a Catholic priest and nun as the only expatriates at their site.

Shortlands seemed too wild. Honiara seemed too tame. Malaita seemed just right. Maybe we would get to visit Laulasi Island from where Jack London had been attacked by headhunters. I knew that the Kwaio had killed Tax Collector Bell and his group on Malaita. Maybe we would get to go to Ngongosila Island and see Mr. Bell's grave. Malaita was where Kansans Martin and Osa Jonson had traveled to try to capture cannibal feasts on film. And now, Paula and I were going!

Peace Corps had arranged for everyone to travel to their work sites to allow us to feel more comfortable during our remaining training time. These brief excursions were called walkabouts. Matt and Margaret had a long trip, so they were scheduled to leave at 6:00 a.m. on Sunday. Paula and I got up early to see them off. We helped them get their things to the plane for their flight to Western Province.

Paula and I flew to Auki for our walkabout the next day and found our way to the Auki Lodge. I asked for the manager and spoke in English. "We're Charles and Paula Sellens," I said. "We're Peace Corps Volunteers and we want to check-in. The Peace Corps office in Honiara made reservations for us to stay for four days."

"Sorry," the manager answered, in English. "I don't have a room for you."

I was perplexed. "Did the Peace Corps make reservations for us?" I asked.

"Yes," he answered. "You have a reservation, but there is no room."

"Why don't we have a room if the Peace Corps made reservations?"

"You're not here in time. I gave your room to someone else."

"But it's only two o'clock in the afternoon. How could we be too late to use our reservation?"

The manager didn't provide an answer. If he had offered one, I don't think I would have found it satisfactory. He left us to solve our problem. He didn't suggest any other place where we might stay, and we didn't know of any. We pondered our predicament. I wasn't about to leave the lodge when we had reservations.

Malaita Airport

I was afraid if we left, they might lock the door. Wandering around all night wasn't an option. What if there were old Malitians who didn't know that headhunting and cannibalism were past customs? There was an Italian couple there in a similar predicament. "Are you staying here?" Paula asked, in English.

"We would like to stay, but they don't have any rooms," the lady answered.

"Did you have a reservation?" I asked.

"No, we just came. We thought we might be lucky."

"We have reservations, but they told us they gave our room to someone else. What are you two going to do?"

Both Italians shrugged their shoulders. I thought our situations were very different. We had reservations. That gave reasonable cause for me to think we should have a room. They didn't have reservations, so the fact that they didn't get a room was not unreasonable. All four of us slept in our clothes on the dining room floor that night.

The manager set chairs and draped blankets over them to make separate sleeping areas for the Italians and us. It wasn't the most comfortable night we spent in the Solomon Islands. Paula voiced an opinion that she was ready to go home. Given the circumstances, it really didn't seem possible.

We woke early and helped a hotel employee transform our sleeping room into a dining room. When breakfast was served, we sat near a guest who was also eating breakfast. After brief introductions and polite chit-chat, I took the conversation to more pertinent topics. "My wife and I are Peace Corps Volunteers," I informed him. "Are you a tourist?"

"No," he answered. "I'm the Solomon Islands' director of taxation."

"Where are you from?"

"I'm English, but I've lived in the Solomon Islands for several years."

"Did you stay here last night?" I asked.

"Yes," he answered. "I checked in yesterday."

"It's not very important, but did you have a reservation?"

"No, I came unannounced and just checked in."

I understood then why our reservations weren't honored. The director of taxation showed up on business. Auki Lodge's manager wanted to get on good terms and gave him the only room that was not occupied. That would be the room that had been reserved for Paula and me. I better understood my place in the Solomon Islands' hierarchy. The director of taxation had higher status than Peace Corps Volunteers. He didn't stay another night, so Paula and I did get our room.

There were also three Japanese men staying there. One of them, Yasuo Isozaki, introduced himself in English that morning. He told us that his wife, Masako, would soon come to the Solomon Islands. Yasuo said he would introduce us to his wife when she arrived. He looked forward to us being friends.

We made our way to the provincial offices and found our supervisor, Paul Kennioriana. Paul was of medium height and heavily muscled. He was clean shaven, and his head was graced with a nicely trimmed afro. His neat, clean, cotton shorts came nearly to his knees. They complemented a colorful shirt that advocated vacationing in Australia on the Great Barrier Reef. His sparkling, white teeth showed he was not a betel nut chewer.

Paul was not wearing shoes. His black feet were heavily calloused. They carried scars and cuts in various stages of healing. "My name is Paul," he said, in English. "I'll be your supervisor when you come to Auki permanently."

"Hello Paul. My name is Paula," she said.

"Hello Paul," I said, shaking his hand. "My name is Charles. I'm very pleased to meet you."

"I'll talk to you in English while you're here on your walkabout," Paul informed us. "But when you come back to Auki after your training, I'll never speak English to you again."

Paul went on to tell us that when we went to villages for our jobs, only Pisin would be spoken. He said that we would also meet many Malitians who did not even speak Pisin. Paula and I both pledged to study hard to learn Pisin. Paul escorted us to an office where we would work.

The windows were louvered to keep out rain, but they were open that day to let in fresh air. Overhead fans hummed softly. Our desks were metal and heavily rusted, courtesy of the Solomon Islands' high humidity. Paul pointed toward a building under construction. "We'll soon have a new building," he informed us. "You'll have a new office when the building is completed."

We returned to the Auki Lodge to better our chances of keeping the room that had been assigned to us. Malaita Province Magistrate David Chetwynd came to meet us late in the afternoon. David told us that he had delivered mail to a Volunteer Service Organization (V.S.O.) married couple from Scotland. They were doing their V.S.O. training on another island.

David said the man, Colin Cameron, would be the provincial legal advisor, but his wife, Alison, wouldn't have a job. David obviously knew that we would be at the Auki Lodge. "How did you know we would be here?" Paula asked.

"I heard on national radio Thursday that you would arrive on Monday," he answered. "Why don't you stop by my house this evening around eight o'clock and meet my wife Stephanie?"

Auki Island man with skulls

"Well, thank you very much!" Paula said. "We would love to come."

David gave us directions and we told him we would eat supper at the Auki Lodge then walk to his house. Our Italian friends told us they were going to visit Auki Island and asked us to go with them. They said the island was occupied by two families who maintained separate living areas.

Both areas had skull houses. We agreed and arranged to get rides on two small, dugout canoes. We were welcomed on the island and shown the skull houses in one of the living areas. We took pictures and returned to Auki.

Paula and I ate supper at the Auki Lodge then began our walk to Chetwynds. We met Stephanie and exchanged family and other information. "There is one thing I should warn you about," David said, as we were leaving. "It's not safe for Paula to walk alone at night. There's always a chance of rape."

"Have there been any assaults recently?" I asked.

"There was a young doctor from Australia raped not too long ago. The rapist broke into her house, raped her, then made it back to his village where he couldn't be found."

"Why couldn't the Solomon Islands' police find him?"

"I don't think they even tried. The rapist was a policeman himself."

We visited a near-by Catholic mission manned by Polynesian brothers. All the men were young, tall, and powerfully built. The brothers relayed an incident that occurred in Langa Langa Lagoon. "Many Langa Langa people are pagans that worship sharks," one brother informed us. "They believe when someone dies, they're reincarnated as sharks."

"Do you believe Langa Langa people are reincarnated as sharks?" I asked.

He didn't answer but smiled widely. "A Langa Langa boy drowned," he continued. "One of the young men was a good swimmer and had to recover the body. The swimmer was supposed to perform a cleansing ritual afterwards, but he didn't do it. The next time he went swimming, he was attached by a shark."

He paused to let us absorb the facts. "Did the shark kill him?" Paula asked.

"No," the brother answered. "The shark bit him on the head and face then let him go. The shark stared at the diver then left."

"How long ago did it happen?" I wanted to know.

"It was recent," he answered. "Those things happen all the time in the Solomons."

He went on to tell us that the swimmer promptly performed the purification ritual when he returned to his island. He didn't have any problems with sharks after that. The Catholic brothers invited us to come back and spend a weekend when we were permanently assigned. We left the mission and spent another night in the Auki Lodge.

We flew back to Honiara on Friday and spent the weekend at the Honiara Hotel. Jimmie, Jim, and Chris met with us on Saturday. "We'll move to Langa Lau, our training village, on Monday," Jimmie said. "But first, I want to hear your impressions about what you learned on your walkabout."

We each gave a summation of what we did and who we met. Paula told Jimmie about not having a room at the Auki Lodge our first night. Paula insisted that Peace Corps not pay for it. Jimmie made a note in her notebook. "Does everyone think they have a good understanding of what they will be doing when they get to their permanent assignment?" Jimmie asked.

Matt and Margaret expressed concerns about the civil conflicts that continued in the Bougainville Islands. Rick, Carrie, Bill, and Tom gave brief descriptions of what their jobs would be. Paula and I felt comfortable in saying that we thought we understood what we would do. Jimmie and Jim exchanged knowing glances. We thought little of it and spent the rest of the day preparing to travel to Langa Lau Village for five weeks training.

# CHAPTER 4

# *Training Village*

Our training group moved to Langa Lau Village for five weeks training on August 6, 1990. We rode in the bed of a truck for over three hours to reach our destination. Paula and I were assigned to live with the Ono family. Samuel Ono, his wife, four children, and extended family lived in a three-room house. When Paula and I moved in, there were a total of eleven people sharing the three rooms. Samuel Ono was the village chief and was a candidate for a provincial elective office.

Samuel Ono and family

The villagers had a feast for us featuring fish, vegetables, cucumbers, fruit, megapode eggs, and baked taro pudding. The food was served on banana leaves.

We sat on the ground and ate with our fingers, Solomon style. "These megapode eggs are very rich," Jimmie said. "Chris, you've been here a long time, what kind of bird is a megapode?"

"Megapodes are birds about the size of chickens," Chris answered. "They have big feet, long necks, and small heads. Megapode hens lay their eggs up to three-feet in the ground. The natural heat from the soil incubates the eggs. When the chicks hatch, they use their powerful claws to dig their way to the surface. They're fully feathered when they hatch and can fly as soon as they are above ground."

"Interesting," Paula said. "I never heard of birds like that. And can someone tell me how this taro pudding is made?"

"Taro is a root crop staple in the Solomon Islands," Jim answered. "It's poisonous if eaten raw. The Langa Lau women had to work hard to make this taro pudding. They first had to pound the taros into a thick dough. Next, they had to scrape and squeeze the meat of ripe coconuts to make milk. They blended the coconut milk into the taro dough to make a creamy texture then baked it."

The Langa Lau villagers made their living by subsistence farming. Both men and women spent many hours each day in their gardens. Most sold what they didn't eat at the open-air market in Honiara. The Anglican Church owned a truck that made regular trips to and from Honiara. Langa Lau women rode in the bed of the market truck to get their produce to Honiara.

There was no electricity in Langa Lau Village. Water was available for about four or five hours every day from four standpipes strategically located throughout the village. A solar powered pump filled a storage tank when the sun was shining. On cloudy days, no water was pumped, and water was severely rationed.

Village women taught Paula how they make custom cakes. The simple, donut-like cakes were made by mixing only flour, yeast, and water then deep fat fried. We often had a commercial chocolate drink and bananas, cucumbers, or other fruit for breakfast. We went to the Anglican Church with the Ono family every Sunday. There was also a Jehovah's Witness church in the village.

Samuel's nineteen year-old nephew, Fred, attached himself to me. He liked to question me about my army service, my weight lifting techniques, and karate practices and bouts. Fred also provided information about Solomon Islands' magic and sorcery. "You know about *Vele*?" he once asked me.

"No Fred," I answered. "What is a *Vele*?"

"*Vele* like man, magic powers. Carries custom bag on little finger. Magic in bag. He bad."

"Can I see a *Vele*?"

"I can see," Fred answered. "You can't see. You don't believe. *Vele* hides by path. Someone gets close, *Vele* pinches."

Fred pinched me to demonstrate what it would feel like if I were to get near a *Vele*. "What happens next?" I asked.

"Man falls down, sleeps. *Vele* makes forget everything. Man goes back to village. Soon gets sick. Maybe dies."

Fred sat silent while I pondered the existence of *Vela* magicians. Fred had assured me that I would never see one because I didn't believe in them. However, if I were to see one, I certainly would believe in them. What conundrums confronted we Peace Corps Volunteers. "Paula and I are going to live in Malaita," I said. "Are there any *Vele* in Malita?"

"No *Vele* in Malaita," Fred answered. "*Vele, piro, kibokibo* in Guadalcanal. *Arua* in Malaita."

"What do *Arua* do?"

"*Arua* looks like man. Has magic. Takes food from someone. Feeds it to snake. Sometimes feeds frog or rat."

"What happens then?"

"Get sick. Sometimes die. *Arua* sometimes gets fingernail or hair from someone. Does magic, make them sick. Sometimes die."

The Ono house was constructed from sago palm leaves. It was built about three feet off the ground on stilts. There was an adjacent, open-air structure that was used for cooking. Our house's three rooms were used primarily for sleeping. Samuel Ono, his wife, and two small children slept in one room. Five assorted children, nieces, and nephews slept in a second room.

Charles and Paula lived in a three-room house in Langa Lau

Paula and I had the middle room where we slept under a mosquito net. We managed to continue the benefits of married life despite the unusual living arrangements. The room also had a small table at which we ate our morning and evening meals. "Where do you think they wash our dishes?" Paula mused one evening, as we ate our simple meal.

"They probably wash them at the standpipes," I answered. "They would have plenty of time during the day while we're having our lessons."

I actually thought they might have village dogs clean the plates by licking. There were other potential problematic issues I observed during training. I often thought I might solve problems with investigation and corrective actions. However, I always convinced myself that it would be prudent to create imaginary, plausible solutions rather that burden myself with truth and facts.

My supposition they were washing our dishes at the standpipes would have satisfied most people but not Paula. She raised the issue the next night. "I know where they're washing our dishes," she said, during our meal. "I followed Mama and saw her washing them in the river! Pigs poop in the river! We might get sick from that!"

I couldn't disagree with her, but it was comforting to learn they didn't have dogs functioning as living dishwashers. I rationalized that accepting our dishes being washed in the river was a part of accepting Solomon culture. Culture lessons were often combined with Peace Corps rules. Examples included: Always take the prescribed malaria prophylaxis at the designated times. Men stepping over another man's legs was implying that the stepper was having sex with the other man's wife.

Women must never be higher than men. Expatriate women must always wear long skirts. Expatriate men must always wear shirts. Never barter for prices when shopping at farmers' markets. Peace Corps Volunteers must never get involved in commercial logging issues. Volunteers must never loan money to Solomon Islanders.

Volunteers must always wear life jackets when riding in canoes. Volunteers can't travel to the U.S. for vacations. Cuts and scrapes need quick attention due to the likelihood of infections. Volunteers must never drive vehicles. Women must never walk alone at night. Single women must never invite a Solomon man into her house. There were many more rules, and all were created for our own good. Rules are rules!

Our Solomon trainers occasionally disagreed with Jimmie. She once told us if we were in a vehicle that hit a Solomon Islander, we must stop and render aid. That seemed reasonable to me, but our Solomon trainers disagreed. "You run away," Ephraim said.

"Yes, run away." Charles agreed. "Solomon man kill you if you stop."

Jimmie ended the discussion by restating our obligation to stop and render aid. At a later date, Ephraim, Charles, and Joseph privately repeated their advice to run away if I were involved in an accident. "Solomon man kill you," each insisted.

Samuel Ono initiated an early discussion with me concerning Solomon culture. "Solomon man higher than woman," he informed me.

"Charles and Ephraim told us about that in our Solomon culture lessons," I answered.

"Peace Corps knows Solomon culture. Everyone learning."

"Thank you, Samuel. We're studying hard."

"Why Peace Corps spoil Solomon customs with boss woman, Jimmie?"

I didn't have a satisfactory answer. Jimmie had been placed in a difficult position that was contrary to Solomon customs. I wished our trainers had prepared me for a question like that. "It's America's customs," I finally answered. "For Peace Corps to send us to Solomons, they must have some boss ladies."

That seemed to satisfy Samuel. He turned the conversation to his campaign for a provincial office. He had a letter for me to edit. His letter was in English and well written. I made a few improvements and wished him luck in his race.

Since Jim and Chris were volunteers themselves and had lived in the Solomons many months, their experiences were valuable. "Things will move very slow for you," Jim told us. "It's going to be hard to make things happen. Your training group is replacing my training group. Chris and I are the only ones still in the Solomons."

"What happened to the others?" Margaret asked.

"They got frustrated and terminated their contracts. Tom and Bill have structured assignments. They know where they will work and what they will do. You others are community development workers. You will have a lot of freedom to develop projects, but you will need cooperation from village leaders, area council representatives, and your provincial supervisors."

"I take it that the previous volunteers couldn't accomplish that," Carrie said.

"That's right. There were always problems, but the major one was funding." The Solomon Islands' government and the provincial governments don't have any money. Peace Corps won't provide funding for your projects."

"Well then, how can we make things work?" Paula asked.

"If you follow the system for needs assessments that we're teaching you, you'll know how to write well-developed action plans. You can use the plans to apply for grants."

"Where will we apply for grants?"

"The granting agency will depend on the project. When you know your needs for your proposed project, the funding agency will become more apparent."

Paula and I talked about our jobs that evening. We decided that we would try to start several projects. We could apply for a grant for each project thinking that if two, or even one, were funded, we would be successful. Terminating our contracts was not an option.

Langa Lau villagers used the bush for their toilet needs. Men used one area and women used a separate area. Peace Corps officials had made agreements with village leaders for them to install four water seals for our use. The structures were to be built by digging holes then setting formed, cement, squat-toilet slabs over the holes. A leaf structure was to be built around the slabs to offer we trainees more privacy. Payments for the scheduled work had been made in advance.

Only two water seals had been built when we arrived. One was close to Samuel Ono's house. Jimmie was aggravated because the Langa Lau men had not built the water seal toilets by the time we arrived. She told us that she would ensure that the appropriate villagers would build the other two promised, and paid for, water seals.

We squatted to use the water seals and flushed with a bucket of water. We men carried water from the near-by river to a barrel set by the structure. Carrie received a surprise one night when she went to use the privy. When she opened the door, a pig squealed and crashed through the wall. Neither Carrie nor the pig was harmed in the incident.

Our days were filled with training in the Pisin language, Solomon Islands' culture, government issues, needs assessments, health issues, and other issues important to Peace Corps Volunteers. We had tea breaks around 10:00 a.m. and 3:00 p.m. Peace Corps provided our lunch. Our breakfasts and suppers were furnished by our host families.

The *wontok* system was a feature of Solomon Island life. This involved reciprocal obligations that began with direct family members and extended to friends, neighbours, and others who spoke the same tribal language. Solomon Islanders often travelled to other villages where they could call upon *wontok* ties for hospitality and help. "Solomon Islands' people will consider all Americans *wontoks*," Chris said. "We're from the same country and we all speak the same language."

"There are positive things to the *wontok* system," Jim added. "But there are also downsides. The system is often abused. "*Wontok* ties are sometimes exploited. Families fulfilling *wontok* obligations can be driven into poverty."

Most of we trainees attended church with our host families. Men and boys sat on benches without backs on one side. Women and girls sat on backless benches on the other side. After one Sunday service, Margaret and Paula had a banana cake demonstration for the village women. There were ample bananas for the cake, and they got the other ingredients from the Peace Corps larder. Margaret and Paula baked their cake in a traditional, Solomon Islands' stone oven. The village women enjoyed the lesson and relished the banana cake.

Mary was a nurse employed by the Peace Corps. She was British and had lived in Africa for some years. She was currently married to a Solomon Islander. Naturally, her job was to teach us about health issues that would confront us in the Solomons. She traveled from Honiara to Langa Lau for our medical lessons. We learned that malaria, hepatitis A, hepatitis B, typhoid, yellow fever, tuberculous, respiratory diseases, and leprosy were in the Solomons.

Mary told us that malaria was the most dangerous. We were instructed to take malaria prophylaxis the entire time we were there. We were to take two paludrine pills each day and two chloroquine tablets on Sunday. Mary gave us each a medical kit that contained blood slide equipment. If we thought we might have malaria, we were to draw blood and make a slide. If our blood test was positive, we would have to take a course of chloroquine.

Nurse Mary had a session on sexually transmitted diseases. She culminated this lesson by teaching us how to put a condom on a banana. During this lesson, Mary introduced the issue of overpopulation. "The Solomon Islands have the highest population growth and fertility levels in the Pacific," she said. "Fertility levels are over five births for every woman between the ages of fifteen and forty-nine."

"Are there organized efforts to initiate birth control?" Carrie asked.

"There's no official government policy. Expatriates like you often talk about the problems. There are even some Catholic priests who advise their parishioners to limit birth numbers."

We slept under mosquito nets nightly and burned mosquito coils to keep the nasty insects away. When we first arrived in the Solomons, we smeared ourselves several times daily with a lotion called RID. Paula and I soon quit using it. RID was recognized as a carcinogen and caused us to break out. We used Skin-so-Soft in-lieu of RID. The Skin-so-Soft worked very well.

Nurse Mary told us that malaria is transferred as parasites from an infected person to a healthy one. The parasites are carried by mosquitoes that inject the parasites into the victim's blood while feeding. The parasites travel to the liver, then return to the bloodstream where they reproduce in red blood cells.

Mary provided professional explanation of how paludrine and chloroquine killed malaria parasites. Translated into simple verbiage, the malaria parasite drowns in its own metabolic products. The thought of malaria parasites drowning in their own wastes was extremely satisfying. I hoped each of the nasty bugs suffered tremendously.

Chloroquine was a medication used to prevent and to treat malaria. Mary told us that common side effects included muscle aches, loss of appetite, diarrhea, and skin rashes. Potential serious side effects includes problems with vision, muscle damage, seizures, and low blood cell levels. Neither Paula nor I ever experienced any of these side effects, but I always felt a little nauseous.

Paludrine tablets contained the active ingredient, proguanil hydrochloride. Proguanil prevents malaria by stopping the parasite from reproducing when it's inside the red blood cells. Potential side effects of Paludrine use included nausea, vomiting, constipation, diarrhea, and/or abdominal pain.

Neither Paula nor I had such negative side effects from using Paludrine. What I did experience was very vivid dreams. I never experienced nightmares or anything erotic. My dreams often consisted of long-lasting, multi-colored, undulating scenes of music. I could see the music in my dreams, but I couldn't hear any sound. I can only describe my dramatic sleep visions as four dimensional. I always woke fully rested and refreshed.

Rick and Carrie were assigned to work in the Solomon Island Development Trust. John Roughan was the founder and director of the organization. He was a former Catholic priest, currently married to a Solomon woman. They had one son, Paul. The Peace Corps had Director Roughan as a guest speaker. "Economic development isn't just about money," he told us. "It's about people's lives. Money is important, but it's an addition, not a substitute, to development."

In addition to working for Roughan, Rick and Carrie were going to live in an apartment under his main house. Roughan had a unique perspective on the economic status of Solomon Islanders. "Solomon Islands has thousands of villages filled with wealthy people," he said. "They own mountains, land, trees, and the Pacific Ocean filled with fish."

When it got dark, we men showered under standpipes in the middle of the village. The women showered under a standpipe in a more secluded area. When Jimmie, Chris, Paula, Carrie, and Margaret took their showers, they manipulated their lava lavas, so they could wash their bodies. Young men and boys amused themselves by watching from the bushes until complaints from the ladies resulted in the village elders putting a stop to it.

We men removed our shirts, shoes, and socks for our standpipe showers. Our wet shorts were later put into a bucket of water to soak with other clothes. We soaked the clothes overnight to aid in washing them. We scrubbed the wet clothes the next day with a brush and soap. Wet clothes took a long time to dry in the humid weather.

One evening, I went to the standpipe to shower and wash clothes. The full moon made it easy to see. After showering, I moved away and began scrubbing our clothes. A young Solomon woman approached the standpipe to begin her own shower. She had her lava lava wrapped around her body including her breasts. She began her shower by facing me then rewrapping her lava lava to expose her upper body. Her brown breasts were large and firm.

She soaped her body slowly. The water trickled down her body and soaked her lava lava. The wet garment soon clung to her shapely legs and buttocks. The light material became easy to see through. There was little left to imagine what she would look like if she were totally naked. This was close to the image of young, scantily clad maidens, dancing in the moon light that was a motivation in my joining the Peace Corps.

However, I recognized that this might not be understood by other interested parties. Perhaps a father or brother might demand compensation for my innocent participation. Maybe a husband would demand that I be beaten to a pulp. Worse yet, Paula might mistakenly think that I had not given proper attention to washing our clothes. The incident ended without further drama. The woman finished her shower, rewrapped her lava lava to cover her breasts, and left.

We had been in the training village for three weeks and had two more to go. Jimmie told us that the appropriate villagers said they would build the other two water seals soon. It was the cool-dry season. We were comfortable most of the time. One-fourth of the training time was spent on Pisin language and one-fourth spent on culture and customs. The rest of the time was spent on individual skills development.

We were told that the Peace Corps programs were evolving into a process-oriented system rather than a project-oriented system. I could repeat the spoken words, but I couldn't identify any lessons on recognition of the current project-oriented system and how we were expected to evolve into a process-oriented system.

Solomon people had adequate food, clean water, and basic shelter. Most lived primarily by subsistence agriculture. They were working toward better functioning government and development skills. Some were embracing the concept of money-making projects.

Tom's and Bill's needed skills were specific to their jobs. Our trainers recognized they were not qualified to instruct Tom on the care and feeding of giant clams or Bill on accounting. Useful non-formal education skills were stressed for we community development workers. I had similar non-formal education training in my M.P.A. courses at K-State.

I felt lucky to have a Peace Corps assignment in the Solomons, but the training was stressful. We were told we must assume the status of children with our hosts functioning as our parents. I lacked any feeling of independence. The food was different from what I was accustomed. There weren't any recreational opportunities. I dealt with the stress by sleeping up to eleven hours every day. I often went to bed promptly after supper and slept.

Paula joined the others for social events when I went to bed early. I also had trouble with language acquisition. I had been stationed in Germany for two years in the Army and learned to speak some German. I began to understand Pisin, but when I tried to speak, German words came out.

We attended a custom wedding while we were in the training village. The bride and her family arrived with lots of prepared food. They carried two live hogs on poles that were to be killed and cooked for the feast. The groom and his family were to purchase his wife in a bride price ceremony. The wedding dress was a blue skirt with lots of shell money draped about her neck to partially cover her naked breasts. She also wore a head piece and initially draped a piece of cloth around her head and face. Everyone waited for the bride's family to barter for additional money.

Solomon bride

When the price was agreed upon, the bride's family picked her up and carried her to the ceremonial umbrella. The groom joined her there and they were officially married. When the bride's family were carrying her to the umbrella, they ran into a tree. The couple had been living together for two years.

Administration Officer Peter Corsey was scheduled to make a presentation. He arrived with his wife and introduced her. "My wife makes better presentations than I do," he said. "I'm going to have her take my place."

Mrs. Corsey made a nice presentation. She was knowledgeable about the topics covered. The Corsey couple returned to Honiara. We took our morning break then moved to the area for our Pisin lessons.

The issue of water seals came up again several days before the end of training. Jimmie started one of the training sessions by informing us that she was angry that the villagers had not built the two remaining water seals. She told us that she had called the village leaders together and gave them a tongue-lashing. Samuel and three other village leaders called on me that evening. "Here about Solomon customs," Samuel began.

I sensed something was wrong. I couldn't think of anything that I had done that would have caused angst. "What customs are you talking about?" I asked.

"Man over woman custom. Woman never boss. Want Jimmie leave. You be boss."

They didn't mention anything about Jimmie scolding them about the water seals. I didn't bring up the issue. I spoke to them in Pisin telling them that Peace Corps in Washington D.C. had made the decision that Jimmie would be boss. My closing argument was that if they managed to force Jimmie out, they wouldn't get the money they had coming from Peace Corps. That caused them to better appreciate a woman boss in their village.

On our last full day in the village, we exchanged gifts and said our good-byes. Samuel Ono gave us a custom spoon and a basket. Fred gave us a bamboo flute. Paula could play the flute immediately. We went to a final celebration at the church and returned to Honiara the next day by market truck.

We stayed in the Honiara Hotel when we returned from our training village. Each of we eight trainees had an individual session with Jimmie. "I don't think I'm going to be able to recommend you for permanent assignment," Jimmie informed me.

I was flabbergasted. "Why can't you recommend me for placement?" I asked.

"I'm concerned that you're culturally insensitive. Being culturally sensitive in very important in Peace Corps assignments."

Cultural sensitivity was subjective and obviously in the eye of the beholder. If there was an objective measure from which cultural sensitivity could be measured, we didn't cover it in our training. I didn't think it was a subject that could be resolved by debate or argument. "Jimmie," I protested. "Paula and I made tremendous sacrifices to join the Peace Corps. We quit good jobs. We sold everything we owned. We left our families. We can't just go back and pick-up where we left off."

"Everyone makes those sacrifices."

I was deeply distressed. I told my fellow trainees about my exchange with Jimmie. "I don't like that!" Matt exclaimed. "We have to stick together. I want Charlie to give the thank-you speech for us."

"I think a woman should give our thank-you speech," Carrie said.

The decision was made that Paula and I would share thank-you presentation privileges. Tom and Bill had individual meetings with Director John Mark. Married couples had a joint, private meetings with him. "My door is always open," John Mark said, when Paula and I met with him. "You can come see me on any issue at any time. I can only think of three times that I've closed my door in all the time I've been here."

"I do want to talk to you about our training," Paula responded. "I don't think Jimmie treated Charlie very well in the end."

John Mark looked surprised. He immediately rose and shut the door. Paula told him that Jimmie said it would be hard for her to recommend placement for me. John Mark looked at the written record Jimmie kept during our training. "I don't see anything here," he said. "What is the problem?"

"I didn't know there was a problem," I said. "All Jimmie said was that she thought I was culturally insensitive."

"If Jimmie thinks you are culturally insensitive, you're probably culturally insensitive."

Issues involved with my cultural sensitivity were not resolved, but there were no further discussions. It became understood, without anyone saying, that I would be permitted to serve.

Nurse Mary took us to visit a sup-sup garden. Sup-sup gardens were small plots beside houses used to grow vegetables. The goal for planting sup-sup gardens was to improve Solomon diets. We bought seeds to take to Auki. We walked to the provincial government office after lunch to find out when we would be leaving for Auki.

We had final evaluations and weighed in at Mary's office. I had lost twenty-five pounds and Paula had lost fourteen. Mary thought Paula looked pale, so she drew blood to check for anemia. "If I had worms, could they cause me to be anemic?" Paula asked.

"It's possible," Mary answered. "Do you think you might have worms?"

"Maybe I do. They washed our dishes in the river in our village. Pigs pooped in the river. Maybe I got worms that way."

"It's possible that you have hook worms. I going to give you both sample kits. We'll find out for sure."

We followed instructions with the sample kits and learned that we didn't have worms. We had a free day that I would have been happy to have spent relaxing and watching a movie. Rick had more energy. "This would be a good chance to see Matanikau Falls," he announced. "They're famous, and we will follow Galloping Horse Ridge to get there."

"How long will it take us?" I asked.

"Just a few hours," he answered. "We might have to swim out. I'm been reading about Matanikau Falls. Following the river is the best way out. The trees and brush on the banks are so heavy that we won't be able to walk."

"Well, I can't swim," I answered. "But if I can't walk out on the banks or wade, I can always go back on the path that we walked in on."

Tom chose to rest while the rest of us opted for a jaunt to Matanikau Falls. We followed a path on Galloping Horse Ridge between what were once Japanese fox holes. We had been warned to stay on the path because there was a possibility that live ordnance was around the holes. Rick was our group historian and told us of the importance of the area in W.W. II. "It was right here that Japanese forces dug in during the Guadalcanal Campaign," he said.

"Were there other allied countries involved in the campaign?" Matt asked.

"No, there were no other allied forces here," Rick answered. "There were native Solomon men helping U.S. soldiers and Marines. The fighting started here in December 1942."

"What were the battles all about?" Margaret wanted to know.

"The Americans were trying to destroy the Japanese forces who were building an airstrip on Guadalcanal. The Japanese were trying to hold out until reinforcements could arrive."

It was easy to imagine how horrific it must have been fighting in the thick jungles and extremely hot, humid environment. The Japanese couldn't get reinforcements or supplies. Many died from malaria, starvation, and lack of medical care. The Japanese eventually withdrew to Guadalcanal's west coast where they were evacuated during the first week of February 1943.

We reached the tropical rain forest and then began descending the mountain. We followed the path by sliding into a deep crevice where we found the falls. The vegetation was thick and lush as promised. It was a long and tiring hike, but the beautiful falls and the comradeship made the trip well worth the effort. I watched while the others swam and played in a large pool at the base of the waterfalls. In due time, we decided it was time to return to Honiara.

As Rick had warned, I could see the trees and brush were so heavy in most areas that I couldn't walk on the banks. In the few locations that it would have been possible to walk, the banks were too steep for me to climb out. My idea to follow the path back was thwarted by the deep, steep crevice where we slid to get to the falls. I had no other option but to begin following the river downstream. The river was so deep in many places that the others had to swim.

As I wrote earlier, I couldn't swim, but I could stay above water by flailing. I wished I had thought to bring one of the life-jackets that I was obligated to wear when riding in a canoe. I wished I had a canoe. I wished I had stayed in Honiara. The others would swim ahead and find a hand-hold or a rock for me to stand on, so I could rest. It was scary for me, but the more I "swam" the better I got.

Rick and Matt were certified life-guards and Rick had a national rating. There were places where we waded in calf deep to chest deep water. The water was clear, flowing, and very cold. The tips of our fingers and thumbs soon became numb. We eventually made it out and back to the Honiara Hotel.

Paula and I saw Peter Corsey at the office. He told us he had a transformer for sale that allowed him to use his American electrical equipment in the Solomons. He offered to sell us the transformer for US$600. We were not tempted to buy.

Later that week, we went snorkeling for the first time. Some Peace Corps Volunteers stationed in Honiara loaned us their equipment and showed us what to do. The white sand beach, fish, and coral were beautiful. Matt pointed out coconut palms that still showed bullet scars from W.W. II. Rick went swimming parallel to the beach. I watched in amazement as he swam farther and farther. He eventually turned and swam back. "How far can you swim?" I asked, when he came ashore.

"It's just like walking," Rick answered, with a shrug. "I can swim as far as I want."

Close-of-training party at Jimmie's house.
Front left to right – Matt, Jimmie, Carrie, Chris, and Margaret.
Back left to right – Jim, Paula, Charlie, Rick, Bill, and Tom

Paula and I prepared to give our thank-you speeches for our graduation ceremonies. Members from our host families were invited to attend the ceremonies. Peace Corps Director John Mark talked to us about our assignments. "Some Peace Corps country directors think their jobs are limited to providing money, medicine, and mail," he repeated. "I hope you know that I want to provide you with a lot more support."

He told us of other benefits available at headquarters. "The most important thing I can tell you is to be safe," he said. "I have two caskets in storage in the event someone is killed. I don't want to ever have to use one of them. Don't ever put yourself in danger trying to do your jobs."

John Mark told us that single volunteers would get a free *Newsweek* magazine each week. Married couples would receive one to share. He also talked to us about making our Peace Corps pledges. He told me that the pledge was like the one that I had given when I joined the army.

Director Mark also informed us the prior to our invitations, the premier had temporarily halted volunteers coming to the Solomons while he determined their value to the country. "I would like for you to consider making individual pledges to the premier," he told us. "You don't have to, but I think it would make the premier happy."

He gave us a written pledge that he had prepared. None of us said anything at the time, but we discussed it later. The consensus was that John Mark shouldn't have asked us to make pledges to a foreign head of state. Regardless, none of us felt strongly enough about it to refuse.

We completed our graduation ceremonies including our Peace Corps pledges and pledges to the premier. Paula and I gave our thank-you speeches in Pisin. We spent the rest of the day saying our good-byes and getting ready to travel to Auki. We were ready for the next phase of our Peace Corps adventure.

Swearing-in ceremony

# CHAPTER 5

# *Kwara'ae Tribes*

We traveled to Auki on an eleven passenger plane the day after our swearing-in ceremony. The airport in Auki had a grass runway that was neatly trimmed. This allowed the pilot to see any pigs or dogs that might be occupying his landing area. The runway was mammal free and we landed early in the evening without incident.

A Malaita provincial driver was there to meet us. It was dark when he got us to the house where we were to live temporarily. The driver told us that his wife was the house girl for the residence. The electricity wasn't working, but I found a kerosene lamp. There was no kerosene, but the driver left and returned with a small bottle of fuel.

The large house was formally occupied by Dr. Marissa, the Australian whom David Chetwynd had told us had been raped. The next day, we found where the rapist had cut a kitchen screen to gain entry. The screen had not been repaired. I constructed a crude system to hold our bedroom door shut when we retired for the evening.

There was also a very functional club in the house. I thought it was likely that Dr. Marissa had obtained it after her ordeal. It was a small club, about eighteen inches long. About twelve or thirteen inches were handle with about five or six inches of round head. I kept it close by me when we went to bed.

Expatriates were expected to have house girls and most in Auki observed the custom. The house girls weren't paid much, but the money meant a great deal to them. Soon after we moved in, a woman presented herself and announced she was the house girl for the residence. She confirmed that she was the provincial driver's wife and had been Dr. Marissa's house girl.

Our house girl's performance proved to be much less than satisfactory. She acted like she owned the house and we were living in it as her nonpaying in-laws. She refused to do anything in the house, but spent her time working in the yard. She insisted that she had to keep it up to be ready when the new doctor arrived. I thought it would have been better for her to do what we were paying her to do. Another Solomon cultural lesson learned!

We quickly recognized the accuracy of Fred's lesson about *Arua* magic in Malaita. There was a commonly held belief that an *Arua* could get someone's fingernail or hair and use it for magic. The *Arau* could make a victim sick or even die. Because of these concerns, only a good friend or close relative was sufficiently trusted to cut hair. I trusted Paula completely, thus she became my barber. In due time, she became the barber for many other expatriates. However, she didn't trust me enough to let me cut her hair. She used the excuse that she and Mary had pledged to not cut their hair until they were together again.

Auki had a harbor where ships came and went several times a week. The city's population was officially 2,950. Auki had a public water system and a public electricity system. A diesel fueled generator produced the electricity. Diesel and gasoline were transported to Auki by ship in fifty-five-gallon drums.

A private company provided telephone service. We lost water and telephone service occasionally. We lost electrical service frequently. When the electricity went off, many Auki men emitted primal screams.

There was an open-air market in Auki six days a week. Saturday was the big market day. Malaita gardeners offered fruit, vegetables, coconuts, taro, kumara, sweet yams, pineapples, tomatoes, betel nuts, and other items for sale. Fishermen brought in freshly caught fish for shoppers to buy. We soon made Saturday shopping a regular occurrence in our routines.

Those of us who did not want to buy freshly caught fish could purchase processed fish in a local shop. A young J.O.C.V. managed the shop and supervised the employees. The employees sold processed fish and used the money to buy fresh fish from fishermen. There were ample funds to pay the employees and pay the bills.

There was also a meat market and a bakery. May Ice Cream Company sold ice cream and a frozen sugar-water. The sugar-water was colored, sealed in stiff, plastic tubes then frozen. Children purchased the sugar-water then discarded the plastic tubes on Auki's streets. The results were children with bad teeth and streets strewn with the unsightly plastic.

There were a few small grocery stores and shops owned and operated by ethnic Chinese. Eric Mason owned a small truck that he hired out. Few Solomon Islanders could successfully operate businesses. The *wontok* system mandated a potential business owner sharing his or her goods with *wontoks* without payment.

The Chinese were descendants of Chinese who traded with Malitians from small ships many decades before. The ancestor Chinese would trade in daylight hours then move to the safety of deeper water at appropriate times. Though the Chinese shop owners had been born in the Solomons, they were not citizens. Solomon citizenship was only granted to those with at least three native Solomon grandparents.

The largest, and most popular, establishment was Margaret's Chinese Store. It had an open, covered porch the entire front length of the store. A large counter ran the inside length of the store separating goods from customers. Margaret sold beer, cigarettes, wine, pop, packaged rice, canned tuna, exercise paper, and various canned goods.

The canned tuna was produced in Western Province by a Japanese company. The other canned goods were mostly imported from Australia. They were usually beyond the expiration date when they entered the Solomon Islands. The beer was always fresh.

Margaret's primary employee was from Isabel, mitigating *wontok* issues. He handled the money exchange duties and supervised the Malitian employees. The Malians managed to respond to customer requests for goods without smiling or speaking. Quickly raised brows signified affirmative responses to questions.

Paul Kennioriana had told us that our work day would begin at 8:00 a.m. On our first day of employment, we walked to work and arrived at the office building before 8:00 a.m. The building was locked. Paul showed up around 8:30 and let us in. "Solomon time," he said, with a shy smile.

We walked to our office arriving around 8:15 the next two days. We had to wait until 8:30 for Paul to unlock the building. From then on, we arrived at work around 8:30. When in the Solomons, do as Solomon Islanders do.

Paula and I shared an office with George Toritelia and Moses Agougka. George was clean-shaven, and Moses had a full beard. Like most Solomon people, both were heavily muscled. George and Moses were betel nut users evidenced by their reddish-black stained teeth. Each wore cotton shorts that came nearly to his knees, a colorful, cotton shirt, and no shoes.

On our fifth day of work, Paul Kennioriana came into our office early in the morning. Moses, George, Paula, and I looked up expectantly. "Central Malaita Area Council meet today," Paul said, in Pisin. "Want you meet them. Tell who you are, why you here."

I started to speak, but I stopped when Paula touched my arm. "Where will we meet?" she asked.

"Not decided," Paul answered. "When ready, will collect you."

Early that afternoon, Paul came to our office. George wasn't in and Moses was busy. Paul instructed us to follow him and led us to a meeting area in the building. George Toritelia was seated with the area council representatives and was taking notes. Paul introduced us as new Peace Corps Volunteers who would be working in Malaita.

Paula and Paul stood aside and looked to me. "We're Charles and Paula Sellens," I began, in Pisin. "We're community development workers. We're here to help Malaita people with development projects. We'll be here for two years. If you want us to try to help, you can arrange with Paul Kennioriana for us to visit your village."

The area council representatives sat stoic. None smiled or responded with comments or questions. Observing Solomon Islands' male dominated culture, Paula did not speak. We accompanied Paul back to our office. George stayed with the council. We spent the rest of the day writing letters home. Our week-end was uneventful.

Paul Kennioriana introduced us to Malaita Province Education Officer Albert Nori early Monday morning. Albert was slender and neatly dressed. He wore long trousers and a colorful, button-up shirt. Albert did not show effects of beetle nut use. He was the only one we had met in the provincial offices who wore shoes. "There was supposed to be two more Peace Corps Volunteers with you," Albert said, in English. "They're not coming. I want you to do work in my community education department."

"Agree with plan," Paul said, in Pisin. "Talked to Peace Corps when you on walk-about. Said our right to assign jobs."

I was ready to agree when Paula spoke. "What exactly will we be expected to do?" she asked.

"I want you to work with the provincial literacy program," Albert said. "You can also be reporters for the *Malaita Nius*. *Malaita Nius* is the provincial newspaper. It's published monthly in English and Pisin."

"If we get too much work from Paul Kennioriana, can we put off some of the things we would be doing for you?"

"Paul is your boss," Albert said. "When Paul has work for you, no work for me."

Paula looked to me and nodded. "We would be pleased to take on these responsibilities," I said. "We want to be productive during the two years we're here."

I later learned that Albert's brother, Andrew Nori, was a member of the Solomon national parliament. Andrew was elected in 1984 representing the West 'Are'are constituency.

The prime minister promptly appointed him minister for home affairs and provincial government. He was re-elected in 1989 and was elected opposition leader.

I also learned that Andrew and Albert's father was Nori Nono'oohimae. He was then deceased, but was one of the founders of the Maasina Ruru movement. Maasina Ruru followers revolted against the British colonial rule that was reinstated after the U.S. left at the end of W.W. II. Nori Nono'oohimae was a famous figure in Solomon Islands' history.

It was our third week at work, and things were going slowly. We had been told in training that we should expect a slow start. However, we did want to have something meaningful to do. We didn't get directions from Albert on what to do to develop a literacy program.

We met a couple from Australia early in our stay. The man was an engineer supervising the construction of the new building where we would have an office when it was completed. They had us over for supper one evening. "We'll be finished with the new building before too long," he said. "We'll return to Australia when it's finished. We think we'll be back to supervise construction of a fence around the market area."

"Why are you building a fence around the market area?" Paula asked.

"Auki officials asked for it. They want to make a charge for venders using the area. Building a fence and entry gate will make the plan more likely to be successful."

Our first request for a site visit came later in the week. Our visitor seated himself in our office and introduced himself. "Name Robert Dettka," he said. "My village has cattle. Sell calves to fatten in Guadalcanal and Australia."

"That sounds impressive," I answered. "We're Charles and Paula Sellens. What would you like for us to do?"

"Come see cattle project. Help us do better. Have guest house where you stay."

"We would be happy to come to your project. Our supervisor is Paul Kennioriana. We have to clear everything through Paul. Paul will have to arrange transportation to get us to your village. Let's go see him."

We three walked to Paul's office. He stopped what he was doing to talk to us. "Hello Paul," I said. "This is Robert Dettka. Robert would like for Paula and me to visit his cattle ranch. We could do a needs assessment to learn if we can help them."

Paul blushed deeply and avoided eye contact with me. "Know Robert," he responded.

We chatted off subject a bit with me bringing the conversation back to the reason for our visit. Paul was very evasive. I couldn't get him to commit to scheduling a needs assessment for Robert's cattle project. I was a bit frustrated when we left Paul's office. I told Robert that I would contact him when we were able to visit his village.

The next day, I returned to Paul's office. He stopped working on his project and smiled. "Paul, when Paula and I brought Robert in yesterday, you didn't seem to want us to go with him," I said. "What was the matter?"

"He's insane," Paul answered, in Pisin. "Doesn't own anything. Can you imagine him owning cattle?"

I was surprised. I hadn't noticed that Robert was different from any of the other Solomon men that I had met. Paul genuinely believed that I recognized that Robert lived in a fantasy world. Every day in the Solomon Islands was a learning experience for me.

Our assignment in Auki made us de facto community development workers for the Kwara'ae tribal group. As with most Malitians, Kwara'ae villagers made their living through subsistence farming and fishing. Men and women shared the work involved in gardening. They periodically cut out undergrowth, burned trash, planted, weeded, and harvested root crops and vegetables.

Men did the more difficult jobs including cutting trees and log removal. After drying, trash was gathered into small piles and burned. The ash was used to fertilize growing plants. The men marked the cleared plots into sections. They used dibble sticks to poke holes in the ground where they planted taro, vegetables, kumara, sweet yams, pineapples, tomatoes, and tobacco.

Most Kwara'ae took up to an hour to walk to their garden plots. Some gardens were even more distant. The job of transporting garden produce was usually performed by women. They grew bananas, plantains, betel nuts, ngali nuts, coconuts, pomelo, and papaya in other areas. Additionally, Kwara'ae people used forest products for building materials, dyes, and medicines.

Area Council Representative Paul Tafqi made the first legitimate request for us to spend a few days in his village. Paul Kennioriana brought him to our office. "Name Paul Tafqi," Kennioriana said, in introduction. "Paul area council representative and Central Malaita Area Council vice-president."

"We're pleased to meet you, Paul," I said.

I rose and extended my hand for shaking. Paul took my hand and held it while we spoke. "Surprised you speak Pisin at meeting," he said approvingly. "Thought you speak hard English."

Paul Tafqi swung our joined hands slightly from side to side as we spoke. "Paul wants village visit," Paul Kennioriana said. "Arrange transportation to Fasileta, November 5."

We traveled to Fasileta on our scheduled day. We met with Paul and other village leaders and described how we did needs assessments and developed action plans. We told them that when the steps identified in our action plans reached the proper point, we could apply for a grant. Paul showed us men drying coconut to make copra.

We spent three days in Fasileta and were constantly followed by children. Many of the children had white hair and the younger ones were naked.

We had brought a deck of cards and showed the children a card trick. The trick enabled Paula to know the identity of a card chosen in secret by the children. They were impressed in an unexpected way. "Arghhh, arghhh, arghhh!" they screamed as they ran away. "Arghhh, Mommy, Daddy, they talk to devil! Talk to devil!"

Men making copra

Early in our Fasileta stay, I saw an old man approach a young man with a betel nut, leaf, and lime box. What was usually referred to as betel nut was actually areca nut. The areca nut was wrapped in a betel nut leaf. The lime had been made by heating, then powdering, coral.

Solomon Islanders chew areca nuts with betel leaf and lime for their effects as a mild stimulant. Users experienced a warming sensation and slightly heightened alertness. The toothless, old man handed the young man the material. The young man chewed it well, then spat it into his hand. He moved his hand to the old man's face and put the soggy mass into his mouth.

Even though chewing betel nut is an important and popular cultural activity in Solomon Islands, I recognized that I would always politely refuse when offered. I was concerned that I would be recognized as an old novice who could not properly manage the task. If my betel nut were first chewed by a young man then offered to me, it would be even more difficult for me to refuse. I decided to cite Peace Corps rules when refusing.

We met Paul's sister, Betty Tafqi, during our visit in Fasileta. Betty lived in a nearby village, Koa Hill. We were staying with Paul and his family and Betty came to cook for us. "Worked for white people," she informed us. "Know what white people eat."

Betty prepared a breakfast that featured fried eggs and included fried tomatoes and onions. That was the first time that I had eaten fried tomatoes and onions. They were delicious. I felt lucky to be in a village where a Solomon woman taught me what white people liked to eat for breakfast. Paula and I later talked to her privately about her life as a Solomon woman. She had an adopted daughter but no husband. "Married before, not married now," she informed us. "Husband beat me. Divorced him."

Divorce wasn't common in the Malaita, primarily governed by the custom of bride price payments. When a man's family paid bride price, the man effectively owned the woman. "What happened with the bride price payment?" Paula asked.

"No bride price," Betty answered. "When marry, mommy said no bride price. Man bad? Leave him. Man was bad. Left him."

We thought Betty's life was worthy of a story in the *Malaita Nius*. Paula told her we would come to her home in Koa Hill Village at a later time for an in-depth interview.

In addition to his own village of Fasileta, Paul represented Buma, a much larger village. After Paula and I visited Fasileta, we made an action plan. I expected Paul to pursue the proposed project for his own village. Instead, he arranged for us to visit Buma Village for another needs assessment. I was impressed with Representative Tafqi's unselfishness.

Area Council Representative Tafqi escorted us to Buma and introduced us to Simon Buarafi. I thought of Simon as the chief, but he preferred the title of chairman. Tafqi also introduced us to Simon's brother, Daniel. Daniel told us that he had worked for the U.S. military during W.W. II. He proudly showed us two medals he had been awarded. "America fought Japan," Daniel said. "Solomon man help America fight Japan."

Children greeted us in Buma

I didn't speak, but raised my brow, Solomon style, to show I understood and agreed. "After war, America help Japan," Daniel continued. "America not help Solomon Islands. Why America help Japan, not Solomons?"

I didn't have an answer for Daniel. He waited patiently for an answer. I waited patiently for him to stop waiting patiently. I eventually waited him out and we returned to discussions about his being awarded W.W. II medals.

Buma was about six or seven miles from Auki and was situated on the ocean. The trail that led from the main road to Buma was intersected by a small creek. A short part of the trail was through an area that had been clear-cut by a commercial logging company. What had been a century-old rainforest was then ugly stumps and unusable scrap branches. Dank water stood in low areas making it even more unattractive and odious. It was a perfect mosquito breeding area.

We spent considerable time on needs assessment practices during our training. The goal was to provide we community development workers with a system for identifying the gap between how things were and how they could be. I can explain our needs assessments and actions plans as creating a set of procedures used to identify needs, determine their nature and causes, then establish priorities for improvement.

I learned similar concepts in my M.P.A. courses at K-State under the title of action plan creation. Creating action plans included establishing defined goals to achieve, identifying those who would be involved, identifying what their roles were, and defining steps to achieve the goals. Each step was to have a due date, person responsible, and an identifier to determine if each step's goal was met.

Our needs assessment findings indicated that a reforestation project would be appropriate for maintaining the cultural and economic stability of the Buma Kwara'ae. An application for a reforestation project could not be construed as interfering with commercial logging operations. The logging operation had already done its damage.

I spent considerable time with Simon while we were preparing our plans. Simon told me that he had worked for British administrators for several years when Solomon Islands was a British protectorate. "English very strict," he said. "Had to wear shoes. Had to speak hard English."

We also got acquainted with another Kwara'ae family early in our stay. "I met a young couple at Margaret's Store," Paula said, when she returned from shopping. "The woman's name is Irene, but I forgot the man's name. Irene's father and mother are big-shots in Malaita. I told Irene to stop by some time."

Irene and her husband, Modesto, did stop by soon. They were interested in our lives in the States, our families, and our work in Malaita. "Father is Jim Misuka," Irene told us. "Mother is Salamai Misuka. Have big garden with cocoa, vegetables, pineapples, strawberries, other things. Come see."

"That's very interesting," I answered. "Yes, we'll come visit your garden sometime."

"Father Chief Saenaua Tribe," Irene continued. "Mother President Saenaua Women's Association."

I was rightfully skeptical. I thought of Robert Dettka and his claims to have a successful cattle operation. "That's impressive," I said. "I'm looking forward to meeting your parents."

Irene promised to come to our house that week-end. She said she would take us to meet her parents and see their garden. Irene did come as promised. We managed to get transportation to get near her garden then walked the rest of the way. Jim and Salamai Misuka were there to greet us. Irene's descriptions of her parents and garden proved to be accurate. The garden was large and well kept. We gave them some of the seeds we had purchased in Honiara. "Have tree project," Jim said. "Come see?"

"Yes," Paula answered. "We would love to see your tree project."

The tree project was even more impressive. Several women were cutting grass between rows of saplings that had been planted in straight lines up steep hills. I wondered

Irene and Paula at Misuka's garden

why the trees had not been planted on the contour. "What are you going to do with the trees when they're grown?" I asked.

"Cut when big," Jim answered. "New Zealand pay money to cut old trees, plant new ones. Pay to cut grass between trees, trees grow better."

"What kind of trees are the new ones?"

"Our name is *Faibaru*. New Zealand people say pencil cedar."

"What do you do with the old trees that you cut down?"

"Nothing. New Zealand don't want old trees. Want pencil cedar. Buy pencil cedar when big."

"Interesting. If you would like, Paula and I could come to your village again. We might be able to make a plan to cut the old trees into lumber to earn you money now."

Jim Misuka liked the idea. We found the names of the New Zealand government officials who were responsible for funding the tree project known as the Saenaua Custom Association. I talked to one of the New Zealand officials and explained our ideas. We received his endorsement to apply for a grant for a portable sawmill to process the downed trees.

We did a cursory needs assessment and developed an action plan in which we would apply for a grant for a portable saw mill. "What about Peace Corps telling us not to get involved in logging issues?" Paula asked.

"We're really not getting involved in logging issues," I rationalized. "I think what they intended was that we shouldn't try to stop any existing logging enterprise. We're only trying to offer an alternative."

Paula agreed with my rationalization, but she wanted our supervisor's approval. When Paul read our action plan, he had us meet with Matthew Kiri and Henry Doro. Matthew was the district forester for Malaita Province and Henry was the minister of land.

Both Matthew and Henry supported our ideas. Our plan identified the receiving organization the Saenaua Custom Association. The association was managed by Benjamin Kiki, one of Jim's many cousins.

Paula and I began getting requests for other village visits. Chief Jim Misuka was often part of the arrangements for some of the visits. He

Jim Misuka, Thomas Misuka, and Saenaua tribe members

sometimes served as a guide to get us to the remote villages. I went without Paula on an early trip and met him at his village. I carried my back pack full of what I considered necessities. Jim carried only what he considered necessary. His necessities consisted of a custom mat that would serve as both umbrella and sleeping mat. "Give Irene back-pack to carry," Jim said. "Job for woman."

I knew Jim was observing Solomon customs of using his daughter as a pack animal, but I had my own pride and customs. I was polite but firm. "Thanks, Jim, but letting Irene carry my back pack would spoil American customs. I can carry my own back pack."

Jim started down a well-worn path and I followed. Irene didn't go because she was not needed as a pack animal. Jim walked, and I struggled, down the path for about two hours. We went up small mountains and down small mountains. The path was slick from frequent rains. It was much easier to go up-hill than down-hill. When we were going down-hill, it was harder to maintain my footing. I occasionally slipped and fell. It was hard traveling. By the time we reached our village, I had changed my mind about the wisdom of refusing to allow Irene to carry my back-pack.

Our village visits were similar and focused on needs assessments that followed the same pattern. Paula usually made written notes for subsequent action plans. We identified village leaders and asked the number of people living there. "How many people live in your village?" I would ask.

Village leaders seldom gave reportable answers. Paula seldom recorded their responses. "One-hundred. No, one-hundred seventy. No, one-hundred forty-six," were typical answers.

We estimated the number of people living there and described the condition of the village. We made note of the number of children in each family. Our training included discussions concerning Malaita's increasing population trends. Village leaders had been exposed to expatriates' opinions concerning birth control. "Think too many children?" we were frequently asked.

"We're not here to judge you," was my standard answer. "But how many children do you have?"

Four or five were typical answers. "How long does it take you to walk to your gardens?" I would continue.

"One hour, more one hour," were typical answers.

"Will your four or five children have places for their gardens when they're adults?"

That usually ended our conversations about population control. Paula and I made special efforts to document health issues. I subtly looked for unknown tribal medicines that I could take back to developed countries for the benefit of humanity and make millions of dollars for myself. We made special notice of any projects that were funded by aid donors.

We never tried to convince them that economic development was in their best interest. "We're not here to tell you should have projects to make money," I often said. "We're not here to tell you to change how you are living. If you like your life style, keep on doing things the same way. But if you want money making projects, we can help you."

Our action plans also followed the same pattern. We created written documents that began with village descriptions. Potential projects were identified and step by step plans were identified. Each step identified who was responsible for performing the step. Our action plans were always identified as the first step and village organization was usually the second step.

High in the list of steps was to have a parliamentary procedure workshop. I had no illusions that they would organize themselves using parliamentary procedures. However, I was confident that documenting the workshop would be positive in grant applications.

Grant application only came when organizers had successfully completed all of their requirements. We made copies for distribution to village leaders, Solomon Islands' Peace Corps, Paul Kennioriana, and one for ourselves.

Solomon men traditionally went naked or wore only the briefest of clothing. They carried their small, personal items in bags hung around their necks. The bags were woven from bush materials. The Pisin names for these bags translated into English as "baskets." When we were there, nearly every Solomon man wore cotton shorts that came to their knees. The shorts all had pockets, but Solomon men continued to carry their personal items in traditional baskets hung around their necks. I began wearing a traditional basket.

We had arranged to have telephone service early on in our stay in Auki. Paula called the Peace Corps office to talk about our village visits. She learned that Administrative Officer Peter Corsey had left. Peter had been replaced by Larry who had worked in South Korea for seven years.

Paula told Larry that our needs assessments pointed toward Buma and Saenaua benefiting from portable sawmill projects. She told him she was concerned about applying for Small Project Assistance (S.P.A.) grants because of Peace Corps instructions to avoid logging issues. Larry told her he couldn't foresee any problems, so we continued our efforts.

# CHAPTER 6

# *Malaita's Expatriates*

We had met Yasuo Isozaki when we were on walkabout. Yasuo and the two other Japanese men we met at the Auki Lodge were working on an ice-house project. The Japanese government was funding the project with the goal of making ice available for Malaita fishermen. The fishermen were being encouraged to buy ice to keep their catch fresh for sale to Japanese buyers and eventual transportation to Japan.

Yasuo introduced us to his wife, Masako, and we became good friends. The other two Japanese families didn't associate very much with other expatriates, but the leader attended Auki's Catholic Church. There were also J.O.C.V.s living in Auki, but they didn't socialize with other expatriates when we arrived.

Isozakis lived in one of the nicest houses in Auki. Yasuo and the other two Japanese men each had new, four-wheel drive, Japanese pickups for their jobs. The project leader had an agreement with Malaita Premier David Oeta that none of the provincial employees would attempt to commandeer the trucks for provincial use.

Paula with Yasuo and Masako Isozaki

Malaita's residents received medical care in Kilu'ufi Hospital. The Solomon Islands was a member of the British Commonwealth allowing Kilu'ufi hospital to be funded by the British government. The British Commonwealth operated by consensus of its member states. Most of the fifty-two-member countries were former colonies or protectorates.

Kilu'ufi was the third largest hospital in Solomon Islands. It was established in 1915 when Solomon Islands was a British colony. It was located three miles north of Auki. Britain recruited and funded British doctors to practice at Kilu'ufi. Solomon Islanders were privileged to use the hospital without cost. Kilu'ufi administrators had a garden designed to contribute to food supplies. Malitians visiting patients were encouraged to work in the garden to help offset food expenses. They seldom complied.

Kilu'ufi was very low-tech with little modern equipment that doctors had in developed countries. The British doctors' dedication allowed them to overcome many deficiencies. Solomon women who lived close enough to Kilu'ufi to walk, or make the journey by canoe, gave birth in Kilu'ufi. Midwives performed the birthing duties.

We met Dr. Graham and Sheila MacBride-Stewart early in our stay in Auki. Dr. Graham was the chief doctor and administrator at Kilu'ufi Hospital. Sheila did considerable volunteer work with women's groups. Both were devout Catholics. "Do you have children?" Sheila asked Paula, the first time we met them.

Charlie and Paula with Dr. Graham and Sheila

"Charlie and I have two sons," Paula answered. "They live in Los Angeles, California. Do you have children?"

"Graham and I have two of our own," Sheila explained. "I had four with my first husband who was killed in a car accident. I soon married Graham and we had two more. The youngest, Vincent, is coming to visit us at Christmas."

Sheila continued by telling Paula that Dr. Graham was originally a dentist. After marriage, he moved the family from England to New Zealand where he trained as a medical doctor. He financed his medical school by working as a dentist on weekends. Some of their children still lived in Auckland.

Dr. Arun Menon was another British doctor who practiced at Kilu'ufi. He was ethnic Indian and always had a smile. Dr. Arun was about 5' 6" tall and weighed about 135 pounds. He was mischievous and jokingly referred to the U.S. as: "The Colonies."

Dr. Arun frequently tried to hold me responsible for what he asserted were historical misdeeds performed by U.S. decision makers. "American was a bigger colonizer than England," he opined, during an early dinner party. "America's primary goal in W.W. II was to acquire all the British colonies."

"My history books tell me that the U.S. entered the war to save England from complete annihilation by Germany," I responded, attempting to be equally illogical. "My history books also tell me that it wasn't the U.S. that colonized India or any other country."

"That's because your history books were written by Americans," he said, with a wide grin.

Dr. Arun was married to Elaine Menon. Elaine was a certified nurse, but she was a stay-at-home mom in Auki. Elaine was about the same height and weight as Arun. Dr. Arun and Elaine had two children, Neil and Sumaita. Neil was

Sellens and Menons

four years old and Sumaita was two. I formed an early opinion that mischievousness was an inherited trait and Neil had inherited the characteristic from Dr. Arun.

Colin and Alison Cameron

Colin and Alison Cameron had finished their training and arrived in Auki a few weeks before Paula and I arrived permanently. The Camerons were from Scotland where Colin had been an attorney and Alison had been a nurse. Colin held the position of Malaita Provincial legal advisor and Alison soon began volunteering at Kilu'ufi Hospital. I got to talk to Colin at a dinner party held at Dr. Arun and Elaine Menon's house. "Is this the first time you have lived overseas?" I asked.

"Not at all," Colin answered. "Alison and I lived in Malawi for several years when we were first married."

"What did you do in Malawi?"

"I was what you Americans would call a lawyer. We have two classes of practicing lawyers in England, solicitors and barristers. Barristers plead cases before the court and solicitors specialize in administrative law."

"Why did you go to Malawi?"

"Alison and I wanted to get married, but the salary I would earn in Scotland wouldn't be enough to support a family. I learned about a job in Nyasaland that would pay much more. I applied and was hired. Alison and I married and moved to Nyasaland in 1957."

"I don't think I have ever heard of Nyasaland."

"The country was named Nyasaland until it received its independence. It's now Malawi."

"When did you leave Malawi?"

"We left in 1964. I was the attorney for a former national cabinet member who sued the president."

"You filed a lawsuit against the president of an African country? Wow, you really had nerve!"

"Policemen came to our house and told us we had twenty-four hours to get out of the country. The policemen told me that if I didn't leave, I would be imprisoned. It's more likely that I would have been killed. Alison and I gathered the children and what we could and left."

David Chetwynd was Malaita's provincial magistrate. He and his wife, Stephanie, had welcomed Paula and me to Auki when we were on walkabout. David was full of energy and frequency organized adventures that required physical exertions. David and Stephanie didn't have children.

Andrew was a single British lawyer who served as Malaita's prosecuting attorney. There was no private attorney for people to hire to represent them court. There was no one assigned to represent defendants in criminal proceedings.

Missionaries provided valuable economic and religious services for the Solomon Islanders. The Roman Catholic Church had a strong presence in the Solomons. About 20% of Solomon Islanders were Catholics. Bishop Gerry Loft and Father Jon Volkers attended to the spiritual needs of Auki's Catholics from the Diocese of Auki. Father Chris Kamphuis and Father Phillip were posted in villages near Auki. There were other expatriate priests in various other villages throughout Malaita.

My first meeting with Bishop Loft was memorable. Paula and I had gone to meet him after we got off work. We sat on his porch visiting about our impressions of Malaita. His accent was different from the English and Scottish people I had met. "Are you from Australia?" I asked.

"Australia?" Bishop Loft looked incredulous. "Am I from Australia? No! I ought to throw you off the porch! I'm from New Zealand. I wouldn't think of living in Australia."

Paula steered the conversation to a less controversial subject. "Have you heard that there is a group here from Australia making a documentary about the Solomons?" she asked.

"I hear something about that occasionally," Bishop Loft replied. "Someone here to worship at the shrine of Roger Keesing, I suppose."

"I read about Roger Keesing," I said. "I know he was an anthropologist that lived with the Kwaio for many years."

"I don't think it's about Roger Kessing," Paula said. "I heard they were in Western Province talking to shark callers. I heard a different rumor they were in Western Province to document the fighting over the copper mine."

"You know how rumors are in the Solomons," Bishop Loft said. "Some turn out to be true. Some turn out to have come from chewing too much betel nut."

Father Jon Volkers was from the Netherlands. We learned that he had spent his entire adult life as an ordained priest in Malaita. "Were you assigned to Auki when you first came to Malaita?" Paula asked, when we first met.

"No, I first lived a small village," Father Jon said. "I served in a small church that didn't have a choir. My altar boys were altar girls that went topless. It was kind of hard to keep my mind on my business."

Father Jon was very popular in the expatriate community. He loved to play canasta and often hosted dinner parties. Father Jon and Bishop Loft asked me about my contact with Malitians at an early party. "You're in villages a lot with your job," Bishop Loft said. "When you're there, have any of the young men asked about the Iraq War?"

"Some of them have talked about it," I answered. "Some ask if they can join the U.S. Army. Why are so many of them interested in the Iraq War?"

"I believe that many of them think that America and Iraq will come to the Solomons to fight," Father Jon answered. "That fits into their customs. Many Malitians worked for the U.S. military during W.W. II."

Father Jon Volkers

"What customs are you talking about."

"Malitians traditionally had battle sites for their tribal wars. They agreed to meet at the site at a stated time. They exchanged arrows and insults until one or two were wounded or killed then they went home to sleep. They came back the next day for another battle."

"Is that why they think that the U.S. and Japan fought in the Solomons?"

"Yes, they're still convinced that the U.S. and Japan agreed to fight in the Solomons, so they wouldn't destroy the other's cities and farms. We're worried that they won't plant their gardens thinking Americans will come here to give them good paying jobs and food."

"Interesting. That's why so many have asked me about the U.S. Iraq conflict."

"If you hear any of them thinking that America is coming here to fight Iraq, convince them it won't happen," Bishop Loft continued. "We're worried that we may have a lot of hungry Malitians in a few months."

"If it does come up again, I'll definitely tell them that the war will not come to the Solomons."

Doug and Cheryl Hicks were Anglican missionaries from Montana. They had three children. Auki's Anglian priest was a Solomon Islands' man ordained by the Church of England. Doug spent considerable time supervising the construction of houses in Auki. The Hicks had been in Auki for some time evidenced by their son's Kwara'ae language skills.

Eric Mason was a single expatriate. Eric had worked for the British government in Africa for two years then transferred to the Solomon Islands. "I worked in the Solomons until I retired," he told me. "I went back to England to live, but I couldn't adjust. I came back to the Solomons. I have permanent Solomon Islands' residency. I'll live here the rest of my life."

Eric was slender and always neatly dressed. His black shoes were always highly shined. He seriously referred to the U.S. as: "The Colonies." Eric owned and lived in a beautiful, new house in Auki. He owned a small, four-wheel drive truck that he hired out. His trucking business operated under the name of Sampson's Transport. Eric employed a young truck driver who lived in a small apartment under Eric's main house.

Bob King was a Peace Corps Volunteer engineer who was designing water projects. Bob was teaching kung fu classes three nights a week and we thought about joining. "Bob, Paula and I are interested in joining your kung fu classes," I told him. "When and where do you have them?"

"I usually have them on Mondays, Wednesdays, and Fridays," he said. "When you're ready to start, I'll show you where we meet. Have you ever had martial arts training?"

"Paula and I both took karate classes in Great Bend, Kansas and I took classes in Garden City, Kansas when I worked in Dighton. I also played football and wrestled at Garden City Junior College."

"There are usually twenty to twenty-five men and three or four women that show up. Why are you thinking of joining kung-fu classes?"

"I like sports and I need to do something for exercise. Expatriates also keep warning me about potential rapes. I thought that participating in your kung fu classes might help build some respect."

"Good idea. I'm sure you heard that Dr. Marissa was raped in the house where you're living. She was my friend and was young and pretty. Since she was a doctor, she had physical contact with men while performing her medical duties. The young men didn't always understand that. Solomon men also like to watch foreign movies in which white women jump into bed with anyone that asks them. These stupid movies create negative images of white women."

Bob had a large, tractor-tire tube stored under his house. "I used the tube a few times when I went on river floats," he said. "You might want to get it when I leave. You'll have plenty of opportunities to use it to float down Malaita rivers."

"Thanks Bob," I said. "We'll get it as soon as you leave."

We started Bob King's kung fu lessons. As Bob had said, there were around twenty young men and four or five women in the class. Bob had a Solomon man as his assistant.

Bob allowed only limited sparing fearful that the Malitians would pursue their matches too vigorously. I sparred the assistant in one of the early lessons. Our skills were similar, but I was taller and heavier, so I could best him quite easily.

I twice sparred with Bob. Bob was taller and had better skills, but I was heavier and motivated by showing the Malitians that my wife was always to be treated with respect. I was also motivated to move around quickly to prevent Bob from kicking and hitting me. I felt that I achieved my goal of showing the Malitian men that Paula was to be treated with respect. My goal of preventing Bob from kicking and hitting me, not so much.

One of the most interesting Malitians we met in the kung fu class was Peter Ufa of Dala Village. Peter dressed and acted differently from other Malitians. He proudly identified himself as a custom man. He made real efforts to live his life in the way of his ancient ancestors. He had good fighting skills and was always anxious to spar others in the kung fu classes.

Graham and Glenda were another missionary couple who lived in Auki. There was another missionary couple living and working in Ontong Java. We never met the missionaries from Ontong Java. There were also the Polynesians we met while on walkabout who lived in a nearby village.

We were getting well acquainted with Auki's expatriates, but we hadn't forgotten our fellow volunteers. We were happy when we learned that Rick and Carrie were coming to visit us the end of October. They spend many of their days touring outside Auki. We celebrated Rick's birthday on October 31.

We toured a house where we were to move when the new doctor came. I didn't think it was very nice. Paula deemed it unsatisfactory. We knew that Bob King was leaving soon, so Paula talked to Mary Alisha in the provincial office. Mary was Fijian and married to National Parliament Representative Sam Alisha. Paula convinced Mary to assign us Bob King's house when he left.

The Australian couple we met early in our assignment finished the new provincial building. They expected they would return so he could supervise the building of the market fence. They invited us to come to Australia and visit them. We saw them off on the *Yu Mi Nou* and began moving into our new office.

Solomon warriors traditionally made shields out of wicker. The shields were oval or rectangular about three feet by one foot. Modern Malitians used wicker to make coasters, hot pads, serving trays, and baskets for sale to expatriates. Young boys were frequent salesmen with wicker ware for sale. We bought several items over the first few months we lived in Auki. I especially liked the small coasters that I could buy for SI$1. At SI$1 each, we were able to send many to the U.S. for presents.

Paula and I saw David Chetwynd as were leaving our office one afternoon. "I'm having a Guy Fawkes party November 5," he said. "We'll eat then burn poor, old Guy in my backyard. Do you know about Guy Fawkes?"

I was confused. I didn't understand that Guy Fawkes was a man. "No," I answered. "What is a guy fawkes?"

"Guy Fawkes was a member of a group of English Catholics who planned to assassinate King James I. They had a goal of restoring a Catholic monarch to the throne."

"I never heard about that. When was it?"

"I think it was around 1604 or 1605. The plotters rented a cellar under the House of Lords and filled it with gunpowder. Fawkes was assigned the job of guarding the explosives."

"Were they successful in destroying the House of Lords?"

"No, they were found out. Authorities learned of the plot and found Fawkes on November 5. He was tortured and sentenced to hang. On his execution date, Fawkes fell from the scaffold, broke his neck, and died of his injury."

"Do English people celebrate this every year?"

"Many English people do. Fawkes became the face of the Gunpowder Plot. His failure has been celebrated on November 5 ever since. We have parties then burn an effigy on a bonfire."

"That sounds like fun. Of course, we'll come."

We did attend the Guy Fawkes party. As David had told us, we ate dinner then burned an effigy of Guy in a small bonfire. "I wonder what Malitians will think about this ceremony?" Colin asked.

"I suspect Malitians' opinions of us change daily," David said. "Missionaries told them for decades that they must be kind and gentle like white people. Then W.W. II came, and the kind, gentle white people killed thousands of Japanese. After the war was over, they were back to being kind and gentle."

Bob King had left to go to Australia, so we moved into our permanent housing.

Bob King, in blue shirt,
says goodbye to Auki expatriates

When Bob left, we stopped going to kung fu lessons. We had been in our new house for about a week when we had a visitor. I answered the door in response to a knock.

There stood a Solomon man that I hadn't before met. He had a rim and mounted truck tire. "Come for money," he said.

I was confused. "Do I owe you money?" I asked.

"Give me SI$50.00 now," he continued. "Pay you later. Work at transportation department. Give tire until pay."

I understood much better. My caller wanted to borrow money from me. He had a rim and mounted tire that he was willing to give me as collateral. It's value far exceed the SI$50.00 that he wanted to borrow. Despite his generous proposal to put me in the banking business, I was not willing to loan him money.

His offer of a tire for security did not give me confidence. The tire wasn't his and I couldn't have converted it to cash when he defaulted on the loan. "Sorry, Peace Corps rules don't allow me to loan money," I explained. "I would like to help you, but it's Peace Corps rules."

Tire Man acted insulted. He turned his back and rolled his tire away. I turned to Paula. "He wanted to borrow money," I explained. "He wanted to give me a tire for collateral until he paid me back. I told him I couldn't."

"Well, I'm glad you didn't give him money," she said. "They told us in training not to loan money. They said we would never get it back."

"I remember very well. I told Tire Man it was Peace Corps rules, but he went away mad."

"Better him mad than you and me."

Bob King's house girl, Betty, came with the house. She and her husband, Able, lived directly across the street from us. Able worked for Malaita Province as a truck driver. Betty wanted to be paid SI$5 per day for her cleaning. A day's work was from four to five hours. Betty was afraid of electricity and wouldn't touch electrical fixtures or appliances.

The weather was warm and humid, but we were getting accustomed to the climate by that time. It rained nearly every day, so we usually carried umbrellas. When there was no rain, the umbrellas served to protect us from the sun. We were comfortable speaking Pisin at all occasions. As Paul Kennioriana had warned us, people in the villages only spoke Pisin or their tribal language.

Our diets were very simple. We bought vegetables and fruit at the Auki market. Paula made yogurt from dried milk and a live-culture starter. We ate rice several times per week. The rice frequently had bugs, but we separated the black bugs from the white rice and ate the rice without harm. The flour we bought frequently included bugs that we usually removed before consuming the flour.

Bill Wasser soon came to Auki to replace Bob King as provincial engineer. Bill had completed two years Peace Corps service in Isabel and had extended to serve one year in Malaita. Bill soon left for a vacation in the United States.

Our house was very close to Colin and Alison Cameron. It had two bedrooms, a kitchen/dining room, and a bathroom. The bathroom had a commode and a shower with cold and colder water. We usually heated water in a bucket and took it into the shower with us for washing. The house also had a screened front porch. A twenty-gallon propane tank stood outside the back door to fuel our propane cook stove.

Our house was owned by the national government and designated for use by census takers. Since the census was only taken every ten years, the national government made it available for Malaita Province's use. Mary Alisha liked to assign it to Peace Corps Volunteers thinking it would be better cared for. A Peace Corps couple that had lived in the house before Bob had screened the porch.

Cockroaches shared our home, much to our displeasure. The home had a small refrigerator and a screened food safe. We always protected our food in the food safe to deter the cockroaches from sharing. However, they occasionally contributed to my entertainment. Paula kept a flyswatter handy to punish the offending insects for invading our home. "I hate you!" she screamed, as she pursued brazen ones who dared show themselves.

She struck mighty blows as they scurried for protection. "I hate you!" she screamed. "I hate you! I hate you!"

Several geckos also lived in our house. The one to two-inch lizards ran up and down walls with ease. They had adhesive toe pads that enabled them to run across our ceiling. Many of the expatriates didn't like sharing their homes with reptiles and threw them out. I was happy to have them because the smaller ones ate small insects, including malaria carrying mosquitoes. The larger ones were able to catch and eat cockroaches that attempted to make our home, their home.

Semi-feral dogs roamed freely. Their exposed ribs provided evidence that they didn't eat regularly. Solomon boys contributed to their misery by throwing rocks at any of the poor beasts that came within their range. Chetwynds had a nice dog named Mange. The unattractive name suggested to me that it was not always so nicely groomed. Mange hated Solomon Islanders because he was often a target for rock-hucking athletes.

Father Jon told us that Mange had been born under the porch of our house a few years before. Bishop Loft had objected to so many new dogs living in the neighborhood and had poisoned them with chloroquine. Mange survived the purge and was taken in by the Chetwynds.

Semi-feral chickens also roamed freely. Ample feathers covered what I suspected was evidence of infrequent eating. They didn't suffer the indignity of being targets for rock-hucking athletes without reason. When an Auki family needed a chicken for the pot, boys were dispatched to get a chicken. They managed their assignments by chasing and throwing rocks until the chicken was injured sufficiently for them to catch and kill it.

We had Paul Kennioriana and his family over for dinner as soon as we settled in. We also invited Yasuo, Masako, Colin, and Alison making a total of eleven for our evening meal. I had offered to provide a chicken, procured Solomon style by neighbor boys, but Paula bought beef instead. We started thinking about Christmas after everyone had left. "What do you want to do for Christmas?" Paula asked.

"I hadn't given it much thought," I replied. "I'm sure that the expatriates in Auki will have Christmas parties that we will be invited to."

"What do you think about inviting everyone in our training group to come here and celebrate Christmas with us?"

I thought it was a great idea. We started making plans and promptly mailed an invitation to Matt and Margaret in Western Province. Tom, Bill, Rick, and Carrie all lived in Honiara and had phones. We called them and invited them to come to Auki for Christmas.

I received notice that we had a package at the Auki Post Office. I went to collect it and found not one, but two, large packages. I picked them up in turn and estimated they each weighed over forty pounds. Two young men lounged in the shade, watching my transaction. I didn't relish the idea of lugging even one of the boxes home. I looked toward the young men. "Would you like to make some money?" I asked. "I'll give you SI$1 each to carry my boxes home."

The men stood. Both were neatly dressed, clean shaven, heavily muscled, and barefooted. Neither spoke, but they nodded to show their agreements. The men easily carried the boxes the entire distance without rest. I gave them SI$1 each and asked their names. The taller one told me his name was Johnathan as he shook my hand and departed. The second one told me his name was Gabriel as he shook my hand. "Gabriel," I said. "If I have some work again, would you like to help me?"

Gabriel didn't speak, but he smiled and nodded. The packages were from Paula's mother. When we opened the boxes, we found our cool walking sandals were included. We tried them on and found perfect fits. I thought we would look as cool as Rick and Carrie when we wore them.

I saw Gabriel a few days later when I went to the post office. "Hello Gabriel," I said, as we shook hands. "I'm going to sand the floors in my house. Would you like to help me?"

Gabriel raised his brow to signify he would. "When?" he asked.

"I'll find you when I'm ready. I'll pay you SI$1 each hour."

We gave an anniversary party for Dr. Graham and Sheila for their twentieth wedding anniversary. David Chetwynd took the opportunity to tell more about the Cameron couple. "Colin told me they moved to Malawi in the late 1950s," David said. "Colin went to work as a lawyer. He represented several Malawians after they were arrested."

"Why were the Malawians arrested?" I asked.

"Malawi was a British protectorate at that time. It had the name of Nyasaland. The men were arrested for trouble they caused the British by demanding independence."

"When did this happen?"

"It must have been in the early 1960s. He and Alison were kicked out of the country after Malawi gained independence. Colin represented a former member of parliament in a suit against the president."

"Interesting, he told me something about that. I'll have to ask him more about it sometime."

Rumors abundant. Rumors flew more frequently in the Solomons than did parrots, warblers, pigeons, and cockatoos. Paula and I had heard rumors that there were Australians making a documentary on native culture in the Solomon Islands. We couldn't be sure if the rumors were true, but we knew they hadn't been to Malaita. The rumors were soon confirmed to be facts.

Paul Kennioriana came to our office and told us there was something he wanted us to do. He informed us that he wanted us to go to Laulasi to serve as advisors to the islanders who would soon be dealing with the Australians film crew. Paul seemed genuinely concerned. His brow sported a distinct frown as he shifted his weigh uneasily on his wide, bare feet. "Worry Australians cheat Laulasi people," he explained in Pisin. "Want film shark callers. Talking big money. Maybe four or five-thousand Solomon dollars."

An Australian film crew wanted to film shark callers on Laulasi Island? We were going to the island from which headhunters attacked Jack London in 1905? Our supervisor wanted us to be there? We were to have positions of responsibility? Wow! I was excited about getting to go to Laulasi. "Great!" I exclaimed. "When do you want us to leave?"

Inexplicably, Paula looked at me rather disdainfully. I saw the face of a loving mother observing her not-too-bright child. I fell silent. "What do you want us to do?" Paula asked Paul.

Paula was right, of course. We did need to have a better understanding of what was expected of us. I was probably going to think of asking him myself in due time. "Will hire canoe, take you Laulasi," Paul continued in Pisin. "Four Australians want to film Laulasi shark caller. I tell Laulasi chief why you there. Stay and help Laulasi people."

Paula and Paul continued their discussion, but Paul's information and instructions remained somewhat sketchy. We were to leave the next morning at ten o'clock, Solomon time. Solomon time usually meant thirty to sixty minutes after the designated time. Occasionally, Solomon time meant up to one hour earlier than the stated time. The concept of Solomon time was made even more uncertain because no one had a watch.

Paula and I walked home after work. We talked endlessly about our upcoming trip over supper. I was anxious and ready to go. After hugs and kisses, we went to bed. Despite thinking of what adventure awaited us, I promptly fell asleep.

# CHAPTER 7

# *The Shark Callers*

A rooster woke us before sunrise. We ate a leisurely breakfast of yogurt, fruit, and bread. We arrived at the dock at 9:40 a.m. making us twenty minutes early or forty minutes late, depending on your point of view. Actually, I didn't have a watch, so I really didn't know the exact time. It was definitely morning in early December 1990. Solomon time.

Our supervisor, Paul Kennioriana, was at the dock with a Malitian who had a canoe that had been manufactured overseas. The colorful canoe was powered with a new outboard motor. George Toritelia was just leaving in another canoe with four white men. "We go Laulasi," Paul said, as we climbed into the canoe.

Laulasi is one of many artificial islands that had been built in the Langa Langa Lagoon over decades and even centuries. Anthropologists believed that the artificial islands were built to avoid other headhunting tribes. The Langa Langa people themselves said the islands were originally built at the instructions of an ancestor god.

The islands had been constructed by gathering large coral pieces from the ocean floor. They used the coral chunks to build holding walls in shallow areas. The coral retaining walls were packed with sand to make a solid base. Traditional Solomon houses were then built. Over several decades, many of the artificial islands were built to a height of ten to twelve feet.

We accompanied Paul to Laulasi where we met Laulasi Chief Wallie Tailu and a contingent of young men. George and the Australian film crew had landed a few minutes before us. The Australians seemed less than pleased to see us arrive. Paul introduced Paula and me to Chief Tailu and explained we were there to help them. The young men listened attentively and respectfully to our discussions. George introduced the four men to Chief Tailu.

George and Paul soon left the island in their respective canoes. Paula and I introduced ourselves to the film crew. They were led and funded by Greg Grainger. Wade Farley, Damon Smith, and Bruce Gee completed the team. Wade Farley was from New Zealand and was kayaking in Solomon waters when Grainger met him. Grainger attached him to his group and assigned Farley duties as sound technician and underwater cameraman.

Damon Smith was Grainger's photographer. Bruce Gee was an Australian who was living permanently in the Solomons. Gee lived in the capital city of Honiara. He had several businesses in the Solomons including the bakery in Auki. It was Gee who had contacted Granger to make him aware of the unique, Solomon Islands' opportunity for a documentary.

Chief Tailu, several Laulasi men, and the film crew were soon seated around a small, rough table. The lumber for the table had been cut with a chainsaw from a downed tree on the mainland. The table was positioned in front of a newly constructed guest house that was to be Paula's and my sleeping quarters. Paula and I sat apart from the negotiations and listened attentively. The negotiations were conducted in Pisin with Bruce Gee translating for the other expatriates.

Most people present knew that deceased Laulasi resident Harry Galegu was universally acknowledged as having been a practicing *Fata'abu*. This status indicated he had special ability to call sharks and interact with them. His skills were believed to have died with him. "Did you know Harry Galegu?" Grainger asked, in the direction of the assembled Laulasi men.

"Yes," answered Chief Tailu. "He Laulasi man. Skull in sacred place. See when we call shark."

The young men nodded and murmured their agreement. I was a bit skeptical that Harry Galegu's skull would be among those that were kept in the skull house. Christians had been mostly successful in curtailing the practice of keeping skulls of deceased ancestors by the time Galegu died.

I fully believed that the Laulasi men would have many skulls to show the film crew. However, these skulls would more likely be older than what Galegu's would have been. I suspected that if Grainger had asked about Aviator Amelia Earhart, and offered adequate money, the Laulasi men would have produced "her" skull for the Grainger documentary.

English Adventurer Ben Cropp had visited Laulasi in previous years. He filmed Galegu calling in a twenty-foot shark. Galegu sat in a canoe, held the shark by its dorsal fin and had the shark tow him about the lagoon. Grainger was going to include this footage in his documentary to demonstrate what had prompted him to come the Solomon Islands.

Greg was seeking something just as spectacular and was willing to pay for it. "After Harry Galegu died, I hear that no one has been able to manage sharks like he could," Greg said. "Do you think there's a new priest that can do that?"

"Yes," Chief Tailu said. "Old man can. Special old man. Cost lot of money."

"Do you think the priest can call in sharks?" Grainger asked.

"Yes," the chief answered. "*Fata'abu* has special magic."

"Will the priest be in the water handling the sharks?"

"Yes, special magic," the chief nodded affirmatively. "Use special pig in ceremony."

"Can he control the sharks, so children can swim and play with the sharks?"

"Old man can. Special magic."

The conversation quickly proceeded to discussions concerning what the people of Laulasi would do. Grainger professed to be only interested in a ceremony in which the priest called in sharks. He wanted to film the *Fata'abu* handling and managing the sharks so Laulasi children could interact with them.

Chief Tailu and his followers insisted that additional activities would be necessary. The entire ceremony would take four days with a pig sacrificed each day. On each day, Laulasi people would demonstrate ancient customs and practices. Greg would film the performance and be obligated to pay. The discussions eventually resulted in an understanding of what Laulasi performers would do. Then, the negotiations concerning payments began. "Cost big money," Tailu repeated.

The observing Laulasi men continued murmuring and nodding in agreement. Laulasi had been a feature of the Solomon Island Adventure Tour some years before. The tour had been organized by the expatriate owner of the Auki Lodge. The program was discontinued when he sold the lodge to another party. The Laulasi men remembered the payments they had received for their limited participation in the Auki Lodge tours. It was obvious to me that they wanted considerably more money for participating in Grainger's documentary.

"I can pay five thousand Solomon dollars," Greg offered. "Cost big money," the chief insisted. "Must pay big money. Need special pigs for sacrifice."

"I could give five thousand, five hundred, but I'll only give the money to you, Chief."

"*Fata'abu* has special magic. Special pig."

"How much do you think that the entire program will cost?"

"First price fourteen thousand. Second price twelve thousand," proposed Chief Tailu, in the unique Malitian way of negotiating prices.

The two men eventually agreed upon a payment of seven thousand Solomon dollars to be paid when the filming was completed. The payment was to go directly to Chief Tailu for redistribution to the participants as he saw fit. I was surprised at the amount of money that Grainger would pay. I had dealt with Malitians for several months and I believed that they would have agreed to Grainger's original offer of five thousand,

Smith films women in canoe while Grainger and Farley film from an adjacent canoe.

The filming began promptly. The first event featured several older women paddling toward Laulasi in a traditional canoe. The women wore lava-lavas made from tapa. Tapa was native cloth made by pounding the inner bark of mulberry trees into functional material.

They had the lava-lavas wrapped around their lower bodies leaving their breasts bare. They sang lovely songs in their Langa Langa language as they paddled. The Australian crew, with their cameras, were in another canoe propelled by Laulasi men. The filming canoe was paddled parallel to the women, allowing the event to be properly recorded. Paula and I stood onshore, taking pictures with our still camera for our personal use.

The next event had several young men paddling toward Laulasi in a traditional war canoe. The cameramen filmed the event in a parallel canoe powered by Laulasi men. Both

Smith films mock battle

canoes landed, and the filming crew exited the canoes. The Solomon men then repeated the landing for the cameras. This time, they were met by other young men in a mock battle.

Most combatants wore only tapa lap-laps wrapped tightly around their lower bodies. The men screamed, shouted, and threw headless, bamboo shafts at each other. The mock battle continued until Chief Tailu gave his own warriors several strings of shell money to ensure the safety of the visitors.

Paula made a quick friend with a young Laulasi girl, Fascia, on the first day. Most Solomon women were short of stature and very muscular, just like Solomon men. They had strong backs and thick waists. An absence of bras contributed to sagging breasts at young ages. Fascia was likely sixteen years old at that time. She stood out among Solomon women generally and Laulasi women particularly.

If there were ever a beauty contest in the Solomons, Fascia would be among the finalists. Bruce Gee also noticed Fascia. "What a beautiful girl," he casually observed to me in English.

"Yes, she's beautiful," I agreed. "She looks much older than her sixteen years."

"Yes, she does. She could do a lot better than marrying a fisherman and living out her life on this island."

I estimated that Gee was in his early forties. I thought it was admirable that he was showing such a fatherly interest in the young girl that he didn't even know. The last event of the day was the pig-sacrifice, so we men moved to the proper area. Paula stayed with the women and learned how to make shell money.

Only men were permitted to observe or participate in the sacrifice because it occurred in the part of the island that was sacred. Chief Tailu introduced Greg Grainger to the *Fata'abu*. The *Fata'abu* was a toothless, old man, clad only in a tapa wrap. He was clean shaven and had close cropped hair. His dark, loose skin seemed a couple of sizes too large for his frail body.

As we walked toward the sacrificial area, we passed several small leaf shelters with steeply pitched thatched roofs. Each was about three feet tall and contained several skulls set rather haphazardly. The film crew captured the scene for later inclusion in the documentary. None of the Australians asked which of the skulls was that of Harry Galegu, the acknowledged *Fata'abu*. None of the Laulasi men took the initiative to provide the information. Given the circumstances, I didn't raise the issue.

Two men entered the area with a pig tied to a pole by its four feet. They presented the still bound pig to the *Fata'abu*. After sufficient incarnations and gestures, the *Fata'abu* suffocated the pig by winding a strong vine around its snout. The porker was not stuck and bled-out as expected by those familiar with Western butchering methods.

The *Fata'abu* removed the viscera and threw it into the sea while standing on land. Small reef sharks soon found the viscera. The pig was cut into pieces to be roasted in an open pit. Knowing it would take several hours to roast, neither the Australians nor I waited for the feast.

Paula and I ate some of the food we brought with us then retired to the guest house for the night. Per Malitian customs, two of the young men, Anthony and Joseph, slept on rough benches outside the house to ensure our safety. The Australians were assigned a leaf house among others on the crowded island.

The second day's filming included women making shell money. Bruce Gee initiated conversations with Fascia. I thought it was likely they were talking about Solomon culture. What a wonderful man. Such fatherly interest in this innocent, young Mali-

Smith films butchering while
Farley deals with sound

tian girl. The day ended with the pig sacrifice ceremony. As before, the *Fata'abu* suffocated the pig by winding a strong vine around its snout after sufficient incarnations and gestures,

The meat was cut into sections and laid in an umu with vegetables. The pork that had been processed the day before was ready for eating. I was recognized as a principal figure and offered what was considered the best part of the porker. It was a large piece of fat, about an inch thick and twice the size of my hand.

It looked far less than appealing. "Thank you very much, but I can't take it," I explained. "Greg Grainger is paying for the privilege of being here. I'm only here because of Grainger. It would spoil white people's customs if I were to eat the best part."

Grainger was then offered the Solomon delicacy. First Grainger, then his assistants refused, in turn, both the fat and the meat offered to them. The four men did eat some of the vegetables. I was happy to take a large piece of pork. It was delicious. Per Solomon custom, we men ate the pork and the deceased ancestors enjoyed the fragrance.

Grainger asked me later in the day about my willingness to eat the pork. I told him I had no concerns as the meat was well cooked and I had eaten pork in other Solomon Islands' feasts without incident. A Laulasi man approached Grainger with a request for direct pay for his participation. Grainger replied that he would only give money to Chief Tailu at the end of the programs.

Paula had been accepted by the Laulasi women as a friend and mentor. They had fed her traditional Solomon food. She was also immediately accepted by the children. That night, Paula and I slept in the guest house with Joseph and Anthony sleeping outside to ensure our safety.

The third day began without the *Fata'abu*. He was obviously not on the island. Chief Tailu was also absent. "Where is the priest," I asked Joseph in Pisin.

"Ran away," Joseph replied.

"Why did he run away?"

"Afraid shark."

Grainger and his crew had already heard the news when I first saw them. I was compelled to agree that the *Fata'abu* was a fraud. His ability to manage sharks existed only in his mind. I didn't want to think about how the documentary making would end without the featured performance. Grainger had Smith and Farley film a mother performing a face-scaring procedure on her daughter.

Smith and Farley also filmed a bride-price ceremony. Grainger filled in the time by interviewing a local fisherman named James. James used English to tell Grainger that his boat had capsized at sea some years before. James called for a shark to rescue them and one appeared. James and two small boys rode several miles on the shark's back to the safety of land. "Who do think the shark really was?" Grainger asked.

"It was my grandfather," James answered, in English.

"That's an amazing story," Greg observed.

James told Grainger that he sacrificed a pig to his reincarnated grandfather to thank him. Had James failed to perform his obligation, he claimed the shark would have eaten him the next time he went fishing. Bruce Gee spent more time with Fascia. I was beginning to suspect that his interest was motivated by something other than fatherly concerns. Actually, he seemed infatuated with the young girl. Before the day ended, he asked her to marry him. "If you like, I'll ask your daddy if I can marry you," he proposed.

"All right," was Fascia's shy acceptance.

Gee proceeded to locate Fascia's father to ask for permission to marry his daughter. If granted permission, Gee would be expected to pay considerable valuables in bride-price. Fascia's father didn't give an immediate answer. He told Gee that his son lived in Honiara and he would ask about Gee's reputation.

The fourth day got off to a promising start with the return of the *Fata'abu*. He brought what he claimed was a special pig for sacrificing. He reported that he had to leave the previous day to procure the pig. He assured Grainger that he could, and would, call in and manage sharks. Greg seemed skeptical that the *Fata'abu* would be able to perform the ceremony that had previously been agreed to, but the event proceeded. We men promptly walked to the proper area and Paula stayed with the women.

The special pig was sacrificed, and the meat was again cut up, wrapped in banana leaves, and laid in an umu with vegetables. The *Fata'abu* spent considerable time murmuring in his tribal language. When he was satisfied, he took the pig offal and slowly entered the water. When he was up to his waist, Farley also entered the water with an underwater camera. Wade was wearing a snorkel, so he could remain submerged during the filming.

The *Fata'abu* drug the bloody offal through the quiet water of Langa Langa Lagoon while murmuring in his tribal language. When he was only about fifty feet from the island, he was up to chest in the salt water. At that time, he flung the offal another twenty feet. He continued murmuring in his tribal language to call the sharks.

In less than a minute, a three-foot long reef shark hit the offal. Another small reef shark quickly attacked the offal. The *Fata'abu* immediately moved to solid footing on Laulasi. Joseph's assessment of the phony *Fata'abu* being afraid of sharks was apparent. Wade Farley continued filming. He was made of sterner stuff than the sham *Fata'abu*.

Grainger was much less than impressed with the ceremony. In due time, he asked for a meeting with the Laulasi principals. The meeting was held in front of our sleeping house. The Laulasi women hustled Paula out of sight when they saw us approaching. I was quickly seated at the small, rough table. A few Laulasi men seated themselves on the rough benches.

Grainger, Gee, Farley, Smith, and most of the Laulasi men remained standing. Several small boys stood in the background observing the proceedings. Neither Chief Wallie Tailu nor the *Fata'abu* who performed the faux ceremony was present. No one said anything for a few minutes then Grainger broke the silence with Gee translating. "Did you think the priest could call in sharks?" he asked, in the direction of the standing men.

"Yes," Moses answered. "Has special magic."

"And did you tell me that the priest would be in the water handling the sharks?"

When there was no answer, Grainger continued. "Didn't you tell me that there would be big sharks?"

The Solomon men didn't answer. They seemed perplexed by the meeting and Grainger's questions. "Didn't you tell me that children would swim with the sharks and play with the sharks?"

"Play with sharks? You crazy?" the men simultaneously shouted in anger. "Children play with sharks? Sharks eat them!"

Greg held his ground both figuratively and literally. "The chief said the priest would be in the water with the sharks when he called them in," Greg argued. "Chief Tailu claimed that the priest would control the sharks so that children could swim with them!"

The Laulasi men responded that no such claims, nor agreements, had been made. Grainger insisted that there was. The men sharply exchanged different opinions and points of view. "You did say the priest would call in sharks and control them," Grainger repeated emphatically. "Just ask your own advisor!"

Grainger pointed toward me. All eyes turned in my direction. "Your advisor knows what happened," Grainger insisted. "He was here! He heard everything!"

Everyone expected me to side with them. The Laulasi men knew that I was assigned there for their benefit. Grainger knew that what he said was true. No one seemed to be willing to compromise. We were alone on an artificial island and needed to resolve the dispute immediately. I had a secondary goal of settlement without bloodshed. I had a primary goal of settlement without Paula's and my own blood being shed. "It's not proper that Grainger speaks for me," I said, quickly and firmly. "When I speak, I'll only speak with Laulasi men."

Four, angry, white men conferenced among themselves. I was confident that Gee understood Solomon customs and recognized that what I said was appropriate. The four men stormed away in the direction of their own hut. Grainger blessed me with a red, disgust-filled, contorted face. I had never before been the subject of such a look. I returned his look pleasantly, believing that his looks could not kill me. However, I had full recognition that there were ample weapons available that could kill all of us white people.

All the Laulasi men turned to face me. Angry men. Angry, young men, with teeth stained black from years of chewing betel nut. Six angry, young men crowded around the crude table where I sat. More angry men stood in the background. The six vented their contempt for what they considered unreasonable demands by the Australian film crew. Their dark eyes flashed with uncontrolled anger.

Their voices transcended shouting levels as they screamed about the absurdity of their tormentors' demands. Gentle Pacific Ocean waves slapped softly against the coral retaining walls of Laulasi. The sound was masked by the intensity of the Solomon voices. "Hear them?" Moses shouted at me.

"Hear what they want?" screamed Anthony.

"Want children swim with sharks for pictures!"

"Children never swim with sharks!"

They gestured wildly and simultaneously jabbered in Pisin and their tribal language of Langa Langa. I folded my arms across my chest in what I hoped would be recognized as a commanding, Charles-in-Charge position. I listened attentively. "Sharks eat children!" they continued.

"White men crazy!"

"Say children swim with sharks!"

"Never let children swim with sharks!"

"They're crazy! White men crazy!" they all agreed.

The men were getting more agitated. They pushed against each other in their eagerness to be the one who could provide the most compelling argument against using their children as shark bait. Their wide-open mouths were bright red from betel nut use. Their eyes seemed to flash fire. Their red mouths made a striking contrast to their ebony faces.

Anthony was one of those closest to me. Red betel nut juice dribbled from his mouth. He spattered betel nut juice in my direction as he spoke. Some landed on the table. A generous portion landed on my shirt and my arms that I had folded majestically across my chest. I feigned disinterest in the red, juice shower with which I was being continually blessed. Other betel nut chewers punctuated their angry statements with ever more powerful and louder huffs.

I was alone. Alone in a situation where the anger now directed toward the foreign filming crew could quickly be focused on me. I was glad that the Laulasi women had sensed trouble and had shuffled Paula to the island's women's area. She was, at least temporally, out of harm's way. "Hear what they want?" the men continued.

"Hear what they want?"

"They're crazy!"

Their rants continued. I waited patiently, silently, and happily for them to tire. I needed time to think of a way out of all our predicaments. I quickly rejected my fledgling idea of trying to reason with them by reminding them that they had claimed that the *Fata'abu* could call and control sharks. I wanted to tell them that they had claimed that their children could swim with sharks. I dared not!

Such is the nature of Solomon Island negotiations. Such is the nature of Malitian culture and men. No contract is binding. No agreement is final. I was sufficiently aware of Malitian customs to know that these Laulasi men should not be reminded of what they had agreed to. I would like to see the man who could take advantage of a Malitian man or hold him accountable for a commitment that he had made. If there are any, I am not among them.

Yet, Grainger seemed determined to get what he had bargained for. I looked directly at the young men. "The white men are crazy!" I shouted, mimicking their intensity and gestures. "Children can't swim with sharks! White people should know that!"

"We keep them. Make pay seven-thousand!" Moses asserted.

"I think they would be missed," I softly cautioned. "I think the police would come looking for them."

There was more discussion among the men in their tribal language making it impossible for me to understand. I was hopeful that they weren't discussing killing the Australians and feeding them to the sharks. I was even more hopeful that they weren't discussing killing me along with the Australians.

Eventually, their conversation ended, and they spoke to me in Pisin. "We keep camera and film," Abraham said. "Keep everything. Make them pay ten-thousand."

"That might work," I said. "But when they got back to Auki, do you think they would go to English Judge Chetwynd and tell him you have their equipment? Even though you're in the right, I worry the white judge would agree with the white men."

There was more discussion in Langa Langa with more suggestions with which I was encouraged to agree. None of their ideas smacked of being driven by rationality. I consistently agreed with their ideas. However, I always had a counter-argument as to why their proposed course of action might end in failure. When they grew silent, I paused to be sure that no more ideas were forthcoming. Hearing none, I had my own suggestion. "If they would pay four-thousand Solomon, would that be enough?" I asked.

There was more discussion in Langa Langa then Moses looked to me. "Take five-thousand," he said.

I wasn't in any position to negotiate for the Australians. However, I thought we had arrived at a place where the Laulasi men were unlikely to cause anyone any physical harm. Joseph sent a boy to tell Grainger and his associates to come back. When the foursome arrived, I told them that Laulasi would accept five-thousand Solomon dollars as payment in full. Both sides had bitter scowls on their faces.

There was not any hint of agreement or accommodation from any man present. The Australians huddled and spoke briefly in English. They spoke softly so I couldn't understand anything. Greg soon broke the huddle. "I'll give you four-thousand," he said. "But I want the chief here. He should be here right now! I will only give the money to Chief Tailu!"

Another huddle among the Laulasi men speaking Langa Langa. They spoke softly so no one could hear. They could have shouted at the top of their lungs and no one could have understood. They responded with a counter-counter-offer. Another Australian huddle, then a counter-counter-counter-offer.

Chief Tailu came during the negotiations, but he did not participate. Both sides eventually agreed to a payment of four-thousand, six hundred Solomon dollars with payment going to the chief. Both sides also agreed to be unhappy with the settlement and very angry at everyone but me. I agreed with myself to be happy with everyone.

Gee received the answer that Fascia's father wouldn't permit Fascia to marry him. It seemed that Gee had a reputation in Honiara of being somewhat insincere when courting and marrying young women. Payment was made and the film crew began gathering their things in preparation to leave. Grainger and his crew soon left in their rented canoe.

As soon as they were out of sight, mild pandemonium broke out. The Laulasi men were jubilant. They were ecstatic at receiving four-thousand, six hundred dollars. They spoke in Langa Langa, but I knew they were congratulating themselves for besting the Australians. Children swim with sharks? Only in tourism books!

Our canoe was soon ready, and Paula and I were heading to Auki. When we arrived at the dock, Grainger and his group were waiting. We exchanged greetings. I wanted Greg to know that the Laulasi men were very satisfied with the conclusion. I also wanted to learn of their opinions of the happenings. I didn't think that the wharf would be a very good place to talk. Paula agreed. "How would you like to come to our house for dinner this evening?" she asked.

"We would," Grainger replied. "What time would like us to come?"

"Around seven o'clock would be good."

"We'll be there. We'll bring some refreshments."

The men arrived around seven with a case of cold beer. We began drinking beer and relived the four day's events. "Bit dicey at the end," Cameraman Smith observed.

"Yes," I agreed. "When I was alone with them, they were talking about keeping you prisoner until you paid the seven-thousand."

"That doesn't surprise me," Gee said.

"They were also considering grabbing your film and equipment until you paid the full amount."

"That doesn't surprise me either," Grainger said. "When we were in our hut, we were taking our good films out of their cases and putting in unexposed films. I was ready to bluff them. I was going to give them unexposed films marked 'Laulasi' and take the good film with us. I was just going to throw the films at their feet and tell them that they didn't do what they said they would. I was going to tell them that the films were worthless."

"I'm glad you came over," I said. "I wanted you to know that the Laulasi men really weren't mad at all. They were very pleased to get a payment of nearly five-thousand Solomon dollars."

Grainger grew serious. "I certainly wasn't hurt on the deal," he said. "We got some excellent footage. I was willing to pay them the entire seven-thousand!"

We ate our dinner and finished most of the beer. They left the remaining beer with us and returned to the Auki Lodge. Paula and I slept very soundly that night. It was good to be in our own beds.

The next morning, we found Paul Kennioriana at work. We gave him a partial report. We left out the part about both sides being fully satisfied with the final result. Paul listened attentively. "Already heard about it," Paul said, his eyes dancing with delight. "Every day, got morning report and evening report."

"You did?" Paula asked. "Who was keeping you informed?"

"Solomon secret," he answered, with a grin. "Knew there would be trouble."

I was dumfounded. "What made you think there would be trouble?" I asked.

"Old man doesn't have magic power," Paul answered. "Not even from Langa Langa Lagoon. He bush man. Couldn't swim with sharks. Can't even swim. Knew there would be trouble. That's why I sent you!"

Bruce Gee returned to his business interests in Honoria. Greg Grainger and Damon Smith returned to Australia. Wade Farley continued his kayaking trip in the Solomons. Greg made a very nice documentary called *In Search of the Shark Callers*. Wade Farley frequently appeared in the film. We never again saw or heard of Wade Farley. We never again saw or heard of the faux *Fata'abu*.

Neither Damon Smith nor Bruce Gee were shown in the film. The documentary relates a somewhat different story of the Laulasi incident than what I document. Paula and I have a copy of the film. I wrote news articles about the events for publication in Kansas newspapers.

# CHAPTER 8

# *Holidays in Auki 1990*

Paula and I woke early Sunday morning and went to mass. Nature graced us with living Christmas trees for us to enjoy on our leisurely walk. The trees were plentiful and sported green leaves throughout the year. In mid-December, they bloomed large, beautiful, red flowers. They helped put us in the mood for Christmas.

Alison brought us a branch from an evergreen tree at Kilu'ufi Hospital. Paula put up a "Charlie Brown" Christmas tree. Carolers came to our house that evening. We gave them navy biscuits and applause.

Dr. Graham's and Sheila's son, Vincent, was visiting for the holidays. Paula and I had plans to float down the Fiu River with Alison and Vincent the next day. I opened the door to the storage area beneath our house to get the tractor tire tube. I moved the tube and discov-

Solomon Island Christmas tree

ered a nest of chicken eggs. "Paula, there's about a dozen eggs in the storage area," I said. "That hen and her eggs are going to be a lot more welcome than that stupid rooster that wakes us up every morning."

"What do you want to do with the eggs?" Paula asked.

"I'm afraid some of them might be spoiled. When I was a kid, we sometimes found a nest of eggs that a hen had hid out. Mom and Grandma Wehrli would make noodles out of them."

"I can make noodles. That can be my weekend project."

"Maybe I can catch that stupid rooster that wakes us up too early. He would make a nice addition for a chicken and noodle soup."

We traveled to the Fiu River the next day in Alison's car. Vincent and I floated down the river on the tractor tire tube and met Paula and Alison at the Fiu Bridge.

Bill, Rick, and Carrie arrived a few days before Christmas. We borrowed beds from Camerons and Isozakis to make them comfortable in our house. "Are the others coming?" Bill asked.

"We know that Tom isn't coming," Paula answered. "He said he had to work. We sent Matt and Margaret a letter, but we didn't hear back. We don't even know if they got it. I worry about them. The civil war in Bougainville might spillover into the Shortlands."

As Christmas day approached, carolers began coming every evening to sing us religious songs. We rewarded them with navy biscuits and fruit. We took our *wontoks* to Misuka's garden. Salamai had planted the carrot seeds we had given her, and they had flourished. We pulled our first bunch of carrots in the Solomons. We picked strawberries then went to view the Saenaua forestry project.

Christmas 1990 in Auki Bill, Charlie, Paula, Rick, and Carrie

Carolers came to our house again that evening. We recognized some of them had been there before. The last ones arrived at approximately 10:45 p.m. They had a fruit bat with them that was likely destined for the cooking pot.

Bill, Paula, Rick, Carrie, and I went to mass on Christmas day. When Father Jon gave his sermon, he spoke about the men who were prisoners in Auki Prison. He told us that no one came to visit them at Christmas time or any other time. He encouraged some of those who were caroling to go to the prison to sing for them.

Father Jon's moving message to remember those in prison had an effect. "Do you think that anyone will go to the prison to sing carols for the prisoners?" Bill asked.

"I doubt it," Paula answered, with a smile. "I don't think that our carolers will go to the prison. I really think they sing where they will get rewards of navy biscuits and fruit."

"I think we should do it," Rick said. "It must be lonely to be locked up in Auki Prison."

Bill, Paula, Rick, Carrie, and I did go to the prison to entertain the prisoners. We asked the guards to allow us in to sing. They opened the gate and we entered and walked near four prisoners. We sang several Christmas carols for the stoic inmates. I don't know if they enjoyed our singing, but we felt good about performing for them.

We all went to David and Stephanie Chetwynds for Christmas dinner. They had their house decorated for the festivities. We played parlor games of black magic, I'm going on a trip, and I like peaches. Some of us drank wine and snacked on chocolates while waiting for dinner time. We had a magnificent meal including lamb, turkey, ham, Scottish and English puddings with cream, and an assortment of fruits and vegetables.

The party was lovely. Stephanie's table was large enough for all us to be seated together. Bill, Rick, Carrie, Dr. Graham, Sheila, Vincent, Stephanie, David, Dr. Arun, Elaine, Neil, Sumaita, Colin, Alison, Andrew, Paula and I bowed our heads for Dr. Graham to say grace. We played dominoes and an English version of trivial pursuit after dinner. Bill, Rick, and Carrie made special efforts to show their appreciation for the hospitality. Our *wontoks* said their good-byes and returned to Honiara.

David Chetwynd lived up to his reputation of activity promoter. He organized a trip to the Fiu River. Andrew, Paula, David, and I spent three and one-half hours rafting down the Fiu River the last day of 1990. We saw children playing as we approached a picturesque village situated on the river bank. When we were near, the children announced our approach. "White people! White people!" they screamed in Kwara'ae, as they ran away.

It was great fun, but we all got sunburns. "Do you think those kids were really afraid of us?" Andrew asked, as we were returning to Auki.

"I think they were frightened," David answered. "Every culture has some kind of bogeyman. I expect Malitians tell their youngsters that if they misbehave, white people will come get them."

We went to a New Year's Eve party at Alison and Colin's home. Everyone dressed in the American 1960s style and we danced to American 1960s music. David had information that piqued my interest. "Do you know that there was a white man that lived in Malaita when headhunting was the sport of the day?"

"I hadn't heard that, David," I answered. "Where did he live?"

"He was on one of the artificial islands in the Lau Lagoon off Malaita. He lived there for years before he was rescued by a blackbirding ship."

"Interesting, David. Where can I find out more about him?"

"There were several newspaper articles about him published in Australia and Scotland at that time. There was also a book written about him. He was a Scotsman and Colin can tell you something more about him."

"Interesting. I'll ask Colin about it sometime."

Dr. Arun and Elaine weren't at the party, but Alison was taking care of Neil and Sumaita. Our visiting was interrupted by a loud smack. Everyone turned toward Alison who was holding Neil. "Once, just once, Neil!" Alison exclaimed. "I wish your mother would lose her temper with you!"

It was obvious that Alison had lost her temper with Neil. No one asked what he had done to deserve the smack. We didn't need to know. It was universally wished that Elaine would also lose her temper with Neil. Neil didn't make a whimper and we returned to our visiting.

Paula and I celebrated New Year's Day with an evening dinner with several expatriates at Bishops Loft's house. Vincent and I played chess while Paula watched a custom wedding video with Sheila. Dr. Graham and I talked about his and Sheila's upcoming trip to New Zealand. "Sheila and I are going to New Zealand next week," Dr. Graham said. "Would you like to use my car while I'm gone?"

I was surprised, and impressed, with Dr. Graham's generosity. "Paula and I would be happy to have the use of your car while you are gone," I said. "Is there something that you would like us to do for you while you're in New Zealand?"

"No, nothing special," he replied. "Father Jon and Bishop Loft will look after our house while we're gone. You can use the car to help with your projects."

Our conversation turned to our visit to Laulasi for the shark calling ceremony. "Did anyone say anything about the Army bombing Laulasi?" Dr. Graham asked.

"Bombing Laulasi? What are you talking about?" I answered, by asking questions.

"The U.S. Army bombed Laulasi during W.W. II. They thought it was a different island where there was a Japanese camp. Laulasi elders asked for compensation, but the U.S. never gave them anything."

"No one asked about compensation for the U.S. bombing Laulasi. Maybe it will come later."

Paula and I talked about their generosity when we got home. "Did you hear Dr. Graham and me talking about them loaning us a car when they go to New Zealand?" I asked.

"Yes, I heard you," Paula answered. "Sheila is also going to let me use her sewing machine while they're gone."

"They're really great people. They do so much to help Solomon people live better lives."

"Everyone here is great. Everyone works very hard and everyone is so nice. Think how nicely they treated Rick, Carrie, and Bill. No one in Auki even knew them, but they opened their doors and welcomed our friends into their lives."

"I only want to use Dr. Graham's car when we need it for something to help others. We can continue to walk to work, market, church, and everywhere else we go."

"I agree. We don't want to let ourselves get spoiled."

Paula selected a day for her noodle making and had me collect the eggs. There were fourteen by that time. I helped her string a line in the guest bedroom. We broke the eggs and threw away three that were bad. Paula made the noodles and hung them on the string to dry.

Two days later, she checked on them. "Charlie, there are ants on my noodles!" she exclaimed. "This place is full of bugs. Our house is full of cockroaches! There're weevils in our rice! There're bugs in my flour. And now, I have ants on my noodles!"

"There're good protein," I countered. "Solomon food charts feature insects as good protein."

"Well, Solomon Islanders can eat bugs if they want, but I'm not going to."

She brushed the ants off the noodles and stored them in our food safe to keep the cockroaches from sharing.

By the end of January 1991, we had performed needs assessments in several villages and three schools. The school assessments included our assignment to develop a literacy program for Malaita Province. School needs assessments revealed they were deficient in everything except heating systems. The school buildings all needed maintenance. There were not enough qualified administrators, not enough educated teachers, not enough books, and not enough desks.

Paula at a typical school in Malaita.

There was no money available to improve the situation. When they completed the available courses, some of the brightest students occasionally received scholarships to attend college overseas. They always had to take remedial classes before they could pursue freshman courses.

Paula and I discussed the possibility of bringing the General Education Development (G.E.D.) program to the Solomons. To addresses the issue of lack of funds, we envisioned Peace Corps Volunteers being recruited. Our idea included volunteers teaching selected, motivated Solomon students in the G.E.D. structured preparatory system after they completed the available courses.

We took our idea to Albert Nori, the Malaita education minister. "Albert, Paula and I did needs assessments in three schools," I said. "Did you get our reports?"

"Yes," Albert answered, in English. "You understand our problems. Solomon Islands needs education but doesn't have money. Malaita doesn't have money. We don't have any way to get money."

Paula and I explained the G.E.D. program and our idea to bring it to the Solomons. Albert was supportive of the plan and encourage us to pursue it. "You'll need Sam Alisia's support and approval," he said.

"The name sounds familiar," I said. "But I can't place him. Who is Sam Alisia?"

"Sam Alisia is the Solomon Islands' education minister," Albert answered.

"Isn't Sam Alisia married to Mary Alisia that works for Malaita Province?" Paula asked.

"Yes, Sam Alisia and Mary Alisia are a married couple."

"Well, that should make it easier. I know Mary very well. I'll see her soon and invite them to dinner the next time Sam is in Auki. We can talk about the G.E.D. program at that time."

Moses and Anthony came to the office. I expected them to talk about organizing tourism for Laulasi. There was another issue. "America bombed Laulasi." Anthony said. "Killed many people."

"I heard something about it," I responded. "I don't know any details."

"America bombed Laulasi. Killed people. Want compensation."

"Do you have copies of any papers that your fathers gave the Army to ask for compensation? If there are any papers, we could take them to the U.S. Embassy in Honiara."

Anthony and Moses looked at each other then spoke in Langa Langa. They looked back to me without saying anything. Their silence indicated they didn't have any paperwork. I asked them to see if they could find documentation for their claim for damages. They nodded and left.

Rocky came in to talk about tourism for Laulasi the next day. He was very drunk, but still thought his visit was appropriate. He also thought it was an appropriate time to demonstrate Solomon customs of men always being higher than women. "News about tourists for Laulasi?" he asked.

"We have written some letters to tourism agencies in California," I said. "But we haven't gotten any answers yet."

"Maybe we should think about getting a provincial tourism officer position established," Paula added.

"Shut up!" Rocky snapped at Paula. "You same Charlie's child!"

Paula didn't look too pleased with the prospect of accepting Rocky's status assignment. Rocky and I continued our conversation while Paula participated by directing disgusting looks at Rocky. She also seemed to direct a few of the mean looks toward me for some unexplainable reason. Despite Paula's less than approving looks, I dealt with the issue observing what I considered appropriate Malitian customs.

When we went to work the next day, I took an early opportunity to go see George. "Do you know that Rocky from Laulasi Island is coming to see Paula and me about tourism for Laulasi?" I asked.

George raised his brow to signify that he knew. "We're glad he comes," I continued. "We want him to come. Laulasi has potential for attracting tourists. Tourists would bring money that would be good for Laulasi and Auki. But when Rocky came in yesterday, he was really drunk. I don't want him to come in when he's been drinking."

George nodded, but didn't give a verbal response. I interpreted the nonverbal communication as: "I understand. I'll take care of it."

Our village assessments in Fasileta, Ura, and Aimeta required overnight stays. I was offered betel nut, but I always refused, citing Peace Corps rules. Our village assessments

71

focused on community development. In all three villages, elders questioned me about the Iraq War. They were anxious for America and Iraq to come to the Solomons for the war.

I always tried to convince them the war would not be fought in the Solomons. I echoed Bishop Loft's and Father Jon's insistence that they continue planting their gardens. "I was a soldier for three years in the Army," I told them. "America is fighting differently. Iraq and America will not come here to fight. Continue planting your gardens or your children won't have anything to eat."

Peace Corps required volunteers to submit quarterly reports. Paula and I submitted separate reports. We worked at the same office, we lived together, we did our projects for Albert Nori together, and we did needs assessments together. Naturally, our reports were very similar.

We used general language to describe what we did during needs assessments and included written copies for the record. We used more specific language in describing our work in the education division. I described our goals of developing a literacy program for Malaita Province and included the idea of introducing a G.E.D. program for the Solomon Islands. I also wrote that I was serving as a reporter for the *Malaita Nius* newspaper.

Since we were going to have Dr. Graham's car for several weeks, we needed Solomon Islands' driver's licenses. Obtaining them was quite easy. We simply went to the post office with passport size pictures and showed them our Kansas licenses. We were issued Solomon Islands' licenses on the spot. "What do you think about Peace Corps' rules that we're not to drive cars?" I asked.

"It doesn't make sense," Paula answered. "We could have an accident just as easily if we were riding in a car with someone else driving. I know Tom Scherer drives from the clam farm to Honiara a lot. I think Bill Wise drives. I bet there are other volunteers who drive."

"You're right. What the Peace Corps doesn't know won't hurt them."

"Do you remember that we are having guests for dinner tomorrow?" Paula asked, changing the subject.

"I remember. Sam and Mary are coming to talk about the G.E.D. program for the Solomons."

We made small talk while enjoying Paula's delicious dinner. Mary was Fijian thus felt comfortable participating in our conversations. We eventually got to the subject of education and the G.E.D. program. We told Sam that we had explained the concept to Albert Nori and had his approval. Sam gave tentative approval subject to approval from American G.E.D. officials.

Our house girl, Betty, came twice a week. She was paid SI$5 per day, but she didn't want paid after each day's work. She preferred Paula keeping track of her money and paying when she asked for it. Betty still wouldn't touch electricity, but she cleaned, washed our clothes, and worked in the yard. She washed our clothes with a scrub brush like we did in training.

We received letters from Chuck and Jason. Chuck sent a Japanese language tape. Jason's letter included our first picture of our granddaughter, Ashley Marie. We agreed that we had a beautiful grandbaby. A young Solomon boy came to our house that evening. He wore only a pair of knee pants and carried a box with two baby parrots. He wanted to sell the parrots.

I had seen many beautiful parrots in many villages and thought these babies would make wonderful pets. However, these two screeched continuously and looked to be too young to thrive. "I like them," I told him. "But they look too young. Bring them back in two months and I'll give you SI$2 for each of them."

The boy nodded his agreement and left. I wasn't sure that he understood but time would tell. I received a letter from Peace Corps Director John Mark later that week. It was addressed only to me and included a form for a cost-of-living survey. Peace Corps Volunteers had discussed the meagerness of our stipends on previous occasions. Everyone agreed that US$165 per month wasn't enough to live on.

John Mark's mail also included a scolding letter. He was annoyed that I was doing work for Albert Nori. He referenced my quarterly report and advised me that he was going to take up the issue with Albert Nori. I promptly took the letter and showed it to Albert. "Do you know what John Mark is mad about?" I asked. "You and Paul Kennioriana told me that Peace Corps officials told you that you and Paul could assign Paula and me any work you wanted."

"Peace Corps told us that," Albert answered, in English. "Paul and I called when you were here on walkabout. There was supposed to be two more volunteers come with you. They didn't come. We asked Peace Corps about your job. Peace Corps told us that you could work in any program we wanted. Now, two new volunteers are coming."

I thought about our exchange. "I think I understand what happened," I said. "When you and Paul called, Peace Corps thought you didn't have jobs for us. That's why Jimmie and Jim acted so smug when Paula and I told them we thought we knew what our jobs would be. I can't imagine why they kept the conversations with you secret. And I really don't like John Mark's butt-chewing letter. He could have easily called. We could have arrived at a quick conclusion without bad feelings."

"Anyway, the new volunteers are coming. I still want you to get the G.E.D. program into the Solomons, write articles, and continue the literacy program."

Gabriel and I began sanding floors in my spare time. We started with the hallway and extra bedroom. We would work an hour or so then take a rest, Solomon style. When we finished the extra bedroom, we varnished the floor and continued sanding another room.

I had a visitor with an artifact to sell that evening. He was wild and fierce looking and didn't speak Pisin very well. He was obviously very nervous. He had a lime container that was complete with a lime stick made of wood. The lime container was made from a short length of bamboo and had finely-carved, geometric patterns etched on it. I thought it was a real artifact. I asked him how much he wanted for it. He only shrugged and handed me the lime container.

I eventually understood that he would take whatever I would give him. I wanted the lime container and gave him what I thought was fair. I told him my name was Charlie and he told me his name was Bo'ogo. I tried to ask him what tribe or village he was from, but I wasn't sure he understood me. I didn't think he was Kwara'ae.

Paula and I went snorkeling with David, Andrew, and Colin that weekend then went to David and Stephanie's house for supper. Stephanie had prepared Indian curry. "This is delicious," Paula said. "I would like to get your recipe sometime."

"It really is good, Stephanie," Andrew agreed. "You're a perfect hostess."

Bill Wasser returned from his leave to the States in January 1991. He had gained weight, but he was quickly losing it on his Solomon diet. "Did you get to know Bob King very well?" Bill asked me, soon after he returned.

"Paula and I got to know him well in the few months before he left," I answered. "I thought he was a great guy. We got a letter from him a few days ago. He is living and working in Australia. He taught kung fu classes in Auki that Paula and I joined. Why do you ask about Bob King?"

"I was looking at the work he left," Bill answered. "He's designed very professional water distribution projects for many villages. If they can ever get funding, the plans are ready to go. Any of those plans would be ideal to include with a grant application."

We traveled to Gwaunoa School for a needs assessment. Like other schools, Gwaunoa needed uniforms, books, paper, pencils, desks, and money to buy additional school supplies. School officials specifically asked for books. We told them we would make inquiries about getting school books from the U.S.

Gwaunoa School Boys

New Peace Corps Volunteers Jim and Clair Millar arrived by ship later in the week. We met them at the wharf and helped them get their bags to our house. They were staying with us until their own house was ready. "We've been invited to the provincial magistrate's house for Chinese food this evening," Paula told them. "We have a great expatriate community here. You'll get to meet some of them tonight."

"That sounds lovely," Clair answered. "I feel welcome already."

There was no electricity, but Stephanie had still managed to have excellent Chinese food. Andrew, Colin, and Alison were also present. "What are you guys doing tomorrow?" David asked, during dinner.

We looked at each other for an answer. "We're planning on going to church," Paula said. "We thought about watching a movie somewhere after church, but we don't have any definite plans."

"How would you like to go to the falls? We can't watch movies if the electricity doesn't come on. We could take a picnic lunch, swim, and explore the falls."

We agreed that would be fun. We went to church and enjoyed Father Jon's sermon and the choir. Auki's Catholic Church had a choir composed of both men and women. Men and women sat separately like men and women sat separately during church services. There were usually between twelve and sixteen singers who sang a cappella. I can't do justice to their melodious harmonization with written words, but the congregation always enjoyed the singing immensely.

After church services, we prepared our picnic lunch. David, Stephanie, Colin, Alison, Jim, Clair, Bill, Paula, and I all managed to fit into two cars. We made our way to the base of the falls where we ate our picnic lunch. We then followed the swift flowing stream up to the falls. We were rewarded with beautiful falls and a pool where swimmers could swim. It was a lot of fun, but I got a lot of bug bites.

Paula and I rode home with David. "I'm going to go to Ontong Java next week," David said. "The Auki provincial ship will drop me off and pick me up. I'll be gone five days."

"I heard there's a wrecked U.S. Army airplane on Ontong Java," I said. "U.S. military personal supposedly often flew low over the islands to see young, beautiful, scantily clad maidens dancing gracefully in the moonlight. One of them flew too low and crashed."

"I heard the same thing. If it's there, I'll see it."

I had read about Ontong Java and knew it was one of the largest atolls in the world. Martin Johnson traveled to Ontong Java with Jack London in 1908. Approximately 2,000 people lived on the atoll when Paula and I were in the Solomons. There were two main villages with nearly 1,300 people in Luaniua and over 600 in Pelau.

When we were back in Auki, I walked to Margaret's Chinese Store to buy canned goods and rice. I saw Tire Man on the way. He stared at me with disdain. I ignored him. There was a young man buying a cigarette. Chinese stores sold individual cigarettes from imported Australia brands. Solomon Islanders would buy a single cigarette, but they would not buy a full pack. Everything for sale was behind a counter to discourage shoplifting. "Roll," was all the customer said to place his cigarette order.

The clerk got one cigarette from a pack without speaking. The young man paid for his cigarette without saying a word. He left the store to take a spot on the porch where he would spend the night. I paid for my purchases and left for home. Paula and I discussed the practice of buying individual cigarettes that evening.

Jim and Sherry called that evening giving us the opportunity to learn what was happening in Kansas. They told us that everyone was well, but that Kansas needed rain. We told them that Malaita didn't need rain, and we would be happy to send them some.

Paul Tafqi had arranged with Paul Kennioriana for us to have another visit to his village of Fasileta. We didn't go because there was no transportation. Gabriel, Paula, and I spent the afternoon working on presentations for Laulasi instead of traveling to Fasileta. We had a visitor late in the afternoon. "Name Abraham," our visitor said. "Chief my village. Want you come my village, Kafo'elia."

"I'm happy to meet you," I answered. "It's part of our jobs to visit villages for economic development projects. Let's go talk to my supervisor to make arrangements."

Paul didn't want me to go because Kafo'elia was far from our assignment in Central Area. I still wanted to go. It would be yet another opportunity to seek primitive medicines to take to the U.S. to benefit mankind and make myself millions of dollars. I reluctantly confess that I also wanted some time away from Paula.

Paula was a lovely Peace Corps partner. She was beautiful and well-liked by everyone who knew her. She never complained about our harsh living conditions, and our love life was great. But we were together virtually twenty-four hours every day. I was beginning to suffer from Solomon cabin fever.

Paul reluctantly consented to my going to Kafo'elia. He said he couldn't arrange transportation because it wasn't in Central Area.

Abraham agreed to meet me at Margaret's Store when he was ready. We were to take a market truck to get close to his village.

Paula had diarrhea for several days, so we drove Graham's car to work. Gabriel and I continued sanding floors while Paula typed a script for our parliamentary procedure

Paul Kennioriana

program. A Malitian came to the door with a war club for sale. "What is the name of this club?" I asked. "Name *sube*," he answered.

Chief Isaac

I wasn't certain if the *sube* was a relic or a replica, but I bought it.

Chief Isaac from Ano Naki Naki was an early visitor. He was from a mixed Kwaio – Kwara'ae tribe. Isaac didn't ask for us to come to Ano Naki Naki, but he was always interested in learning about the projects we were working on.

Isaac had broken his ankle some years before. The break didn't heal properly causing him difficulty in walking. Isaac gave me a wooden mortar and pestle the second time he visited.

The pestle was about nine inches long and pointed on one end. The mortar was about eleven inches long with an opening of only about one inch. "What are these used for?" I asked.

"Betel nut," he said, demonstrating a grinding action.

Isaac went on to explain that when men lost their teeth, they couldn't manage to begin the chewing operation. He told me that the man would put betel nut, leaf, and lime into the mortar and grind it into a paste. It looked like an artifact. "How much do you want for it?" I asked.

Isaac only shrugged. He didn't seem to want any money, but I gave him a small amount and some vegetable seeds. He smiled and promised to come again.

It was Andrew's birthday, so we had him and Father Jon over for supper and canasta. Andrew and I were partners. Andrew told us that he had applied for a job in Hong Kong as a policeman. Father Jon told us that the provincial ship had trouble and David Chetwynd was stranded on Ontong Java. Father Jon and Paula won two out of three games.

We learned that the Darien Book Aid Plan World Wise School Program had books they would send to Auki. We would be required to pay shipping costs. We developed an action plan for Gwaunoa School with its obligation to raise SI$150 to pay for shipping.

I varnished floors Saturday morning while Paula went shopping with Alison and Claire. We ate supper with Bishop Loft and Father Jon then played canasta afterwards. Bishop Loft and I won two out of three. We got a telephone call when we got home. "Hello, this is the Sellens' residence," Paula said.

She paused for her caller to identify themselves. "Just a minute," she said. "I want your dad to hear."

She motioned for me to come to the phone. "It's Chuck and Jason," she told me.

She held the phone between us, so we could both hear and speak. "Dad's here boys," she said, into the phone. "We can both hear."

Chuck and Jason sang happy birthday with gusto. "Is it January 27 there?" Jason asked.

"No, but it will be in about two hours," Paula said.

We exchanged news of what we were doing in the Solomons and what they were doing in California. Paula's siblings, Jim Coyne and Linda Shalberg, called the next day and wished her happy birthday. Claire and Jim delivered birthday presents and Paula cut Claire's hair. Dr. Graham brought presents from Sheila and himself. Andrew called and wished her happy birthday. I gave her flowers. We topped off her celebration by watching *Blues Brothers* at Father Jon's home.

That evening, I watched a large gecko that waited patiently for a large insect to come near. There was none in the vicinity. Suddenly, the large gecko leapt forward and grabbed a small gecko to eat. I was not pleased. Small geckos were supposed to eat small bugs. Large geckos were permitted to live in our house, so they could eat large bugs. If I allowed large geckos to eat small geckos, there would soon be no geckos to eat bugs.

I caught the large gecko and threw it out the door. From then on, I threw all large geckos out of our house and my life. That event was enough excitement for one day. I kissed Paula and went to bed early to be well rested for my trip to Kafo'elia.

# CHAPTER 9

# *Kafo'elia Village Visit*

Chief Abraham at his mother's grave

I got up early as it was the day that I was to go to Kafo'elia with Chief Abraham. As planned, I met Abraham at Margaret's Chinese Store. I was wearing my cool walking sandals and carried my backpack filled with necessities. We rode in the bed of a market truck for several hours to a stopping off area.

I followed Abraham to a simple footpath that led into the jungle shade. The path ran straight up, deviating only to go around large trees. He stopped on the way to point to a well-marked grave site. "Mother buried here," he said.

We continued slowly. Tree roots occasionally crossed the path for me to use as footsteps. Most of the trees beside our path were mature, but a few were only three or four inches in diameter. I didn't use them for hand holds because I would have likely provided biting insects a way to get onto my body.

My cool walking sandals were not suited for trekking in the wet jungle. The velcro straps quickly filled with mud and didn't hold. I tried tying my sandals to my feet with vines. That didn't work. I tried taking them off and walking barefoot. My feet got cut and bruised. After about two hours of me struggling, Abraham stopped and waited for me to catch up. "You swim?" he asked.

I thought that was a strange question, but I knew the answer. "No, I can't swim," I said. "Why do you ask?"

Abraham didn't answer, but he continued leading me up the slippery path. He walked, and I hobbled, for another hour. I was confident that Abraham would have taken only an hour to cover what had taken me three. Then, I saw the reason for his swimming ability question. We had come to a beautiful river. It was swift flowing and about seventy-five yards across. "Have to cross here," he said.

"I can't do it," I protested. "The river is running fast. That water looks deep. I can't swim."

"Not deep," he answered. "Look over there. Children playing in river."

"I see the children playing in the river. I see children swimming in the river. That means that they can swim. I can't! I can't cross that river!"

We stood without talking. We each looked to the other for a solution. I thought about going back to the road. I could hobble for another three or four hours on my bruised feet to get back to the main road. I could then sit by the road, without any cover, until morning. I would eventually get a ride on a market truck to return to Auki. That didn't seem like a reasonable plan. Drowning in the river didn't seem like a reasonable plan either. "I help you," Abraham finally offered. "We walk across. I hold your arm. We do it."

I decided that drowning would at least be quicker, so I consented. We entered the water with Abraham grasping my arm. The river bottom was covered with small stones that made very poor footholds. I was downstream from Abraham in the swiftly moving water. The water came high on my chest and near Abraham's neck in some areas. I was amazed that Abraham could keep his footing, but we did make it across.

It began to rain as we neared the river bank. The children watched with interest as we clambered up the bank. "What's the name of that river?" I asked.

"Aluta," Abraham answered.

"Aluta seems like a fitting name. Does the name translate into English?"

"Only name. No meaning."

As we continued up the path, the melodious pitter-patter of rain on the nearby foliage almost caused me to stop thinking of my bruised feet. The smell of fresh rain moderated the more powerful odor of decaying vegetation drifting from the near-by forest. Parrots and macaws displayed colorful plumage as they flew by.

Abraham walked, and I hobbled, for another hour to reach Kafo'elia. By the time we reached the village, the rain had stopped. Several women saw us coming and pulled their ankle length skirts to cover their previously bare breasts. It was getting dark and I was tired. Abraham gave me a light supper of bananas, popo, hot tea, and cold kumara. I was pleased when Abraham showed me to the men's house where I was to sleep.

The men's house was a one-room, sago-palm structure on stilts. As in many other houses where I had slept, bamboo strips had been tied together to build the floor. I slept on the commercial sleeping mat that I had brought and used my backpack for a pillow. Five other men slept on pandanis sleeping mats. None of us had any covers.

Crowing roosters announced it was time begin my day. Abraham gave me a breakfast of fruit and cold kumara. I made a special effort to learn everything about Kafo'elia. I thought I might need to stay there until the river dried up. I thought I might have to stay there for the rest of my life. The thought of braving the raging river again was not appealing.

As in other villages that I had visited, pigs, chickens, dogs, and white-headed, naked children wandered about freely. The dwellings were raised on stilts and constructed from sago-palm thatching. Most them had separate kitchens for open-stove cooking. The houses were rectangular, and all had windows for ventilation to take advantage of the frequent breezes. Colorful parrots flew overhead. The village was clean, and the houses were well kept.

I felt grubby after my previous day's travel. I told Abraham that I wanted to take a bath. He directed me to a small, nearby stream. I hobbled to the stream, stripped and sat in the cold running water to allow the previous day's grime to wash away. I soaped my body and used a small bottle of shampoo to begin washing my hair. I sensed a presence.

I looked toward the bank where a small girl watched intently. I was confident that it was the first time she had seen a naked white man taking a bath. I was equally confident that I didn't want it to continue. I gave her my shampoo and sent her away. I dried my body with my dirty clothes and put on clean ones. I felt refreshed and ready to begin my day.

I spent the day visiting with Kafo'elia elders. They asked when the U.S. and Iraq would come to the Solomons to fight. The notion that the U.S. and Iraq would have their battles in the Solomons coincided with their ancient customs. I knew that previous gener-ations had designated battlefields where waring villages would meet for fights. Their organized battles ensured that their villages and gardens would not be destroyed. "I don't think that America and Iraq will come to the Solomons to fight," I said.

"America and Japan came," they argued. "Malaita man helped America fight Japan. Young Solomon man want join American Army."

This was the issue that greatly concerned the expatriate community. Father Jon, Bishop Loft, Dr. Graham, Colin, Father

Charlie visits with men

Chris, David, and others had voiced opinions that Malitians might not plant gardens thinking that Americans would come to the Solomons as they had during W.W. II. It was possible that some of these elders had themselves participated in the war effort.

Previous conversations with Malitian men caused me to believe that explanations why Japan and the U.S. fought in the Solomons would not convince them America was not coming with cargo ships. I offered more convincing evidence. "I was in the Army for three years," I said. "American Army fights differently today. Iraq won't want to come to Solomons to face both American and Solomon soldiers." America will have to fight Iraq in Iraq."

My military planning strategy saved the day. I was also asked about other weighty, international issues. "America put man on moon?" one asked.

"Yes," I answered. "We put a man on the moon about twenty years ago."

"How he do that?"

"He flew in a rocket."

"How rocket fly?"

That question made me think deeply. I could foresee two problematic issues concern-ing my answers. The first was that the Malitians would not understand complex expla-nations about flight dynamics from a rocket scientist. The second problem was that I was not a rocket scientist. However, I did my best. "Do you sometimes see airplanes fly overhead?" I asked.

I raised my hand and moved it slowly across the sky to imitate an airplane. The men all nodded affirmatively. "Do you know how airplanes fly?" I asked.

The men all nodded affirmatively. I was pleased to learn of their knowledge because I didn't know how airplanes flew. However, I did know that I was then on firmer ground.

"Rockets work the same way," I said, moving my airplane hand to the ground. "Only rockets fly straight up toward the moon."

I moved my rocket hand from the ground toward where I thought the moon might be. "Airplanes fly across the sky," I said, transforming my rocket hand into an airplane hand to simulate flying across the sky. "Rockets fly straight up to the moon," I continued, retransforming my airplane hand into a rocket hand to simulate a rocket flying to the moon. "They work the same way."

That explanation satisfied the elders. I was pleased that I had been able to provide satisfactory, technical information on flight technology. I moved around the village in the event that others were seeking to learn about advanced rocket technology.

I included a visit to a garden and learned that they tended their gardens the same way as Kwara'ae. The path to the first garden was dry, allowing me to keep my cleaned sandals on my feet. The path to the second garden was wet, allowing mud to transform my walking sandals into carrying sandals.

Young men also sought me out for my expert opinions. I modestly complied and sat with several of them. "You join Army?" one asked.

"I was in the U.S. Army for three years," I said. "When I was your age, the U.S. had the draft. That meant that every young man had to be ready to go to the Army when called. Two years of my service were in Germany."

"Germany bigger America?"

"America is much larger than Germany."

"Germany bigger Solomon Islands?"

"Individual islands in the Solomons are far apart. However, Germany has more land area than Solomon Islands."

"Can I join American Army?"

"It might be possible. There was a Canadian and a German on active duty in the U.S. Army with me in Germany. You can check with the American Embassy in Honiara. You will need to be healthy and speak English."

Our exchanges seemed to satisfy the young men. I pondered how I might get word to Paula and Paul that I would be stranded until the river dried up or at least dropped four feet. I hadn't developed a satisfactory solution by the time I went toward the men's house for my night's slumber. I sat outside and watched a beautiful Solomon sunset before climbing the steps into the house.

A symphony of crowing rosters told me it was time to get up. I gathered my meager possessions and packed them into my back pack. I had cleaned my sandals and thought the velcro straps might hold them in place while I sloshed over the muddy path. I left the men's house and headed toward Abraham's house. I admired the colorful sunrise as I walked.

Chickens and pigs paused their searches for something to eat to allow me to pass. A bare-breasted woman was picking lice from a friend's head as I approached. They changed places to allow for reciprocal grooming. When I found Abraham, he asked if I had given a little girl a bottle of hair shampoo. The girl was his daughter and he was concerned that she had stolen it. I confirmed that I had given it to her. After our Solomon breakfast, I thought about my return trip to Auki.

Our trip to the river went as expected. The path was slippery making it difficult for me to keep my footing. Abraham's bare feet and toes clung firmly to the ground in most places. On especially steep, wet places, he jammed his heels into the mud as he strode down the path. His method made a temporary step to prevent him from slipping.

I thought I would try the method when I had better footwear. For this trip, I continued to slip and fall.

Abraham didn't say anything about crossing the river as we walked. Perhaps, he mistakenly believed that I had forgotten that this trip had put my life in danger. We arrived at the river and stopped. "You ride canoe?" he asked. "Take canoe to Atoria. From Atoria, take market truck to Auki."

Charlie launches canoe
Backpack lies in the path

Abraham pointed to a dugout canoe about twelve feet long. "Ride in Solomon canoe?" He asked again.

"This will be the first time," I answered. "It looks great. I'm afraid to cross the river again."

I quickly helped Abraham get the canoe into the river. Abraham had me sit in back facing him as he stood in the bow. He didn't expect me to do anything more than help him counterbalance the long, narrow canoe.

I thought it was peculiar that Abraham stood, but I didn't know anything about the proper way to propel a Solomon canoe. A little water began to splash into the canoe. We didn't have anything to bail out the water. I thought began to better understand the reason for him standing.

Very soon, he handed me the paddle and I stood, balancing myself in the dugout. I was impressed at how well the canoe tracked considering that it didn't have a keel. We didn't have to paddle very much because the swiftly flowing river propelled us quite nicely.

The rainforest scenery was beautiful. I saw many birds that I didn't recognize. That didn't surprise me because I hadn't made any effort to study Solomon Islands' bird species. I did know that there were birds in the Solomons that were unique to the country and some that were unique to individual islands.

The flowers, butterflies, and trees were equally stunning. We eventually reached Atoria where Abraham got us ashore. I laid in the shade of a tree waiting for a market truck. A Solomon boy brought me a pillow. It didn't have a pillow case and was obviously well used. I used it gratefully without a whit of worry about getting head lice. Solomon Islanders also waited with their market goods. We didn't have to wait long before a truck arrived.

I waited while those with market goods loaded their items and took their positions. I got on board positioned myself on a comfort-

Charlie paddles canoe standing

able bag of copra. The truck headed toward Auki stopping occasionally to let someone on or off.

The time seemed to pass quickly, and I was in Auki. I got off at Margaret's Store and went inside to buy beer. There was a white stranger in the store. He was about sixty years old and dressed like we long-term expatriates. "Hello," I said. "Are you new in Auki?"

"I don't live here," he answered. "I'm Australian. I like it here. I would live here if I could get a permanent visa. Do you live here?"

"Yes," I answered. "My wife and I are American Peace Corps Volunteers. We've been here about nine months."

"I don't smoke," he confided in me. "But when I'm in Malaita, I can buy single cigarettes. Since I can buy singles, I always smoke one."

I nodded as if I thought that made sense. He didn't smoke, but he smoked in Auki because he could buy single cigarettes. I smiled and left the store to walk home. Paula greeted me with hugs and kisses. I was very tired after three days in the bush. I took a shower and sat down to rest and drink a beer. She promptly noticed my feet. "What did you do to your feet?" she asked.

"It's a long story," I said. "I'll tell you tomorrow. But let me tell you about an Australian that I met at Margaret's Store."

"Well, your feet look terrible. But what about your new friend?"

"The guy told me he liked living in Auki because he could buy single cigarettes. He said that he didn't smoke, but he bought a cigarette to smoke because he could buy singles."

"He does sound a little strange. On second thought, he might think that you traveling to a primitive village in Malaita for no good reason might be a little strange."

I'm confident that I had a clever response, but I can't remember what it was at this time. I went to bed and immediately fell asleep.

I woke refreshed from my Paludrine induced, happy dreams. "What did you do while I was gone?" I asked Paula, while we were eating breakfast.

"I was really busy," she replied. "I attended women's group meetings and had Jim and Claire over for lunch. I spent the nights with Alison. We had suppers with Papa Jon, Bishop Loft, and Dr. Graham. One more interesting thing, I talked to Malaita Premier Oeta while you were gone. If no other P.C.V.s come to Malaita in April, you and I might start working for other area councils."

"That's just what we need, more work," I said. "Anyway, if we get assigned to other area councils, I've already visited Kafo'elia Village. I could write an action plan in three hours."

"Something else happened while you were gone. Have you heard of Ben Burt?"

"The name is familiar, but I can't place him."

"Ben Burt is a famous British anthropologist. He has a Ph.D. in Anthropology. He works for the British Museum in London. Dr. Burt often comes to Malaita for research on the pagan Kwara'ae. He spent several months with them at Siele some time ago."

"He sounds like an interesting man. I'd like to meet him sometime."

"He came to the office while you were gone," Paula continued. "I met with him and two Solomon Islanders at the Auki Lodge to talk about a Kwara'ae cultural center. He might want us to help manage the Kwara'ae center if he gets funding."

"Everyone knows about the Kwaio," I said. "But the Kwara'ae aren't so well known. The Kwaio are famous because they're remembered as the fierce ones that killed Mr. Bell, Cadet Lillies, and thirteen native policemen. Roger Kessing wrote articles and books about the Kwaio. I haven't heard of the Kwara'ae killing any tax collectors."

"Maybe we'll get to go to Kwai and Ngongosila Islands someday and see where Mr. Bell is buried."

"Maybe we will," I said. "Malaita isn't so large, but it's so hard to get around."

"Anyway, we're not here for tourism," Paula said. "We're here to help Malitians with development projects."

"I know there're other tribes in the interior that reject Christianity and economic development," I continued, steering the conversation away from work. "The Kwaio are the most famous. I think that the guy that brings artifacts for me to buy is from a Begau village. I think his name is something like Bo'ogo. I hope that Burt can get funding for his cultural center. It's taking so long to get funding for our sawmill projects. Where can we get some of the books that Dr. Burt wrote?"

"He said he was going to send us some things."

Our conversation drifted back to my meeting with the Australian in Margaret's Chinese Store. "He told me he didn't smoke," I repeated. "But he bought a cigarette to smoke because he could buy singles."

"He would fit into Malitian society very well," Paula said, laughing. "Maybe he doesn't drink, but he drinks beer because he can buy just one."

"Beer is different! It's sensible to buy beer because we can buy them one at a time."

I had a visitor with several wicker pieces that he wanted to sell. They were large and round and could be used for hot pads. Paula and I had bought several of them, but only hung them for decorations. I had told other salesmen that we didn't want any large ones, but I would buy small ones for SI$1 each. At SI$1 each, we could send many to the U.S. for presents.

I told this man I would buy many small ones. He was back the next day trying to sell the large ones. I didn't buy any. The vendors continued to bring large wicker pieces that I wouldn't buy, but they seldom brought small ones that I did buy. Some brought baskets that we bought.

We continued our meetings and visits with our ever-growing numbers of Kwara'ae friends. We often visited area villages despite not having any official business. We were always well accepted and simply wanted to be with our friends. Paula and I spent two night in Buma with Simon. His house was constructed of cement. He called it his "German house." It was quite clean and comfortable.

I spent two days and one night in Ano Naki Naki with Chief Isaac. He told me that several years ago, an English doctor had advised him to have his broken foot amputated. Isaac had refused. I told Isaac that it was possible that the doctor was offering to operate to fuse his foot bones together rather than amputate. Isaac seemed to understand, but he didn't commit to talking to Dr. Graham about the possibility.

A young Kwaio man came to our office with a request for help in developing a money-making project. He was small and was missing an arm. He said his name was Jacob and that it was hard for him to survive in his traditional Kwaio village. I explained that our system for organizing aid was for villages rather than individuals. I advised him that if his village chief would make a request, Paul Kennioriana might approve of Paula and me traveling to his Kwaio village.

Missionaries Graham and Glenda had us over for tea one afternoon. They concentrated on ministering. "There are many Rice Christians in Malaita," he said. "We avoid giving them anything that might be considered payments."

"What do you mean by Rice Christians?" I asked.

"Early missionaries found Solomon Islanders would attend their church meetings when they fed them rice after their sermons. Those missionaries that didn't serve rice had few attendees. Those Solomon Islanders that came for rice became known as Rice Christians. Glenda and I want to avoid that."

We had Father Jon and Andrew over to celebrate Andrew's birthday. We had dinner then played canasta. Andrew and I were in partners. "Did you know that the Chetwynds are going to be leaving us?" Father Jon asked, as he shuffled the cards.

"No, I haven't heard that," I answered. "Where are they going."

"I haven't heard about what they'll do next. David's contract is finished, so he's leaving Malaita. He might have an offer to come back to Honiara for more work in the judicial system."

"I hope they do get to come back. Paula and I really like them. They're fun to be around. David has almost as much energy as Neil Menon."

We were prepared for our Laulasi parliamentary skit, so we made our canoe trip to Laulasi. We toured the island again and saw it through the eyes of potential tourists. I thought that they should build a more traditional skull house.

I didn't mention it, because they would have asked me to apply for a grant to build it. I was loath to apply for a grant to preserve their culture. If they had to be paid, their culture was effectively gone.

That evening, the man I thought was from the Begau village brought a nose bone and comb to our house and asked me to buy them. He didn't look so wild and fierce looking, but he still seemed nervous.

Laulasi skull house

Even though he couldn't speak much Pisin, we were able to communicate a little. The nose bone and comb looked very old and I was happy to have them. "I've seen that man here before," Paula said, when he left. "Is he from a Kwara'ae village?"

"I don't think so," I answered. "He doesn't speak Pisin very well. I couldn't understand for sure, but I'm sure he's Begau from some village in the middle of the island. His name is Bo'ogo."

"What did you buy?"

"I bought a nose bone and custom comb. I think they're very old. I wonder if the nose bone is made from human bone. I hope he comes again. He's the only Begau man I've met. I'd like to go to his village someday."

Our work days were routine. We performed needs assessments then created action plans to address the needs we identified. Paula cut Stephanie's hair after work one day. Stephanie talked about their upcoming departure from Malaita. Paula made an appointment for us to go to the Chetwynd home to buy some things they didn't want to take with them.

Stephanie thanked Paula for cutting her hair and left. "Do you remember that we're going to Dr. Arun and Elaine Menons to celebrate Neil's birthday?" she asked.

"I remember," I said. "I got a couple of beers yesterday to take with us."

Menons had a barbeque and side dishes for the party. Neil was his usual mischievous self. We sang happy birthday and gave him a present. I had always thought of Dr. Arun as an Englishman, but he had different status. "The U.K. had many colonies and protectorates," he told me. "Now, the U.K. has different citizenship classes. Each class has a different passport."

"I never heard of that," I responded. "What class of passport do you have?"

"I have a third-class passport. I was born in East Africa and trained as a medical doctor in London. Passport types are different depending if holders are classed as being a dependent territories citizen, a British overseas citizen, a British subject, a British national overseas, or a British protected person."

"The Solomon Islander were a protectorate until independence. Does that mean that Solomon Islanders have British passports?"

"I don't know about the Solomon Islands. But it's not right that I'm classed as a third-class, British citizen."

I went Margaret's Store later that week to get some canned goods. Two young men each bought one beer and one cigarette and left. Yasuo Isozaki was shopping for rice, tuna, and wine. "Masako is going back to Japan soon," he said. "She would like you to come for dinner sometime before she leaves."

"Thanks for the invitation, Yasuo," I answered. "I'm sure that we can come. Just let us know when."

Paula saw Masako a couple of days later. They set a date for our dinner party. We took a bottle of wine and a cake. "I'm going to Japan for a vacation soon," Masako informed us, during dinner. "Our daughter, Haruko, is going to visit Yasuo while I'm gone."

"We'll miss you," Paula said. "But it will be nice to meet your daughter. We'll have Yasuo and Haruko over for dinner sometime."


Gabriel and I continued sanding floors to get them ready for varnishing. I took the opportunity to tell him about my trip to Kafo'elia. When I told Gabriel about Abraham standing in the canoe, he told me that Abraham was able to guide the canoe by shifting his weight.

Visitors continued to come with large wicker pieces that they wanted to sell. I continued telling that that I didn't want any large ones, but I would buy small ones for SI$1 each. At SI$1 each, we could send many to the U.S. for presents. I changed my strategy.

I told each of them that I knew Solomon warriors traditionally made shields from that same wicker. I showed them pictures of the traditional oval or rectangular shields. I showed them how large a three-feet by one-foot shield would be. I offered to pay handsomely for one or more of them. None of them ever brought me a shield for me to buy. They continued to bring me large, round wicker pieces that I wouldn't buy.

Paula and I continued writing letters to tourist agencies in the U.S. encouraging them to develop tours to the Solomon Islands. I kept copies for the men from Laulasi. Eric Mason brought Paula living orchids that week. I later tied the orchids onto a tree outside our house.

We invited Yasuo and his daughter, Haruko, over for supper. Jim and Claire were still living with us making six for our meal. The electricity went off while we were eating, so we finished our dinner by candlelight. Jim and Claire did the dishes afterwards. "Haruko is a very beautiful, young woman," Jim said, after Isozakis went home. "She speaks English very well."

"You haven't met her mother yet," Paula said. "Masako is beautiful herself. She's in Japan now."

"I think that Haruko also speaks French," I added. "I don't know what she does for a living in Japan, but she's special."

Paula used Sheila's sewing machine when we had electricity. She made a dress and a slip for herself and bought more material for a dress. Jim and Claire moved into their own house. Dr. Graham and Sheila returned from New Zealand. I washed Dr. Graham's car, cleaned it up, filled it with gas, and took it back to their house.

I went to the bush for needs assessments in three villages that week. I was well received. Old men talked about the U.S. and Iraq coming to the Solomon Islands to fight. Young men asked me if they could join the Army. One man announced to his friends that his grandfather would have liked for me to come to his village for dinner. I was to be the main course. "Did your grandfather like to eat fat men?" I asked.

"Not fat man, tall man," he said. "Solomon man like eat tall man. That's why no tall Solomon man today."

Paula stayed in Auki to type business letters and attend a women's group organizational meeting during my three trips to the bush. I told her about the Malitian who told me his grandfather would have liked to have me for dinner. Paula laughed at my story. Our unique lives were beginning to seem normal.

# CHAPTER 10

# *Ready for Australia*

Other than the Malitian telling me his grandfather would have liked to have me for dinner, the village needs assessments were uneventful. I had made notes for the action plans I would create. I began creating the action plans and worked for two days. When my plans were finished, I took them to Premier Oeta's office to have copies made.

The only copy machine in Malaita was in the premier's office. There was a designated operator and that woman was the only person permitted to make copies. Her responsibility had quickly evolved into authority. It often took bribes to get her to make copies. I managed to get the copies made and returned to our office about quitting time.

Paula and I stopped by Margaret's Chinese Store for supper supplies. When we got home, I sat down at the kitchen table to watch a gecko stalk a fly. Paula was reading her Women in Development newsletter. Both the gecko and the fly were upside down on the ceiling and I was watching carefully. I had formed an opinion that when geckos got close enough to their pray, they leapt forward with all four feet leaving contact with the ceiling.

I always watched them carefully to try to understand how geckos could accomplish that feat. My scientific observations were interrupted when Paula spotted a cockroach. She leapt to get her flyswatter and went after the fleeing insect. "I hate you!" she screamed, as she pursued the offending bug. "I hate you! I hate you!"

The cockroach made it to safety despite Paula's Amazonian efforts. Paula returned to reading her newsletter and I went back to my scientific, gecko study. "Look at this," she said. "There's a United Nations Environment Program on Sustainable Development. We could nominate Salamai or Betty for awards."

She handed me the newsletter. It said that winners chosen would receive an all-expense paid trip to an international women's conference in Miami, Florida. "We could nominate both Salami and Betty," I said. "It would be unlikely that either would be chosen. But if we nominate them, the article says each would get a certificate of recognition."

"Let's get started on the applications. We already know most of the information we will need."

I returned to my more important, scientific, gecko study. Just when the gecko was getting ready to pounce, the electricity went off. "Arghhh, arghhh," a Solomon man emitted a primal scream from some distance.

"Arghhh, arghhh," a Solomon man answered from a nearby house.

"Arghhh, arghhh," again from a distance.

"Arghhh, arghhh, arghhh, arghhh," I responded.

"What do you think you're doing?" Paula demanded.

"I'm doing what Solomon men do when the electricity goes off," I patiently explained. "I've always wondered why they do it. Actually, it's very satisfying. Arghhh, arghhh, arghhh!"

"Well stop it! You're not a Solomon man! People will think you're crazy!"

I thought that I was being culturally sensitive by observing Solomon customs. However, I did have to remember that I was still married to an American woman. "Well, what can we do in the dark?" I innocently asked.

"You can work on our cost-of-living survey. Everyone knows US$165 per month isn't enough to live on."

"I can do it, but it won't help us. By the time Peace Corps would increase stipends in the Solomons, we would be gone. It's too dark to see anyway."

We went to Kwaineketa village the next day for a needs assessment. A young man held his infant son as he listened to my introductory speech. He slowly chewed betel nut as he observed. He removed a cud of betel nut from his mouth and gave it to his son to chew. The Kwaineketa people were excellent hosts and served us a delicious meal with chicken for the main course. Paula bought a custom fan from one of the men.

Paula and Charlie in back of house with baby parrotsin cage

When we got home, I fed the baby parrots. They stopped screeching long enough to eat. We went to Father Jon's house to watch a movie that evening. We were watching a movie on Australia when the electricity went off.

I refrained from joining the Solomon men in their primal scream contest. Since Paula had rejected my efforts to be culturally sensitive, I doubted if Father Jon would understand.

We went to Chetwynds that Saturday and bought their key board. They invited us to stay, but we soon left to go to the market for our weekend shopping. We had another surprise when we returned home. In addition to not having electricity, we didn't have a phone. "What do you think is wrong with our phone?" Paula asked.

"I have no idea," I responded. "There was an underground line cut a while back. Maybe it's something like that. I'll check with Camerons to see if they have phone service."

Paula and I walked the short distance to Camerons and knocked. Alison came to the door. "Hello, Paula and Charlie," she said. "We were just thinking about you. What are you doing this afternoon?"

"We don't have any plans," Paula answered. "But we came to see if your phone was working."

"I don't know. I haven't used it today. I'll check."

Alison checked and told us their phone was working. We made plans to return to Chetwynds that afternoon and I committed to calling the phone company Monday. I made my call to Honiara from Camerons early Monday morning. "This is Charlie Sellens from Auki," I said. "I lost phone service Saturday. I'm calling to see what the problem is."

After some time, I had an answer. "Phone disconnected. Didn't pay bill."

"I paid my bill," I protested. "I always pay my bill on time and I pay by check. I know my bill is paid."

"Where you pay?"

"I took the check to the phone company office in Auki."

"Didn't pay in Honiara."

"I just told you that I paid in Auki. I live in Auki, my phone is in Auki, so I paid my bill in Auki. I always pay my bill in Auki."

"Didn't get check from Auki."

"Well, call Auki and ask if I paid my bill, please. They'll tell you I paid then you can reconnect my phone. Next time, don't disconnect my phone. I don't complain when I lose my phone service because of problems, but you shouldn't disconnect my phone. I always pay my bill on time."

"I know. White people pay on time. Japanese pay on time."

Our phone was reconnected that day. Our electricity came on and went off for several days, but we did little complaining. Other volunteers lived in villages without any electrical service. We were eating supper by candlelight that evening when we had a knock on the door. "Hello, anyone home?" someone called out.

"I'll get it," Paula said. "It's Papa Jon."

I joined her at the door. Father Jon carried three small packages. "Come in and have supper with us," Paula said.

"Thanks for the invitation," Father Jon responded. "I'll come in, but I can't stay long. I brought you some meat from Bishop Gerry's and my freezers. It's starting to thaw, and it doesn't look like the electricity will be back on soon."

Auki church

"Well thank you," Paula said. "We'll go to church tomorrow. I could bake it and have you and Bishop Loft over for dinner."

"That would be nice, but I'm planning a dinner at my house to use up some more of the meat. I would invite you, but you can have your own party with this start."

We went to church then went home immediately after the services to prepare for our dinner party. Alison, Colin, Andrew, and Bill came at noon and helped us enjoy our gifts. We went to Chetwynds for tea in the afternoon. "Did you hear the latest report about the electricity?" Stephanie asked.

"I know it's been off for several days, but what's the latest?" Paula asked.

"It's expected to be off until the end of March."

"The end of March? Arghhh," Paula voiced her displeasure with her own primal scream. "That's over six more weeks without power! What's the problem?"

"I heard that the generator is down. They had to order parts from Australia."

"We won't be in Auki too much in February," I said. "We have our early service conference in Guadalcanal. We'll also spend some time in Honiara on the G.E.D. program."

"David, this is the first time we've seen you since you came back from Ontong Java," Paula said, changing the subject. "How long were you there?"

"I was there for five weeks. It was some of the most interesting times I've spent in the Solomons."

"Was there a wrecked, U.S. Army airplane there?" I asked.

"There had been one many years ago. Most of it has been taken by junk dealers or souvenir hunters. Souvenir hunters are terrible for taking all that stuff. Would you like to see a piece of the plane?"

David laughed and showed us the piece of downed airplane that he had himself collected.

Paula and I were becoming much better known and accepted in Malaita. Paul continued to bring us requests to visit villages for needs assessment. We stayed busy most of the time with village visits for needs assessment, subsequent development of actions plans, writing articles for the *Malaita Nius*, literacy, women's in development issues, house maintenance, and other things.

Chief Isaac from Ano Naki Naki came to our office that week. He brought a boar's teeth necklace. "Is this old?" I asked.

"Belonged to Grandfather."

"I would like to have it, but I don't know if it's right to take cultural artifacts from the Solomons."

Isaac smiled then explained that I should take this artifact. He told me that people in his village weren't Christians. When the villagers converted to Christianity, church leaders would destroy all the old artifacts that had connections to the ancestor spirts.

I nodded and raised my brow to show I understood. "How much do you want for the necklace?" I asked.

Isaac shrugged and smiled. He didn't seem to want any money. I gave him a small amount of money and some more vegetable seeds. Other Solomon men frequently stopped in the office just to talk. Many visitors were eager to share stories of

Charlie, Isaac, and Paula

their ancestors. Others questioned us about life in American. Several were interested in learning about my military service. Peter Ufa, the custom man from Dala Village, was a frequent visitor. He brought us a custom basket as a gift on one occasion.

Gwaunoa School had completed its obligations identified in our action plan. Its final act was to raise enough money to pay for shipping books. The school secretary, John Osi, brought us the agreed SI$150. Paula wrote a check on the Kearny County bank for shipment from Darien Book Aid Plan World Wise School Program. She went to the post office to mail the letter and check. Paula picked up our tickets for our flight to Honiara for our early service conference while she was out.

Paula's sister, Mary Eddy, called that week. Paula told her about getting books from the Darian Book Organization. Mary worked for the school district in Ulysses, Kansas. She told Paula that she was going to try to get school books sent from Ulysses to Malaita.

Paula got a late birthday card from Augusta S.R.S. Jim and Sherry Coyne sent us a letter that included packages of Kool-aid. Since we didn't have electricity, we couldn't

Mary Eddy and Darian Book Organization
sent books to Malaita.

make ice. I took a pitcher of water to May Ice Cream Store where they agreed to cool it. May Ice Cream Company had its own emergency generator knowing Auki was frequently without electricity. We made Kool-aid the next day when I got home with the cool water.

Colin gave us a ride to the airport for our ride to Honiara for our early service conference. As we approached Henderson Field, I was impressed with how the appearance had improved. When I saw the airport a few months before, I thought that it was not deserving of an international airport designation.

But that day, it was beautiful. It was amazing how much improvement that had been made in the few months that we had lived in the Solomons. In retrospect, maybe my idea of what constituted a modern airport had evolved.

The first day of the early service conference was held at the Honiara Hotel. Nurse Mary gave us shots early in the afternoon. We spent the afternoon at Jimmie's house where we watched a movie and ate super. She confirmed that John Mark had left and that she was the acting director. Jimmie took us back to the Honiara Hotel where we spent the night.

Peace Corps had planned a special place for our conference. We rode a bus to a departure point where two commercial canoes with outboard motors waiting to take us to Velulua Island. I dutifully wore my life jacket. Rules are rules.

Other volunteers used their life jackets for seat pads and found them very comfortable. It was raining, but we arrived without incident. It rained lightly all day, but we continued our conference in an open-air dining area.

Our conference continued the next day. Several of us enjoyed playing volleyball before lunch with several Velulua Island employees. Jimmie said she wanted to talk to me, so I left the volleyball game and followed her to a quiet area. Others continued the volleyball game.

I thought Jimmie might want to raise the issue of her and John Mark's mistaken opinions that I was culturally insensitive. I was ready to document cultural assimilation by referencing my screaming when the electricity went off. I thought she might want to acknowledge that Paula and I were doing good jobs as community development workers. I thought she might want to offer apologies on behalf of John Mark for his butt-chewing letter over my working for Albert Nori.

She didn't raise any of those issues. We didn't talk about anything meaningful. I returned to the volleyball game. Our evening ended with a talent show that was great fun. We watched *Teenage Mutant Ninja Turtles* and went to bed.

We left Velulua Island for Honiara in two canoes. The sea was rough creating problems for the first boatload of volunteers. The canoe nearly capsized and Jimmie lost her purse. Everyone was soaked, but our pilot got us through without drama. Naturally, I was wearing my life-jacket. Rules are rules. We took a field trip to see a portable sawmill and watched a performance by Gilbertese dancers at the hotel that evening.

Paula and I went to I.C.L.A.R.M. with Tom to spend a few relaxing days. Tom and I talked about Kwara'ae tribe's lineage that I was documenting. Paula cut his hair, then Tom took us to a party.

He gave us a guided tour of the clam farm the next day. "How would you like to go scuba diving?" he asked. "I use scuba gear nearly every day for my work. I have plenty of equipment. We will go about fifteen feet deep and see giant clams."

Tom and Paula with giant clams

"I would love to go, Tom," Paula answered. "I've never done anything like that."

I also wanted to go, but I knew my life-jacket would interfere with the scuba gear. "Thanks Tom," I said. "But going fifteen feet under-water doesn't appeal to me. Maybe next time.

Paula went scuba diving and enjoyed the experience. I finished two articles for the *Malaita Nius* while they were gone. We took a market truck to Honiara in the afternoon and bought snorkeling equipment. We spent the night with Bill Wise then went to Peace Corps office the next morning. We waited almost an hour before we realized it was a U.S. holiday.

We took the opportunity to go to the national parliament building to see Sam Alisia. Sam introduced us to several people in the education department. We discussed the Solomon education system generally and the G.E.D. program specifically. After the formal meetings, we returned to his office. "Would you like to come to dinner at my house?" he asked, in English. "Mary has a nice dinner planned."

"We would love to come," we simultaneously answered. "How will we get to your house?

"I have a car and a driver. Meet me at the parliament building after work."

As Sam said, he had a nice car and a Malitian driver. Sam rode in the front with the driver while Paula and I rode in the back. Sam's driver was skilled and responsible. We met another car whose driver was less skilled or drunk or both. He approached us at a rapid speed. Sam's driver moved as close to the shoulder as he could and decreased speed.

The other driver seemed to increase his speed and moved to occupy the space forfeited by Sam's driver. We passed close enough that our mirrors hit resulting in Sam's mirror being knocked from his car. Sam didn't show any emotion. "My krangie," was all our driver said, as we continued to Sam's house.

Mary had prepared a delicious meal and we enjoyed our conversations. We continued to discuss the Solomon education system generally and the G.E.D. program specifically. After dinner, Sam's driver took us to Bill Wise's house where we spent the night.

The next day, Paula got medication from Nurse Mary for an ear infection. We ate lunch at Madonna Hotel where we saw Kim, Paul, and two other P.C.V.s stationed in Honiara. We took a red bus to the Honiara Airport and flew back to Auki. All we passengers got a ride to Auki on a market truck. "Leave bags," the driver said. "Come back for bags."

When the driver delivered our bags, he held out his hand. "Pay for bags," he said.

"I don't think I should have to pay for the bag delivery," I protested. "There was plenty of room for us to take the bags when we came in on the truck. It was your idea to have us leave the bags."

After much discussion, I didn't pay for the bag delivery. I walked to the post office and asked for our mail. We had several letters including one from Jason with pictures of our beautiful granddaughter, Ashley.

We spent the next day at home recouping from our trip. Dr. Arun and Elaine had invited us to a going away party for David and Stephani. Nearly all of Auki's expatriates were there to wish them well in their next adventure. We were having a wonderful time when Dr. Arun motioned for me to join him.

I began preparing for a spirited exchange obligating me to defend against charges of perceived wrongs committed by long-dead Americans. He had his usual mischievous grin, but a new topic. "We're very busy at Kilu'ufi," he said. "Would you be willing to help us sometimes?"

"I know everyone at Kilu'ufi is overworked and I'm willing to help," I said. "But the only medical training I've had are first aid courses and an Emergency Medical Technician course that I took when I worked for Lane County. Elaine is a nurse and would be much better suited to help."

We continued our discussion. I eventually suggested Paula and I take care of Neil and Sumaita to allow Elaine to help at Kilu'ufi. Dr. Arun and I approached Elaine and Paula where our idea was presented. Paula was willing. Elaine was enthusiastic. I quickly formed an opinion that she relished the idea of some time away from Neil.

Paula and I went to Chetwynds the next day to pick up things we bought. They gave us many books. We had a picnic lunch with Father Jon and Chetwynds, then we watched the movie, *Gandhi*.

Paula attended a women's club meeting the next day. She went with Sheila to the airport to wave goodbye to Chetwynds. David had been offered a job in Honiara, but he hadn't accepted. We received a package from Paula's folks and Jim and Sherry. They included a canned ham with their goodies. Paula had to pay SI$13 as an import fee.

Paula bought twelve customs combs. She sent two rolls of film to the U.S. to be developed and mailed a letter to her parents. We ate supper with Camerons and introduced them to tomato beer, a combination of beer and tomato juice. They introduced us to shandies, a combination of beer and lemonade.

I planned on going rafting with Elaine and Dr. Arun while Paula took care of the children. It was raining so I used the indoor time to install a light in the closet per instructions from Richard Kimberly. Even thought it was raining, Paula and Cheryl Hicks walked. I thought I was getting ample exercise without extra walking. We watched movies in the afternoon.

The day before our scheduled trip to Buma, we did interviews for *Malaita Nius*. I was writing two articles for publication when Simon and two other men came into our office. "Problem in Buma," Simon said. "Land dispute. Maybe stop sawmill project."

"There're always land disputes in Malaita," I answered. "We expected that when we started the project. We'll just work around it."

"What we do?"

"I think we should talk to Colin. He knows about the project and he understands land disputes. If Colin says it's alright, we'll continue."

Paula with market purchases

Colin came by the house that evening. He was very supportive and even agreed to go to Buma with us. Paula stayed home and worked with Betty while we waited for transport to Buma. Our plan was to travel in the afternoon and spend the night. Early in the afternoon, we learned that the transportation was having mechanical problems, so it was not coming. We watched a movie in the evening.

Paula and I got up early because a rooster had disturbed our blissful sleep. We sat on our screened porch until it was time to go with Camerons to the Auki Market for our Saturday shopping. We bought green coconuts, pine-apples, tomatoes, green peppers, cucumbers, shallots, and other vegetables. Colin gave us a ride to the shop where we bought speedy-gas. "Did you hear about Sol Air's first commer-cial, international flight?" Colin asked, on our return trip.

"No, I didn't know Sol Air had started international flights," Paula answered. "Where are they going?"

"The first flight will be to Cairns, Australia. Cairns is a tourist resort city on the Great Barrier Reef."

"When is the flight?"

"The flight leaves from Honiara on March 19. It will arrive in Cairns in a few hours."

"Are you two thinking about going?" I asked. "If you go, I'm sure we would want to go with you."

"We talked about it," Alison answered. "But Colin has too much work to think of a vacation. Of course, we're always short of help at Kilu'ufi Hospital, so I shouldn't leave."

"March 19 is nearly three weeks away," Paula said. "That gives us plenty of time to think about it."

Paula and I discussed advantages and disadvantages of going. The advantages included having fun. The disadvantages included not having money. We soon decided to go. We had a credit card and money in the Kearny County Bank. Paula's mother could pay our bill when it came due from money in our account.

Paula called Sol Air and reserved tickets to Cairns for March 19. She also called the Australian consulate to begin the process of getting visas. That evening, we went to Father Jon's house to watch movies. Father Jon didn't watch movies with us, but he provided information concerning our upcoming trip. "Cairns is a very popular tourist destination," he said. "Tourists go there from all over the world for the tropical climate. Cairns is close to the Great Barrier Reef."

"I wouldn't go anywhere to be in a tropical climate," Paula said, with a chuckle. "We live in a tropical climate every day in the Solomons. "But what can you tell us about the Great Barrier Reef?"

"The Great Barrier Reef is one of the seven natural wonders of the world," he answered. "It's the world's largest coral reef system. It's made of coral so it's alive. It's huge. It's made of nearly 3,000 individual reefs and 900 islands."

We finished watching our movie then excused ourselves. "Thanks for having us, Father Jon," I said, as I stood to leave. "But we need to get home. We're going to Buma tomorrow. We're going to give a presentation on parliamentary procedures."

"Why are you doing that," Father John asked.

"We're working on an S.P.A. grant application to get them a portable sawmill. We need to be able to identify a community organization to accept the funds for our application to be considered. We can document that we did a skit to teach them how to conduct a meeting using parliamentary procedure."

"I want to hear how it goes. I'll be surprised if they organize themselves in the way that you would like. That's not their custom."

"I don't expect it, Father Jon. We've done parliamentary procedure workshops in other villages. I know they created governing bodies in their custom ways. But if we get to the point to apply for grants, I'll be able to document that we had the workshops to help them organize in ways that will be acceptable to the granting agency."

We did travel to Buma the next morning for our presentation. Jim Miller, Clair Miller, Colin Cameron, and George Toritelia participated. The workshop went well and the Buma residents were very attentive. When we were finished, Chairman Simon Ruarafi of Buma Village North stood and assigned committee appointments.

Father Jon would not be surprised when we told him about the committee organization. When in the Solomons, do as the Solomon Islanders do. It rained on the way back. We men were riding in the back of a pickup, so we all got soaked.

Yoshimi, a J.O.C.V. nurse, came to see us late in the afternoon. Yoshimi said she wanted to learn to speak better English. Paula agreed to help her. Paula took Yoshimi into the extra room to get her a book to read. "We're accumulating a lot of books," she said. "We don't have a good place to put those that Chetwynds gave us."

"We do have a lot of books," I agreed. "Maybe I should build a book case after we finish the floors."

We continued getting ready for our trip. Gabriel and I sanded floors the next day while Betty did our washing and worked in the yard. Paula continued working on visitors' visas to Australia. She also made a call to Cairns and made reservations for us at Cairns Village Resort. I made a call to Sol Air. "I'm Charles Sellens," I said. "My wife called a couple of days ago and made reservations to go to Cairns. I want to make arrangements to pay for the tickets."

"Yes," was the response. "Name Thomas Sogavare. Bring cash Sol Air office. Get tickets."

"Thomas, Paula and I live in Auki," I protested. "We can't just walk to your office with cash to pay for the tickets."

"Pay cash, get tickets. Bring cash tomorrow."

"I'm not able to come to Honiara with cash tomorrow or any other day. I'll send you a check for the full amount."

"Come Sol Air office. Pay cash by March 13. Way Sol Air does business."

"That's rubbish! Sol Air is presenting itself as an international airline! International airlines don't require customers to carry cash into their office to get tickets! I can mail you a check today for the tickets! If you won't accept that, I'll cancel the reservations right now!"

"Send check. I book flight. You pick up the tickets March 18 for flight to Cairns."

Our days continued as usual. Things were slow in the office, so Paula started a letter to the Kansas Behavioral Sciences Regulatory Board about renewing her social worker's license. I looked out the window and noticed a Melanesian woman whom I thought was likely from Fifi. Her hair was smartly styled and sported plastic combs. She wore shoes, stockings, and a long, colorful dress. Her stride was quick and powerful.

I saw George the next day. "George, I saw a stranger walking in the street yesterday," I said. "She looked like she might be from Fiji. Do you know why she was in Auki?"

"From Australia," George said. "Grandparents from Malaita. Grandparents go Australia on blackbird ship. Didn't come back. She speaks some Kwara'ae."

"Why did she come to Malaita?"

"Look for her people. Knew grandparents' names."

"Did she find her relatives?"

"Kwara'ae people shunned her. Thought she might claim land rights."

Another Solomon Islands cultural lesson learned. I told Paula about my conversation with George as we prepared to go to bed that evening. She agreed that we learned something new every day.

We went to church on Sunday then spent the rest of the morning babysitting for Menons because they were very busy at the hospital. When Dr. Arun and Elaine returned for lunch, we ate with them and watched a movie. Paula went walking with Cheryl Hicks in the early afternoon. We got a phone call from Kansas that evening. "Hello, this is the Sellens' residence," Paula answered.

She paused for the caller to speak then continued. "Hello Jim, hello Sherry; how is everything in Lakin?"

She listened carefully to what Jim and Sherry said then answered. "Good, we're well here. We are going to go to Australia in a couple of weeks. We'll be there eight days. We'll send you something."

Another pause while Jim and Sherry spoke. "Of course, we want to talk to Chuck," Paula eventually said. "Put him on, please."

Paula held the phone, so we could both hear and talk. "Hello, Mom and Dad," Chuck greeted us. "How are things in the Solomons? Do you need any rain?"

"Hello Son," we replied in unison.

"Things are great here and we don't need any more rain," Paula said.

"I remember when we were farming in Kansas," I added. "We always needed rain. I pledged that no matter where I lived, I would never complain about having too much rain. I'm not complaining now, but many of my Solomon friends do. What's new in your life?"

"I'm working as a security guard at the meat packing plant in Garden City. Everyone is fine. I heard from Jason recently. Grandma and Grandpa Coyne said to say hello. Grandma Sellens talked to me about her and me going to the Solomons to see you guys."

We continued our conversation exchanging news of what was happening in Kansas and the Solomons. That evening, Yoshimi came for her first English lesson. Stuart-McBrides came over for supper. Paula had baked the canned ham that her folks has sent us for Christmas. We chatted about our trip to Australia. "We will be leaving soon to go to Cairns," Paula said. "I'm cutting Charlie's hair tomorrow afternoon. If you're ready for haircuts, I could also cut yours."

"Thank you, Paula," Sheila responded. "I think I'm about ready for a trim."

"I could also use a haircut," Dr. Graham added. "We'll come over after lunch."

Paula cut my hair early the next morning. As promised, Dr. Graham and Sheila came over and Paula cut their hair. We said our goodbyes. Cheryl Hicks also came for a haircut. We said our goodbyes. Chuck called to wish us a safe journey. We said our goodbyes. We were ready for our trip to Australia.

# CHAPTER 11

# *Australia Visit*

Anthony and Moses from Laulasi came to our office and talked about tourism. George Toritelia was with them. During the time George and the Laulasi representatives were in our office, they sometimes spoke in the Langa Langa language. Anthony and Moses left, but George remained. "Are you from Laulasi?" I asked him.

Office visitors

George's smile featured his betel nut stained, black teeth. "Not from Laulasi," he answered. "Me Langa Langa man, different island."

"What did you talk about when you were speaking Langa Langa?"

"Talk about you leave. Help with tourism, then leave. What happen when you leave?"

"What do you think we should do, George?"

"Maybe new Peace Corps. Maybe get Malaita tourism man."

I thought about his answer. "I don't know if there will be new Peace Corps Volunteers to replace us," I said. "If there are replacement P.C.V.s, we don't know if they would continue our projects. How can we get a Solomon man to work in tourism?"

"Tell Malaita Premier Oeta. David Oeta get tourism man."

"All right, George. I'll talk to David. In the meantime, Paula and I'll continue writing letters to tourist agencies in the U.S. Maybe we can find an agency that will develop tours to Malaita."

We did a site visit to the artificial island of Laulasi and made our written reports. Our action plans always required the village to organize a group to accept any grant funds. This was a typical requirement of aid donors. We always did our best to have them organize using parliamentary procedures knowing it was unlikely that they would comply. We started working on a written skit. We also began scribing a constitution and bylaws.

We were scheduled to travel to the Busarain School area to do three needs assessments. Our transportation was canceled, so I took the opportunity to talk to Albert Nori about his father, Nori Nono'oohimae. "What was it like to grow up with a famous father?" I asked.

"We were just children when father was working with Maasina Ruru," he answered. "We didn't see him much. He was always away from home. I didn't understand what Maasina Ruru meant at that time."

"I read that the British put him in prison to destroy the Maasina Ruru movement."

"I didn't know it then, but Father was jailed. Many other leaders were jailed. That stopped Maasina Ruru. Solomon people wanted America to stay and look after the Solomons. Solomon people like America better than they like England. Solomon people can't understand why America helped Japan after the war, but it didn't help Solomon Islands."

I did take an early opportunity to talk to Premier David Oeta about getting a Malaita Province tourism officer. I explained that I was writing tourism agencies in California with descriptions about Malaita generally and Laulasi specifically. I told David that if he could establish a tourism officer, I would give him all the contacts that I was making in the U.S. David listened attentively, but he didn't make a commitment.

Malaita Province provided us with housing, electricity, water, and propane. Malitians called the propane "speedy-gas." Speedy gas was purchased in twenty-gallon tanks from a commercial business. The commercial business imported gasoline, diesel, and the speedy gas from Honiara. Colin and I obtained vouchers from Malaita's financial officer, Fred Fono, to get our speedy gas. "Fred is a financial magician," Colin said. "Malaita never has enough money, but Fred always finds a way to pay the bills. I don't know how he does it."

It was Chloroquine Sunday and we woke to the crowing of a rooster. Paula and I walked to church in a soft rain. Father Jon was gone, so Bishop Loft conducted the service. We had St. Patrick's lunch with Dr. Graham and Sheila at their house. The electricity was working during our lunch. Sheila had the lights on even though we would have had ample light without the artificial assist. She must have wanted to take advantage of the opportunity to use her electricity. "How are your projects going?" Dr. Graham asked, during our meal.

"Things are going slowly," Paula answered. "I'm not surprised. They told us in training that it would take time to be accepted. We've met a lot of people and we always get good responses when we go to villages. We've applied for some grants, but we haven't gotten any big applications approved."

"We know you're being well received in the villages," Dr. Graham continued. "I do want to talk to you about a grant I applied for from the United Nations Children's Fund. It's for a nutritional improvement program. If my application is approved, I'll need someone to manage it."

"That sounds interesting," Paula said. "Do you see us being involved?"

"I envision you two being the project directors. The general plan is to take an education program to villages who ask for it. There would be three phases for each village. For the first phase, you would go to each village and make presentations on nutrition and growing vegetables. You would want to recruit Solomon Islanders to go with you to give demonstrations on how to plant and take care of vegetables."

"I bet we could get Irene Misuka to help us," Paula said. "She would be great."

"This sounds like something we would like to do," I said. "And Paula's right. Irene Misuka would be an asset. She's young, energetic, and she helps her family with a beautiful garden. That's where we get the strawberries that we have for some of our dinners."

"You would give interested people vegetable seeds and tell them that you would be back," Dr. Graham continued. "In the second phase, you would go back and give a repeat lecture on nutrition and health. You would view the gardens and give them more seeds."

Paula and I listened attentively without speaking. "In the third phase, you would go back to each village for a cooking demonstration," Dr. Graham continued. "You would take some food items that you bought from a store. If this works, you'll show them how to prepare the vegetables and store-bought foodstuffs to make nutritious meals. Of course, everyone would eat the meals and hopefully continue good nutrition practices."

"You would be great for the cooking demonstration, Paula," Sheila said. "You always make such delicious meals and dishes for our parties."

"I feel very positive about working in the project," I said. "How do you feel about it, Paula?"

"I like it and would be happy to participate. When will we know if you get funding?"

"We could hear anytime," Dr. Graham answered. "I'll let you know as soon as I learn something."

We were in final stages of preparation for our trip to Cairns. We took our screeching parrots to Camerons. Paula spent the afternoon packing and included our typewriter that needed repaired. Gabriel and I varnished the rest of our floors. Since we couldn't walk on the wet floors, we spent the night with Jim and Claire Miller.

Alison and Colin took us to the airport for our flight to Honiara. We spent the day in Honiara getting our tickets, visas, money, traveler's checks, and doing other things necessary for our trip. We went to the Peace Corps office, got our Peace Corps passports, and checked for mail. Rick and Carrie had gone to Isabel Island for a vacation. They had given us permission, so we spent the night at their apartment.

We woke early and made another trip to the Peace Corps office where we met Tom Scherer. "Hello Tom," I said. "It's good to see you. How's your work at the clam farm going?"

"The same as always," Tom answered with a wide smile. "I'm in a routine. What are you two doing in Honiara?"

"We're getting ready to go to Cairns," Paula said. "Sol Air has initiated international flights and the maiden voyage is to Cairns."

"Have fun," Tom said, as we departed.

We took a red bus back to Rick's and Carrie's apartment to pick up our suitcases and then on to the Honiara Airport. The maiden voyage to Cairns hadn't attracted much attention or business. The only passengers were three Solomon couples, a young son of one of the couples, and Paula and me. We had assigned seats, but we were free to move to other seats.

Before we landed, a steward gave each of us a cloth to cover our mouths and noses. He then sprayed the plane with an insecticide to kill mosquitoes. We arrived in Cairns and took a taxi to the Cairns Village Resort. The Solomon families were also staying at the Cairns Village Resort. The resort had excellent service and facilities. It was located on five acres of tropically landscaped gardens. The low-rise buildings were constructed in the Australian Colonial style. There were 195 rooms with singles, doubles, and family accommodation.

Our first full day in Cairns was busy. We went to the Cairns City Center to look for interesting things to do. We looked at some brochures for ideas on places we might like to visit. We also took our typewriter to a repair shop to be fixed. The clerk was very friendly. "Where are you from?" he asked

"We're Americans," I answered. "But we're living in the Solomon Islands at this time."

"What are you doing in the Solomons?"

"We're American Peace Corps Volunteers. We've been in the Solomons for eight months. We will leave in September 1992."

"I know about the American Peace Corps. I hear you Yanks do decent work, but you should have come here later in the year. You have a good chance of getting rained on. Our wet season runs from November to May and our dry season runs from June to October. I say dry season, but we still get some rain."

"A little rain won't hurt us," Paula said. "We get wet a lot in the Solomon Islands."

One of our first destinations was to the Cairns Museum. The museum featured a history of living conditions when Europeans settled Australia. We picked-up brochures that told of sweltering heat, sugar cane production, building railroads, and Aboriginal resistance to European settlements.

The brochures told there would be stories of tourists, hippies, local celebrations, cyclones, toads, mold, and mozzies. I didn't know what to expect from a story about mozzies. "What are mozzies?" I asked, when Paula and I paid for our entry tickets.

"Mozzies are what you Americans call mosquitoes," she answered. "Diseases transmitted by mozzies include Dengue fever, RR virus disease, encephalitis, and BF virus disease."

"We're Peace Corps Volunteers in the Solomon Islands," Paula responded. "I know the Solomons has Dengue fever, but malaria is our biggest worry. I don't know about the virus diseases, but if they're in Australia, I suppose they're also in the Solomons."

"I imagine so. Well, enjoy your stay in Cairns and come again. Watch out for mozzies!"

We decided to walk back to the city center and started our trek. We stopped in a park to listen to a two-man musical group. When we arrived at the center, we picked up brochures for several tours we were interested in. We decided to book a tour for the Spring Mount Cattle Station. We paid for our tickets and arranged to meet our minibus early the next morning.

We went shopping and bought groceries at Woolworths. We included Australian meat pies in our purchases. Australians eat meat pies with even more gusto than Americans eat hamburgers. Aussies reportedly eat over 250 million meat pies annually.

The Aussie meat pies were similar to the pot pies Americans buy and consume. The meat pies we bought were about six inches in diameter. They were just the right size to hold in one hand. They were filled with a course ground meat with enough thick gravy to hold them together. We covered our pies with ketchup like we saw Aussies doing. When in Australia, do as the Aussies do.

Paula went window shopping with the Solomon women who were also staying at the Cairns Village Resort. I sat down with the Solomon men. Our common language of Pisin made us *wontoks* in Australia. "You know Oliver?" one of the men asked. "Oliver Peace Corps four, five years ago. From Chicago."

I pretended to think for a moment before I answered. "No, I don't think that I know Oliver," I said. "I just came to the Solomons Islands last year."

"Oliver wrote letters when back Chicago. Didn't write anymore. Maybe, because I didn't write back. Maybe see him when back America."

"Oliver from Chicago. Yes, if I see him when I go back, I'll tell him you asked about him."

We got up early for our trip to the Spring Mount Cattle Station as we had to meet our minibus at 7:10 a.m. Unlike the Solomons, 7:10 in Australia was 7:10. There were ten of us on the tour. The cattle station was a working ranch covering 60,000 acres. We toured the ranch and shot clay pigeons with an old, 12-gauge, Remington shotgun. We also shot a five-gallon can with a Chinese assault rifle.

After a barbeque lunch, a horse ride was a scheduled part of the activities. The station owner assigned Paula and me spirited animals after we told him that we had owned horses on our farm in Russell County. Novice riders were given slower mounts for their first ride. Paula and I ran our mounts for a considerable distance, pleasing both the horses and us. Half way through our ride, we rode through a cluster of cylindrical mounds.

Charlie and Paula ride among termite mounds

The mounds were made of soil and clay. Some were up to five feet wide at the base and ten feet high.

After our ride, we asked the owner about the mounds while we curry-combed the horses. "While we were riding, we passed through about 100 mud mounds," I said. "What made them."

"Those are termite mounds," he said. "There are lots of them on my cattle station. They're all over Australia."

"They're so huge," Paula observed. "How many termites does it take to build and maintain one of the mounds?"

"I don't know," he answered, with a laugh. "I've never taken the time to count them. What I do know is that every mound has workers that feed and groom the other termites in the mound. There are soldier termites that defend the mound against invaders. If you tore into one, the soldiers would bite you and their bites are poison. There's a king and a queen in every mound. They continuously reproduce to keep up the number of workers and soldiers."

We saw a wallaby on our return trip to Cairns. We did a walking tour after freshening up in our hotel. We saw several Aboriginal Australians lying on the sidewalk. They had obviously drunk alcohol until they were extremely intoxicated and passed out. It was a sad sight. "I saw several Aboriginals while we were out walking," I told the clerk, when we returned to our hotel. "They were drunk and passed out on the sidewalk. It that common?"

"All too common," the clerk answered. "The police don't pick them up. The Aboriginals can't stand to be locked up. Even though they know they would be let out in the morning, they can't stand to be confined. Many have killed themselves before the sun rose."

We began our next day by doing our laundry then went swimming. We went to the horse races where we found the Australians were dressed very elegantly. Men wore suites, ties, and hats. Women wore elegant gowns. The ladies' hats were large and ornate.

Paula and I were limited to wearing our poor clothes that we had brought from the Solomons. The Aussies did a lot of betting. We didn't waste our money betting on horses about which we had no knowledge. For our evening entertainment, we bought groceries, including meat pies and ketchup. We ate our meat pies in the room and watched movies.

We went to Kuranda Village by bus for our next daytrip. Kuranda is a picturesque little village tucked in the rainforests surrounding Cairns. Kuranda featured art, crafts, and replica, indigenous artifacts. We first went to the Australian Butterfly Sanctuary. The sanctuary was the largest butterfly flight aviary and exhibit south of the equator. It was listed in the Guinness Book of World Records. We also visited a nocturnal museum.

Paula at the horse races

The next day, we went to see the Tjapukai Aboriginal dancers in a corroboree celebration that first opened in 1987. There were three full-blood and two mixed-race dancers. One of the mixed-race dancers served as a master-of-ceremonies. He explained the significance of each dance. He shared stories about hunting through the dances of the kangaroo, brolga, and cassowary. The dancers introduced us to the Aboriginal Djabugay language through interactive song and dances. They finished their show with a fire-making ceremony.

After the dances were completed, the master-of-ceremonies turned to a more contemporary subject. "I'm a member of the stolen generation," he said. "From about 1910 into the 1970s, mixed-race children like me were taken from our mothers."

The audience grew quiet. We somberly waited for more of the story. "The white government believed that indigenous Aboriginal people were a dying population," he continued. "There were written policies and laws that allowed government officials to forcibly remove us from our mothers."

He went on to tell us that European Australians believed their culture was superior to that of indigenous Australians. Most considered recognition of mixed-race children to be a threat to the nature and stability of the prevailing white civilization.

"We were called half-castes, quadroons, crossbreeds, and octoroons," he said. "Those names were derogatory then and they're derogatory now. We're doing everything we can to preserve our heritage. By being here today, you've contributed to better understanding. I hope you can take our messages back to your own counties and share our stories."

We left the theater and went shopping. We bought Aussie hats for Jim Coyne and our sons, Jason and Chuck. We rode home on a train that took a route along the Kuranda Range. We marveled at the spectacular scenery of the Barron Falls. We were late getting back and were a little tired of meat pies, so we ate at McDonalds then returned to our room. "What did you think of the Aboriginal dancers?" I asked, as we got ready for bed.

"I know how they feel about losing their culture," Paula answered. "I know I'm of Cherokee descent, but I really don't know enough about Cherokee culture. There are very few full-blood Cherokee today. Most are mixed-race like me."

We woke well rested from our Paludrine assisted slumbers. "What shall we do today?" I asked, as we were getting dressed. "We've done about everything we wanted to do except go see the Barrier Reef."

"We have two more days," Paula answered. "Let's just take it easy today and go to the Great Barrier Reef tomorrow."

"A slow day sounds good to me. We've been on the run since we arrived."

We went shopping and Paula bought a few souvenirs for friends in the Solomons. We mailed the hats to Kansas and picked up our typewriter. We went swimming in the afternoon then returned to our room. We ate then watched the movie, *Lady Beware*. We kissed good-night then went to bed early to be ready for the next day's adventure.

We left Cairns at 7:10 for a day trip to Fitgray Island, Green Island, and the Great Barrier Reef. We climbed to the light house on Fitgray where we met a couple from Canada. After eating lunch, we traveled by boat to Green Island. Green Island features white sandy beaches and crystalline waters. The island is part of Australia's Great Barrier Reef National Park.

We did a whirlwind tour including a ride on a glass bottom boat, underwater observatory, aquarium, and a crocodile farm. We saw a variety of coral reefs, exotic fish, and marine life. We ate our supper at our motel, did our laundry, watched a movie, and packed to get ready to leave the next morning.

We arrived at the airport on time for our flight. We had another surprise. "Isn't that Bruce Gee?" Paula asked.

"Yes, it sure is," I agreed.

"Hello Bruce," I said, as we approached him. "We're really surprised to see you here."

"Hello Sellens," he said. "And I'm surprised to see you here. What brings you to Cairns?"

"We flew in on Sol Air's first international flight. It was a good chance to see Australia. We really had an enjoyable time. We fly back to Honiara today."

We chatted a bit then made our way toward the screening area. We bought duty free liquor and boarded our plane. We went shopping at Chinatown when we got back to Honiara. Rick and Carrie were still in Isabel. They had told us that we could spend another night at their house, and we did.

We went to the Peace Corps office for mail the next morning. We met two people from Australia while pricing portable sawmills. We tried to get tickets on the *Iu Mi Noa* to return to Auki, but the ship was fully booked because of Easter. We went to the Sol Air office tickets and bought tickets to fly to Auki the next day. We spent another night at Rick and Carrie's apartment. Paula was sick, so she went to bed early.

We packed in the morning and called Colin to ask him to pick us up at the airport. We met Kim and Paul for lunch at Mendana Hotel. We took a taxi to the Honiara Airport and flew home. The Camerons picked us up and took us to their house for supper.

Bo'ogo came to our house with an artifact for sale that week. He didn't seem nervous, but still struggled to speak Pisin. He made me understand that he was from a Begau tribe in the middle of Malaita Island. I examined the artifact carefully. I wasn't sure, but I thought it was a woman's belt. It was made of black fiber, interwoven with white shell beads.

I had read about Malitian women's attire before Christian influence. Women and girls wore belts like this one and little else. Young women wore these belts and similar armbands. They often adorned them with flowers or feathers. After marriage, a woman would tuck an apron-like piece of tapa cloth into the belt to cover her genitals. This designated her as a married woman.

I again asked Bo'ogo how much he wanted for the belt. He only smiled and shrugged. I wanted the belt and wanted him to come back. I gave him as much as I could afford. I tried to make him understand that I would like to visit his village. He nodded and smiled, but I wasn't confident that he understood.

I was showing Paula the Begau belt when the electricity went off. "Arghhh, arghhh," a Solomon man emitted a primal scream from across the street.

"Arghhh, arghhh," a Solomon man emitted an answer from far away.

"Arghhh, arghhh," again, from across the street.

"I know what you're thinking!" Paula asserted. "Don't you dare!"

"Arghhh, arghhh, arghhh, arghhh," I answered.

"Arghhh, arghhh, arghhh," another primal scream from across the street

"Arghhh, arghhh, arghhh," I answered. "That's what Solomon men do."

"You're not a Solomon man! I think you're crazy! I better get you out of here before you want to get Solomon Islands' citizenship and build a house in the bush."

I knew that observing Solomon customs was the right thing to do. I also knew that staying married to my lovely wife was the right thing to do. I moved to the kitchen to get candles to replace the erratic electricity.

Dr. Arun and Elaine Menon organized a trip to Alita Reef. The reef was nearly six miles long and underwater at high tide.

The Menons had hired a Solomon man, Michael, to use his large commercial canoe for the event. Michael took the Menons, Colin, Jim, Claire, Paula, and me to the sand reef. It took about an hour to get there.

Picnic at Alita Reef

Michael's wife had made a turtle soup for our lunch. It was delicious. The water was crystal clear and shallow, only about chest deep, around the reef area. I found a giant clam shell while I was snorkeling. Our return trip to Auki included pleasant conversation with our friends.

Paula was very tired and had fever blisters coming on. She went to bed early while I stayed up and read. We were interrupted by our ringing phone. I'll get it," I said. "Hello, this is the Sellens' residence."

"It's Bill Wise here," came the reply. "What's happening in Auki?"

"Nothing much happening now. Our projects are moving slowly. We lose our electricity frequently and sometimes lose our water. What's new in your job?"

"I have more than enough work. I just learned that I will be sent to Auki on April 12."

"Great! We'll be happy to see you again. Do you want to stay with us?"

"Thanks for the offer. I'm happy to stay with my *wontoks*. We can catch up on what's happening in the world."

Charlie found a giant clam shell

We were spending more and more time with the Misuka family. Irene cleaned house for us that week while her brother worked in the yard. Paula taught women's literacy in the afternoon. Bill Wasser came over for conversations and beers in the evening. He always had funny stories to tell and was in a good mood. "Did I tell you about the time the Catholic priest thought we had too many dogs in our village on Isabel?" he asked.

"No, I didn't hear your dog story," I answered. "What happened in Isabel?"

"There really were too many dogs in the village. They were dirty and mangy. They didn't belong to anyone. The Catholic priest wanted me and another Peace Corps Volunteer to start killing the dogs."

"What did you do?"

"We told him we didn't want to. We also told him we had never killed a dog, but that didn't change his mind. He was determined that we were going to be the village dog exterminators."

Paula and I listened attentively. "What happened next?" Paula asked.

"He came to our house later that week and told us he would teach us how to kill dogs. He took us to his house where he had a dog tied by a rope around its neck. He gave us bush knives and told us to get after it."

Bill was a masterful story teller. He paused, waiting for us to urge him to continue. "We didn't have killing dogs in our training program," I said. "Father Jon told us that Bishop Loft poisoned several dogs with chloroquine. Why didn't you use chloroquine?"

"We didn't even want to kill dogs. It was solely the priest's idea. But we did try to kill the mangy beast with the bush knives."

Bill swung his imaginary bush knife to demonstrate their techniques. "We tried to hit the dog, but he kept dodging. The priest was hopping around and yelling at us all the time."

"What was the priest yelling about?" Paula asked.

Bill continued his bush knife wielding demonstration while answering. "He was calling us cowardly wimps! He was jumping around screaming that he couldn't believe that Americans defeated the Japanese at Guadalcanal when Americans were such pansies and weaklings."

"So how did it end?"

"The priest took the bush knives away from us and gave the dog a whack. That ended the dog and our training lesson. He gave us a scolding for being so worthless. Fortunately, he gave up on his idea that we would rid the village of unwanted dogs."

When I had Sheila's car inspected, they found that it needed some repairs. Sheila had me keep it until the repair shop could schedule it for the needed work. Paula and I used the car go to Kilu'ufi hospital the next morning. We took a tour of Kilu'ufi and talked to Dr. Arun about malnourished children in Malaita. Dr. Graham had a receptionist make copies for the literacy program.

Paula helped a Japanese J.O.C.V. study English in the afternoon. We went to Doug and Cheryl's for fajitas that evening. Cheryl made excellent Mexican food that we enjoyed. Doug brought up our participation in the Laulasi shark filming event. He told us that Fascia had moved to Honiara under the pretext of attending school. She soon moved in with Bruce Gee.

Dr. Paul and Dr. Teresa van den Bosch had arrived in Auki while we were in Australia. They had three children, Katie, Peter, and Elizabeth. Dr. Paul and Dr. Teresa had moved to Auki from England. Both had practiced medicine in Zambia with V.S.O. from 1984-86. Dr. Paul would work at Kilu'ufi Hospital and Dr. Teresa was going to be a stay-at-home mother.

We had the van den Bosch family and Colin and Alison for supper soon after the van den Bosch family arrived. Paula had a delicious meal that we enjoyed immensely. "Did you hear about the latest land dispute?" Colin asked, as we ate.

"I know there's an ongoing land dispute among the Buma area people," I answered. "It may be a problem because we're working on a reforestation grant for the community. Is that what you're talking about?"

"No, this is different. There is a typical land dispute involving six groups and one individual. Instead of having expatriate judges make the decision, the judicial authority created an ad hoc committee to hear the dispute. Do you know Henry Doro?"

"I know Henry. He has a prominent position with the Malaita government."

"Henry Doro is the minister of lands for Malaita. He is chairman of the ad hoc committee. They're going to render their decisions this coming week. You should come hear the decisions."

We walked to church in the rain that Sunday. Father Jon and Bishop Loft were out of town so Father Chris from Dala conducted the service. The Hicks family came over for brunch after church. Dr. Graham and Sheila were returning from a trip to Honiara, so we used one of their cars to collect them. Menons were leaving on a trip, so we took them to the airport.

We often had leisure activities after work. We enjoyed picnic lunches at swimming areas, swimming, playing volleyball, and dinner parties followed by canasta. We often spent the mornings at the office with Paula teaching literacy to Solomon women in the afternoon.

I visited the open-air courthouse for the land dispute findings. Henry Doro gave introductory remarks and summed the issues claimed in the dispute. Henry referenced Mr. Bell's early work when reporting on the committee's research. The committee awarded varying percentages of land rights to the tribal litigants and nothing to the individual. I saw Henry after the session was completed. "Was nervous," he said. "First time for that."

"I was impressed with your report and findings," I said. "I think it was wise to have Malaita men make the decision. You understand Malaita, history, culture, and land dispute better than any white judge."

Henry smiled and nodded. "Your position of minister of lands for Malaita made you the ideal man to chair the committee," I continued. "The dispute was among only Kwara'ae. It was also important that there were no Kwara'ae men on the ad hoc committee."

"Maybe same plan next land dispute."

"I hope so. Whoever is in charge should recognize the wisdom of letting Malitians solve Malitian problems."

# CHAPTER 12

# *Nutrition Program*

When Bob King moved to Australia, he left several paperback books for us. David and Stephine Chetwynd gave us several more books when they left. Most expatriates in Auki valued books. When we had guests, we would ask them to choose a book and take it home. They usually returned the book and often brought one or two more. That gave other expatriates easy access to the books. Our extra bedroom was evolving into a mini-library. Books were setting randomly throughout the room.

It was Saturday and I knew that I needed to build a bookshelf to get things better organized. I curbed my ambition to coincide with Solomon Islands' leisure-time customs. Paula and I went to the market with Colin, had rolls and fruit with Cheryl and Doug Hicks, watched movies with Dr. Arun and Elaine, and visited with Jim and Claire. That was enough activities for Saturday.

We attended Easter Service at the Catholic Church on Sunday. After services, we joined an expatriate party at Sheila's and Dr. Graham's house. We later went swimming with Alison and Colin in the Fue River. That was enough activities for a Sunday. Monday was going to be different. We were to have a day off because of Easter holiday. As I laid in bed watching geckos stalk flies, I made plans to build book shelves the next day.

Paula was up and dressed when I woke. I had borrowed a circular saw from Dr. Graham with intentions of cutting boards for the book shelves. "Do you remember that we have Easter holiday today with no work?" Paula asked.

"I remember," I answered. "I'm going to work on book shelves."

"You might be out of luck. We don't have electricity and we don't have water."

"Oh great! Well that's life in the Solomons. By now, we should be accustomed to not having electricity or water. But it's still aggravating!"

"April Fool! You fell for it! We have both electricity and water!"

I used Dr. Graham's saw and cut the boards for book shelves. Paula had an appointment with Jashimie and Masako to study English. Jashimie didn't come, but Paula and Masako worked for two hours. We enjoyed our holiday and we went to work the next day as scheduled. Paul Kennioriana came to our office with an announcement. "Representative from Kwai and Ngongosila Islands my office," Paul informed us. "Wants you come get grants."

We accompanied Paul to his office where we met Area Council Representative Silas Muala. He was likely in his early forties, athletic appearing, barefooted, and neatly dressed. "Kwai half-mile from mainland," Muala informed us. "Have canoe, take you Kwai."

I was very excited about the invitation. "Isn't Ngongosila where Mr. Bell is buried?" I rhetorically asked.

"Mr. Bell, Lilies, and policemen buried on Ngongosila. Kwaio killed them."

Paul and Representative Muala agreed that we would make the trip in three days. On the appointed day, Paul informed us that there was no transportation and that the visit had been rescheduled. Our appointments that depended on provincial transportation were frequently postponed. That was the nature of Solomon Islands' culture and lack of resources.

I took an early opportunity to question Dr. Paul and Dr. Teresa about the United Kingdom's medical system. I told them that there was a doctor shortage in western Kansas. I believed that British doctors would make a good fit into rural medical programs. Since medical personnel like the van den Boschs, Stuart-McBrides, and Menons were happy in the Solomon Islands, I thought they would be contented living and working in rural Kansas communities.

We began receiving mail directly from the U.S. rather than the official system of having mail sent to the Peace Corps office in Honiara. The Peace Corps did forward our mail, but it took extra time. We ate supper with Dr. Graham and Sheila and talked about sawmill projects. We continued making telephone calls regarding our sawmill applications.

Dr. Paul, Dr. Teresa, the van den Bosch children, Alison and Colin came to our home Sunday morning for breakfast. Paula had prepared waffles and fruit salad for the occasion. We all went to Buma for snorkeling in the afternoon. It was great to get to walk on the beach where there were no foot-prints but our own.

Buma children followed us and were especially interested in the van den Bosch children. We ended the wonderful day setting on our porch watching a lovely Solomon sunset. We had popcorn, cokes, and read with electric lights to end our evening.

Dr. Graham and Sheila came for supper later that week. We had electricity, so being able to see each other made our conversations easier. "I just got notice that my application for a SI$10,500 grant was approved," Dr. Graham said.

"That's great news," I said. "I know you told us before, but what organization funded the grant?"

"It came from the U.N.I.C.E.F. Nutritional Improvement Program Funds. Are you ready to go to work?"

"Yes, we are," Paula said. "We're working on applications for portable sawmills and I have my women's literacy program. Charlie is spending a lot to time on tourism and getting a G.E.D. program established in the Solomons, but we'll have time to do this."

"As I said earlier, you'll be project managers. You can find interested villages, arrange private transportation, and hire Solomon help for gardening techniques training. You've been in enough villages to know that you should expect the unexpected. One new issue that you may be confronted with is sitting fees. They may expect you to pay them for their attendance. You might be able to convince them that free seeds and a feast are payment enough. You can call on me whenever you need help."

As they were leaving, Dr. Graham asked me to get their vehicles safety inspected. I was happy to do it. He had let us use one of the cars when he and Sheila were in New Zealand. Both he and Sheila had more work than I did.

Our second scheduled trip to Kwai and Nogsellia was cancelled, so I took one of Dr. Graham's vehicles for its safety inspection at the transportation department. It passed the Solomon Islands' inspection without needing any repairs. Paula worked on her women's literacy project while I was gone.

We completed plans for our nutrition program and were ready to schedule our first workshop. Irene Misuka agreed to work in the program. We also received a commitment from Irene's cousin, Pauline, to help. There were to be three workshops with each workshop being one day long. For our first workshop, we planned on showing a nutrition film followed with discussion. We were to next talk about the three food groups, breast feeding, and first foods for babies. We were also to discuss growth charts, diarrhea, malaria, and malnutrition prevention for school children.

At the end of the first day, we were to talk about small garden care and maintenance. Our workshop ended with us giving the participants garden seeds. I tried to convince Paula that Solomon Islanders would flock to the programs to hear our interesting presentations. Paula insisted that they would be motivated to attend because of videos and free seeds.

Kilu'ufi Hospital had a nicely boxed television and a generator suitable for traveling. We were to use the equipment to show the video. Our first workshop was scheduled for Fouia Village. Fouia was located at the end of the road on the north end of Malaita. We talked to Eric Mason and arranged for his driver to take us to the village. We got an early start and arrived at Fouia shortly after noon.

We unpacked our things into the provincial medical office where we were to spend the night. Village leaders soon approached us, and we discussed our plans. We told them that we would have a video and do a health and nutrition survey during our presentation. We told them about what we would do for our second and third visits. The men listened attentively until we finished. "You pay SI$50 for meeting house," the leader informed me.

SI$50 was only about US$17 and the U.N.I.C.E.F. grant was for US$3,800. We had the money and I was not surprised that they wanted us to pay. "Setting fees" was a concept ingrained into Solomon culture. Rewards, or bribes if you prefer, had been customarily given to entice Solomon people who might have otherwise been unwilling to participate in any given lecture.

It was ingrained in my value system they should be happy to have us there. We were there to present a program to benefit them. "I talked to your village chief about our program," I answered. "Fouia's chief invited us. There was no discussion about us having to pay for a place to have our program. Where's the chief?"

"Not here," the leader continued. "Program not part village. Pay SI$50 use community building."

I wanted them to be reasonable. Being reasonable meant doing things my way. "We're here to help you," I argued. "The United Nations gave us money to bring a program to improve women's and children's health in your village. We have movies, lectures, and seeds for you. The chief asked us to come and do the program. We'll have a feast the third time we come. We shouldn't have to pay. Where is the chief?"

"Not here. Program not part village. Pay SI$50, use building."

I paused and had a brief conversation with Paula. She supported my stubbornness. I returned to the village leaders. "We won't pay to use your community building to put on the program," I told them. "We don't need your community building."

"Where do program?"

"We'll do it here in the medical building. The medical building in owned by Malaita Province, not Fouia Village. We're part of Malaita's medical system. We'll have our program here and we won't pay you for using the building."

"Not big. Medical building not big for people."

"That's not my problem. We'll have the program here. It's up to you to tell the people that there just won't be enough room for them to see the video."

The leaders left, and Paula and I sat down and rested. The leaders returned in about two hours. "Use community building," the leader said.

"Can we use the community building without paying you anything?"

"No pay."

We completed our program without further drama. Because of our late start, we were late when we finished. Villagers fed us without any request for payment. Irene and Paulene made a nice presentation on planting and caring for gardens. We settled down in the medical building for the night. We woke to the crowing of roosters and ate a leisurely breakfast. We packed our things and returned to Auki.

Charlie rests while villagers gather for a nutrition program

We organized more nutrition workshops and always felt we were successful. We contacted John and Lottie in Small Malaita about doing a nutrition workshop in their area. They thought it was a great idea and said we could stay with them.

Small Malaita was also known as South Malaita Island. Eighty percent of the islanders spoke 'Are'are. 'Are'are was spoken by about 18,000 people, making it the second-largest language group in the Solomons, second only to Kwara'ae.

Malaita Province owned a small boat that could be used for this trip. I negotiated a price for a round trip for Paula, Irene, Pauline, and me. We rented the boat for five days, Monday through Friday. We were going to be crowded, but the boat could go six knots per hour. I expected to make the trip in seven hours.

We arrived at the wharf with snacks and water for our trip. Our captain had brought another man. He also had a large canoe with an outboard motor in tow. "Why is this man here?" I protested. "We're going to be crowded with just our group."

"Teach him pilot boat," the captain said.

"This isn't meant to be a training exercise. We paid Malaita Province money to lease this boat for a week. We'd be crowded with just you and the four of us."

"I don't say how many you bring."

"The issue isn't how many I'm bringing. I leased the boat and paid money to use it. That gives me the right to bring the people I need. We'll be crowded, but there's room for the people I'm bringing. The issue is you want to make our trip even more crowded and uncomfortable. And why do you have that canoe? It's nearly as big as our boat. The canoe will slow us down."

"Need canoe, boat breaks down. Use canoe, get to shore."

"We don't need the canoe if we break down. We'll never be more than eighty or ninety yards from the mainland."

Our captain looked at me with seeming pity. I reluctantly agreed to the unexpected arrangement and we left. We traveled south and were never more than sixty or seventy yards from the mainland. When we passed Radefasu village, we saw several people cutting mangroves. Langa Langa people used mangroves for food, firewood, and building materials. The mangroves also protected the shorelines from erosion.

Our captain struggled unsuccessfully to teach his trainee to properly operate the boat. Our trip was slowed considerably by the canoe and took eleven hours rather than the expected seven hours. John and Lottie met us at the wharf. Irene, Paulene, Paula, and

Paula with baby crocodile

I moved our things into their modest home.

We left our pilot and his trainee to arrange their own accommodations. There was no electricity on Small Malaita, so we used the Kilu'ufi generator to treat John and Lottie to electric lights. Later in the evening, we sat on their porch enjoying the beautiful sunset. We watched our pilot and his trainee use the canoe to go fishing in the bay.

Our first day's nutrition workshop went as planned. Irene and Pauline performed their jobs admirably. Afterwards, we visited a crocodile farm.

The villagers had gathered crocodile eggs and allowed them to hatch. They had several small crocodiles that we were permitted to handle. There were several much larger crocodiles in a twelve-foot deep hole. The crocodiles were being grown to sufficient size to be killed for their flesh and hides.

Our two-day nutrition workshop was successful, and we prepared to return to Auki. John and Lottie thanked Irene and Pauline for their participation. We had met an Englishman, Peter Moss, who was vacationing in the Solomons. Peter was working in Hong Kong and had published a novel. We agreed to give Peter a ride on our boat when we returned to Auki.

I piloted the boat for an hour on our trip back to Auki. I couldn't understand why the pilot's trainee couldn't manage the feat. Paula piloted the boat for several hours without difficulty. The pilot told Paula that her operating skills were better than mine. We arrived in Auki late Thursday. "I have the boat rented for a week," I

Charlie, Lottie, John, and Peter

said. "I want to use it tomorrow for you to take several of my friends to Alite Reef. I'm going to invite several people, so you're not to bring anyone."

Our pilot looked at me as if I was being unreasonable. Paula and I invited Dr. Tereasa, Katie, Peter, Elizabeth, Masako, and Peter Moss. When Dr. Arun and Elaine arranged the previous trip to Alite Reef, we arrived at about 11:00 a.m. I scheduled our departure time, so we would arrive at Alite Reef at about the same time.

We chugged toward Alite Reef at six knots per hour. We were making better time because we weren't towing a canoe. The women and children sat in the open hold while

Peter Moss and I sat cross legged on the deck. Paula held baby Elizabeth while Dr. Teresa managed Katie and Peter.

There was a long, heavy fish line with a large hook wrapped around a piece of wood. I thought I should go fishing since I was in the Solomons. "Can I use this fish line to go fishing?" I asked.

The pilot raised his brow and nodded to indicate approval. There was no bait, but I didn't expect to catch anything. However, I was not deterred. My goal was to go fishing, not to catch fish. I strung out the line to a length of about forty yards. The line rippled through the water with the line and hook about two feet under water. I was content with my efforts. I thought to ask Paula to take my picture, but she was busy taking care of Elizabeth.

I was very surprised when the line jerked taunt. I didn't think it was possible that a fish had taken the baitless hook, but I knew something was on the line. I began quickly pulling in the line. I let it fall to the boat deck in a sloppy fashion. I was doubly surprised when I pulled in a large fish. It was about twenty inches long and weighed eight or nine pounds.

I grabbed the flopping fish by the tail while searching for a way to subdue it. I quickly located a piece of galvanized pipe about one inch by twenty-four inches. I smacked the fish on the head and released it. It continued to flop causing me to be concerned that it would flop itself back into the ocean. I kicked the fish into the cargo hold where Dr. Teresa, Paula, and the children sat.

The fish flopped powerfully and sunk its spiny, dorsal fin into Paula's foot. Paula flinched, but only tightly clutched Elizabeth to her breast. The fish quit flopping before I finished with my profuse apologizes. I tried to get people to think of other things by casting the line back into the water. The line rippled through the water again with the line and hook about two feet under water.

I was not surprised when the line jerked taunt. I believed that another fish had taken the baitless hook. I began pulling in the line and pulled in another large fish. This fish was about eighteen inches long and weighed six or seven pounds. I grabbed the flopping fish by the tail and smacked it on the head with the galvanized pipe. I held it by the tail until it quit flopping. I stored the two fish in the cargo hold away from the passengers.

I continued fishing, but I didn't catch any more fish. When we arrived at 11:00 a.m., there were several people in water up to their knees and waists. "Where are we?" I asked.

"Alite Reef," our pilot answered.

I was puzzled. "Alite Reef? There's no reef. People are up to their knees in water."

"It's the tides," Peter said. "When the tide recedes, the reef will be above water."

"I was here once before at this same time. The reef was exposed."

"The tide changes every day. The reef will be exposed sometime today."

I thought to make excuses asserting that I didn't know about tides changing times because I'd lived in landlocked Kansas most of my life. I expected that someone might have cause to think that I should know because I had lived in the Solomons for several months.

We began our return trip to Auki. The wind blew Peter van den Bosch's hat into the water. I attempted to salvage what little reputation I might have had. I convinced the pilot to turn around and guide the boat near Peter's hat. I reached down into the water and retrieved it.

As we approached the wharf, our pilot asked me if he could have the fish. I laughed at him and told him when I had a fish for everyone on the boat, he could have the next one. When the boat reached the wharf, we debarked. "Do you know how to butcher fish?" Masako asked.

"I know I won't be very good at it, but I'll manage," I said. "I butchered bullheads that I caught when I was a kid."

"You can bring them by my house. Yasuo will butcher them when he gets off work."

We stopped by Margaret's Chinese Store on our way to Isozaki's home. I bought a bottle of wine and continued on to Isozaki's house. Yasuo soon arrived and began butchering the fish. We enjoyed our fresh fish, wine, and time spent with our good friends.

Elaine and Dr. Arun came over for supper later that week. "I'm applying for a job in New Zealand, Charlie," Dr. Arun told me, over a forkful of quiche. "I'll be finished with my resume' soon. I'd like for you to edit it for me."

"I'd be happy to," I said. "When do you want me to do it?"

"I'll finish it soon and drop it by some day after work."

We continued performing our established routines of village visits, needs assessments, and creating action plans. Paula taught literacy to Solomon women three times each week. We exchanged letters with a Dr. Fielding in the U.S. about obtaining pack animals for the Solomons. We submitted a partial application for the reforestation portion of the Buma project.

Bill Wise came to Malaita for his job and stayed with us. Father Jon joined us for supper then we played canasta afterwards. Bill and I were partners and we were getting the better of our opponents. Father Jon offered me tongue-in-cheek card playing advice. His advice was clearly based on an assertion that he knew to be false. I acted shocked. "Father Jon," I said, looking at him sternly. "Will you go to hell for telling lies like you would go to hell for those other sins?"

"If I tell you a lie and you know it's a lie, it's not a sin," he answered, with a wide smile.

Bill and I won both games. Father Jon said good-bye and left for his own home. "You really have a great bunch of expatriates to work with in Auki," Bill observed. "Everyone was so nice when Rick, Carrie, and I were here for Christmas."

"Everyone is much more than nice," Paula agreed. "Did you notice that car out front?" It's Dr. Graham's and Sheila's. They let us use their cars a lot."

"Are you concerned about Peace Corps rules prohibiting us from driving?" Bill asked.

"Not really," I answered. "What they don't know won't hurt us. I've heard that you also have to drive for your job."

"Yes, I do drive," Bill answered, with a grin. "What they don't know, won't hurt me. Do you play canasta with Father Jon very often?"

"We do play a lot. Probably two or three times a month. We have a dinner party then play canasta. What do you think of his idea that if he tells me a lie, but I know it's a lie, it's not a sin?"

Bill thought a moment. "I have to agree with him," Bill said. "Lies are met to deceive. Since he knew that you knew it wasn't true, he wasn't trying to deceive you. Therefore, it wasn't even a lie."

Bill was quite the intellect. I would have probably thought of that myself if I had more time. We stayed up till 1:00 a.m. visiting about life in the Solomon Islands generally and our jobs specifically.

Sheila had gone to Honiara and we still had her car. Bill completed his assignment the next day, so I used Sheila's car and took him to the airport. Elaine brought over her sewing machine for Paula to use. We went swimming with Dr. Paul and Dr. Theresa to complete our day's work.

Dr. Arun brought his resume' by for me to critique. He waited while I read it. "It's very well written, Arun," I opined. "Of course, you used British spelling, but that's to be forgiven."

"You should learn to spell so properly," Dr. Arun said. "It might make some people mistakenly believe that you're intelligent."

"I can offer a real criticism," I continued, pretending I didn't notice he was winning our insult contest. "You use grammatically correct sentences throughout your resume'. I was taught that you shouldn't do that. For example, you write 'I worked at Kilu'ufi Hospital in Auki in general practice.' I think you should drop subjects and make brief descriptions. For example, write: 'General medical practice at Kilu'ufi Hospital'."

"That seems like a good idea. I'll try it to see how it reads."

"Can I write on this?"

"Yes, go ahead. This is just a draft."

Dr. Arun and I edited his draft together. "Are you doing anything about your idea to encourage Kansas hospitals to recruit British doctors to work in Kansas?" he asked, as we worked.

"I've started drafting letters," I said. "I'm going to work on some more tomorrow."

I worked on doctor recruitment letters the next day while Paula baked pumpkin pies. That evening, Father Jon, Paula, and I used Sheila's car to go to Dala for dinner and canasta with Father Chris. Father Jon and Father Chris were partners and they won the first game quite easily.

Paula and I were doing well the second game and I expected we would win. The last hand made a dramatic change in the outcome. Father Chris and Father Jon snatched victory from the jaws of defeat. "How did you manage that comeback?" Paula asked.

"Divine intervention," Father Chris answered, with a laugh.

"It must have been," Paula agreed. "I was sure we were going to win."

We left Dala early because we were scheduled to go to Kwai and Ngongosila the next day. Three Solomon men were walking toward Auki. One of them attempted to force us to stop by stepping close to where we would pass. I was able to drive around him without slowing.

We were up and getting dressed when the nuisance rooster started crowing. Our screeching parrots added to the din. We got to the office early because we wanted to be ready for our trip to Kwai and Ngongosila. Paul came to our office with a smile. "Don't have transportation today," he said. "I get message to Representative Muala. Make new time."

"Thanks Paul," I said. "We have plenty to do here today. I'm sure we'll get to Kwai and Ngongosila someday."

"You work hard. Good for Malaita people."

I didn't think we worked so hard. We did stay busy and we had accomplishments. That must have passed for arduous work in the Solomons. Since we couldn't go to Kwai and Ngongosila, we made other plans.

Paula made a picnic lunch and we used Shelia's car to go to N.A.T.I.T. Training Institute for a tour. We stopped at Kilu'ufi Hospital on the way to talk to Dr. Graham about the nutrition program. We also wanted to let him know what we were doing with Sheila's car.

Jim and Claire had gone to Honiara for their jobs. They called and told us they were returning, so we picked them up at the airport. We took them home and had popcorn with gin and tonics after our meal. "You seem to have Dr. Graham's cars a lot," Claire observed. "How do you rate?"

"Dr. Graham and Sheila are just great people," Paula answered. "They do so much for Solomon people. Maybe they let us use their vehicles, so we can accomplish more things for Solomon Islanders."

Irene brought us a huge watermelon that week and I bought a live chicken at the market. I butchered my bird late in the afternoon. Camerons were returning from Honiara and I had agreed to use their car and pick them up at the airport. Paula made granola to go with the watermelon and chicken while I was collecting Colin and Alison. We traveled to our house where we enjoyed Paula's delicious meal.

Charlie was given tapa cloth and beetle nut

Paula was quite free to schedule her own activities. She sometimes went to an expatriates' house to cut someone's hair or have tea. We also had a regular schedule for teaching English to J.O.C.V. nurses.

We soon went back to our routine of making needs assessments for villages and schools. When we arrived, I was often offered beetle nut. I always explained that Peace Corps' prohibition against me chewing the nut.

The village chief or areas council representative would next give us a tour of the village. The villagers would eventually assemble, and the village leader would introduce us. Many made claims that I had fought Nazis in Germany during W.W. II. They usually said I was there to get them money.

It didn't seem likely that any would believe I was old enough to have been a soldier in W.W. II. There were many Malitians who had worked for the U.S. military during the war. The listeners should have easily recognized that these men were twenty years older than me. Most of the Malitians served as laborers, but a few of them had taken on combat roles and were decorated.

Solomon men were very stoic. They seldom laughed or even smiled. When we were in Rufoki Village for a need's assessment, I again experienced their sense of humor. After being introduced, one listener had an observation. "Grandfather like you come our village," he said. "Grandfather kill you, eat you!"

He laughed uproariously at his own joke. The other Rufoki men enthusiastically joined the laughing. I laughed with them, but with much less enthusiasm. We didn't spend the night in Rufoki.

We were getting more requests for nutrition program workshops. We soon began to feel overwhelmed. Two J.O.C.V. nurses recognized our plight. "Would you like us to help?" Jashimie asked. "We could take off from our work at Kilu'ufi and go with you on your tours."

"We would love to have your help," Paula said. "We'll contact you when we have our next one scheduled."

We received a call from Acting Director Jimmie Wilkerson. Paula answered the ringing phone. "I'm coming to Malaita in two days," Jimmie told her. "We have two new volunteers coming in to be assigned to Atori sub-station. I need to see what accommodations are available for them in Atoria. I also want to see you and Charlie while I'm there."

"Great," Paula answered. "Do you want to stay with us?"

"That's very nice of you to offer. I'll take you up on it. I'll stop in and see Paul Kennioriana first. Provincial Assemblyman John Sala is going with me to Atoria. Paul is going to make arrangements for transportation."

Paul came to our office the next day and repeated that Jimmie was coming to Auki and would go on to Atori. He told us that he would arrange provincial transportation for Jimmie and John Sala for the trip. "You scheduled go Kwai and Ngongosila," he said. "Always transportation conflicts. You ride with Jimmie and John?"

"I want to go to Kwai and Ngongosila," I said. "We can be ready at a moment's notice."

"Can you get a message to Representative Silas Muala that we will be in Atori?" Paula asked. "We will need for him to have a canoe ready to take is to Kwai."

"I send message."

"Then we should go. I'm sure Jimmie won't mind."

That was just like Paula. Always trying to be practical. It was possible that Paul thought I would really get myself into trouble if it wasn't for her. I would have probably thought about getting a message to Representative Muala if they would have given me more time.

Jimmie arrived in two days and met with Paul in his office. She eventually made it to our office, and we walked home at quitting time. The electricity was working, so we had ice to make iced tea with our meal. We told Jimmie that we would be riding with her to Atori. We played cards until we were tired then went to bed. I dreamt of our upcoming trip to Kwai and Ngongosila.

# CHAPTER 13

# *Kwai and Ngongosila Islands*

We had fruit, bread, and coffee for breakfast then Jimmie, Paula, and I began our leisurely walk to our office. I was enthusiastically looking forward to our trip to Kwai and Ngongosila. We had been scheduled to go Kwai and Ngongosila Islands on previous occasions, but our trips had always been postponed. This time we were going to get to go. I was going to get to see the graves where Mr. Bell and his group were buried.

We didn't need our umbrellas, but we carried them knowing that they would be needed before we returned to Auki. Provincial Assemblyman John Sala soon arrived. Jimmie and Paula chatted about our upcoming trip until our driver arrived. A light rain arrived simultaneously with our driver.

Solomon house building

John Sala took the front seat with the driver. Jimmie, Paula, and I crowded into the back seat with our backpacks and umbrellas. The five of us were more than cozy in our four passenger Japanese model. Solomon men don't like to talk, so only Jimmie and Paula exchanged thoughts. The fresh smell created by the rain moderated the powerful odor of decaying vegetation drifting from the near-by forest. The melodious pitter-patter of raindrops on the car's roof created a natural music to entertain us.

Malaita only had two roads. The longer road circled about three-fourths of the island. It avoided some construction difficulties by running parallel to the South Pacific Ocean. The other road intersected the main road near Dala. It crossed volcanic mountains and a deep gorge to get to the other side. It terminated in Atori at the provincial sub-station. The sub-station sat next to a lagoon where a canoe would take us to villages on Kwai and Ngongosila Islands.

Solomon Islanders ostensibly drove on the left side of their roads. In reality, there was very little traffic and drivers steered their vehicles anywhere on the roads in vain attempts to avoid pot holes. Our driver deftly steered our well-used import toward our destination. He did manage to miss a few of the pot holes. Our trip took us past Buma Village where we often visited, allegedly to work on the portable saw-mill/reforestation project. We really went to Buma more because we enjoyed being with the village people.

By the time we reached the Atori lagoon, the rain had stopped. We said our good-byes to John Sala and Jimmie. The pair walked toward the small house where the new volunteers were to live. This was the first time we had been in Atori, so we made a brief tour of the area. There were not very many houses and no children came to greet us. The houses were typical of Solomon Islands' construction. We moved to the beach where a native in an outboard powered canoe soon arrived.

We loaded our backpacks and umbrellas into the canoe and departed for Kwai Island. Kwai Island was only about seven to ten feet above sea level. It lacked any protection from the often-powerful tides resulting in noticeable coastal erosion. When we arrived, Area Representative Silas Muala and a native displaying a large conch shell greeted us.

The native blew through a hole that had been reamed into the top of the shell. His effort resulted in a loud, melodious blast that reminded me of deep, horn blasts from expensive American cars. The booming blast could be heard on both islands. Everyone was on notice that we had arrived.

Representative Muala cordially asked us to tour his village and we proceeded. Doves, parrots, and macaws left the numerous coconut palms on the mainland to observe our progress. Their colorful plumage and shrill calls seemed fit for an adventure movie shot.

Most of Kwai Island's closely packed huts were built on the ground. Unfinished poles had been buried upright in the ground to make frames. Cross-pieces had been lashed to the uprights with *logia* cane. The cane looked and felt remarkably like bailing twine. The builders next fastened *sago* palm leaves to the cross pieces with more *logia* cane to complete the structure. The construction method gave the walls and roof a shingled appearance and function.

I knew the dirt floors would be damp. This was usually the situation in houses built on the ground due to frequent rains, high humidity, and lack of proper ventilation. We knew that we must always refer to the one-room structures as houses. Solomon Islanders would likely be insulted it they heard their homes were being identified as huts.

One of the houses was built on stilts and stood about three feet off the ground. Several 10' X 3' sheets of corrugated iron were stored under the house. "What's the sheet metal going to be used for?" I asked Muala.

"It's stored," Muala answered. "Australia gave after Cyclone Namu. Cyclone Namu wrecked Kwai and Ngongosila."

Tropical Cyclone Namu was often cited as the reason for lack of greater development in Malaita. "I see that it's stored, but Cyclone Namu was five years ago," I persisted. "Is the man going to use the sheet metal to build a better house?"

Muala only shrugged and continued walking. Cyclone Namu was considered to be the worst tropical cyclone to have ever battered the Solomon Islands. It hit the Solomons on May 15, 1986. The storm lasted for days and reached speeds of up to eighty miles per hour. The storm moved slowly resulting in phenomenal flooding. Entire villages were destroyed on Malaita and Guadalcanal.

People on Kwai Island led traditional, substance lives. They grew root crops and vegetables on the mainland and caught fish in the lagoon and open ocean. A bare-breasted woman staggered past us burdened by the weight of a large basket of yams. The woman had dug the yams in her mainland garden then transported them in a small canoe to Kwai. She eyed us curiously but didn't speak.

A few blond-headed, naked children tagged along. They seemed fascinated by the only white people that many of them had ever seen. The children would begin wearing clothing around the age of five or six.

Their first clothes would only be cotton shorts. When they neared puberty, their blond hair would begin turning color until it was as dark as their bodies. Paula talked to several school girls about their school work.

A few chickens and pigs searched carefully among the houses looking for something to eat. Their diligent efforts were

Solomon school girls

usually unsuccessful. We came into a clearing that featured the village church. It was a large, frame building with a recognizable steeple. It was by far the most superior structure on the island. A prominent, brass plate identified the church's funding coming from the First United Methodist Church in Brisbane, Australia.

Representative Muala took us into the church. He guided us through a large area where church services and community events were held. He next showed us to a small room that was to be our sleeping area. "Sleep here tonight," Muala informed us.

"Can we leave our back-packs?" Paula asked.

"All right," our host answered.

When we left the church, I asked to see the graves holding the remains of Mr. Bell and his group. Remains might have been an apt description because some reports of the incident state that considerable quantities of the murdered tax collector and his entourage had been eaten. Muala agreed and we headed toward the adjacent island of Ngongosila. Fortunately, it was low tide, so we waded with the water coming up only to our knees.

Ngongosila was a small island and we soon arrived at our destination. The island, like Kwai, was only about seven to ten feet above sea level. Coral rock walls had been built around the western and southern sides. I didn't see any coastal erosion in those areas. The island had small houses built on the ground like those on Kwai. Ngongosila seemed even more populated than Kwai.

Two women observed our coming. They pulled their ankle length skirts to their chins to cover their previously bare breasts. We wound our way among the closely packed houses. "Mr. Bell and Lillis buried there," Muala said, pointing to a small, clean space. "Policemen buried there," he said, pointing to an adjacent area.

The graves were crudely marked and were crowded on all sides by the houses. Men rested in the shade of the houses smoking Malaita-grown tobacco and chewing betel nut. The betel nut/lime mixture turned blood red and slobbered out of their mouths onto their beards. A young, bare-breasted woman used bamboo tongs to turn yams being baked over an open fire.

We continued our tour and traveled to the edge of the island. Muala stopped to show us an old man working on a dug-out canoe. We could see burned areas where hot coals had been used to weaken the wood. He was using a traditional Solomon tool to gouge out the charred wood. Two women sat in the shade of a house. The younger one was picking lice from the head of the older one. "White people don't get lice," Muala informed us.

"White people do get lice," Paula said, in disagreement. "Lice don't recognize skin color."

Muala changed the subject by telling us how poor the islands were. He made assertions that Kwai and Ngongosila were always ignored by aid donors. To the contrary, I had noticed numerous projects bearing signs stating they had been funded via donations from various aid donors. It was obvious that Ngongosila and Kwai had received substantial grant aid for many years.

Fearing the rising tides would make our crossing back to Kwai difficult, we soon started an uneventful return to Kwai. As dusk approached, we slowly meandered to our meeting place in the middle of the village. Malitian sunsets are magnificent. Vivid shades of browns, oranges, rusts, and reds compare favorably with the beautiful sunsets in Kansas. Sunsets often provided Paula and me with entertainment in lieu of movie theaters and television shows. The sunset flaunted its beauty only briefly, and it was soon dark.

Man making lumber with chainsaw

Representative Muala, Paula, and I were promptly seated at a small, rough table in an open area in front of the church. The lumber for the table had been made with a chainsaw from a downed tree on the mainland.

The table held a kerosene lamp that made us somewhat visible to the assembled villagers. The lamp wick needed trimmed resulting in considerable smoke being emitted. The smoke had created a black, sooty lip on the lamp globe.

Representative Muala was on my right and Paula was on my left. Muala rose and began addressing our audience. He introduced us as Peace Corps Volunteers from Auki who were there to get them money. He informed the listeners that I was a W.W. II veteran who had fought the Nazis in Germany.

He next elicited pity from his constituents by whining about how they, and only they, among all people in developing counties, had never received any grant aid. At that time, he assigned problems associated with poverty on his islands directly to me. "You never give anything!" he shouted. "Malaita gives Kwai and Ngongosila nothing! Don't get aid from anyone! Get back to Auki, get money! Get us money quick!"

Representative Muala momentarily halted haranguing me to catch his breath. I was stunned. I looked toward Paula to see her reaction. She was immobile, a pencil held motionless over her loose-leaf notebook. I considered our burning lamp's value as a weapon if a weapon became necessary.

I studied the table carefully, seeking meaning and understanding for my life generally, and what was happening to Paula and me particularly. The table provided no answers. I didn't think it would make a useful shield if we were attacked by the estimated 200 villagers who were attending the meeting. Muala caught his breath and continued berating me. He majestically raised his fist to the sky. "Never give anything!" he bellowed in Pisin. "Malaita Province does nothing for Kwai and Ngongosila!"

Muala was standing and speaking in the direction of the villagers who were seated in an open area to our immediate front. He turned his attention and wrath toward me. "Don't get aid!" he raged, shaking his fist at me.

I sat stoic, stunned by his outburst. I didn't have any logical recourse that might improve the awkward situation confronting us. "Paula, would you make a note of that?" I asked.

I hoped my feigned interest in his assertions would better our situation. I hoped this attempt at pretending Muala's behavior was reasonable might better the chance of us getting off Kwai Island with our heads still attached to our bodies.

As scribed before, Paula is a descendent of Cherokee Indians. Her heritage might have made it easier for her to give lip-service to accepting the male dominated cultural norms when in the presence of Malitian men. "Get to Auki, get money!" Muala shouted. "Get money fast!"

I immediately resolved to never apply for any grant aid money for Kwai or Ngongosila. I also resolved to get Paula and myself back to the safety of our modest home in Auki. "Write that down!" Area Rep Muala ordered Paula, as he jabbed his finger at her. "Write that down!"

Paula's lips began forming into a sneer, but she started making pencil marks in her notebook. I furtively peeked to determine what she had scribed. I didn't see any written words, but I imagined that she had made a drawing of Peace Corps Volunteers shooting arrows at a Malitian man.

I thought her imagined artwork for the Malitian was a good likeness of our tormentor. I especially liked the horns, hooves, and tail. She showed me what she had actually written. "AND YOU WANTED TO COME HERE?" she had printed in uppercase letters.

By that time, her lips were parted, panther like. The smoky lamp emitted enough light for me to clearly see her pearly, white teeth. Beautiful teeth that had been repaired and maintained with thousands of dollars of dental work. Her smoldering eyes exuded disgust that might have illogically been directed toward me.

Her rhetorical question about my desire to come to Kwai and its sister island of Ngongosila could only be answered affirmatively. I had yearned to visit Ngongosila for a long time. I wanted to come ever since I read about the history in the tourist book sent by Solomon Islands' Peace Corps officials.

The tourist book explained that Bell and Lillies had been buried on Ngongosila after being assassinated by Kwaio warriors. Understandably, at that precise moment, I was no longer interested in the burial sites for Bell, Lillies, and their native policemen. I was very interested in Paula and I avoiding having our own burial sites on Kwai Island.

I thought of our supervisor, Paul Kennioriana. If I could only get a message to Paul, he could get us out of the predicament. At the time Paul organized this outing, we had made some twenty previous trips to villages for needs assessments. Some of Paul's trips had gotten us into some dicey situations. In fairness to Paul, I had gotten myself into more predicaments than he had. In fairness to Paula, her steady guidance had often kept us out of trouble. But not this time.

The haranguing continued for what might have been five minutes. It seemed like five hours. Muala alternated shaking his fists at the dark sky, the watching villagers, and me. I wondered how I could give him a lightning rod to draw the punishment from the sky that I wanted him to receive. When he tired and sat down, I rose slowly.

I faced the audience and peered intently into the darkness trying to convince them that I could see them clearly. I waited a little to build expectations. "Thank you Representative Muala," I eventually began. "Thank all of you for sharing your time with Paula and me today. When we get back to Auki, we'll remember the kindness and hospitality that you have shown us. I'll do my very best to get you what you deserve."

Getting them what I thought they deserved was going to be difficult given restriction imposed by Solomon Islands' laws. I eloquently waxed and waned on our lives generally and our jobs in Malaita specifically. I explained our system for needs assessments and action plans. I spoke for some time without saying anything that could be construed as a commitment to apply for grants.

I knew that I wasn't going to apply for any grants on their behalf. If I learned that any grant money was coming to Kwai or Ngongosila, I would inform the donor and ask them to divert the program and money to another village. I questioned how successful I would be if I attempted to call in the Australian Navy to blow the islands off the face of the earth, but I thought I might try.

Importantly, I had the immediate challenge of getting us back to Auki. I was somewhat comforted by the knowledge that there wasn't enough room to bury us next to Bell, Lillies, and the policemen. Paula stood to join me. I thought that she likely had her own plans for getting the islanders what they deserved.

Representative Muala escorted us to our sleeping accommodations in the church. He soon returned with cold kumara and hot water. "I bring more," he said. "You pay SI$1 each."

One Solomon dollar was worth about thirty-five cents in U.S. money, but we were invited guests. Asking us to pay anything was totally contrary to Solomon customs. Asking for payment was most certainly contrary to arrangement that Paul Kennioriana would have made when he committed for us to travel to this island paradise.

I would have rather starved to death than submit to the humiliation that Muala was heaping on me. I was not hungry at that time, being full of anger, disgust, and adrenalin. My brain knew that I would soon be famished, but my mouth took charge. "We don't want anything to eat," I responded. "We're not hungry."

I stared at Muala with a fervent hope that looks could kill. I envisioned striking him stone-cold dead with my piercing glare. Try as I did, I didn't accomplish my goal. Representative Muala remained alive. He left us to fend for ourselves, again refusing to observe niceties required by his own culture. He should have offered to sleep in our room to ensure our safety through the night.

It was a not-so-ancient Malitian custom to kill visitors in their sleep. Thus, an invited guest was the responsibility of the village chief. While Muala was not the chief, he was obligated to sleep with us to ensure our safety. Muala likely understood that I was very aware of Malitian customs. He probably knew that it would be his own life that would be in danger if he slept in our room.

I thought to make a search of the church to see if the mice had overlooked any small morsels that might sustain Paula. I couldn't help but feel somewhat responsible for her not having anything to eat. Paula lit three mosquito coils to deter mosquitoes from sharing Solomon Islands' malaria with us.

We sat on our sleeping mats and discussed what had brought us here and how we might get back to Auki. If Paul only knew, he could come to our rescue. Colin Cameron had excellent relationships with the Malaita police. Maybe David Chetwynd was back in the Solomons. If any of the three knew, they could get the police to come and straighten the matter.

Unfortunately, we didn't have any way to contact our potential saviors. We fumed and sulked for about thirty minutes when a village woman entered. "Brought something," she said, smiling shyly.

She gave us several freshly baked yams and fish. "Thank you very much," Paula said with a larger smile.

"Thank you," I echoed. "Thank you."

I gave her SI$5 then snuck a peak above her head. I wanted to see if I could detect a halo. There was none, but she deserved one. When we were alone, we ate most of our simple meal in silence. Our angel's dinner of yams and fish was delicious. Despite our situation that should have kept me awake worrying, I went to bed and slept like the proverbial baby.

I woke with the crowing of rosters. I felt no compunction to leave the comfort of my sleeping mat and the sanctity of my church room. I rested peacefully until a small earthquake woke Paula. We dressed then ate a leisurely breakfast of left-over yams and fish. When we opened the door to leave the church, we found Muala sitting on the steps. He made us an offer we couldn't refuse. "Car here soon," he said. "Pay SI$20 for canoe ride to mainland."

My brain knew that I shouldn't refuse the offer. However, my pride asserted its dominance over my brain. A primal instinct caused me to reject all influences of common sense. I disdainfully pushed past him without speaking. I knew that the only sensible thing to do was pay the extortion demand. I could not do it.

Twenty Solomon dollars was only about US$6.60, but I refused to pay. I admit that I may have acted a little stubbornly. I knew that Muala might be correct when he said that our ride would soon be there. It was equally likely that our ride might not be there for two hours. Paula and I walked to the water's edge and sat down on a small log. We waited for divine intervention. The mainland was only about half a mile away, but it might as well have been a hundred miles. We were stuck.

Waiting for transportation

Intervention came in about twenty minutes in the form of an approaching village woman. She told us that a man would come soon and give us a ride in his canoe. As announced, the man soon appeared. We tossed our back-packs and umbrellas aboard and climbed in. His motorized canoe soon had us standing on the mainland. I thanked him and gave him SI$20.

Our driver arrived in less than an hour, quite punctual for Solomon time. "That was interesting," I said. "Now that I know we are going to live through it, I think we should do it again."

"You do it again!" Paula responded. "I never want to see or hear of Silas Muala again!"

Our trip back to Auki was uneventful. It did, however, give me ample time to consider my options in the likely event that Australian naval officers would refuse my request to bomb the islands.

I could devise no more sinister revenge than to try to halt grant aid until Muala had been better punished. It would be easy to refuse to apply for any grant for him, but I wanted to go further. I wanted to ensure that no granting agency would go near Ngongosila and Kwai until Silas Muala was no longer area council representative.

The next day, I gave Paul an oral report of how terribly Paula and I had been treated. Paul listened attentively, then smiled widely. His dark eyes flashed with tiny, grinning stars as he spoke. "Thought might happen," he said. "Same thing happened me year ago when I there."

I was flabbergasted. "Paul, why did you send us there," I asked. "If the same thing happened to you, what did you think would happen to us?"

"You want see Mr. Bell's grave," he said, smiling even wider. "Know you like villages. Muala asked for you. Knew you know what to do."

Paula convinced me that asking for Australian intervention was not a practical idea. In lieu of this, I wrote an action plan report on our trip as usual. I scribed that Kwai and Ngongosila were very prosperous. I truthfully reported on the successful grants that they had received. I also made up "facts" about some non-existent ones.

My praise was very lavish and made with a goal that anyone reading the report would never consider sending any aid money. I went to the extreme of writing that Representative Silas Muala recognized that the islands had already received more than their share. I claimed that he wanted grant aid to go to other Solomon Islands' villages.

I sent a copy of the written report to Peace Corps headquarters in Honiara, kept a copy for us, and gave a copy to our supervisor. I waited while Paul carefully read my fictional report. He looked at me and smiled widely. "You know what to do," he said. "You know what to do."

# CHAPTER 14

# *Community Development*

Paula continued teaching her literacy classes to Solomon women three times per week. She came home with news after one session. "Do you know that Yasuo and Masako have returned from Japan?" she asked.

"No," I answered. "I didn't know that. Let's go see them."

"Of course, we should. I really missed them."

We took a few cold cokes and walked to their house. Masako had brought back a key board and many gifts for us. She told Paula that she wanted to continue Paula's English lessons. They agreed on a time for the next lesson. "By the way, do you know that Dr. Graham's birthday is this weekend?" Paula asked Masako.

"I didn't know that," Masako answered. "We just got back today. You're the first ones we have seen."

"We're going to have a birthday party for him. Of course, you're invited."

"I don't think we can make it. We need to get settled in after our long trip."

Our birthday party for Dr. Graham was enjoyable. Everyone sang happy birthday and gave him small presents.

Dr. Graham and Sheila at the birthday party

"There are two United Service Organization (U.S.O.) Volunteers coming to Auki soon," Colin told me, as he took a piece of birthday cake. "I'm arranging a canoe trip for them to go to Buma. Would you like to go with us?"

"Of course," I answered. "It would give us a chance to talk to Simon about our grant application. Do you know why U.S.O. Volunteers are coming to Auki? I thought the U.S.O. mission was to provide entertainment to military personnel."

"I didn't hear why they're in the Solomon Islands. Maybe there's a U.S. naval ship docking in Honiara."

We did travel to Buma by canoe with Cameron's and the U.S.O. Volunteers, David and Morgan. They were very nice and told us that they were just vacationing. We snorkeled and had tea with Father Phillip. We lunched in the evening then went to Camerons for tea with David and Morgan.

We made another trip to see Jim and Salamai Misuka. We wanted to talk about the Saenaua Reformation Project and Saenaua Women's project. After we arrived, we went to see the tree nursery and garden. Jim invited us to spend the night and we accepted. "Jim, since we have a lot more time, Paula and I can walk to Cane then on to Naoasa," I said. "It's not too far and we can be back before it gets dark."

The sun was shining making our brief walk to Cane enjoyable. We talked to Cane's chief about his progress on completing the next step called for in the action plan. The sun was still shining when we started to Naoasa, but it soon started raining. We stopped in a school house to wait until it stopped.

When the rain eventually ended, we continued to Naoasa. The path was slippery and muddy, but we made progress by using walking sticks. Naoasa's chief offered me betel nut, lime, and leaf when we arrived. I declined, citing imaginary Peace Corps rules. Rules are rules.

When we returned to the Misuka house, we found that Irene had cooked a chicken with vegetables from their garden. We enjoyed the Solomon meal with our friends. Irene and Salamai picked up the dishes and left. Jim, Paula, and I sat in their house and visited about life in the United States.

Salamai soon reentered wearing the simple, Solomon dress held with elastic at the waist. She didn't have it pulled to cover her breast as Solomon women usually did in the presence of expatriates. "Oh, showing nakedness," she said, smiling shyly.

A young boy entered and announced that Jim's brother, Thomas, was coming. Thomas was recognized as an authority on Solomon Islands' flora. He was being paid by a New Zealand entity to identify Solomon trees and other plants by their Kwara'ae names. He soon arrived and joined our conversation. Everyone spoke Pisin, so Paula and I could participate.

Solomon Islanders frequently gave themselves new names that they found attractive. Jim and Thomas discussed their cousin, Benjamin Kiki's, new moniker. "Said name Catalog," Thomas said, with a laugh.

"Don't know meaning catalog." Jim said, joining in the laughing.

"Catalog Chairman Saenaua Association."

"Use catalog, buy chainsaw. Catalog's chainsaw for Saenaua Association."

Jim had built a new house on stilts where we were to spend the night by ourselves. It was quite modern by Solomon standards with a nearby outhouse. We grew tired and retired to the new Misuka house for the evening. "Jim and Thomas enjoyed making fun of Benjamin Kiki's new name," I said, when we were alone.

"Catalog is a funny name," Paula answered. "I wonder if they'll tell him the definition of catalog."

"I doubt it. They seemed to enjoy making fun of him too much to tell him he sounds silly calling himself Catalog."

"I was surprised that Salamai didn't have her breasts covered," Paula said, changing the subject.

"I was surprised too. I can only think that we have been accepted as members of their family."

We ate breakfast with the Misuka family after a good night's sleep. Paula went to the tree project nursery and garden with Salamai and Irene. The trio worked in the garden and gathered vegetables. Paula had a cooking and nutrition demonstration when they returned.

Jim took me a short distance to a shower area. Water for the shower came through a pipe driven into a small spring. The pipe ran into a stone wall enclosure that had been laid without mortar. Jim told me that an old man had built it some years before. Jim shared the Malitian men's opinions on the status of women. "Men higher than women," he said. "Women don't think good. Women's heads soft."

I raised my eyebrows to acknowledge his opinion. If he understood my nonverbal communication to mean that I agreed, it was his privilege. I had heard Malaita men make such comments before. I had never taken the opportunity to share them with Paula. On our way back to the house, I took the opportunity to ask Jim about the pagan Kwara'ae. "Jim, do you know where the pagan Kwara'ae live?" I asked.

"Live mountain shrine Siele," Jim answered. "Have magic staff. Worship *Debil*."

Jim's description of worshiping the devil would be better understood as worshiping a deceased, paramount ancestor. Christians

Jim, Salami, Irene, and Paula

discouraged the traditional religions and identified the practices as worshiping the devil. Solomon Islanders began using "*Debil*" in Pisin to identify their paramount ancestors. "I would like to go there some time," I said. "Would you take me?"

Jim thought a bit then answered. "I take you," he said. "Paramount Chief Osifera keep magic staff. Old things in custom house."

"Thanks, Jim. I'll contact you and make arrangements soon."

Salamai gave us lots of lots of vegetables for our trip home. We got a ride on the N.A.T.I. transport truck and arrived late in the morning. We found that we had received several letters and processed pictures from our trip to Australia. Gabriel brought us a chicken and some limes and Masako brought us carrots. We appreciated having such nice friends.

We called our son, Jason, the next day. He told us that he, Mary, and Ashley were fine. We received a packet of information in the mail about the pagan Kwara'ae from Ben Burt. Paul came to our office with information. "Made plan visit two villages," he said. "Go Nanoa Village May 7. Go Foawnasufu Village May 10."

The trip to Nanoa would be a repeat. The trip to Foawnasufu would be a first. We went to Menons to celebrated Sumita's birthday. "Can I come to your house tomorrow to talk about the nutrition program," Dr. Arun asked.

"Of course, you can come." Paula said. "We're ahead of schedule on implementing the nutrition grant that Dr. Graham received. We can talk more about it."

"We're scheduled to go to Nanoa tomorrow for a needs assessment," I said. "We should be back around quitting time."

We walked home after Sumita's party. We sat on our screened porch and watched neighborhood activities. Our house girl, Betty, was busy washing her own clothes across the street. Two dogs threw up puffs of dust as they trotted by our house. "Oh darn," Paula exclaimed. "Yasuo and Masako invited us for supper to celebrate our twenty-fourth wedding anniversary. Now, we told Dr. Arun that he could come over."

"Work before play," I answered. "We'll have to cancel our anniversary celebration with Isozakis."

"I'll call Masako before we go to work tomorrow."

Paula called Masako and canceled our anniversary party as soon as we woke and had breakfast. We walked to work and were soon informed that we wouldn't have transportation to Nanoa Village for our May 7 needs assessment. We walked home after work, ate supper and got ready for our meeting with Dr. Arun. He soon called and said he wasn't coming. Paula and I celebrated our anniversary by having popcorn and cokes on our screened porch.

As we walked to work the next morning, we saw a unique Malitian walking near our office building. He was an old man in full, custom regalia. Despite his age, he was very fit with neatly trimmed, white hair. He had a colorful loincloth tied to cover his genitals, a large nose bone, dangling earrings, and an elaborate clamshell neckless.

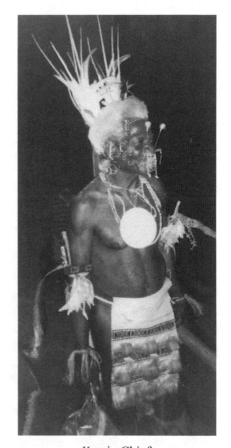

Paul Kennioriana came to our office later in the morning. He told us that our needs assessment to Foawnasufu was postponed because there wasn't any transportation. "That's not a problem, Paul," I said. "We have plenty to do here. Do you have a new date set?"

"No yet," he answered. "Let you know when."

"Paul, when Paula and I were coming to work we saw an old man. He had white hair with an elaborate adornment fastened to his head. He had yellow feathers stuck in arm bands and wrist bands. Do you know who he is?"

"He Kwaio chief. Here for land dispute."

"We could use this time to go see Misukas at the Saenaua Association. They will need to open a checking account at the bank, so we can deposit the grant check when it comes in."

We traveled to Saenaua Association area and found Jim and Salamai. A young woman from Holland was visiting Auki, so we took her with us. We took care of our business then separated into men's and women's groups. I took the opportunity to ask Jim about ancient customs. "I've read some books about old times when Solomon men collected heads," I said. "I'm not going to judge, but I would like to know if what I read in the books is true."

Kwaio Chief

"True," Jim said. "Old men know. Christians say no talk about it. Ask old men."

I had already asked old men, but no one would provide details. Some ventured that Christians told them that head-hunting and cannibalism were wrong, but they were practiced before they knew Jesus. Christians discouraged the younger generations glamorizing the practices. They were concerned with possibilities of them reverting to old ways.

While Jim didn't want to talk about old customs, he did share his opinion on the athletic differences among races. "White men better black men," he said.

I raised my eyebrows to acknowledge his opinion. If he understood my nonverbal communication to mean that I agreed, it was his choice. That was the first time anyone had offered that opinion. I questioned how he arrived at that conclusion knowing how muscular and fit all Solomon people were.

I thought the Solomon opinion might come from comparing gun toting W.W. II Marines against average Solomon men. I also thought he might be comparing Solomon people with white Peace Corps Volunteers who were noticeably fitter than average Americans. I observed cultural sensitivity by not disagreeing with him.

We returned to our office where we found Chief Isaac waiting for me. He had another necklace for me to look at. It was much more elaborate than the boar's teeth necklace that he had previously given me. He wouldn't set a price, but I gave him what I had in my wallet. He asked me why I wasn't wearing the boar's teeth necklace, so I promised to begin wearing it.

Paula had applied for a grant for her literacy class. She didn't know if her application would be successful, so the class organized a bring-and-buy fund-raiser. Paula participated by baking cakes for the raffle.

She spent the afternoon and evening baking cakes, but she couldn't get icing to stay on the cakes. She finally gave up and went to bed.

We woke early in the morning to a moderate rain. By the time we went to market, the rain had stopped. Paula's literacy class sold SI$60 in tickets for drawings

Clair Miller and Paula with Paula's cake at bring and buy

for her cakes. They took in a total of SI$223. Alison and Colin had us over for supper. The phone rang soon after we got home. "Sellens residence," Paula said, for her greeting.

She listened a bit then called me to hear the conversation. Her brother, Jim Coyne and his wife, Sherry, were on the phone. They had called to wish Paula a happy Mother's Day. Jim and Sherry told us they were thinking about coming to the Solomons in the fall. We encouraged them to come. We told Jim about the opportunities for fishing.

We had invited Paul Kennioriana and his family to dinner one evening. Betty didn't

Paul and family come to dinner

show up to clean the day before, so Paula stayed home to tend to the duties. She did the laundry, cleaned house, and made homemade chicken and noodles for supper.

Paul and his family enjoyed Paula's American style cooking. Paula and I did card tricks after supper and we all played dominoes. The children relished Paula's chicken and noodles. It was the first time for them to drink iced tea.

Paula stayed home the next day, so she could talk with Betty. When Paula got to work, she told me she had explained Betty's responsibility to come to work when she was supposed to. She said that Betty promised to do better.

We began a three-day week-end by babysitting for Dr. Arun and Elaine. We went to their house and they soon left to go to Kilu'ufi. I had developed sophisticated parenting skills by raising Chuck and Jason to adulthood. Given my advanced expertise, I appointed myself in charge of Neil. "I'll take Neil out to the porch," I told Paula. "I'll sit at the small table and read. Neil can run around all he wants without anything in sight that he can destroy."

"That's a clever idea," Paula answered. "I'll stay inside with Sumita and watch a movie."

My plan worked remarkably well for over two minutes. Neil searched the porch for something he could break while I smugly read my book. Suddenly, he sprang into action! With the quickness of a cheetah, he rushed the table. Neil demonstrated incredible strength for a thirty-five pound, four-year-old by grasping the table by the leg closest to me and tipping it over. He eyed me with a self-congratulatory look of accomplishment.

I demonstrated my advanced parenting skills by leaping into action. I grasped him by the shoulder and gave him a loving smack on his butt. His look of accomplishment changed to a look of awe. He made not a whimper, but he dropped to his butt and continued to stare at me. I set the table on all four legs and returned to my chair and reading. Neil spent the rest of our session staring at me with reverential respect, mixed with wonder. I thought it best to refrain from sharing my advanced parenting theories with Elaine when they returned.

Paula and I left and began preparing for our upcoming three-day, White Monday holiday weekend. Paula borrowed Cheryl's sewing machine for an anticipated project. I went to market while Paula baked a banana cake for an upcoming party at Doug and Cheryl Hicks. We played volleyball and had a barbeque party at the Hicks.

Dr. Arun and Elaine had an expatriate dinner party during the White Monday holiday. We seated ourselves in a large circle after our dinner. Neil prowled the large room looking for mischief. Suddenly, he charged across the room toward me. The room fell silent to enjoy entertainment by Neil.

Neil's lips curled into a snarl as he jammed his teeth onto my knee. I didn't flinch or move to stop him. He kept his eyes fixed on mine and I kept my eyes fixed on his. He paused. His thoughts were easily read. He was pondering what I would do if he bit me. He wondered if I would dare to smack him in the presence of his parents and the expatriate community. "Are you sure you want to do that?" I asked, menacingly.

Neil paused but just a moment, then began ardently kissing my knee. When he seemed satisfied that he had outsmarted me, he left to look for mischief elsewhere. Conversations resumed in the room. No one questioned what had occurred or why. There were no surprises when Neil was involved.

Dr. Arun sought me out and mischievously asked me if the U.S. would colonize Iraq and steal the oil. I told him we would if I were put in charge. My answer seemed to puzzle or satisfy Dr. Arun. Paula and I were among the last to leave. "Did you see what Neil did at the party?" I asked, as we walked toward our home.

"I saw him," she said. "I thought he was going to bite you. What would you have done if he had?"

"May you never know. I love that little kid. I really think he's a genius and doesn't know how to behave as a child. I hope we can stay in touch with Dr. Arun and Elaine, so I will always know what becomes of him."

A pan pipe band performed during our Sunday church service. Colin, Sheila, Dr. Graham, Dr. Paul, and Peter came to our house after church and ate waffles with us. We ate supper with Father Jon that evening and played canasta. "You know Father Philip and Father Chris Kamphuis from Dala, don't you?" he rhetorically asked, during our game.

"Of course, we know them," Paula answered, expecting a story. "What happened in Dala?"

"They got in an argument over something in the morning. They argued all day long. They agreed to an interlude in the evening so that Chris could give Phillip a haircut. Father Chris gave Father Phillip the worst haircut ever performed in the Solomons. Father Phillip is now wearing a hat at all times."

We discussed going to church in Dala, ostensibly to hear Father Phillip's sermon, but to actually see his haircut. Our three-day week-end passed quickly. We packed our backpack and went to work on Monday. We waited patiently for the provincial truck to take us to Foawnasufu for a needs assessment. The truck finally came just before noon to take us to the village. By the time we got there, the villagers had left. We went back to Auki, ate a late lunch, and went back to work.

That week, we went to do the needs assessment on the Saltwater Association. We visited five, seaside villages and a ship building project. The Langa Langa carpenters were building a large ship using designs and techniques taught by an Australian ship builder. When finished, the large ship would be suitable for commercial travel in the Solomons.

We were treated to a delicious meal and returned late in the afternoon. We didn't have water for two days, so Paula went to the Fiu River with Sheila. She took a bath, washed her hair, and brought water back for me. I heated water then took a sponge bath in the shower.

Yasuo and Masako had invited several expatriates to their house for supper. Sheila, Dr. Graham, Alison, Colin, the van den Bosch family, Paula, and I were among those present. Supper included dry sea weed that we ate after spooning rice into it. I liked the rice, but I didn't like the dry sea weed. Masako also had tempura that I loved.

We discussed the report that the water pump was fixed. We had been told that water was being pumped into the storage tank and that we were expected to have water the next day. "They told us not to drink the water for a few days," Yasuo said, over tempura. "They said to use it but not drink it. That would let the system clean itself."

When it was time to go, we put on our shoes and stepped out on the landing. As usual, the steps were very slick from the constant Auki rain. Dr. Teresa held Elizabeth in her arms as she started down the stairs. Without warning, both feet slipped from beneath her. Dr. Teresa landed on her butt without making any attempt to break her fall. She only clutched Elizabeth to her chest. "Are you hurt?" I asked.

"I'm not hurt," she answered. "I slipped so quickly that I didn't have time to react."

"I'm impressed with your bravery. You didn't give any thought to yourself, but only acted to protect Elizabeth."

It was Chloroquine Sunday, so we readied ourselves for a long day by taking naps after church. Desire and Bob Renner called to see how we were doing. Masako brought us sashimi and gave me a Japanese lesson. I walked to Margaret's Chinese Store for cokes. I thought of the silly, old Australian who didn't smoke, but bought and smoked cigarettes in Auki because he could buy singles. Silly old man.

We went to Nifimia via province truck for a needs assessments Monday morning. The driver confirmed that he would be there the next day at noon to give us a ride back to Auki. We performed needs assessments for Nafinua, Nafinua School, and two nearby villages. The Nifimia chief provided us with a delicious Solomon meal and a nice house where we could spend the night. The chief slept in our room to ensure our safety.

We got up late and had a leisurely breakfast, courtesy of the Nifimia chief. Our province truck was to be there at noon to collect us. We waited until midafternoon then hitched a ride back to Auki via the Watts Company truck. We arrived late in the afternoon and had the driver drop us at our house rather than at the office. Solomon time was observed. We were adapting to Solomon culture quite well.

I continued typing letters to Kansas hospitals asking them to develop programs to employ British doctors. Anguished crying began with the wailing of an adult woman. Another woman joined. The crying continued with more adults and children joining.

Yasuo and Masako came for brunch the next day. "Did you hear the crying last night?" Paula asked. "It kept us awake for an hour after we went to bed."

"It kept us awake too," Masako answered. "A four-year old child died of cerebral malaria. The child didn't want to take the medication and the parents didn't make him. It's so sad."

Masako, Yasuo, Paula, and Charlie
picnic at Bina Harbor

Isozakis took us to Bina Harbor for fishing that afternoon. Yasuo had expensive rods and reels for us to use. Many Solomon Islanders were fascinated by we foreigners and Yasuo's expensive fishing equipment.

The fish were less impressed and didn't attach themselves to our hooks. Several people rode back to Auki in the back of Yasuo's pickup.

Betty came to clean house and do our wash. She still wouldn't touch anything connected to electricity. She told Paula that she wanted her pay at the end of the day. She was outside washing our clothes when we received a telephone call. "Hello, this is the Sellens' residence," Paula said, when she answered the phone.

She listened then spoke again. "We would be happy to have guests. We'll meet them at the wharf."

"What was that about?" I asked when she hung up.

"That was Jimmie," Paula said. "The Peace Corps medical officer from Pakistan and her husband are visiting in the Solomon Islands. I told Jimmie they could stay with us. They'll be here tomorrow."

We borrowed a bed from Camerons and got the extra room ready. Masako came in the early afternoon for an English lesson. Masako and Paula combined their English lesson with a yogurt making lesson. We received a letter from Jim and Sherry Coyne. They wrote they were making plans to come to the Solomons in October or November.

Jimmie Wilkerson called the next day and told us that new P.C.V.s, Katherine West and Glen Nashimori, were coming to Malaita for their walkabout. She asked us to meet them at the wharf and help them find the Auki Lodge. Jimmie told us that Paul Kennioriana would arrange transportation for Glen and Katherine to get to Atori.

Pakistani Peace Corps Medical Officer Marge Huxtable arrived with her husband, Jack. We met them at the wharf and walked them to our house. It was a six-hour ship ride from Honiara, and they were tired. Marge and Jack were to be in Auki for three days, so we gave them our house key. They rested and showered while we fixed supper. Bill Wasser, Claire, Jim, Colin, and Alison joined us. "How long were you in Pakistan?" Bill asked, during supper.

"We were there over two years," Marge answered. "We went there in February 1989 and it's now June 1991."

"Pakistan is a Muslim country," Claire said. "How did you fit into their male dominated society?"

"I got along just fine," Marge said laughing. "They assigned me the status of honorary man and treated me as an equal."

"Maybe there's hope for the Solomons," Paula said.

Katherine West and Glen Nashimori, came the next day for their walkabout in Atori. The couple arrived at Solomon time and we met them at the wharf. We walked them and their luggage to Auki Lodge. "Did the Peace Corps make reservations for you?" I asked.

"Yes, Jimmie said everything was arranged," Glen answered. "She said we were to meet with Paul Kennioriana who would be our supervisor. Jimmie told us that Paul would have transportation to get us to Atori."

"I hope you have a room at Auki Lodge. When Paula and I came on our walkabout, management had given our room to someone else. We had to sleep in the dining room on the floor the first night. You could stay with us, but Pakistan's medical officer and her husband have our spare bedroom."

Glen and Katherine were able to check-in without drama. "We'll stop by on our way to work tomorrow," Paula said. "You can walk with us to our office. We'll introduce you to our supervisor, Paul."

"Thanks Paula," Glen said. "We'll see you tomorrow morning."

We woke to a light rain and got dressed for work. We stopped by Auki Lodge and found Glen and Katherine ready to go. We introduced them to Paul Kennioriana when we got to our office then went to our own office. Salamai came to the office and gave us several huge tomatoes grown from the seeds we had given them. She said the strawberries were ready, so Cheryl Hicks and Paula went to the garden and picked the delicacies in the afternoon.

Paula wasn't back at quitting time, so I started home alone. I stopped by the Auki Lodge to see if Glen and Katherine had made it back from Atori. They were sitting on the porch drinking iced tea. "What did you think of Atori?" I asked.

"We haven't made it to Atori yet," Glen answered. "Paul Kennioriana talked to us in his office, then told us that there's no provincial transportation. He said we could take a market truck, but that sounds a little primitive."

"I'll talk to Paul tomorrow. Would you like to come to supper tonight?"

"We would love to," Katherine answered. "It's a little slow at the Auki Lodge."

When Paula got home from picking strawberries, I told her that I had invited Glen and Katherine for supper. We had our usual simple meal topped with Paula's special strawberry shortcake. We taught them to play canasta after we did the dishes. Glen and I were real gentlemen and let Paula and Katherine win the two games we played.

We arrived at work the next day at our usual starting time. I soon went to see Paul Kennioriana. He smiled as I came in. "Hello Paul," I greeted him. "Do you have a minute to talk to me?"

Paul didn't answer verbally, but he smiled and raised his brow to indicate an affirmative answer. "I saw Glen Nashimori yesterday," I said. "He and his wife don't want to take a market truck to Atori."

"No transport," Paul said. "Asked them get market truck. They afraid market truck. You take them Atori?"

I thought for a minute then said we would take them the day after tomorrow. We went swimming with Alison, Colin, Neil, and Sumita after work. We took Neil and Sumita home after swimming and watched Menon's home video. Sheila had us over for supper and discussion of our nutrition program. The pharmacist from Honiara, his wife, and child were also there. I finished typing some letters to Kansas hospitals asking them to consider initiating a program to hire British doctors.

I stopped by Auki Lodge and found Glen. "I talked to Paul Kennioriana today," I said. "I told him that Paula and I would take you and Katherine to Atori by market truck. Paul said it would be all right."

"When do you want to go?" Glen asked.

"Paula and I have things to do tomorrow. We'll come to the Auki Lodge the day after tomorrow to help you get to Atori. We'll come early, so we'll be sure to get the first truck out of Auki."

Marge and Jack had toured Auki and nearby villages for two days. We took Marge to Kilu'ufi on the third day to meet with doctors and tour the hospital. Dr. Paul said he would get the Huxtables to the airport, so we went to work. They left in the early afternoon and took our house key with them.

We had a normal work day then Father Jon and Brother Taber came over for supper. We played canasta until after midnight. Brother Taber and I were partners. We won two and Paula and Father Jon won two.

Glen and Katherine were ready to go when Paula and I arrived at the Auki Lodge. We got Katherine situated in the seat of honor in the cab of the truck. Glen, Paula, I shared the truck bed with several Solomon Islanders who had spent the night in Auki. The driver picked-up and let-off passengers on the way. The trip to Atori took several hours. "I'm glad to get off and stretch my legs," I said, when we arrived. "Katherine was riding first class and we were in the economy section."

"That was rough," Glen agreed. "Jimmie told us that Paul Kennioriana would have provincial transportation for us."

"Paul does schedule provincial transportation," Paula said. "But we're in the Solomon Islands. There're always conflicts. You're going to find that market trucks are often a lot more dependable."

We took a brief tour of Atori sub-station. Glen and Katherine expressed misgivings about what they could accomplish. We assured them that they would learn techniques in training that would allow them to be busy and successful. We boarded the next truck back to Auki and arrived home late in the afternoon. We had Glen, Katherine, Alison, Colin, and the chief justice from Honiara over for supper.

Glen and Katherine left by ship the next morning for continued training. Paul was scheduled for a trip to Ontong Java. He was finishing a project when I entered his office. "Paul," I said. "I know you're busy, but I wanted to remind you that Paula and I have a trip to Koa Hill scheduled for June 18. Is there going to be transportation available?"

"Transport scheduled," Paul answered. "Leave 9:00 in morning."

"Thanks, Paul. We'll be ready. Have a safe trip to Ongtong Java."

I wanted to go to Ontong Java with Paul. David Chetwynd was stranded on the island for five weeks, but I had confidence that there would be extraordinary efforts to ensure that Paul wasn't stranded. My secondary goal for being in his office was to give him the opportunity to invite me to accompany him. He didn't extend the invitation I had hoped for.

Paula received a survival kit in the mail from her coworkers in Augusta. It had come by sea freight and had taken several months to arrive. It included gum and candy, but the goods had been chewed on by a critter. We had the afternoon off because the next day was June 14, Queen Elizabeth's birthday. I thought it was more important that June 14 was my birthday.

I didn't hear what the queen did, but Dr. Paul and Dr. Theresa had a birthday party for me. Katie and Peter made me a birthday card. Yasuo and Masako also gave me a birthday card. We had Sheila's car, so we picked up Colin, Claire, and Jim at the airport and went snorkeling at Buma in the afternoon.

We met two new volunteers from New Zealand. Maria and Andrew were a young married couple assigned to Malaita. Andrew was an engineer, but Maria didn't have a work assignment. We went to Kilu'ufi in the morning to watch films on sup sup gardens since we would begin teaching the concepts in our nutrition workshops.

Father Jon came over in the evening for a haircut. "Would you like to play a game of canasta?" Paula asked him, after her barber duties were completed.

"I would love to, but I have to get home," Father Jon replied. "I have a busy day tomorrow. By the way, are you drinking Auki water now?"

"Yes, we are," I answered. "Yasuo told us not to drink it for a few days, but we're drinking it now."

"Did you hear why we weren't supposed to drink it for a while?"

"No one said exactly, but everyone knew not to drink it for a few days."

"The reason why we were told not to drink the water was when the men were repairing the pump, they found a dead dog floating in the storage tank. They drained the tank and took the dog out. Makes me wonder how long we were drinking water that was floating the dead dog."

After Father Jon departed, Paula cut my hair and her own bangs. "I have a sore throat," she said. "I'm going to go to bed early."

"I'm going to go to bed too," I said. "We need our rest because we're going to Koa Hill in the morning to take pictures and finish our interview for a story on Betty Tafqi. I hope you feel well enough to go."

Paula drifted off to sleep. I relaxed by watching geckos dart up the walls and across the ceiling. There was a small one that was missing part of its tail. I watched closely to see if it would get the bug it was stalking. I don't know if it was successful because I fell asleep.

# CHAPTER 15

# *Mid-service Conference*

I woke before Paula and laid quietly. I watched her and listened to the soft rain until she woke. "How do you feel this morning?" I asked.

"I feel great," she said. "I know today is the day that we're going to Koa Hill to take pictures and finish the story on Betty Tafqi."

"Do you think we'll have transportation?"

"Paul said he had it arranged. We'll know when we get to the office."

Our transportation not only came, it was there on time. When we got to Koa Hill, we told the driver that we would spend the night. We made sure he understood that we wanted him to come back for us the next morning.

We finished our interview with Betty and continued chatting. "Was in bush for church work," Betty told us. "Saw many Kwaio women walking. White woman with Kwaio. Naked like Kwaio."

We were amazed by her story. "How long ago was that?" Paula asked.

"Three years back. Maybe five years back. Thought Kwaio stole white woman. She Peace Corps."

"She was a Peace Corps Volunteer?" I asked incredulously. "A naked Peace Corps woman was with Kwaio women?"

"She Peace Corps," Betty repeated. "Naked, same Kwaio."

Paula and I returned to Auki the next day then went to Buma to get papers signed. We went snorkeling while we were in Buma. Father Jon Volker and Colin Cameron came for supper and canasta. "Have you noticed that big pumpkin growing in my backyard?" Colin asked, during our first canasta game.

Paula with Betty Tafqi, Betty's daughter, and Betty's neighborhood children.

"I've been watching it grow," I answered. "It's really getting big."

"Alison doesn't want to use it. You can come get it if you want it."

We continued our game and I brought up the subject of naked Peace Corps Volunteers. "Father Jon," I said. "Paula and I spent the night with Betty Tafqi in Koa Hill Village. Betty told us that there was a Peace Corps woman living with the Kwaio some years ago. Do you know anything about that?"

"There was an American couple that lived with the Kwaio a few years back," Father Jon answered. "Do you know who Roger Keesing is?"

"Yes, we know about Roger Kessing. He's a famous anthropologist who lived with the Kwaio for several years."

"That's the man. When Kessing was ready to leave the Kwaio, he wanted his work to continue. He convinced the Solomon Islands' Peace Corps to get a married couple to come to the Solomons as Peace Corps Volunteers. Both applicants were to be working toward a Ph.D. in anthropology. A couple did come and live with the Kwaio for about three years."

"Did you ever meet them?"

"I never met them, but people talked about them. I don't remember their last names, but I think their first names were David and Kate. It would have been Kate that Betty saw with the Kwaio women."

When Father Jon and Colin left, we talked a bit about what it would have been like to live with the Kwaio. "That must have really been hard," Paula said. "I don't think I could do it."

"I don't know if we could do it," I added. "But I don't think I would like to try. I'd like to visit the Kwaio for a few days, but not for two or three years."

We drifted off to sleep and woke when a small earthquake shook our house and beds. We went to work and finished writing six action plans. I finished organizing my presentation for the nutrition workshop that we were planning for Buma. Paula spent the afternoon with Masako working on English lessons. I picked the pumpkin from Colin's garden and brought it home.

I started wearing the boar's teeth necklace that Chief Isaac gave me. Usually stoic Solomon men commented on the necklace. I was puzzled by their responses and took my question to George Toritelia. "Hello George," I said, when I entered his office. "Have you seen me wear this boar's teeth necklace?"

George smiled and raised his brow to signify an affirmative answer. "I wear it all the time," I said. "There have been four times that Solomon men have admired it. They thanked me for understanding and respecting their culture. What does this boar's teeth necklace represent?"

"Worn by ramo," George said.

"George, these men know I'm not a ramo. Why do they say I respect their culture?"

"Know Solomon man in ramo line gave you necklace. Man respects you, give necklace. Every Solomon man respects you."

I was humbled by the status that Chief Isaac had assigned me. I put the necklace away with a pledge to wear it only on special occasions. I began wearing the ornate necklace that Isaac had also given me.

Rain! Rain! Rain! I had pledged to never complain about having too much rain, but I was getting closer to breaking my promise. We had to postpone our trip to Buma for our nutrition workshop because of the rain. We had Sheila's car all week, but we were afraid to go to Buma because we would have had to cross a creek. We didn't want to let her car set idle, so we went to Saenaua in the afternoon and picked strawberries. I cleaned Sheila's car and filled it with gas to have it ready to return the next day.

I gave Paula a ride to work, returned Sheila's car, and walked back to the office. As I entered the building, I saw Paul Kennioriana walk into our office. He was talking to Paula when I entered. "Leave house unlocked tomorrow," he said. "Malaita health officials spray mosquitos."

"What do they spray with?" Paula asked. "How do they do it?"

"Spray walls. Mosquitos set on wall. Then die."

"Paula and I talked to Father Jon that evening. "Paul Kennioriana told us today that health officials would spray our houses tomorrow," I said. "What do you know about what they're doing?"

"They're using D.D.T.," Father Jon said. "D.D.T. is a carcinogen. It's been officially banned since 1983. Most expatriates don't let them into their houses."

"Do you let them spray in your house?"

"I used to, but I don't let them spray anymore. There's always something to worry about in the Solomons. Malaria is the least of mine."

The problems with spraying with D.D.T. were on our minds when we went to bed. "I don't like the idea of them spraying a banned pesticide in our house," Paula said. "On the other hand, I don't like the idea of malaria carrying mosquitoes sharing our rooms."

"I can foresee another problem," I said. "D.D.T. would probably kill my pet geckos."

We continued our discussions of the pros and cons of spraying with D.D.T. over our breakfast of fruit and yogurt. We eventually decided to let them spray. We didn't know of anyone who had contacted cancer from D.D.T., but we did know there were many who were sick or had even died of malaria.

Our participation with Dr. Graham's nutrition program evolved into positions as board members of Malaita Province Primary Health Care Committee. The committee met monthly to discuss all aspects of health care and nutrition. Our goals included developing strategies to meet the basic health care needs of the population.

Dr. Graham gave us a ride to Kilu'ufi hospital for the monthly primary health care meeting. We gave a report on the nutrition program. Dr. Graham attempted to use our successes as motivation for the Solomon committee members to improve their own performances. The Solomon men didn't seem motivated by what we had accomplished.

There was a party for Menons at Dr. Graham's and Sheila's house. Menons were going on a small vacation, thus deserving of a going away party. Paula spent the day baking and decorating a cake. She used the pumpkin from Cameron's garden to make two pumpkin pies. We committed to taking care of Menon's cats while they were going to be away.

I talked to Dr. Graham about the Solomon members at the primary health care meeting. "You saw Solomon Islands' culture in action today," he said. "The Solomon nurses have decent training and know what to do. But it's nearly impossible to motivate them to work the way I need them to work."

"Are they concerned you might fire them?" I asked.

"The threat of losing their jobs doesn't worry them. If I really tried to force them do something they didn't want to do, they would quit and go back to their villages."

The Small Project Assistance (S.P.A.) grant application instructions required us to submit pro forma invoices with the application. Getting the invoices required another trip to Honiara. We made last minute arrangements and flew to Honiara on an eleven-passenger plane. The pilot let Paula sit in the copilot's seat and fly the plane. Fortunately, he assumed control for landing. We got pro forma invoices from Morgan Supply for walkabout sawmills.

We had supper at a Chinese restaurant where we met two expatriates. We initiated a conversation with the men and learned that they were from New Zealand. "What are you doing in Honiara?" I asked.

"Our wives work for the New Zealand government here," the taller one answered. "We don't have any jobs ourselves."

"What do you do to fill your days?"

"We play a lot of golf and watch movies a lot."

Paula and I spent the night with Kim and Paul. I told Paul about our meeting with the New Zealand men. Paul said he didn't know them, but that New Zealand was a woman dominated society. It seemed natural to Paul and Kim that the men didn't work, but that their wives were employed.

We went to the Peace Corps office the next day to discuss our S.P.A. grant applications. I met Gus Comstock, the new director. Gus informed us that our application for a literacy program had been granted. He told us to make an appointment for face-to-face presentations when our applications for portable sawmills were completed. Gus told us to bring representatives from the Buma and Saenaua projects. We went shopping for things that we couldn't get it Auki. Paula wanted to make Mexican food, so she included avocados, flour tortillas, and salsa in her purchases.

We returned to Auki to get ready for our third nutrition workshop for Nafinua Village. We knew that Paul Kennioriana couldn't arrange transportation, but we planned it for the next day. We went to Auki Market and bought several lots of kumara. We also went to Margaret's Store and bought ten kilograms of rice for the program. Paula also bought a curry paste knowing that curry was popular in the Solomons. Irene went with us to buy the supplies.

Dr. Paul and Dr. Theresa had been assigned a better house. We spent the afternoon helping them move. Paula's brother, Jim, called in the evening. He still wanted to come to the Solomons. He told us that he might have to come by himself. Paula started growing three avocado plants from the pits she saved from her latest Mexican dinner.

We received a box in the mail from Washington, D.C. Peace Corps. It contained 100, small copies of the U.S. Constitution. We were asked to give individual copies to our Solomon friends. We began making presents of the copies. They were very popular and always created situations in which we were asked about the rights of being U.S. citizens. We kept the copies in a box in the spare bedroom.

We had rented Eric's truck for our trip to Nafinua. Irene had made it to Auki and helped us load our equipment and supplies. We stopped by Pauline's house, and Irene knocked on the door. She returned and told us that Pauline was sick and couldn't go. Paula was not accepting of Solomon culture and confronted Pauline. "You're not sick!" she insisted. "You're going with us! Now, get on the truck!"

Pauline reluctantly joined us in the back of the truck. It seemed that Paula's association with Kilu'ufi Hospital staff members had granted her healing powers. We stopped by Kilu'ufi and picked up Nurse James. Another Solomon nurse that was scheduled to go claimed he was sick and refused to come.

We traveled to Nafinua for the nutrition workshop. The villagers had ample vegetables to supplement our rice and kumara. Paula's cooking demonstration went well, and everyone enjoyed the feast.

Nurse James made a presentation that was well received. Paula and I agreed that if Dr. Graham could only get him motivated, James could manage the nutrition program very well.

Loading truck for nutrition workshop

140

I went to the Auki fish shop and found it was closed. I stopped by to talk to Yasuo on the way home. "Do you know why the fish shop is closed?" I asked.

"The J.O.C.V. that was managing the shop went back to Japan," Yasuo said. "It only took four days for the shop employees to break the place. When they sold some fish, they pocketed the money. When fishermen brought in fresh fish to sell, the staff didn't have any money to pay for them. They were soon out of fish to sell, so the shop had to close."

I came home thinking about the unique things we dealt with in the Solomons to find Paula very upset. "I got a call from Jim Miller," she said. "Clair was in an accident in New Zealand."

"What happened?" I asked.

"Clair was riding in a vehicle that had a head-on collision with another vehicle. She has two broken legs. Her car was on the wrong side of the road."

"That's terrible. Was Jim hurt?"

"He didn't say anything about being hurt. I'm not sure he was even in the car that was in the accident."

We later learned more details. Jim and Claire had gone to New Zealand for the holiday the last part of June. They met with two of their daughters and other friends from the U.S. The third day they were there, Claire was in a vehicle that had a head-on wreck resulting in her having two broken legs. The van she was riding in was on the wrong side of the road.

Claire was flown to the U.S. to recover. Jim asked us to take care of some of their business in Auki because they wouldn't be coming back. Of course, we agreed to take care of everything. We expressed our condolences and condolences from the many other friends they had made in Auki.

Paula stayed home in the morning to work on our nutrition project while I walked to work. I picked up the mail on the way including two *Newsweek* magazines. I was surprised when we started getting two, because we had been receiving only one. I continued walking to the office wearing the ornate necklace that Isaac had given me. A Solomon man glanced at the necklace without reaction. Paula called Jimmie from home and set up an appointment with the S.P.A. committee for July 23, 1991.

I took our mail and walked home to have lunch with Paula. "Look what came in the mail," I said. "We got two *Newsweek* magazines again," I said. "Do you know why we're getting two?"

"I don't know why, but I'm glad we are. We have a lot of Solomon friends that like to have them when we're finished with them."

When July 23 came, we traveled to the Peace Corps office in Honiara to present our S.P.A. proposals. Simon Ruarafi went with us to represent Buma. Irene, Jim, Thomas, and a man named Fred were there to represent Saenaua. We met in Country Director Gus Comstock's office. We made our presentations to Gus, Jimmie, and Larry.

Paula and I didn't know Fred, but he insisted that he be allowed to offer a prayer to begin the meeting. Paula and I gave a brief, oral description of the applications. Simon and Jim spoke about their individual projects. When we were finished, Director Comstock told us that he would recommend approval of the applications and send them to Washington D.C. for consideration. He told us that the reforestation portion of the Buma project had been funded.

Since I was thinking more about writing a novel based on Scotsman's John Renton's life in the Solomons, I took the opportunity to walk to the National Library of Solomon

Islands. I wanted to learn more about what life would have been like when John Renton lived there. I left Chinatown and easily found the library located near the Mataniko River.

There were only a few people there reading magazines. The employees were pleased to learn that I was interested in their history and culture. I found an old book that mentioned John Renton, but there were few details. It said Renton had lived on the artificial island of Sulufou for seven years. That was interesting because we had nutrition workshops planned in Fouia Village near the island of Sulufou.

Another source stated Solomon Islands was called the "Cannibal Isles." Other sources acknowledge that cannibalism existed, but it suggested that Europeans exaggerated its prevalence. Most sources stated that cannibalism was not practiced for the sake of eating flesh. The practice demonstrated extreme vengeance or done to acquire the "*mana*" of the one eaten.

The library didn't have a copy machine, but I took many notes from the old books. Among them were reports that early missionaries reported cannibalism on Nggela. Coastal people from Isabel reported cannibalism by inland groups, but they denied they participated in the practice. Anthropologist Douglas Oliver identified the Western Solomons as a place where cannibalism was practiced.

The Makira natives were recognized as not only practicing cannibalism, but there were ramos who would charge a fee for participating in a feast of human flesh. In the early 1800s, sailors believed that they could not survive separation from their ship. There is evidence that their concerns were well founded. One report stated that in 1829, twenty shipwrecked sailors made it to Malaita. They were promptly captured and soon eaten.

Cannibalism was reportedly practiced on Malaita to show disdain for a slain enemy or to acquire his power. One source reported that District Officer Bell, Cadet Lillies, and their fifteen native policemen were partially eaten after being killed by the Kwaio.

I left the library and met Paula in Chinatown. We went to I.C.L.A.R.M. to see Tom Scherer. Tom was busy with his job, so we continued working on the V.O.C.A. request. "What did you think about our S.P.A. proposals?" I asked.

"I thought everything went well," Paula answered. "I was surprised when Fred wanted to start with a prayer."

"That surprised me too. There's a time and place for prayer and that wasn't the right time. I don't even know who he is or why he was there. Anyway, Gus said he would send the applications to Washington D.C. with a recommendation for approval."

We finished writing our proposal for the V.O.C.A. program while we waited for Tom. We also finished writing our nominations for Salamai Misuka and Betty Tafqi to the United Nations Environment Program on Sustainable Development. We continued working on constitutions and by-laws for the Saltwater Association and the Laulasi Cultural Tour Community Committee.

Tom entered and provided welcome relief from our paperwork. "Would you like to see the dolphins?" he asked.

"That sounds like fun," Paula said. "We see dolphins swimming beside us when we travel on ships, but we've never seen them just swimming near the shore."

We walked to the ocean edge and watched the dolphins swim and play. Tom lived near a W.W. II museum owned by a Solomon man. Paula and I walked to the area. The war relics were in poor shape, but the owner was very proud of his museum. He told us that many American W.W. II veterans had been there to visit.

We returned to Auki to continue our work. We got our applications for Salamai and Betty for awards of the United Nations Environmental Program on Sustainable Development ready to mail. "I know the applications won't have much chance for winning," I said. "But both of the women will get a certificate."

"Getting certificates will mean a lot to them," Paula said. "They're very unique women who deserve to be recognized."

We went to the post office the next day to mail our V.O.C.A. Farmer-to-Farmer program request and the nominations for Betty and Salamai. I paid with a SI$10 bill and the clerk gave me change. I thought it was likely that there was either too much or too little. The first few times it happened, I called attention to the errors. The clerks were always embarrassed, but they made it right and thanked me.

I soon developed a practice of taking my change without looking. They weren't trying to cheat me, but simply lacked the skills to make proper change. Father Jon was just arriving as we were leaving. "Did you hear about the kid getting bit by a dog last week?" he asked.

"I didn't hear anything about it," Paula answered. "What happened?"

"One of these dogs that run around bit a child. Teresa van den Bosch put several chloroquine tablets in a piece of meat and poisoned the dog."

"Was it one of Dr. Teresa's children that got bit?"

"No, it was a Solomon boy. He's not hurt too badly. Teresa didn't want a dog running around that bit children. That dog's biting days are over."

"I've been tempted to kill some of those dogs with chloroquine myself, but I've always been afraid to do it. I'm too low on the hierarchy chart. Bishop Loft poisoned dogs without repercussions, so I know clergy are exempt. I'm confident that medical personnel have higher status than Peace Corps Volunteers."

We had fourteen months to go in the Peace Corps and the next month was our mid-service conference. We were looking forward to seeing our fellow volunteers from our training group. I was especially interested in talking with Matt and Margaret about potential danger from the Bougainville civil war spilling over into their area. "We're close to being half done with our Peace Corps lives," Paula said. "What do you want to do when we complete our two years?"

"Fourteen months will pass quickly," I answered. "Some volunteers talk about flying to Singapore then taking a train ride from Singapore to Moscow. After that, we could travel on to Western Europe. What would you think about that?"

"It would be fun. We would see some places where we will never get to any other way. We'll talk more about it when time gets closer."

It was Chloroquine Sunday, so we took our two tablets then went to church. Bishop Loft conduced the service. He dropped by afterwards and gave us some rehydrated vegetables and fruit. We went snorkeling with Yasuo and Masako. They invited us to their house for supper with gin and tonics afterwards.

We went to Maoa for another nutrition workshop. Irene and Pauline went with us and performed their jobs very well. The Solomon nurses wouldn't participate, but two J.O.C.V. nurses agreed to go. The J.O.C.V. nurses made excellent presentations about health issues. Everything went smoothly. We spent the night in Maoa and returned to Auki the next day.

My mother had written us about her and Chuck coming to the Solomons. I took time from my work that afternoon and wrote her. I told her what to expect if she made it to the Solomons. Paula went to Saenaua Association to attend to business. She brought back vegetables and strawberries. We didn't have running water, but Masako and Yasuo brought us some. We went to their house and took showers. They had us stay for a traditional Japanese meal.

Maria and Andrew came for breakfast. Andrew told us about him and Bill Wasser going into Kwaio territory to do an engineering survey for a water project. He was a little annoyed that Bill insisted on going to the trouble of doing a proper survey when it was apparent that the project wasn't feasible from an engineering standpoint.

Andrew seemed to have easily adjusted to Solomon culture. Since he hadn't had any training, he couldn't speak Pisin. His language limitations didn't cause any problems, because he was working with Bill. Unfortunately, Maria was having trouble adjusting. "My mother is coming to visit us here," Maria said. "I'm looking forward to seeing her."

"When is she coming?" Paula asked. "I'd like to meet her."

"She's working on flights and visas now. She'll come as soon as she can make arrangements."

Paula and I had a visit scheduled in Dukwasi Village. We planned to go to Dukwasi sometime in the future to see the Riba Cave, but our purpose for this visit was a needs assessment. We took Maria and Andrew with us. Villagers had prepared a feast for us after our survey.

A young chief offered Maria a bird about the size of a pigeon. It had been plucked and cooked but not gutted. The flesh was dark, and the head and feet were still attached. Maria was already stressed by just being in Malaita. The idea of eating the bird was a bird too far. She started crying, upsetting the villagers. Paula and I thanked them for their hospitality and quickly got ready to leave. We told the villagers we would return another time.

It was Chloroquine Sunday, but we didn't go to church. I started writing my book about John Renton by writing paragraphs about my first impressions of Solomon Islands and Malaita. I planned on transferring my own impressions to Renton in addition to assigning Renton justifiable fears of being killed and eaten.

Dr. Paul, Dr. Teresa, and their children came over. Dr. Paul gave Menon's cat a shot. We all went to Masako and Yasuo's house then went on to Misuka's garden. Paula received

Bo'ogo shows bow and arrow

a letter from Judy Tatum from the Augusta S.R.S. Everything was well with our friends in Augusta and El Dorado. We went snorkeling at the airport after our garden trip. We still didn't have water, so Paula and I showered at Maria and Andrew's house.

Bo'ogo brought a bow and three arrows for me to look at. I didn't know if they were artifacts or replicas, but I gave him some money. I tried to ask about Begau customs, but we didn't have much success because of language difficulties.

Maria and Andrew came to our house in the evening for a Chinese food dinner. They told us that they were going to return to New Zealand. We were sorry to see them go, but we understood that Maria was under considerable stress. They gave us their mosquito net and we put it up in the guest room. We gave them a going away present.

Irene and Pauline came to the office to talk about a nutrition program. "We want you to learn everything about the way we do things," I told them. "We will leave some day and we want the program to continue."

"If you learn everything, you can continue the program," Paula added. "I think that Dr. Graham can get another grant. This could be a good job for both of you and you could help Malaita people."

Both Irene and Pauline indicated they were interested. Paula went to the van den Bosch home in the afternoon to cut Dr. Teresa's hair. After cutting Dr. Teresa's hair, Paula was swinging with Elizabeth. The swing broke, but neither Elizabeth nor Paula were hurt. I learned that an article I submitted to the *Solomon Star* about grant applications was published.

Paula baked a cake, so we could have strawberry short cake. I read and researched for my book on John Renton. Dr. Graham and Sheila were going on vacation, so we went to a going-away party at van den Boschs. We took the good ship *Iu Mi Noa* to Honiara to take Miller's things to Peace Corps. We spent the night with Bill Wise and played cards into the early morning.

We had guests for brunch after Sunday church service and guests for our evening dinner. The weather had turned dry in Malaita for the first time we were in the Solomons. Solomon Islanders began to express wishes for rain. The kapok trees were in full fruit. We wanted to collect pods to make new pillows. Paula had worn her walking sandals so much that one had split crosswise. It pinched her foot every time she took a step, but she continued to wear them.

The van den Bosch family came over for brunch the next Sunday. We went snorkeling in the afternoon with Isozakis and the van den Bosch family.

Paula read the rest of the day and I worked on my John Renton book. We got a call from our son in the evening. Paula answered the phone and talked a little then gave the phone to me. "Hello Chuck," I greeted him. "How are things going in California?"

"It's about the same," he answered. "Jason and I go to work every day. It's pretty routine."

"There is nothing routine about our jobs. Are you and my mother still thinking about coming to the Solomons Islands?"

"I talked to Grandma Sellens a couple of days ago. We think we'll come in March or April."

The van den Bosch family

"That's six or seven months away. You'll have plenty of time to plan. That will be a hard trip for my mother. She's close to seventy years old, but she's a tough old gal. She can do it with you there to help her."

"It'll be exciting. I'm looking forward to it. Anything new in your lives?"

"I do have something new planned."

"What are you going to do that's new?"

"We have applications for grants for money for portable sawmills. One of them is for funds for the Saenaua Reforestation Project. If we get approval, your mother will go to Honiara to pick up the checks. I'm going to stay in Malaita and visit the pagan Kwara'ae."

"Pagan Kwara'ae? I don't understand exactly what that means, but it sounds interesting. You did say that your lives aren't routine."

We spent the next few days getting ready for our mid-service conference. We traveled to Honiara a day early to get to see everyone. Tom invited everyone to his home at the I.C.L.A.M. Several of us walked to the nearby W.W. II museum. Owner Fred Kona charged us SI$1 each and gave us a tour. "Cyclone Namu big problem," Fred said. "Namu spoiled museum."

Fred's tour included what was left of several U.S. airplanes. He proudly showed us a few Japanese field guns. Fred also had W.W. II rifles, helmets, knives, and other memorabilia from both U.S. and Japanese soldiers.

Fred Kona shows a plane

We returned to Tom's house with the W.W. II museum on our mind. "It's too bad that Fred doesn't have money to rebuild some of the airplanes," Bill said. "Can you imagine how much work it was just to move the stuff to his land."

"I'm glad he did it," I said. "Scrap iron dealers have already taken out most of the war artifacts they could get to."

We spent the rest of the day visiting and celebrating Matt's birthday by drinking iced tea, pop, and beer. I did get to talk to Matt privately. "I remember you telling us about your prior Peace Corps service while we were in training," I said. "You predicted that some of us wouldn't complete our two years. We're half way through and we're all still here."

"Yes, no one has had to terminate," Matt agreed. "We're an unusual group. I hope we're still together at the end, but I doubt it."

"How are things in your area?" I asked. "We don't get any news in Malaita about the Bougainville Conflict. I'm worried that the civil war might spill over into your area."

"We talk about it all the time. The fighting between the Bougainville Revolutionary Army (B.R.A.) and Papua New Guinea forces continue. The B.R.A. also fights with other armed groups on Bougainville. It's a real mess."

"Is the Peace Corps in Washington D.C. monitoring the situation?"

"I don't know. I hope so."

"Do you know if the Peace Corps gets any information from Australian or other country sources?"

"I don't know about that, but the Peace Corps is concerned. Margaret and I have been at Jimmie's house for a few days. She's talked to us a lot about it."

We traveled to Tambaea the next day for our conference. We had our Peace Corps physicals. Paula weighed 135 pounds and I weighed 220 pounds. I didn't think I weighed that much because my Kansas driver's license, my Solomon driver's license, and my Peace Corps application proved I only weighed 215. We got our physicals and dental examinations, took T.B. tests, and got Hepatitis B shots.

I got an opportunity to talk with Gus Comstock. Gus had served in the U.S. Navy and had also been a Peace Corps Volunteer in the Solomons. He had married a woman from

Western Province, and they had two children. "Gus, there were two volunteers that lived with the Kwaio a few years ago," I said. "Were you here when they were here?"

"We were in the Solomons at the same time," Gus said. "Their names were David and Kate Akin."

"Did you know them?"

"I never met them. We weren't in the same training group. They never came to any Peace Corps event that I know about."

"Didn't they even come to their early-service, mid-service, or close-of-service conferences?"

"Not that I know of. I heard that Kate went to the Peace Corps office once. About twenty Kwaio warriors escorted her to make sure she was safe."

Our mid-service conference was finished, and we had our tickets to return to Auki the next day. I took the opportunity to go to the National Library of the Solomon Islands to continue reading about ancient history. I learned that Malitians took or were given adult names based on some special trait or habit. Seventy-five percent of men's names came from fighting techniques in their tribal wars.

One nineteenth century Malitian had a name that translated into "Snatch Guns." He earned his name from his practice of laying in ambush for an enemy tribesman to come into range of his own rifle. The victim had to be alone and had to be carrying a rifle. Snatch Guns would kill him, grab the dead man's rifle, and run.

There was another old Malitian who had a name that translated into "Snatch Women." There weren't any details explaining precisely how he earned the name. A ramo from the artificial island of Adagege in Lau Lagoon was named Kwaisulia. Kwaisulia translated as "Cuts-off-Bits." Kwaisulia earned his name from his practice of capturing a victim alive and tying him up. Kwaisulia would get him to a special location then cut off bits of flesh for eating while the victim suffered in terror.

Kwaisulia was recruited as an indentured laborer for work in Queensland, Australia. He worked on sugar plantations in Queensland for about six years then returned to Lau Lagoon around 1880. Kwaisulia became a labor recruiting middleman in Lau Lagoon. He accompanied recruiters on blackbirding ships to convince Malitians to agree to work in Queensland.

His influence was enhanced by his status as a ramo, evidenced by many contract killings. Kwaisulia was regarded as the most powerful Malitian of his time. He was involved in several wars in the Lau Lagoon, notably in a war against Sulufou after Kabbou died in 1887. Kwaisulia was killed in 1909 when dynamite he was using for fishing exploded prematurely. I wanted to read more, but I had to leave to be ready for my trip back to Auki.

# CHAPTER 16

# *Pagan Kwara'ae*

We traveled to Auki without incident. Colin picked us up at the airport and dropped us off at our home. I organized my notes and made brief comments about what I had read in the library. Both Paula and I were tired, so we went to bed early. We woke when our beds and the house shook with a small earthquake. We were accustomed to earthquakes and went back to sleep.

We walked to work and was having a typical day until we came home for lunch. We were getting ready to eat when there was a knock on the door. "Hello Glen," Paula said, when she answered. "Come in. We're getting ready to eat lunch. Would you like to join us?"

"Thanks, but I can't," Glen said. "I stopped by to tell you that Jimmie called. She said you weren't answering your phone."

"Our phone isn't working. Other people in the area don't have service either."

"Katherine and I are staying with Bill Wasser. His phone is working. Anyway, Jimmie wants you to call her. It's something about a woman from Malaita winning a trip to Florida."

We quickly got to a working phone and we called Jimmie. We held the receiver so both of us could hear and speak. "I got a call from someone from the United Nations," Jimmie said. "She said the application you submitted for Salamai Misuka won. She's won an all-expense paid trip to Florida."

"Wow, that's great!" Paula exclaimed. "When will she be expected to leave?"

"She has to be on the plane in five days. That's why they called me. The lady said she sent Salamai a notification letter."

"I can't believe they wrote to Salamai," I said. "We didn't put Salamai Misuka's address in the application. Salamai doesn't even have an address for them to notify her. We had our names on the application for submission and notification. I don't think that Salamai can even read."

"I don't know about all that. They faxed a notification letter and travel voucher. I'll send you what I've received. Do you think that you can get Salamai ready?"

"I don't see how we can possibly get her ready," Paula said. "I know that Salamai doesn't have a passport. If we managed to get her a passport, she would need a visa. She's only been off Malaita three times in her life and those three times were for trips to Honiara. She doesn't have suitable clothes. She's never worn a pair of shoes in her life. But we'll try."

"Jimmie, please keep the documents in the office," I said. "If we're going to make this work, we'll have to come to Honiara tomorrow. We'll get them at that time."

We told Paul Kennioriana about Salamai winning the award. We told him we would need to spend the next few days trying to get her ready. Paul was very supportive and complimentary. We promptly started to Misuka's home. "What do you think Salamai will say?" Paula asked, on the way.

"I think she'll be thrilled!" I said. "She'll want you to go with her. What do you think Jim will say?"

"Solomon Islands' society is very male dominated. But if there's any man in the Solomon Islands that would let his wife travel to the U.S. for a function like this, it would be Jim."

We found Jim and Salamai at their home and told them about Salamai being a contest winner. Salamai was excited and overwhelmed. Jim seemed very pleased and promptly consented. We got a passport application form at the post office and returned to the Misuka home.

Paula asked Salamai questions while I wrote her answers on the form. I had to declare that I completed the form from information Salamai supplied. We went to the Auki police station where Salamai used an ink blotter to put her left thumb print on the application in lieu of her signature. Salamai didn't have a birth certificate, so we asked Thomas Misuka and Mathew Kuri to sign statutory declarations confirming her date and place of birth to meet application requirements.

Paula, Salamai, and I took the first plane to Honiara the next morning. Paula went to the Peace Corps office to get the documents from Jimmie. Salamai and I located a photo shop and had two passport photographs made. We three met at the proper office for passport issuance and explained the situation. The men seemed impressed and promptly issued Salamai a passport.

We took the passport to the U.S. consulate and asked to see Charge d' affaires Dan Vernon. We asked Dan if he could issue a visa for Salamai to travel to the U.S. "I can't issue a visa here," he said. "We would have to send her passport to Australia."

"I don't think there would be enough time to mail it to Australia and get it back," I said.

"I can make it happen faster through official channels. Leave the passport here and I'll see what I can do."

Dan made a copy of the United Nations' selection letter and the travel voucher. We thanked him profusely and left the passport. We went back to the Peace Corps office where Paula asked to see Gus Comstock. She asked Gus if Peace Corps would pay for her to escort Salamai to Florida. Gus was sympathetic but refused. "You might want to ask the New Zealand High Commission," Gus said. "New Zealand sometimes has funds for things like this."

We traveled to the New Zealand high commission and got to speak with Joyce, the head of missions. We're Peace Corps Volunteers posted in Malaita," Paula said. "We applied for an award for a Malaita woman who we know. She won an all-expense-paid trip to Florida."

"Salamai isn't capable of traveling by herself," I added.

"Don't interrupt while she's speaking!" Joyce snapped at me.

I didn't protest. I had been told that New Zealand's culture assigned women with greater status than men. I fervently hoped that Paula wouldn't be too supportive of the culture. Joyce's admonishment for me to remain silent was tantamount to Rocky telling Paula to shut-up, that she was only like my child.

Paula was very accepting of her New Zealand assigned status. She continued explaining the situation and showed Joyce the acceptance letter. "Salamai isn't capable of traveling by herself," she said. "I'm here to ask if New Zealand will fund someone to go with her."

Joyce seemed skeptical. "What's the organization that gave your friend the award?" she asked.

"It's a United Nations' program. It's called the Environmental Program on Sustainable Development."

"Are you asking New Zealand to fund a trip for you?"

"I would be happy to go if you wanted me to. But the important thing is for Salamai to get to go."

"Let me check on some things. I'll get back to you soon."

Joyce continued to exhibit skepticism. Paula gave her our address and telephone number. We left her office and traveled to the Sol Air office. We were lucky there was room for us on the last plane leaving Honiara for Auki.

It was raining when we walked to work. It was raining when we walked home for lunch. I opened our pantry door to get a can of out-of-date corn. Every can in the pantry was missing its paper label. "Paula come look at this," I said. "Every label of every can is missing. Did you do that?"

"I'm not going to look," Paula said. "It's not April 1, and I know that what you consider a joke is usually lacking humor."

"I'm not joking. There is not a single label on any can."

Paula eventually joined me. We puzzled over our latest Solomon Islands' mystery. We eventually arrived at the conclusion that cockroaches had eaten the labels. We randomly chose a can and had string beans for lunch. We consoled ourselves by rationalizing that it might not have been out-of-date. We received a call while we were doing the dishes. "Hello, this is the Sellens' residence," I said. "How may I help you?"

This is Joyce from the New Zealand High Commission," she said. "I would like to speak to Paula Sellens."

"Paula, it's for you from the New Zealand High Commission."

Joyce told Paula that she had researched the credentials of the United Nations Environmental Program on Sustainable Development and learned it was very prestigious. New Zealand would provide funds for a Malaita woman to escort Salamai but not Paula. The young Solomon woman, Beverly, had studied in New Zealand and was highly thought of.

When Paula hung up the phone, she looked at me and relayed the message. "I wonder why Joyce didn't give you the information," Paula asked, with an impish grin.

"You know very well why she didn't want to talk to me," I answered. "I'm just the same as your child."

We got a call from Dan Vernon telling us that Salamai's passport and visa had been returned. Paula took Salamai to the Auki Second Hand Store and bought her a suitcase, clothes, and shoes. Salamai commented that the shoes were pretty, but they hurt her feet. Paula offered to cut Salamai's hair, but she said Irene would cut it before she left.

Paula and I escorted Jim and Salamai to Honiara on her departure date. We traveled to Dan Vernon's office and got Salamai's passport and visa. We traveled to the Honiara airport by Red Bus where we met Beverly. Salamai and Beverly got on the plane without incident. Jim, Paula, and I returned to Auki.

Our work week was normal. "What shall we have for supper?" Paula asked, as we were leaving work on Thursday.

"Do we have any chili tuna?" I answered her question with a question.

"We don't have any, but it sounds good."

"We have plenty of time. Let's stop by Margaret's Store and buy some."

"I could make tuna salad sandwiches. I'll go by the bakery and buy bread while you get the tuna. You can also pick up some long-life milk while you're shopping."

As I approached Margaret's Store, I saw a white man sitting on the porch with several Malitians. He was wearing long trousers, a long-sleeved shirt, and a wide brimmed hat. As I got closer, I recognized that he was an albino. Several expatriates had told me that there were several albinos in Malaita, but he was the first one that I had seen.

I went into Margaret's and asked the clerk for tuna. I thought of the silly, old Australian while I was waiting for the clerk to fill my order. I couldn't get the silly old Australian out of my mind. It seemed implausible that he would buy and smoke cigarettes in the Solomons because he could buy singles. Without warning, strange words came out of my mouth unsolicited. "Two rolls," I said.

The clerk removed two cigarettes from a pack and placed them on counter with my tuna. "I don't smoke," I informed him. "But I'll smoke one today because I can buy singles."

I walked home. I was happy with the recognition that I was becoming more accepting of Solomon Islands' culture. We enjoyed our tuna fish sandwiches with iced tea that evening. "Let's get more iced tea and move to the porch," I said. "I have a surprise for you."

We moved to the porch with our tea and sat down. I produced the two cigarettes and matches. Paula seemed less than pleased with my surprise. "Why did you buy cigarettes?" she demanded. "We don't smoke! Cigarettes are bad for our health."

"I know that," I said. "But we can buy singles in the Solomons. Let's smoke these, just this one time."

"You're worse than that silly, old Australian that you told me about. I don't know why I stay married to you."

We smoked our cigarettes with iced tea and popcorn. Paula insisted that we both brush our teeth before she would kiss me good-night. We went to bed and slept soundly.

The next two days at the office was a little slow. Things picked up when got a call from Gus informing us that our grant applications for portable sawmills for Buma and Saenaua were approved. "I'm sure that the trouble makers will continue to try to scuttle the Buma project," Paula said. "There's so much jealousy in the Solomon Islands."

"I know," I said. "Most of the men are primarily concerned that someone else will get something. They're satisfied with not having anything if their neighbors don't get anything."

Salamai and Beverly returned to Honiara from the Florida conference. Salamai traveled to Malaita alone by ship. Jim and Salamai came to see us the day after she made it home.

Salamai had difficulty telling us about what had occurred on her trip. She could relate that she saw Peace Corps Volunteers in Fiji. Paula and I soon understood that Beverly had left Salamai in the home of their host family while Beverly attended events and parties.

Wharf in Auki

We told Jim and Salamai that the Saenaua grant application had been approved. They opened a checking account to receive the S.P.A. money on behalf of Saenaua Association. I took the opportunity to speak to Jim about the pagan Kwara'ae. "Jim, we talked about the pagan Kwara'ae some time back," I said. "Paula will go to Honiara September 9, 1991 to get the Saenaua money. Can you take me to meet the pagan Kwara'ae while she's gone?"

"We can go," Jim said. "Talked to Chief Walasina. Talk to him again. Take you Siele Shrine."

Paula and I discussed Salamai's trip to Florida that evening. We knew that Salamai and the Seanaua Association was unique in the Solomons, but we hadn't thought it would receive international recognition. We decided to nominate the Saenaua Association for a Global 500 Award. The ceremonies were to be held in Rio do Janeiro.

We got a message to Simon that the Buma grant application had been approved. We told him that he would need to come to Auki and open a checking account to receive the money when it came in. A man we didn't know came to our office two days later. "Stop Buma sawmill project," he instructed me.

"Why do you think we should stop the Buma project?" I asked.

"Land dispute. Project on my land."

I struck a Charles-in-Charge attitude. I majestically folded my arms across my chest. "There's nothing in the sawmill application about land. Your claim to a land dispute has no bearing on the project."

"Project has trees. Trees on my land. Must stop."

"There was nothing in the application about trees," I said, trying to be as illogical as I thought he was. "The project is only about portable sawmill equipment."

Our visitor eventually recognize that I was deliberately being illogical and left in a huff. I was quite satisfied with the result. Paula and I talked to Colin that evening. We informed him about the issues with what should have been non-involved persons trying to scuttle the project.

We told Colin that both the Buma project and the Saenaua project had been funded. We emphasized that we would not be deterred from proceeding. Colin reminded us that Andrew had left and there was a Solomon man from Western Province serving as provincial attorney. Simon Ruarafi and Paul Tafqi arrived in the office three days later. "Problem with project," Simon said. "Must stop."

"What's the problem, Simon?" I asked. "Why do you think we have to stop?"

"Law says stop."

Simon handed me a letter written on Malaita Province stationary. It came from Malaita's new provincial attorney. The letter was well written and addressed to Simon Ruarafi, Chairman Buma Village. The message was clear. Buma Village was ordered to cease the portable sawmill project because of a land dispute. "We'll just go see about that!" I asserted. "The provincial attorney has no authority to make such an order! We'll go see him right now!"

Simon, Paul, Paula, and I promptly left to confront the provincial attorney. The attorney was in, and he invited us into his office. We stood while I introduced everyone. "I'm here about a letter that was sent to Simon Ruarafi," I said. "It's signed by you. Did you send this letter?"

I handed him the letter. He glanced at it and acknowledge that he sent it. "I'm the provincial attorney," he said, in proper English.

"I know you're the provincial attorney. That's my point. You're not a judge. I don't think you have the authority to issue what is effectively a court cease-and-desist order."

I paused to let him answer. He didn't speak or change expressions. "Our position is that only a court has the authority to stop this project," I continued. "If you want to stop it, go file an action with the court! We'll see you there! Until there's a court order, the project continues!"

The attorney didn't have a response. We waited patiently for a little time then left his office and returned to our office. "The project will continue," I said. "Go ahead and open a checking account while you're here. Paula will go to Honiara on September 9 to pick up your grant check. I won't go with her because I'm going to visit the pagan Kwara'ae at Siele Shrine.

I had read about the pagan Kwara'ae in publications that Ben Burt had sent. I talked to Paul Kennioriana at that time and told him that that I wanted to see Siele Shrine. Paul was a practicing Christian and didn't want me to go. I explained that if I understood more about the Kwara'ae culture, it was easier to assimilate into the society and do my job as a community development worker.

Paul seemed skeptical for some reason. I claimed that I believed that modern Kwara'ae had adapted their ancient customs to fill existing needs in their ever changing, complex society. I told Paul that I needed to learn how modern Kwara'ae were meshing their ancient customs with Christianity.

Paul was yet to be convinced. I cleverly changed the subject. "Paul, when I was in Honiara, I went to the Solomon Islands National Library," I said. "I read about Solomon history. One book said that in old days, when boys matured to adulthood, they were given names that reflected their characters. Is that true?"

Paul raised his brow and nodded. "The book said that about seventy-five percent of the names came from how warriors acted in their tribal wars," I continued. "Is that true?"

Paul again raised his brow and nodded. "I read that Kwaisulia was a famous Malitian," I said. "His name means 'Cuts-off-Bits' because he cut off pieces of flesh from living enemies that he had captured."

Paul raised his brow and nodded. "Kwaisulia from Adagege in Lau Lagoon," he said. "Many young Lau men take Kwaisulia for names."

I raised my brow and paused. "Paul, what does Kennioriana mean?" I asked.

Paul blushed deeply and smiled broadly. "Kennioriana means 'Hides-Behind-Women.' Grandfather 'Ari'Ari man."

I thought deeply about Grandfather Kennioriana and how he earned his name. After sufficient reflection, I returned to more pressing issues. I told Paul that when I was a political science student, I was taught that academics needed to study ancient political systems to better understand modern systems. I rationalized that very few trained administrators ever have opportunities to observe ancient government systems first hand. It was an academic responsibility to pursue the opportunity. Paul didn't seem to believe me.

In truth, my claims were not true. I was just interested in the personal lives of the pagan Kwara'ae. I was fascinated by the unblemished Solomon Islands' cultures. I had already made arrangement with Jim Misuka to schedule a visit and a date was set. I was going.

I was looking forward to my trip to the pagan Kwara'ae, but normal activities continued. I often wore the ornate necklace that Chief Isaac gave me. I didn't get responses from Solomon men like I did when I wore the boar's teeth necklace. I took my question to George Toritelia. "Hello George," I said, when I entered his office. "Have you seen me wear this ornate necklace?"

George smiled and raised his brow to signify an affirmative answer. "When I wore my boar's teeth necklace, Solomon men admired it," I said. "What does this ornate necklace represent?"

"Worn by virgin daughter of chief," George answered, with a wide grin.

I removed the necklace and gave it to Paula. I thought she was better suited for wearing a princess necklace. I assigned her the title of: "Peace Corps Princess."

Paula and I walked to Father Jon's home late in the afternoon. "Father Jon, I've been thinking about asking you to baptize me," Paula said. "My dad is Catholic, and I attended the Catholic Church as I grew up. Is it possible for you to baptize me?"

"Of course, it's possible," Father Jon said. "Catholics are usually baptized when they are babies. The ceremony starts when the parents ask a priest to baptize their child."

"I'm definitely beyond the child age, but I'd like for you to baptize me. I've attended baptisms ceremonies before, but I really don't understand what they represent."

"Catholic baptisms are complex, ritualistic ceremonies. Catholic theology is incorporated into the baptism. Our baptisms are built on theological beliefs that make the ceremony very important to both parents and the infant."

"My parents live in Lakin, Kansas. They couldn't come to the Solomon Islands. Would I need to have my parents here?"

"You could ask a Catholic couple to take the role of your parents. If you do decide to be baptized, you could ask Sheila and Graham to stand in for your parents."

"I'm sure that I'll want to continue. I'll ask Sheila and Dr. Graham if they'll stand in for my parents."

On September 9, Paula left to go to Honiara. I made it to Chief Misuka's home, and we began our trip. We went by market truck to the end of the Busarata road then continued on foot. "Walk one hour, see Chief Wilson Walasina," Jim said. "After talk with Walasina, go on."

Jim explained that we were to wade across the Fiu River and climb a mountain to the interior of Malaita where we would find the ancient Kwara'ae. The river crossing and mountain climb was expected to take another four hours. We were going to spend the night at Siele.

Jim was not a betel nut chewer, but he began to peal a nut. He was providing himself with stimulation for the difficult journey. Jim took the opportunity to share his opinion on size differences of male genital organs between races. "White man penis bigger black man," he said.

He didn't say anything else but looked at me. He was obviously waiting for my response. I wondered how he might have arrived at his opinion, but penis sizes weren't the cultural exchanges that I was seeking.

I observed cultural sensitivity by not disagreeing with him. I nodded to show I understood without confirming or denying agreement to his opinion.

It took close to two hours to get to Chief Walasina's village. I was confident that Jim could have made it in an hour if he had been alone. Jim and Walasina spoke in Kwara'ae then Jim spoke to me in Pisin. "Walasina said no go," Jim said. "Walasina say Ben Burt go. Timi Ko'oliu die. Can't go."

Jim often served as a guide

154

Chief Misuka continued by telling me that a visit to the interior wasn't possible at that time but maybe later. He said that the pagan Kwara'ae believed that their participation in a visit by Dr. Burt had been the causative factor in the death of Senior Priest Timi Ko'oliu. There was a concern that a visit by me might trigger other deaths. The pagan Kwara'ae believed the ancestors caused the death of Priest Ko'oliu to punish him for this association with Dr. Burt.

At the time of Ko'oliu's death, Paramount Chief Osifera feared for his own life and converted to Christianity. I understood that Timi Ko'oliu was an old man at that time. That gave me reason to believe that the man died from the complications from old age. However, there were many documented cases of the power of old Malitians' abilities to cause death with sorcery.

To explain this, I learned that academics cited modern, medical casebooks that contained many documented anecdotes where healthy patients believed they had an incurable disease. Despite professional assurance that there was no disease, the patient's health declined until they eventually died. Medical theorists accounted for this by assuming that unrelieved negatives and suggestions could cause death. They cited primitive medicine men and witch-doctors as being able to use this power to cause illness and death.

I accepted the decision that I couldn't go as cheerfully as I could. I understood their belief systems and didn't want to do anything to harm the Kwara'ae people or change their customs. Perhaps, because of this feeling of a need for isolation, there may always be some Kwara'ae who continue to observe their ancestral way of life. I learned more about these people by being denied admittance than if I had been welcomed. "I understand the reasons I can't go, Jim," I said. "Maybe we can come back later."

Jim decided to stay in Chief Walasina's village, but I wanted to go back. The Busarata road back to Auki was infrequently traveled, thus I had to walk. I took about six hours to walk out, knowing it would have taken a Solomon Islander only three or four. I confess to being proud that I could do it. I was in much better physical condition than when I first joined the Peace Corps.

Paula returned from Honiara and I caught up on the news. I gave her a brief report on my failed effort to see the pagan Kwara'ae. "What happened in Honiara?" I asked.

"I have lots of good news!" she answered. "I accomplished everything that I went to Honiara for. I got a pap smear and picked up checks for the Buma project and the Saenaua Association. The Global 500 that is to be awarded in Rio do Janeiro likes our Saenaua Association nomination and asked for references."

"Is there a form that we're to use to furnish references?" I asked.

"There's no form. I'll draft letters for David Oeta and Paul Kennioriana to sign. They basically want confirmation that what we put in the nomination was true."

"What else did you learn?"

"I talked to Gus Comstock while I was in the Peace Corps office. He said he would write a letter for me for renewing my Kansas social worker's license. Gus also wants you and me to help train new volunteers in Western Province. He also wants us to be logistics coordinators for Peace Corps training in N.A.T.I."

"Just what we need, more work. I remember Jim and Chris telling us in training that everyone in their group quit because they didn't have anything meaningful to do. Where are those volunteers now? Did anything else happen that was exciting?"

"Gus Comstock told me about a Peace Corps program that gets minorities and women into staff positions. Gus said I would be a viable candidate and he was interested in nominating me when we are close to our end of service. If I were selected, I would spend a year training in Washington D.C. then be assigned to a country staff position."

"You would be a great candidate! I bet you would get it. You're a woman with Cherokee Indian ancestry. Just think of all the successes we're having as volunteers. It's something that we can look forward to. Anything else happen?"

"That's about all that was exciting. I spent the night at Jimmie's house and helped at the office the next day."

We stopped by the post office on our way home. We picked up our mail and found a letter from Australia. The letter was from Greg Granger's cameraman, Damon Smith. Smith had sent us a Christmas card and a hand-written note. He and his family invited us to come visit them. He offered us hospitality and the use of his own home. Paula and I decided to send him a return Christmas card and invite him and his family to come to Auki.

It began to rain when we were halfway home. We had our umbrellas, so it didn't create any problems. "What shall we have for supper," I asked, when we got home. "I know you like to play Russian roulette with the cans without labels, thanks to the cockroaches."

"We need long-life milk, rice and chili tuna, Paula said. If you'll go get those things and anything else you think of, I'll make a guess and open a can of mystery food."

I walked to Margaret's Store for shopping. Two young men were at the far end of the counter when I entered. They had apparently already consumed more beer than they needed, but they were buying more. They cast sideways glances at me. "Big karate man," one of them said, softly and dismissively."

I ignored them. I was satisfied. Neither of the men had attended Bob King's karate classes. I recognized that one of my goals for joining the karate class had been achieved. The respect I had earned had lasted for these many months.

We had a dinner party at Isozakis that week. It was well attended, and we had fun. Yasuo told me that Japanese rice was much sweeter and tastier that the rice we were eating in Auki. We were among the last to leave.

I saw Father Jon at Margaret's Store the next day. "Did you hear what happened last night?" he asked.

"I didn't hear of anything unusual," I said. "What happened."

"Were you at Isozaki's party last night?"

"Yes, we were there. We must have left well before midnight."

"I heard that Cheryl Hicks left the party to walk home by herself. There must have been a man following her, but she didn't notice him. She climbed the stairs and went into her house. The man pushed in right behind her. He was grabbing her, and she was screaming and fighting. The commotion woke up the children who started screaming. The man ran out the door and broke through the railing. He fell to the ground and ran away."

"Did the police catch him?"

"No, he ran back to his village. I don't expect the police will even try to find him. The assailant was a policeman himself."

"That doesn't create a lot of confidence in the police force. It was also a policeman who assaulted Dr. Melissa."

We began preparation for the November 4, 1991 Women's Week. Paula had a leading role in the organization. We took

Yasuo and Masako at their dinner party

the opportunity to do a nutrition workshop without the logistical problems of getting to a village. We didn't have electricity, but we did have the use of Kilu'ufi Hospital's generator.

Paula continued with Women's Week activities the next day while I went to Bina with the Saenaua men to negotiate timber sales. When I returned, I thought I should consult with George Toritelia with an update on our efforts to get a tourism official. "Hello George," I greeted him. "How are you today?"

George gave me a big smile. Instead of showing reddish-black, beetle nut stained teeth, his teeth were sparkling white. I was overwhelmed! It was the primitive medical treatment that I had been searching for. I could take this treatment to the U.S. to benefit mankind and make myself rich and famous. "George, your teeth are so white!" I exclaimed. "They're beautiful! How did you get them so white?"

George rewarded me with another big smile. "Steel wool," he replied.

George used a finger and thumb to demonstrate how held the steel wool for his teeth cleaning. I smiled with him and nodded somewhat approvingly. I quickly rejected my notion of taking this teeth-whitening method to the U.S. to benefit mankind. I also decided it would be better if I curtailed my efforts to discover primitive medical miracles to make me rich.

We went to a dinner party at the van den Bosch home that week. During the after-dinner conversations, the discussion turned to Kilu'ufi Hospital. "We had a strange accident recently," Dr. Paul said.

"I'm sure you deal with strange accidents every day," I said. "What's the latest?

Father Jon, Eric, and Colin at dinner party

"We had a man that had a serious chest injury caused by being impaled by a flying fish. These accidents are not uncommon in the Solomons. Being impaled by flying fish is a real risk for night fishermen."

"Amazing! I've never heard of anything like that before. Did he die?"

"No, he had a collapsed lung, but he will survive. Michael Wale said that the standard advice is for fishermen to stand up in the boat when they know such fish are about. The fish don't elevate high enough to hit them in the chest. Our man clearly failed to do this or didn't have sufficient warning."

"What about getting hit in the legs?"

"We once saw someone with a penetrating leg injury from the same cause. The wound was deep and painful but not life threatening. It's better to be hit in the leg than the chest."

Alison was working the late shift at Kilu'ufi that week, so Paula called Colin. "I know Alison is working late today." She said. "Would you like to come over and eat pistou with us?"

"I would be delighted," Colin answered. "I don't know what pistou is, but I'm sure it will be delicious."

"Pistou is heavy soup made from beans, pumpkin, and kumara. I'm sure you'll like it."

Colin arrived, and we began eating. We got a knock on the door during our meal. I opened it to find Bo'ogo. Instead of showing me artifacts, he made me understand that I was to go with him to his village the next day. Stall. I tried to stall. I wanted to go, but I needed some time to make plans and arrangements. He was insistent that we had to leave early to the next morning.

I had frequently asked him questions about ancient Begau customs. He was willing to teach me, but we struggled with communication because of our language limitations. When I bought artifacts and souvenirs from him, I tried to make him understand that I would like to visit his village. I thought that my interest in Begau customs must have been what prompted Bo'ogo's invitation. This was my opportunity, I decided I had to go.

# CHAPTER 17

# *Begau Adventure*

I woke up early, even before the stupid rooster started crowing. I was anxious to begin my trip to the Begau village. I thought about my supervisor while we were eating breakfast. "I won't have time to talk to Paul about missing work for a few days," I said. "Maybe you can explain what a unique opportunity I've been offered."

"You know that Paul wouldn't approve of you going to a Begau village," Paula said. "Paul is a Christian and you know very well you're going to a pagan village."

"I know you're right, as usual. But I want to go. It's better to ask Paul for forgiveness than permission."

"I don't suppose anything you do will surprise Paul. Nothing you do surprises me."

I met Bo'ogo at Margaret's Chinese Store where he had spent the night. Bo'ogo had joined regular visitors to Auki who often slept on the covered, open-front verandah of the store. He didn't have benefit of a mat or even a blanket. I bought six bags of rice in Margaret's Store for presents to those who would be my hosts.

I gave the driver of a market truck SI$6 to pay for Bo'ogo's and my ride. Our truck ride took about three hours to get to our debarkation point. We began walking and climbing. The discomfort of riding in the back of the truck was promptly traded for the difficulties of mountain climbing. Volcanic mountains reaching 4,000 feet above sea level ran the length of Malaita. Warm moisture collected above the small mountains, forming heavy clouds. This created conditions for frequent rains, thus we were often rained on as we trekked.

We went up one small, relatively steep mountain then down the other side. We were then confronted with another small, relatively steep mountain to climb. Our crude path meandered through ancient, indigenous, hard-wood trees. Their leaves and branches overlapped, resulting in a dense canopy. Our path was usually damp or muddy because the heavy forest prevented sunlight from reaching the ground. Several species of orchids provided colorful and beautiful accents to the background of dark green foliage.

The dense forest had infrequent breaks where there had been commercial logging or long-established gardens. We walked and climbed without speaking. In a couple of hours, we came to a small village of thatched houses where I met Toga. Toga was Bo'ogo's nephew and spoke Pisin very well. I shook hands with Toga and his wife. Both were short and very fit due to their simple diets and the constant activity necessary to survive by substance agriculture.

Both Toga and his wife were bare-chested. Toga wore a heavy cross around his neck. Their two small children were naked as were the other small children who crowded around to gawk at me. I was obviously the first white man they had ever seen. The children had extended bellies caused by their high starch, low protein diets.

A bare-chested, older girl proudly displayed a baby, likely her brother, for my inspection. The baby was sickly, but I had nothing to offer in the form of medicine. I didn't take a picture and moved away. I was concerned that if the baby died, I would be held responsible.

I went into Toga's house and rested with him, his family, and Bo'ogo. The one-room house featured two kerosene lanterns. Bo'ogo soon stood to leave.

Togo, his wife, and child
inside his house

"Bo'ogo go ahead," Toga informed me. "Help get ready."

I knew Toga would make a better guide because of our ability to communicate. Toga and I went outside with Bo'ogo and watched him stride away at a pace that I could not have matched for any extended period. Toga walked with a very pronounced limp due to one leg being considerably shorter than the other. We reentered his house where I showed Toga the rice I had brought. "These are for the chief," I said.

Toga put two of the bags in the rafters among other stored items. He gave the other four to his wife who returned them to my back-pack. I observed Malaita customs by not looking at, or speaking to, his wife or children while we men chatted.

"Why did you leave the village where you were born?" I asked.

"Leg hurt," he answered. "Couldn't live in village."

Toga explained his handicap resulted from a broken leg he suffered when he was a child. He was fighting with an older brother and lost the fight. As he matured, his broken leg didn't grow well. It was now four or five inches shorter than the other. His father, the paramount chief, encouraged him to leave the village several years ago.

The chief instructed Toga to find a Christian village and wife, so he could lead an easier life. Easier life had to be in the eye of the pagan Begau chief. Toga's life didn't look any too easy through my eyes, the eyes of an American Peace Corps Volunteer.

After our brief conversation and my much too brief rest, we began the second leg of our trek toward the pagan village. Toga carried my back-pack and their larger child. His wife carried the smaller child in a sling and a cooking pot. We walked for around two hours when we passed a sago-palm, leaf house. It was newly constructed and sat beside an older, burned out house. The two houses were the only ones I could see. I commented on the obvious. "It looks like someone had the bad luck to have their house burn," I said.

"Brother's house," Toga said, with a snicker. "Name William. Meet him at village."

Toga pushed close to me and whispered, so that his wife couldn't hear. "With William when house burn," he confided. "Wife came time of *sikie-moon*."

*Sikie-moon* is the Pisin expression for menstruation. Women traditionally had separate houses where they went during their periods. By their customs, Toga's sister-in-law had committed a grave offense that had defiled the entire house. My curiosity was aroused as to how her entering the house while she was menstruating could cause it to catch on fire. "How did that make the house burn?" I asked.

"William beat her," Toga said, while laughing hardily. "Beat her and beat her. Then burn house."

"What happened to his wife?" I asked.

"Screamed and screamed," Togo replied, while continuing laughing.

"Thought William kill her. She ran away, screaming and crying. Saw house burn, William and I throw furniture out door. William burn house, build new one."

We continued our journey toward Toga's old village. Though Toga and his wife were carrying everything, and Toga was semi-handicapped, I still struggled to keep up with them. They seemed to glide while I struggled to even keep my feet on the slippery path. I thought we were making satisfactory progress until I forced a rest stop. A Begau family soon passed us. The woman was carrying two small children and a full, native bag that hung around her neck. The man was carrying two, five-gallon cans of kerosene.

I was amazed how strong they were and how they could travel so quickly. They eyed us curiously but didn't speak. My group continued up the slippery path. Despite going slowly, I worried that I might slip and break my own leg. If I had, it would have been very difficult for someone to get me back to the hospital in Auki. As we trekked, I carefully watched for scorpions, centipedes, and other biting insects. I was rewarded with seeing large, beautiful, colorful butterflies and moths flitting about.

Whenever we crossed a swiftly running stream, we splashed water on our arms and legs to cool ourselves and rinse off some of the sweat. We drank deeply of the sweet, cool water to replenish what we had lost in the jungle heat. Maybe I should have been apprehensive about drinking from the streams, but I had done it many times before with no ill effects.

River water was what I knew that I would drink when I got to the village. The difference would be that it would have been collected by women and girls and stored in bamboo tubes. Bamboo gives the water a strange taste, but many generations of Solomon Islanders had survived on this water. I had also drunk stale water from bamboo canteens many times with no ill effects. At each of those times, I wondered why the Peace Corps didn't furnish we volunteers with water purification tablets.

Darkness was approaching. I didn't have any idea how far we had to go to get to the village. I was exhausted, but I couldn't even sit down to rest as I knew there would be blood-sucking insects waiting for me. Toga sensed my tiredness and quickly surged ahead looking for something that only he could find. He returned then led us to a crude shelter where we could spend the night. "Why is this shelter here?" I asked. "It has to be far from the village."

"Harvest *ngali* nuts," Togo answered. "Rain comes, people use shelter."

"I'm glad it's here. I'm glad you found it."

I retrieved my back-pack and slipped into the darkness while Toga built a fire. His wife began heating water to cook one of the packages of rice. When I was out of sight, I attended to my toilet duties then removed my filthy, sweaty socks, tee-shirt, and shorts. I used them to dry my then naked body. I put on clean, dry clothes and joined Togo and his family by the small, crackling fire.

We listened to the night sounds and watched the same twinkling stars that Solomon Islanders had been watching for centuries. I felt very satisfied and peaceful. Soon, we all fell asleep in our *ngali* nut shelter. I slept long and deeply and woke knowing the sun would have been visible had it not been for the heavy foliage.

We continued our trip toward the village to the screeching of parrots, warblers, and cockatoos. We followed the narrow dirt footpath that usually ran straight up and down the mountains. The path occasionally deviated to go around large trees or large stones. In many spots, the slick mud made it difficult for me to stay upright. Toga quietly moved ahead and darted into the bush.

He soon returned with a green nut, about the size of an English walnut. He broke it open to reveal a black, paint-like, pasty liquid. He dipped a small stick into the thick liquid then painted a cross on his chest. I watched with interest. "What is that, Toga?" I asked.

"*Tita*," Toga answered.

"Why are you making crosses on yourself with *tita*?"

"Afraid *debil*," he explained. "Might kill me because I left him."

He continued to paint crosses in various places on his body during the two hours it took us to reach the village. I was surprised to see over two-hundred people as the village would likely only house thirty people. Many of the men were busy with various tasks. None of them paid any attention to us despite me being the only white man that had ever been in the village. Toga and his family were known Christians making us even more of an oddity. "Why are so many people here?" I asked Toga.

"Here for ceremony," he answered.

"What is going to happen at the ceremony?" I asked, fearful of his coming answer.

"Many dances. Father sacrifice pigs to *debil*. Can't stay. Me Christian. Afraid *debil* make me die. Find William. He brother burned house."

Toga soon found his brother and introduced us. William had worked for a logging company in Western Province for several years. He spoke Pisin very well. Toga was obviously nervous. It was the first time that he had been in the village for several years. I recognized the extreme sacrifices that were being made to allow me to be there. "I go now," Toga said. "Afraid *debil*."

Toga and his family started down the path from which we had just came. I felt sick to my stomach. I believed that the ceremony had been organized for my benefit. I had asked Bo'ogo on several occasions to invite me to his village, so I could participate in their primitive lives.

Since Bo'ogo's Pisin skills were limited and I couldn't speak Begau, I was rightfully fearful that he had understood me to say that I would pay to observe a unique, Begau ceremony. I knew that the news of Greg Grainger's trip to Laulasi and his payment of thousands of dollars would have spread throughout Malaita and half of the Solomon Islands by this time.

I thought it was very likely that I was going to be expected to pay thousands of dollars, because I had asked for this ceremony. I feared that I would be held captive until someone paid a huge ransom to free me. I feared worse. I couldn't decide if my fear came from potential scrutiny by the deceased, paramount ancestor, or from my belief that a major event had been organized for my personal benefit.

I couldn't think of anything I could do better my situation. I couldn't possibly pay if I was expected to fund the upcoming ceremony. I longed for the relative safety and security of my modest home in Auki. I longed for the relative safety and security of the *ngali* nut shelter.

I was no longer interested in learning any more about Solomon Islands' traditional culture. I accomplished a pathetic look without any effort. "Does the paramount chief want payment from me for being here?" I asked William.

"Me ask later."

William, wearing shirt and hat,
watches the ceremonies

William drifted away leaving me to ponder my predicament. After some time passed, I saw William approach an elderly gentleman wearing a sailor's cap. After a brief conversation, William returned with news. I cringed in anticipation. "Chief Tomama said you guest," William said. "You no pay. If take pictures, pay forty dollars, give chief copy."

Relief. Profound relief is the only way to describe my emotions. I was ready to dance, run about, scream, and shout with joy. However, such overt displays would have been totally unacceptable in the Solomons. I quickly gave

William forty Solomon dollars. This display was totally acceptable in the Solomons. "Give this money to the chief," I said. "Tell him that I'll give him copies of the pictures when I get them developed."

The relief I felt was overwhelming. I was not likely to be sacrificed to the *debil* in lieu of pigs. I wandered freely around the village taking pictures. Every person was interesting in their own way and I captured many on film. People, dogs, and chickens, with traditional houses in the background made unique photography opportunities.

Women watch the ceremonies

The houses themselves with the forest as a background were worthy of photographs. Women and girls gathered some distance away from men's activities. I paid them scant attention, but I did snap a few pictures without benefit of a zoom lens. Most of them wore skirts, but many were bare-chested.

"Women usually naked," William informed me.

Most rifles appeared old, but
this one appeared to be a more
modern shotgun

"Why are they dressed today?" I asked.

"Because you here."

A few of the on-lookers carried ancient rifles. The original owners had likely brought them back from Australia during the black-birding period. Naturally, I took pictures. Owning rifles was contrary to Solomon law, but there were no policemen with enough courage to travel to Begau country to disarm them. If the weapons were from black-birding days, I though it unlikely that they would have powder that would allow them to shoot.

Begau men dance in
traditional regalia

Dancers were accompanied
by panpipes

The dancing soon started with only men performing. The dancers were in formation and they kept time to the beat of a rhythmic cadence. Some made loud, booming sounds by striking the end of a large piece of bamboo with a coconut husk as they danced.

The men danced in a semi-stooped position, legs flexed, while simultaneously shuffling their bare feet making a unique dance.

During the activities, William informed me this celebration was second highest in rank of four distinct ceremonies. The fourth, and lowest, ranking ceremony allowed women to participate. Women danced with women in this fourth ceremony. Men also participated in the fourth ceremony and performed their own distinct dances. Dances in the third ceremonies were performed only by men. These two, lower-ranking ceremonies were performed when payment was made by a native seeking special favor from the deceased ancestor.

Payment of shell money, pigs, or Solomon dollars was made to Paramount Chief Tomama who performed the ceremony.

Occasionally, individual property, like a chain saw, was given in payment. I thought the chief was more deserving of an additional title of pagan priest. "What about this ceremony that we're watching?" I asked.

"Special one," William answered. "Number two. Done for *debil* Sometimes, chief sees *debil* in dream. *Debil* tells chief make sacrifice. Chief must pay everything. Must pay pigs. Must pay dancers. Cost plenty."

I was very interested in what I was learning about Begau culture. I wanted to understand as much as I could. "What is the first, the highest, ceremony about?" I asked, continuing my questioning.

Paramount Chief Tomama

Chief Tomama directs
sacrificial activities

"Don't know. No one knows. Only paramount chief and *debil* know."

"What will happen after the dancing we're watching is finished?"

"Chief sacrifice pigs to *debil*."

The dancing continued. I couldn't distinguish one dance from the next, but I was confident that each was unique and was being performed for a special purpose. When Paramount Chief Tomama was satisfied that the ancestor was satisfied, we moved to the sacrificial area. There, six pigs were bound, awaiting their own necessary part in the ceremonies.

Men began the process of killing the pigs by tightly wrapping their snouts with vines in a centuries-old butchering method. I moved about taking picture as the pigs struggle mightily and breathed their last breaths. "$#*tabu*\*&^%^) *tabu* +_@@!" came a sharp command in Begau from one of the men.

"Don't go there!" was William's sharp translation in Pisin. "*Tabu!*"

I immediately stopped my progress and retreated. Taboo is the English word that evolved from the South Pacific *tabu*. Of course, taboo in English means forbidden. However, the original word, *tabu*, means sacred. The *tabu* area was indistinguishable from other areas in the sacrificial area where I had been moving about without incident. I believed then, and still believe, that this was a special location where men had been sacrificed and eaten in earlier years. I could think of nothing else that would give this place its sacred standing.

In due time, the pigs were cut into pieces and wrapped in bananas leaves. Holes had been previously dug and fires had been allowed to burn to coals in the bottom of the shallow pits. The meat was wrapped in banana leave and placed in the umus with vegetables. The umus were then covered with dirt allowing the food to bake like had been done in Laulasi.

The ceremony was an all-day event and I moved about freely. Boys ran abound laughing and screaming. Several played with balloons created from blown-up pig bladders. Dogs and chickens hid from the unusual ruckus. The women and girls maintained a respectful distance.

William was often near to answer questions for me. The paramount chief was old, so I thought to learn who would succeed him. "William, who will be made chief when the old man dies?" I asked.

Elders watched the ceremonies

I expected him to name Bo'ogo, himself, or one of the chief's other brothers. Perhaps one of the chief's sons would become the new paramount chief. His answer came as a complete surprise. "Not decided," William answered.

"When will it be decided?" I asked.

"After old chief dies."

"How will the secret ceremony be passed on to the new chief?" I thoughtfully asked. "How will the new chief be chosen?"

"*Debil* give secret in sleep to some man," William informed me. "Man knows, do number one, secret ceremony. Be paramount chief."

"What if someone pretended to get the secret in a dream?"

William was obviously shocked by my question. "No one dare!" he exclaimed. "*Debil* kill him!"

"What if the *debil* doesn't give the secret ceremony to anyone?" I asked.

"Everyone convert Christianity," William answered, with a shrug.

I seized the opportunity to ask another question about ancient customs. "I read in books about the time Solomon Islanders hunted heads and ate men," I began. "Many men have told me that they were the first in their line that hadn't eaten human flesh. When I ask Kwara'ae men, they say they don't know any details. Do you know the customs when old Begau ate men?"

"I know," William answered, showing no emotion.

"Well, I read about a man named Kwaisulia," I said. "Kwaisulia meant Cut-off-Bits. The book said he had that name because he liked to capture an enemy and take him to a special place. Then he tied him up and cut off pieces of flesh while the enemy was still alive. Did old Begau men do this?"

"Begau man did this," William answered, matter-of-factly.

His eyes grew wide. His nostrils flared. He spoke quicker. "Many Begau catch man," William said. "Tie him, carry on pole. Call him long pig. Take special place for killing."

William went on to tell me that the customs of cannibalism were very serious affairs. Only men in certain families practiced the custom. William provided me with answers to all my questions. Sometimes, he told me what I had read was correct. Other times, he told me what I had read was not the Begau custom. On those occasions, he informed me what Begau had done. "I read about ramos in old books," I said. "Did Begau have ramos like Kwara'ae and Kwaio?"

"Begau have ramos," he answered. "Lead in wars. Man sometimes pay ramo to kill man."

We continued our discussion of Begau customs generally and ramos specifically. William told me many things that I had not read in books. "Begau have secret woman, kill ramo," William told me. "Special Begau woman kill ramo."

"I never read anything about women killing ramos," I said. "How did women kill ramos?"

William explained that Begau tribes occasionally trained a young woman for assassination duties. Ramos were often hated and a contract to kill one would command a high price. The training was secret, so that ramos didn't know about the special woman. Ramos were naturally suspicious of everyone. The suspicion made it difficult for a man to get close enough kill a ramo.

The young woman was trained to perform sexual acts in the manner of a prostitute. When the ramo utilized the special services and was sexually satisfied, he would go to sleep. The woman would kill him by smashing in his head with a special club. "What kind of special club did she use?" I asked.

"Small club," William answered gesturing with his hands. "Short handle. Big head."

The description sounded like the club that I found in Dr. Marissa's house when we first came to Auki. I drew a full-size likeness in the dirt. "Did the club look like this?" I asked.

"Look like that," William answered, nodding his head. "Woman carry in sleeping mat."

William and I continued our conversation. He told me of another custom that I hadn't read about. "Eating man serious," he told me. "Go special place."

William told me that a man would occasionally be overcame by the gravity of eating human flesh and feel he had to vomit. Vomiting would be interpreted as a rejection of the custom and of the members who were participating. Even though the vomiting man would be a friend and relative, others would be obligated to kill him for his offence.

The tragedy could be averted by a quick-thinking good friend or brother. If a man were seen to be ready to vomit, a brother could act. The brother would place his mouth to the mouth of the one ready to vomit. When vomit came, the receiving brother would catch and consume the vomit. This selfless act mitigated the offending act of vomiting.

The custom seemed to be well-known among the Begau men. William told me that any argument might escalate to fighting words. "You're not fit to eat the vomit of your brother!" might be uttered, in the heat of the argument. This was a grave insult that might end in physical violence.

The pigs were not completely cooked as darkness approached. William escorted me to a men's house where I thought I would spend the night. It was nearly dark when I climbed the steep steps to enter. The steps had been hewn from a small log about eight inches in diameter.

I had to tread carefully lest I fall on the slippery footing. The one-room house was built on stilts and stood about four feet above the uneven ground. The poles were connected with jungle material to form a pen beneath the house. The pen held several small pigs. I was seated among the Begau men. It soon turned completely dark, preventing me from seeing anything. There was no lamp or candle and certainly no electric lights.

The floor was constructed from strips of bamboo lashed together with vine harvested from the nearby forest. There were gaps in the floor up to an inch wide in some places. Native pigs grunted contentedly from their pen below the house. Their odor added to the uniqueness of my experience. Bo'ogo was one of the men present.

I sat cross-legged on the floor in the crowded room. I was confident that all the other men were also setting cross-legged. It was culturally mandated for men to keep their legs close to themselves. If a man stepped across the legs of another man, it was tantamount to asserting that stepper was having sex with the sitter's wife. Violation of this cultural observance by Solomon men would result in immediate violence. Seated men always arranged their legs to avoid awkward situations. I didn't ever want to learn what would happen if a white man violated the same norm.

Someone gave me something to eat from one of the six pigs that had been sacrificed that day. I couldn't see well enough to know if it was Bo'ogo who gave me the meat, nor could I see well enough to identify the food. I took a bite, but I still couldn't tell what it was. I thought that it might be pig lung from the texture and the odd taste.

I had previously been given many rather exotic foods in Solomon villages and had eaten everything. I wasn't squeamish about eating something without knowing what it was, but I didn't want to swallow the bitter mass that was in my mouth. I certainly didn't want to offend my hosts.

I imagined they could see me despite the darkness. I suspected that every man in the one-room house was watching me as I may have been the only white man some of them had ever seen. I put more "pig-meat" to my lips and spat what was in my mouth into my hand. I cupped my hand and lowered it into my lap. In due time, I silently slid my finger to locate an open space between the bamboo slats. When I found a wide enough space, I dropped the "meat" through the floor to the pigs that were living below.

The men exchanged pleasantries using grunts and minimal words. I knew they were smoking village-grown tobacco from the unique smell of the smoke. The fragrance added to the unique olfactory stimulation of pigs and unwashed bodies. I could hear lime sticks being dipped into lime boxes as they chewed betel nuts. Rain fell softly on the thatched roof.

Dropping the "pig meat" between the slats to the pigs living below didn't create any stir. I believed that my action went unnoticed. The men smoked, chewed betel nut, and exchanged brief comments. In due time, several of us moved through the light rain to the men's sleeping house.

The sleeping house was built flat on the ground with little thought given to site selection. There were sleeping platforms on the two, long sides. Each platform was about ten inches off the ground and could hold about nine or ten men. The center section was packed dirt with a large stone protruding from the ground.

It was possible that the stone had magic powers and had been placed there for some purpose. The ground had not been leveled requiring we sleepers to rest on a slight slope. I would have preferred to spend the night near the small fire in the *ngali* nut shelter. Despite the unaccustomed accommodations, I did manage to sleep.

Crowing roosters woke me before sunrise. Most of the men had already left the sleeping area. The village was virtually empty. I was given some of the pork from yesterday's sacrifices for my breakfast. Toga waited for me at the edge of the village as I said my good-byes. He escorted me back to his house following the same path.

During our trip, I asked Toga more about Begau customs during the earlier days of headhunting and cannibalism. He confirmed information that William had given me and provided information on other customs. "William told me about the custom of tying up a captive and cutting off bits of flesh while he was alive," I said. "Do you know about the custom?"

Togo smiled and raised his brow to signify he knew. "I read about it in an old book," I continued. "The book said the victim was sometimes forced to eat some of his own flesh."

Togo looked at me incredulously but didn't speak. "Did Begau men do this, I asked?"

Toga and family outside his house

"No!" Togo said angrily. "No, never! Book lie!"

When we got to his house, I rested for some time, then we continued to the road. I didn't have wait too long before a provincial truck came in to view.

The truck had a canvas cover that enclosed the front and sides of the truck bed. I recognized the driver as Abel who was married to our house girl, Betty.

Abel's daughter and a woman I didn't know rode in the cab with Abel.

Abel stopped and motioned for the woman in the cab to get out. I got into the cab while the woman climbed onto the truck bed with other Solomon Islanders. I settled myself in the cab without comment, as I fully understood the Malitian custom.

We continued down the road without speaking. We had traveled about eighteen or twenty miles when the truck started drifting to the left. I looked toward Abel who was looking at me with a puzzled look. He turned the steering wheel to correct the direction of travel, but the truck continued to drift to the left. Abel quickly applied the brakes and continued to try to correct the direction of travel.

The truck's speed had slowed considerably by the time it began leaving the road. I quickly pulled his daughter to my chest and turned my back to the dashboard. The truck ran completely off the road and came to an abrupt stop in a small creek. No one was seriously hurt, but those in the back were shaken more than those of us in the cab. Abel and I looked under the truck and saw that a tie rod had become disconnected making the truck impossible to steer.

We all waited until a market truck appeared. The driver stopped, and we all piled on top of the bags of copra that were being hauled. I was not offered a ride in the cab this time. It was dusk when we arrived at Margaret's Store. I walked home where Paula greeted me with hugs and kisses. I related brief parts of my latest adventure. I took a cold shower and headed to bed. My bed was very welcome after my Begau sleeping arrangements.

I didn't make a report to Paul because my trip didn't have any relationship to my job. Paul didn't approve of me associating with pagan people as he was a devout Christian. He never asked me anything about the trip. I didn't talk much about the trip, but many Solomon Islanders and expatiates soon knew. They were surprised that I had been invited to travel to a Begau village since I was associated with the Kwara'ae tribe.

I wrote articles about my unique experience and submitted them, with pictures, to a few Kansas newspapers. The articles were published and picked up by other newspapers. Some pictures were not used because they were deemed more appropriate for *National Geographic*.

I had the film developed and had copies made for the paramount chief. The pictures came from the U.S. in due time. The next time I saw Bo'ogo, I gave him the pictures for delivery to his brother. Bo'ogo continued to stop by my house occasionally with Begau artifacts that I eagerly acquired.

# CHAPTER 18

# *Training in Western Province*

Eric Mason invited Alison, Colin, Paula, and me to his house for dinner. During our delicious meal, Eric informed us we were eating millionaire salad. The salad featured the heart of a coconut palm, thus the palm had to be destroyed for the sake of the one salad. He told us about an incident years ago during which a group he was with had captured and killed a large crocodile.

We exchanged opinions about what was happening in the world generally and Malaita specifically. I gave a brief synopsis of my failed efforts to visit the pagan Kwara'ae. "I heard you also went to a Begau village," Eric said. "Did you have any trouble?"

"It was hard physically, but I didn't have any trouble," I answered. "I didn't understand many of the things I experienced. The ancient practices they told me about and the ceremonies that I saw are better suited for an anthropologist to understand and explain. I took a lot of pictures."

"I've lived in the Solomon Islands for over twenty years. I don't know how you could be invited to a Begau village. You're associated with the Kwara'ae. These Malitian tribes just don't mix. The old customs of headhunting and cannibalism are still in the minds of the current generations."

"Other expatriates told me similar things. It's never been an issue."

Later in the evening, Eric returned to the subject of me visiting pagan communities. "You have a lot of friends who are devout Catholics," he said. "Have any of them ever said anything about you associating with pagans?"

"I haven't had any feedback from expatriates," I said. "Paul Kennioriana doesn't like me associating with non-Christians, but he's the only Solomon Islander who has said anything about it."

We had surprise visitors the next day. Paula was working on a S.P.A. grant application for a sewing project for Dala women. I was attempting to repair a manual typewriter. John and Lottie from Apico appeared. We exchanged greetings and hugs then Lottie brought up the issue for their visit. "Did you get our letter?" she asked. "We're on our way to Honiara for our early service conference."

"We didn't get a letter from you," Paula answered. "When did you mail it?"

"I don't remember the date, but it was the end of October."

"Today is November 12, so it must have been over two weeks ago."

"In our letter, we asked if you would make arrangements in a nearby village for us to do a nutrition workshop," John said.

"Sorry, we didn't get the letter," I said. "We don't have anything set up for your workshop. Anyway, we're happy to see you. Of course, we want you to spend your time in Auki with us. I'll have to borrow a bed from Camerons. I'll go see Colin now."

Colin loaned us a bed and helped me carry it to our house. He met John and Lottie for the first time and stayed for supper. "It's too bad that we didn't get your letter," I said. "Anyway, a day off for you to rest should be welcome."

"Since we don't have anything organized for a nutrition workshop, I have another idea," Paula said. "We're going to Dala to put on a parliamentary procedure workshop. Would everyone like to go with us?"

John, Lottie, and Colin agreed to help us. I gave them scripts that we used for these events and we chose our parts. "I'm glad you're willing to go," I said. "Glen and Katherine are staying with Bill Wasser, but they didn't want to go. Glen said they didn't want to interfere with our projects."

The workshop went well without any thought that anyone was interfering. Everyone made good actors and actresses. We returned to Auki for another joint supper. Bill Wasser joined us and entertained us with a juggling act after our meal. "Bill, did you take any vacations outside of the Solomon Islands during your first tour?" John asked.

"I didn't leave the Solomons," Bill answered. "I thought about going to New Zealand, but I never made it."

"Lottie and I are thinking about a trip to New Zealand. It's not so far and we don't think we'll ever have a better opportunity."

"Charlie and I went to Australia once," Paula added. "I think a vacation to New Zealand would be nice."

We walked Lottie and John to the wharf the next day for their trip to Honiara. We went to our office after we waved good-by. I worked on an article for the *Malaita Nius*. Paula worked on her S.P.A grant for Dala women. We walked home in the rain, had supper, turned in for a good night's sleep.

A crowing rooster woke us very early Wednesday morning. "What is that stupid bird crowing about?" Paula asked. "It's four in the morning, it's dark, and it's raining."

I had no answer for her. A rooster crowing at 4:00 a.m. in the rain wasn't the strangest occurrence that we had seen in the Solomons. The rooster crowed again, triggering affirmative action. Paula leapt from the bed and stomped out of the house. The ensuing commotion convinced me that that Paula had vanquished the rooster to a different location.

I heard her reenter the house and stomp into the bathroom. She washed her muddy feet in the cold shower, then began cleaning the floor where she tracked in mud. I got up and we quickly cleaned up the mud. We went back to bed and managed to get back to sleep.

Paula and I continued discussing the possibility of a vacation in New Zealand. We soon decided we would take the vacation. We sent a letter to Paula's mother telling her of our plans. We wrote that we would write a check on our Kearny County Bank account to pay for our initial expenses. We began scheduling our flight and applying for visas. We also wrote to Dr. Arun and Elaine Menon in Dunedin to tell them we were coming to New Zealand.

We had another surprise when we picked up our mail at the Auki Post Office. We received notification that our Global 500 nomination for the Seanaua Association's had been successful. The Global 500 winners were to be recognized in Rio do Janeiro, Brazil at a United Nations Conference on Environment and Development. Representatives from the Seanaua Association were invited to attend, but there was no funding provided.

We didn't pursue efforts to get funding as the ceremonies were scheduled to be held in the near future.

Paula and I had a visit scheduled in Dukwasi Village that week. We planned to go to Dukwasi sometime in the future to see the Riba Cave, but our purpose for this visit was a needs assessment. The villagers had prepared a feast for us after our survey. We asked for permission for our group of expatriates to visit the Riba Cave in the future. The chief graciously consented.

Bill Wasser came over that evening "I got a call from the Peace Corps office today," he said. "They were calling for you, but you didn't answer your phone. There's an inspector general coming to the Solomon Islands from Washington, D.C. Have you heard about him coming?"

"No, we didn't know that," I answered. "Why is he coming here?"

"They didn't say, but I suppose it over squabbles between Jimmie and Gus. Anyway, his name is Steve and he's arriving November 22. They wanted to see if you could pick him up at the airport."

"It seems Peace Corps is willing to ignore its own rule about volunteers not driving when they need something. Anyway, Paula and I are going to Honiara November 23. We've been asked to help with and early-service conference and a mid-service conference for other groups. But we'll be here to talk to him November 22. I'll ask Colin if I can borrow his car. What does the inspector general do?"

"It's an important job. He reports directly to Congress and the Peace Corps director. He keeps them informed about Peace Corps programs and operations. Maybe someone made complaints about something in the Solomon Islands."

"We've heard rumors there are conflicts between Jimmie and Gus," Paula said. "Making Jimmie acting director when John Mark left might have made it hard for Jimmie to accept not being in charge when Gus came. Maybe that's what it's all about."

Bill grew serious and changed the subject. "Do you remember when I stopped in a while back?" he asked. "It was late in the evening."

"I think I know the time you're talking about," I answered. "You didn't say too much, and you didn't stay too long."

"Well, that was the night that there were six or seven Malitians after me. They thought I had whacked up their dog with a bush knife."

"They just thought you had whacked up a dog with a bush knife?" I asked. "I remember you telling us about the priest in Isabel trying to teach you to kill dogs with a bush knife. Come on now, level with me. Did you really whack up the dog?"

"I didn't do it," Bill protested. "I don't know what made them think I did."

I was a little suspicious about how several Malitians could erroneously think that Bill had tried to dispatch the dog with such crude methods. We civilized expatriates used chloroquine as a canine population control method. Bill and I continued our conversation about Malitian customs when responding to unusual events. "Did you hear about the Korean logger that hit a Malitian with his truck?" Bill asked.

"I don't think so," Paula answered. "Did it happen recently?"

"Not too long ago. The guy works for Marvin Brothers Timber Company. The Korean was driving back to the logging camp. It was dark, and he ran over a Malitian who stepped out in front of the truck. The Malitian was trying to get him to stop, so he and his friends could get a ride. The man was killed."

"Did the Korean stop after the accident?" I asked. "I remember Solomon Islands' Pisin instructors telling me not to stop in a situation like that. They said if I ever had an accident, I should keep going and get to the nearest police station as quickly as I could."

"He didn't stop. He drove back to his logging camp as fast as he could. The Malitians followed him. The guy was afraid he would be killed. He locked himself in a metal storage building. He stayed locked up until the logging company made compensation payments to the family of the guy that had been killed."

"Bill, I know you've been to Kwaio villages at least twice," I said, changing the subject. "What were your experiences?"

"I was in two different villages," Bill said. "I went to the first one to do the preliminary survey for a water project. It was pretty straight forward, but there was one strange thing that happened."

"What was the strange thing?"

"I was there three days and two nights. I had to sleep in the men's house. When I started to go into the house, there was a Kwaio sprawled on the steps. I had to squeeze by him to get into the house."

"Why didn't he move?"

"It was attitude. He was wearing blue jeans, a blue jean jacket, and sunglasses. He had a red bandana tied around his head. I found out later that he had killed a man in Honiara and ran back to his village, so the police couldn't get him."

"Andrew told me that he was in a Kwaio village with you. He complained that you insisted on doing a preliminary engineering survey even though it was apparent that the project wasn't feasible. What about that trip?"

"Andrew was right. We got there and could quickly see that the village was above the water source. To make a gravity system work, we would have had to make water to run up-hill."

"So why did you do the engineering study?"

"I was afraid to tell the Kwaio that it wasn't going to work. We did a preliminary survey and got the hell out of there."

We spent the next few days working on reports for our S.P.A. grants. We received a letter from Menon's inviting us to spend a few days with them while we were in New Zealand. They included their address and telephone number. We wrote back and told them we would likely be in Dunedin in late February and said we would call.

We occasionally worked at home when we needed privacy. Solomon men often stopped in our office just to visit making it difficult to complete what we were working on.

We had two earthquakes while were working at home. One registered 6.2 on the Richter Scale and the other registered 5.6. They didn't do any damage in Auki and there was no tsunami. Our house was considerably above sea level, so I wasn't ever very concerned about tsunamis.

Peace Corps Inspector General Steve arrived on November 22, as scheduled. I used Colin's and Alison's car to pick him up at the airport. Steve had a structured

Back row L to R Charlie, Moses Agougka, and George Toritelia. Three visitors came just to socialize

agenda and first wanted to interview Bill Wasser. After Steve visited with Bill, he came to our office. He didn't ask direct questions and we didn't volunteer any information. We told him that we were going to Honiara the next day. He stopped talking about Peace Corps when we agreed to meet with him there.

Steve wanted to see our S.P.A. grant projects, so we took him to Buma. We introduced him to Simon Ruarafi, Simon's brother Daniel, and other village leaders. I mentioned that Daniel served with the Americans in W.W. II and was decorated. We then went to Seanaua where we introduced Steve to Jim and Salamai. We picked strawberries while we were at Seanaua. "Your forestry projects are impressive," Steve commented, while picking strawberries. "What are you going to do next for these projects?"

"We don't have definite plans," I said. "Logging and timber production are new businesses to us. There is a volunteer program called Farmer-to-Farmer. We've sent an application for a forester."

"I know about the program," Steve said. "The organization sends American agriculture experts to help Peace Corps Volunteers. With the programs you have going, I'm confident that you have a good chance of being approved."

We finished picking strawberries and returned to Auki. We stopped by our house for a glass of iced tea. Steve told us a little bit about his job with the Peace Corps. We walked Steve to the Auki Lodge where he was to spend the night. Paula and I spent the evening packing for our trips to Honiara and Ugheli.

Colin had agreed to take care of our screeching parrots while we were away. When I went out to transfer them, both were dead. I suspected foul deeds had been committed to dispatch the fowl, but I didn't investigate. No harm, no foul. No foul, no fowl.

We flew to Honiara the next day and spent four additional hours with I.G. Steve. Again, he didn't ask any direct questions and we didn't volunteer any information. We ate supper at the Mendana Hotel then went to Jimmie's house to spend the night.

We played canasta while Jimmie told us about her being transferred. "I really tried to get along with Gus," she said. "He was impossible to work with. He was critical of everything I did. I was ready to resign. I informed my supervisors in Washington, D.C. that I was turning in my resignation."

I studied my cards carefully. I couldn't think of anything appropriate to say. Jimmie had paused and was waiting for a response. "I know you're being transferred," Paula said. "So what happened when you said you told them you were resigning."

"Peace Corps, D.C. authorities didn't want me to resign. That's why the Peace Corps I.G. came here. I was promised a transfer to another Peace Corps assignment if I would stick it out until they could find me a new assignment."

Jimmie didn't ask about our conversations with Steve and we didn't volunteer any information. Paula and I thought her new assignment would to be better than her current job as training officer in the Solomons. We were happy for her, and we wished her well.

We traveled to Vulelua Island the next day for Group 41's early service conference. Vulelua was owned by an Australian named Brendon. Brendon had been living on Vulelua for several years. He had a staff of about five or six local Solomon Islanders. We swam in the afternoon, or rather laid on a raft, and enjoyed the sun. We had a delicious Thanksgiving dinner with Group 41 including turkey and cranberry sauce.

We had an extraordinary talent show after dinner. John and Lottie performed a skit they called Camp Malaria. Glen and Katherine performed Shakespeare in Pisin. Dot and Jimmie performed one act plays and Nurse Mary sang a song. Others had equally interesting talents to share. A Solomon Islands' couple did a serious skit in which the man was a wife-beater. Wendy played three songs on her harmonica. Paula and I ended the contest with card tricks.

The consensus was that John and Lottie's malaria skit was great, but Glen's and Katherine's Shakespeare performance was the winner. We returned from Vulelua and worked in the Peace Corps office in the afternoon. We went to Jimmie's house after work. Group 41 came over to say good-by to Jimmie, but they soon left to go to another party.

We went to the Peace Corps office the next day and worked on flip charts. "This would be a good time to talk to Sam Alisha about the G.E.D. program," Paula said. "I could call him and see if he's available."

"I would like to see Sam," I said. "We're about done with these flip charts."

Paula made the call and was told that we should come as soon as we could. Sam was anxious to see us. I was pleased to think that maybe he had heard directly from G.E.D. officials in the U.S. "Come in, sit down," Sam greeted us, when we arrived. "I'm happy to see you. I have been wanting to talk to you."

We seated ourselves and exchanged pleasantries then Sam raised an unexpected issue. "I heard you have funding for a portable sawmill project for Buma," he said. "Is that true?"

"Yes, it's true," I said. "We've been working on the application for some time. We were recently notified that our application was successful."

"Good. I want you to transfer the project to Dala."

I was shocked. I peered at him to see if he was going to smile to let me know he was joking. He held my gaze without smiling. "Sam, are you serious?" I asked. "We can't transfer the project to Dala. Buma is approved, but we could apply for another project for Dala."

"I don't want a new project. I want you to transfer the project to Dala."

"I can't do that, Sam. I'll start on a new application for Dala as soon as we get back to Auki."

"No new project. If you don't transfer the project to Dala, I'll stop the G.E.D. program."

I was silent. I took time to compose my thoughts. "Sam, there's no connection between the sawmill project and the G.E.D. program," I argued. "The G.E.D. program isn't for Paula and me. It's to help Solomon people. You're the minister of education. I'm sure that you want to do everything you can to better the Solomon Islands' education system."

Sam and I exchanged views and opinions. Neither of us could see merit in the other's position. Paula and I left without expressing our true thoughts of Sam's unyielding stance. The Buma sawmill project remained in Buma and the G.E.D. program didn't come to the Solomon Islands.

Larry had a going away party for Jimmie at his house that evening. Most of the Honiara based volunteers were there. We talked to Bill Wise early in the evening. "There's a professional boxing match tomorrow," Bill said. "Tom and I are going. Would you like to go with us?"

"I would like to go," I answered. "I didn't even know the Solomon Islands had professional boxing."

"I haven't been to a match, but I heard there are some good boxers."

Paula agreed, and we made plans to meet them at the site of the match. We spent the night with Jimmie and accompanied her to the airport the next morning. We said our good-byes and wished her well. Paula got pro forma invoices for a sewing project grant she was working on. I spent the rest of the day at the Honiara National Library and Paula went shopping.

We went to the boxing match where a Solomon man fought a boxer with the moniker of Gentleman Jim. Gentleman Jim was from Fifi. He showed class in addition to boxing skills. It was a good match and I thought the Solomon Islander won. However, the three Solomon Islands' judges awarded the match to Gentleman Jim. Gentleman Jim immediately announced that he would give the Solomon fighter a rematch in Fiji.

After the match, a dapperly dressed white man was one of the first to leave. He was wearing a white suit, white shirt, black tie, white hat, and black shoes. He created a mild sensation by waving and bowing to the crowd as he slowly meandered toward the exit. "That's the Solomon Islands' director of prisons," Bill said. "He's English and is a known character."

There was a greater sensation when a powerfully built, young Solomon man confronted the prison director. He began to smack the director around the head and shoulders. The prison director didn't try to fight back, but only crouched and covered his head with his arms. The vigorous plummeting continued until two uniformed policemen appeared. They promptly apprehended the assailant and hustled him toward the exit. "They're going to beat the hell out of that guy when they get him outside," Tom opined.

We went to La Paruce for ice cream after the boxing match. We exchanged thoughts about our visits with the Peace Corps inspector general. We all agreed that he didn't ask direct questions, but he seemed satisfied to give us the opportunity to complain if we were so inclined. None of us admitted to offering any criticisms.

We took the opportunity to talk about our upcoming vacation to New Zealand. "Tom, Paula and I are going to go to New Zealand for a vacation in February," I said. "We'll need a couple of days in Honiara to make final preparations before we leave. Can we stay with you for a couple of days?"

"Of course, you can stay," Tom answered. "I always enjoy your company and I love Paula's cooking. It will be a good time for her to give me a haircut. When will you be here?"

"Our flight leaves on February 12. That's on a Wednesday. Could we come Monday and spend Monday and Tuesday with you?"

"I'm going to be in Isabel for work on those days. But you're welcome to stay at my house. You know where I keep my key."

Paula and I spent the night with Bill Wise. We got up early to get our places on the *Iu Mi Noa*. It was scheduled to leave at 7:00 a.m. for our trip to Ughele, Western Province.

Trip to Ughele on *Iu Mi Noa*
Photo courtesy Paul & Monique Hartman

Most of the trainees were also on the ship. Paula and I entertained Solomon children with card tricks during our voyage. The trip took about twenty-four hours, and we didn't get much sleep.

We arrived at Ugheli early in the morning and were greeted with a welcome ceremony. Everyone was assigned a host family. Our host family lived on a small island separate from the mainland. The host parents were a young couple with a four-year old daughter named Waba. Waba had luxurious, wavy hair and was already wearing shorts. The host father's adult sister also lived with them.

We had the use of a small canoe when we needed to travel to the main island. Two new trainees, Howard and Dee, arrived the next day. Howard and Dee were a married couple and were assigned to live with the same host family. One of the trainees soon began taking a special interest in our host's sister. The trainee joined us for evening meals several times.

Terry Marshall was the training director. He had previously been the country director in the Solomon Islands, so he spoke Pisin and understood Solomon customs. Joseph, our group's logistics coordinator, had been replaced by a young Polynesian man named Marou. There was a beautiful, young Pisin instructor from Sulufou. Sulufou was the artificial island east of Malaita that hosted John Renton for seven years. Pisin Instructor Ephraim from our own training had returned.

Monique Incitti's host family. L to R Angelo, Jonath, Nolay & Mayokay
Photo courtesy Paul & Monique Hartman

There were about thirty trainees in the group. Monique Incitti, Dean Winchell, Tony Glucksman, and David Duane were going to be assigned to Malaita. A few trainees were going to be assigned to Vanuatu. Paul Hartman was among those going to Vanuatu.

Paula and I began our duties in the kitchen preparing morning and afternoon tea and snacks. The snacks included navy biscuits, jelly, and peanut butter. We were to teach the trainees about gardening, use of hand tools, how to make nurseries, and nutrition needs for themselves and Solomon Islanders. I also wanted to teach them how to gauge how much propane was left in a tank and how to butcher chickens. I ordered six chickens for my butchering lesson.

The butchering lesson began early the next morning. David Lally, Leigh Lally, Monique Incitti, Dean Winchell, Tony Glucksman, David Duane, Paul Hartman, Fred Anderson, Dave Gogliana, and David Johnson were among those present. I had boiled water ready for scalding the chickens to make them easy to pluck. I also had a small ax that some people might want to use to begin the procedure. "This training is voluntary," I began. "If you don't want to kill chickens or see them killed, you don't have to stay."

None of the assembled trainees left. I demonstrated my own chicken killing style by gathering the wings and legs then placed the chicken's head on the ground. I laid a stout stick over the neck of chicken. I put one foot on each end of the stick and pulled quickly. The chicken was separated from its the head with little drama. I then plunged the chicken into the hot water for scalding. I quickly plucked the chicken to demonstrate my craft prowess. "Who would like to try next?" I asked.

"I would," one of the men answered.

He gathered the wings and legs per my excellent instructions. However, he only put one foot on the stick then pulled. The poor chicken's head slipped out the unsecured end.

The injured bird managed to free its wings and began fighting and flopping. I helped get the chicken under control and back to its proper position. This time, he put both feet on the stick and was successful. He scalded the bird and participated in plucking. "Who would like to try next?" I asked.

"I would," Fred Anderson answered. "I'll show you how I do it."

Fred gathered the wings and legs in the approved manner. He laid the head and neck on a block, took the small ax, and tried to chop off the head. His aim was poor, and he only took off about a third of the head. This chicken also struggled, flopped, and freed its wings. I again helped get the chicken under control and assisted in better, and complete, head removal. The scalding and plucking proceeded without further drama. The rest of the trainees performed their butchering properly, much to my relief.

Paula organized a banana cake baking demonstration for the Ugheli women. She and Margaret Ottinger had a like demonstration in Langa Lau in our own training. There were ample bananas for the cake. Paula got the other ingredients from the Peace Corps larder. She baked the cake in a traditional stone oven. As in Langa Lau, the Ugheli women enjoyed the lesson and relished the banana cake.

Many of the same problems we had in our training village of Langa Lau were being repeated. Someone from the Peace Corps negotiated with Ugheli village leaders to install water seals. The leaders took the money, but they didn't build all the toilets.

Terry Marshall repeated Jimmie Wilkerson's failed efforts to compel the villagers to perform. "I've talked the village leaders every day since we've been here," he said. "They promised they would get them built soon."

"Water seal toilets are easy to build," Howard interjected. "I could show some of the other trainees what to do. Let's just get the shovels, and get the job done!"

"That's a political statement!" Marshall exclaimed. "I don't know if it's right on not, but that's a political statement."

I joined other listeners who were exchanging puzzled looks as to how Howard's comment could be construed as a political statement. No further progress was made building water seal toilets by either the trainees or the villagers. No one identified any other political statements.

Our host family members were Seventh Day Adventists, so their sabbath was on Saturdays. We went to church with them then spent the rest of the weekend resting and reading. We didn't make a canoe trip to the main island to socialize with other Americans.

We had been in Ugheli for a week and thought things were going well. We talked to Terry Marshall about staying longer. Terry liked the idea and managed to make radio contact with Gus, so Paula could talk to him. Paula told Gus everything was going well. "We would like to stay another week," Paula said. "Would that be all right?"

"Yes of course," Gus replied. "I'm glad everything is going well. You can stay the whole training time it you want. I'll contact Paul Kennioriana and tell him you'll be gone a while longer."

Most of the trainees were college educated, young men. They were cheerful, lively, and athletic. Many organized and played softball games and volleyball games. One of the trainees, Dave Gogliana, was quickly going native. He had begun going barefoot as soon as he had arrived in Ugheli. I noticed he was taking a special interest in the pretty, Pisin instructor from Sulufou.

Marou had formed an immediate friendship with the young daughter of a village leader. I noticed that he was discreetly filching some the peanut butter that we had for the trainees' snacks. I suspected the peanut butter was being used for presents to the girlfriend and her family. The supply of peanut butter was soon being depleted. Marou approached Paula and me with a solution. "Trainees using too much peanut butter," he told us. "You put peanut butter on biscuits. Trainees don't eat so much."

"I'm not about to do that!" I replied. "Those trainees are undergoing tremendous changes in their lives. They're under a lot of stress. If peanut butter makes their days go easier, peanut butter they shall have!"

"Don't have enough peanut butter. Eat too much peanut butter."

"The only reason that there isn't enough peanut butter is because you're stealing it! Get more peanut butter! I'll be happy to explain to Gus Comstock why you need more money for peanut butter!"

That ended our conversation about rationing peanut butter. I thought our cross-cultural exchanges were very beneficial. I also noticed that some of the ladies who had jobs preparing trainee lunches were discreetly taking some of it home for their families. These foodstuffs had been purchased with Peace Corps funds. No one suggested that we would have to begin rationing food for Peace Corps trainees' lunches. No harm, no foul.

A couple of days later, I didn't see Ephraim during the breaks or at lunch. I broached the subject that evening with Howard and Dee. "I noticed that Ephraim wasn't in the village today, Howard," I said. "Do you know where he is?"

"I know he's gone, but no one said anything about why he left," Howard answered.

"We're kind of out of the loop," Dee added. "Living on this island away from the main village doesn't give us much chance to learn what's going on."

Our host family organized a canoe trip to Munda for Howard, Dee, Paula and me. Munda was the largest settlement on the island of New Georgia in Western Provence. It was located at the southwestern tip of New Georgia and consisted of several villages. The world famous Roviana Lagoon was just offshore.

We stopped at a small island on the way back. The local name for the uninhabited island was Kasolo. Kasolo was where John Kennedy led his crew after their PT-109 was wrecked by a Japanese destroyer. Kasolo was better known as Kennedy Island. A small shrine dedicated to the Kennedy ordeal stood on the island. We spent some time taking pictures on Kennedy Island then returned to Ugheli.

Our host mother approached Paula as soon as we arrived. They left for some task while Howard and I discussed water seal problems. Paula was gone for most of the rest of the day. "Do you know who Waba is?" Paula asked me later.

"I know Waba," I answered. "She's our host family's little girl."

"Well, the little girl is a little boy. Our host mother had me give him a haircut. He said he wanted a haircut like yours. The haircut I gave him is the only one he's had in his life."

"Really? I thought Waba was a girl."

"I thought so too. His hair was full of head lice. They were jumping all over the place while I was cutting. I hope none of the nasty critters stay with me. The children wanted me to go swimming with them afterwards, so I did. It wasn't the best place for swimming. It's near the toilet beach, and they clean fish there."

Gus Comstock arrived unexpectedly and began a tour of Ugheli. He began by talking to Terry Marshall then talked to the Solomon staff members and some of the trainees. He eventually came to the kitchen where I was working. "Ephraim came back to Honiara a couple of days ago," Gus said. "He said things were a mess here and quit his job. What do you know about any problems?"

We left the kitchen, so we could talk more privately. "We have an issue over the water seal toilets," I said, "Someone from the Peace Corps negotiated with the Ugheli village leaders to install water seals. The leaders took the money, but they didn't build the toilets. We had the same problem when Paula and I trained in Langa Lau Village on Guadalcanal."

"Have the toilets been built?"

"Not all of them. Dee and Howard are staying with the same host family as Paula and me. Howard is an engineer and he wanted to take charge and build them. Terry Marshall discouraged it."

Gus paused, deep in thought. "I talked to Marou when I first got here," Gus said, as we walked. "He thinks that you don't respect him,"

"Marou thinks I don't respect him?" I rhetorically asked. "Let me be very clear about my opinion of Marou. I have absolutely no respect for him. I don't like him. He's stealing food that is supposed to go to the trainees. He's taken up with a young Ugheli woman. I think he's giving the Peace Corps food to her family to cater favor."

"Marou is the logistic coordinator. He's in charge of those things. You'll have do things to show you respect him."

"I'll show him respect when he earns it. I don't owe anyone respect because of a position they hold."

Gus and I continued our mini-debate. "There are other things to consider," Gus said. "Peace Corps' employment of host country nationals is designed for skills transfers. Marou will learn a lot with his employment with Peace Corps. Solomon Islanders go a long way to understand our own culture and accept our presence here."

What Gus said was logical. I couldn't think of an appropriate counter-argument. I felt I was losing our mini-debate, so I resorted to taking my ball and going home. "I think that Paula and I should leave as soon as we can make arrangements," I said.

"You don't have to do that," Gus said. "I really want you to stay. You and Paula are having a positive impact on the training."

"Thank you, but it's really time for us to leave. Christmas in coming soon, and we have our own projects in Malaita to take care of."

Gus spent another day in the village then returned to Honiara. I booked tickets on the *Yu Mi Nou* for our return trip to Honiara. Paula had another banana bread baking demonstration for village women. In the afternoon, we talked to a group of trainees about needs assessments, reforestation, and nutrition. We started packing to get ready to leave.

Several people came to see us off. Our host family gave us hats, a carved canoe, and two baskets of fresh fruit. Janelle and Fior gave us a carved wooden bowl. I was

grubby, so I took a shower in the men's, public shower area as soon as I got on the ship. I knew that it would soon be too messy for me to use. We didn't sleep much on our trip because it was too crowded to spread out.

One of the trainees, David Johnson, had decided to terminate his service and was on the ship with us. I talked to him during our trip, but I didn't ask why he was leaving. Paula broke out with impetigo during out trip. "I know how I got impetigo,"

Peace Corps Volunteers rebuild a bridge in Ughele
Photo courtesy Monique & Paul Hartman

180

she said. "I shouldn't have gone swimming with the children. Their swimming place is near the toilet beach, and they clean fish there."

"We can't do anything now," I said. "We can go the see Nurse Mary when we get to Honiara. I'm sure she will have something for it."

We arrived in Honiara after another twenty-four-hour trip. We bought tickets on the *Iu Mi Noa* to leave for Auki at 6:30 the next morning. We contacted Bill Wise to see if we could spend the night with him. "Of course, you can spend the night," Bill said. "I always enjoy your company. That will give me a chance to learn what is really going on in the Western Province training village."

Paula and I took turns looking after our things and running errands. Paula went to the Peace Corps office and saw Nurse Mary. Mary gave her a salve for the impetigo. We bought a turkey, cheese, and other goodies for everyone in Auki. We completed everything we needed to do and went to Bill's house. "Ephraim came back from the training village a few days ago," Bill said. "Ephraim told everyone that the training was a mess."

"I know that some of the villagers were pilfering Peace Corps food," I said. "I didn't think that was so terrible."

"Ephraim said that everyone hated Terry Marshall. He said that Marshall and one of the trainees were vying for the attention of one of the language instructors. Ephraim also said that several of the trainees were having sex with the village girls."

"Bill, if that was happening, I don't know about it. Paula and I weren't in the main village. We had to take a small canoe to get to our host family's house. I know that the logistics coordinator was also pilfering Peace Corps food. He was having a fling with the chief's daughter and was using peanut butter for presents to the family."

"Did Gus Comstock go to the village?"

"Gus was there. He didn't ask any direct questions about what I knew. If he had, Paula and I didn't know much. I did tell him that the logistics coordinator was stealing peanut butter, but Gus didn't seem too concerned."

"Some of that's acceptable in Solomon culture. I see it all the time in Honiara."

"I'm sure that aid donors factor that in when awarding aid. Gus must know that Nurse Mary is pilfering medicine and giving it to Solomon Islanders. But we're not out of medicine. No harm, no foul."

We stayed up late talking to Bill, but we managed to get up early enough to get to the dock to claim places on the *Iu Mi Noa*. The ocean was calm, but some Solomon Islanders still got sea-sick. We watched four dolphins swimming by our ship for considerable distance.

They matched the ship's speed and leapt completely out of the water as part of their playful antics. We arrived in Auki early in the afternoon and made it back to our house. We took showers, relaxed, played cards, and went to bed early. We wanted to be rested for the upcoming Christmas holidays.

# CHAPTER 19

# *Holidays in Auki 1991*

We didn't have much time to think about the friends we had made in Western Province as we quickly settled back into our normal routines. Dr. Teresa's parents, Joy and Peter Wells, came to visit the van den Bosch family soon after we returned to Auki. We met them at a party at the van den Bosch home. "My parents would like to see something outside of Auki," Dr. Teresa told me. "Would you take them to see Misuka's garden?"

"Of course," I answered. "We can go this coming Saturday."

Dr. Teresa let us use their four passenger Suzuki for the trip. The trail leading to Misuka's garden was steep and narrow. Traveling downhill to the garden in vehicles was always easy, but a long, steep hill sometimes made returning problematic. We traveled down the trail toward the vegetable garden through large patches of cocoa.

Jim and Salamai were there and proudly showed their garden. Joy and Peter took pictures of the garden. I used their camera to take pictures of them with Jim and Salamai. We bought vegetables and prepared for our return trip to Auki. I put the car in the lowest gear and started up the steepest part of the trail. I soon realized that the van den Bosch import lacked adequate horsepower to make it to the top.

We ground to a stop flanked on both sides by large, white, trumpet flowers. I held the brake and had everyone get out of the car. I then easily drove to the top of the hill. My passengers walked to the top, got back into the car, and we returned to Auki without any more trouble.

We went to mass the morning before Christmas to hear Father Jon's Christmas message. Paula spent the rest of the day baking. She made donuts to give to everyone for Christmas presents. She made and decorated a fruit cake for Dr. Teresa and made a gingerbread family for the van den Bosch children. "Let's take the baked goods to the van den Bosch family now," Paula suggested. "We're going to be busy tomorrow with Christmas dinner at Dr. Graham's and Sheila's house."

"I'll get my shoes on and I'll be ready," I answered.

We walked to the van den Bosch home and knocked on the door. Dr. Teresa came to the door holding Libby. "Come in," she said. "Paul is at work, but the children are here."

"I have something special for the children," Paula said.

Katie and Peter promptly joined us. "Look what I brought for you," Paula said. "This is a gingerbread family."

The children pushed in closer. "This is the father," Paula said, pointing to the largest one.

Peter and Katie smiled and waited for Paula to continue. "And this is the mother," she said, pointing to the next one. "Do you know who this is?"

"It me!" Katie said, laughing and clapping her hands.

"And who is this one?" Paula asked, pointing to a forth one.

"Me!" Peter said, laughing and clapping his hands.

"And who is this one? It looks like a baby."

"It's Libby!" they both shouted. "She's the smallest one."

"The children have something for you." Dr. Teresa said. "Give Paula and Charlie the present you made for them."

Katie left and soon returned with a handmade Christmas card. It was signed by the children. We chatted a bit then left for home. Paula continued with her baking tasks.

Paula and I began our Christmas Day celebration by opening presents from our friends. We went to mass and everyone came by after church for banana bread and coffee. There were twenty-two of us for dinner. We received a call from Mom Sellens and Chuck that evening.

Christmas dinner at Dr. Graham's and Sheila's. Colin, Alison, Masako, and Yasuo were among the twenty-two present

We called Jason and Mary the next day and wished them Merry Christmas. They said everything was going well. Mary held the phone to Ashley's ear, and we talked to her. Ashley didn't make a sound, but Mary said she smiled. Jason sounded happy and well.

Colin and Alison invited everyone to a New Year's Hogmanay party. Alison had a Scottish sausage called haggis. "Haggis is made from sheep's liver, heart, and lungs," she said. "It also has minced onions, oatmeal, and spices."

"Haggis was traditionally cooked and served in a sheep's stomach," Colin added, with a smile. "But this casing's probably artificial."

Most of us tried it, but few seemed to take any more than what was necessary to be polite. During our tasting, Colin told us that haggis is the national Scottish dish made famous by poet Robert Burns' poem: "Address to a Haggis."

Colin also told us about the famous Edinburgh's Hogmanay street parties. He said that people from around the world welcome in the New Year at one of the world's biggest and best outdoor parties. The parties feature live music, disk jockeys, street entertainment, and the ultimate fireworks display from Edinburgh Castle. We made sincere efforts to duplicate the extravagant Edinburgh's Hogmanay street parties. We ate, danced, and imbibed until 3:00 a.m. After a few hours of sleep, we felt well enough to share a champagne brunch with Alison, Colin, Robin, and Vickie on New Year's Day.

Tom Scherer called that evening to wish us happy new year. "If you're going to be home this weekend, I'd like to come visit you," he said. "I have a present for you."

"We're going to be home," I said. "What do you have for us?"

"I can't tell you. It's a surprise."

Tom did come and spend the weekend. He brought Vickie's lap top computer. "Vickie is going to the bush for several months," Tom said. "She'll be without electricity making her computer useless."

"Wow! That's great," I said. "Can you show me how to use it?"

"It's really easy. Vickie thought you two would be ideal volunteers to use the computer. You have electricity and you also have that dryer rigged up in your closet. She's worried about it getting damaged with mold."

"We'll keep it in the closet when we aren't using it."

"I have another present for you. I've lost too much weight to wear these slacks. You've lost enough weight, so that you can wear them."

I tried them on, and they were a good fit. We invited Eric Mason, Yoshimi, Alison, and Colin over for a spaghetti party. Colin had a lot of questions for Tom about his work at the clam farm. Yoshimi seemed to take a personal interest in Tom.

Paula and I had a surprise going away party for Bill Wasser that week. His third year was nearing completion, and he was leaving January 23. "It's really been nice knowing you," I said. "You've made great contributions for the Peace Corps and the Solomon Islands. Do you know where you are going to live when you get back to the States?"

"I don't have a job yet," Bill answered. "I'll write and let you know when I get settled in."

Dr. Paul and Dr. Teresa had another party that week. I enjoyed getting to talk to Dr. Teresa's father, Peter Wells. "I'd like to paddle a Solomon Islands' canoe sometime," Peter said, during our conversation. "I'm an accomplished canoeist. I would like to see how one of the dugouts handles. Can you make arrangements?"

"I'm sure I can," I said. "I'll come by Saturday morning. We can walk to Ambu'i'asi. I'm confident that I'll see someone there I know."

Saturday came, and Peter and I took a leisurely walk to Ambu'i'asi. We wandered among the leaf houses and noticed children watching us curiously. Peter examined several dug-out canoes that were resting haphazardly on the beach. We continued walking and soon saw Moses Agougka. Moses always wore a shirt when he was at work, but he was shirtless that day.

He was chewing betel nut and approached us slowly. "Hello Moses," I said. "This is my friend, Peter Wells, from England. He would like to paddle a Solomon canoe."

Moses and Peter shook hands then Moses led us to a one-man dugout canoe. There was a paddle stored inside. Moses and Peter pushed the canoe to the water and Peter shoved off. Peter rapidly paddled the canoe away in a straight line. "Paddle from one side," Moses said.

Moses was puzzled. I was puzzled because Moses was puzzled. "What do you mean?" I asked.

"Paddle one side. Solomon man paddle two sides. Make canoe go straight."

Peter paddled for some distance then turned and came back to where Moses and I waited. I later asked Peter about his paddling techniques. Peter told me that he rotated the paddle as he propelled the canoe through the water. This allowed him to move straight without needing to paddle from alternate sides. He opined that Moses was puzzled because Solomon Islanders didn't know the technique.

The next day was Chloroquine Sunday, so we took our medicine and went to church. Dr. Graham and Sheila asked us to come for tea that afternoon. We accepted and sat in their living room in comfortable chairs. "Would you like to watch my leprosy film?" Dr. Graham asked, as we sipped our tea.

"What do you mean by leprosy film?" Paula asked.

"I receive funds from Australia to attempt to eradicate leprosy in Malaita. The funding agency knows that if there's leprosy in any South Pacific country, it can always get into Australia. There are funds designated for photography equipment. I use it for education and to document for the funding agency that I'm having successes."

"Do you think there's leprosy in any of the villages where we go?" I asked.

"It's possible. That's why I want you to see the film. I want you to be able to recognize leprosy. If you see anyone you suspect might have the dread disease, just let me know."

Dr. Graham started the film. In the first scene, he was walking in a village while talking about leprosy. "Leprosy is an infectious disease," he reported, in the film. "It causes nerve damage and severe sores in all areas of the body. People have known about the disease for centuries. It has terrible negative stigmas to the point that patients are often isolated in leaper colonies."

In the second scene, Dr. Graham was walking in a different village. "That village looks like Fasileta," Paula said. "Do you know the name of the village, Dr. Graham?"

"I'm not sure," he answered. "It might be Fasileta, but I don't remember."

Dr. Graham moved to a house in the film. "That's definitely Fasileta!" I exclaimed. "That's Paul Tafqi's house! We've been in Fasileta many times."

The scene moved into Paul's house where we saw Paul and his family. "That's Paul Tafqi! Does Paul have leprosy?"

"No, Paul doesn't have leprosy. His wife did, but I'm treating her now. She's Kwaio from the central part of Malaita."

"We've slept in Paul's house several times," Paula said. "Could we get leprosy from sleeping in the Tafqi home?"

"I wouldn't worry about it. Leprosy isn't really that contagious. You have to come into repeated contact with nose or mouth droplet from someone with untreated leprosy to catch it."

We finished watching the film and returned home. We talked about watching for leprosy symptoms when we went to villages. We trusted Dr. Graham, but we agreed that we wouldn't sleep at Paul Tafqi's house again.

We returned to our normal work routines after the holidays. Paula was teaching literacy to her class when Paul stopped in our office. He sat down, and we exchanged holiday greetings. Paul soon got to the reason for his visit. "What Glen and Katherine job?" he asked.

Glen and Katherine are community development workers," I said. "They have the same job descriptions as John and Lottie have in Small Malaita. Paula and I are also community development workers."

"Same job, but what they do? Stay in Auki. No work. Go Honiara. No work. No project."

"Atori is isolated. There's no electricity. They don't have any expatriate friends. It's probably hard to get something started."

"John and Lottie on Small Malaita. No electricity. No expatriate friends. Make project. Help people. You make Glen and Katherine project?"

"I don't have any influence over other volunteers, Paul. We could work together if they wanted to. I did ask them to work with us on some of our projects. They said no. I can't force them to do anything."

Paul thought for a moment then stood. "I talk to Peace Corps," he said, as he was leaving.

Monique Incitti, David Duane, Toby Glucksman, and Dean Winchell completed their training and arrived in Auki that week. Monique was to live and work in a school near Auki. The three young men were assigned to teach at Andava School in North Malaita. Monique stayed with us while the three men worked on her house to improve its livability.

David Duane confirmed the stories about how some of the volunteers behaved wildly during the training. "I was right there," he said. "I didn't know anything about it at the time. I later heard that some of the fathers beat the tar out of the girls for playing with the volunteers."

"We didn't know anything either," Paula said. "We lived on that small island away from the main village. Western Province customs are dramatically different from Malaita. I think there would have been serious repercussions had those things happened in Malaita."

"Terry Marshall was not well liked," David continued. "He gave everyone a language acquisition book at the beginning of the training. He had authored the book and was proud of it. Most of the volunteers returned the books when we left."

"We invited Premier David Oeta and his wife, Seneth, for super Friday evening," Paula told the four, new volunteers. "This will give you a chance to meet the premier. I've also invited Colin and Alison Cameron. You'll like them."

Premier Oeta and Seneth were late for supper. We drank iced tea, snacked, and visited until 8:00 p.m. We thought we were close to starving to death, so we all ate. David and Seneth never came or even called. Monique's house was some distance from ours, so she, Dean, Toby, and David spent the night with us.

David and Leigh Lally arrived in Auki on Paula's birthday, January 27. We had a birthday party at our house. There were thirteen of us for supper and Paula received many presents. Alison and Colin gave her a tee-shirt.

Monique, Sheila, and Alison were among those attending Paula's party

Dr. Teresa, Dr. Paul, and their children gave her brownies and a card. Dr. Graham and Sheila gave her a battery-operated nail kit, a necklace, and a fan. Monique gave her a book with blank pages that she began using for her diary. Father Jon brought her a bottle of wine.

David, Leigh, Paula, and I spent a week working on a logistics manual for future trainings. I loved Vickie's computer and we used it for the manual. I had already begun writing my book about John Renton's life in Malaita. Paula and I were also using Vickie's laptop to enter recipes for a cookbook.

Our goal was that each new Peace Corps Volunteer would be given a cookbook.

Paula began making curtains for Monique's house. She told Monique that she would also make chair pads and a curtain for her cupboard when we got back from New Zealand. We ate sushi with Masako and Yasuo one evening. They ate Mexican food with us the next evening. We read our two *Newsweek* magazines then gave one to Paul Kennioriana and one to George.

We received a letter from the V.O.C.A. Farmer-to-Farmer program saying our application had been approved. They were sending an experienced forester who would be

accompanied by his wife. The program would pay for all his expenses. We were expected to have a house located for them to stay during their three-month stay. Paula quickly went to see Mary Alicia to arranged for a short-term rental house.

Masako had a joint birthday party for Yasuo and Paula. Paula taught everyone to do the macarena dance. We ate, imbibed, and danced. It was a lot of fun with twenty people celebrating their birthdays.

Colin, Igumi, David, Yasuo, and Masako were among those doing the macarena dance at the birthday party

We went to church Sunday, but Paula had to leave early. She was vomiting and had diarrhea, a headache, fever, and cold chills. "I think I have malaria," she said. "I know I'm going to miss supper and canasta with Father Jon and Monique. I hope I'm all right by the time we leave for New Zealand."

"I'll call Dr. Graham and tell him you're sick," I said. "He might want you to go to the hospital."

Dr. Graham came by and checked her. He said she had an acute case of gastritis. We had to cancel our date for supper and canasta at Father Jon's. She was sick for three days and spent a lot of time in bed. She didn't complain about my nursing and cooking skills.

A young couple came to see Paula after she returned to work. They wanted Paula to meet their baby that was named after her. The parents were showing they admired Paula by naming their baby "Paula Joy."

Three Polynesian men from Ontong Java came to our office later that afternoon. They visited with us then extended an invitation for us to visit their island. The islanders were Polynesians making a potential visit exotic.

I knew they had different culture and customs. "I read in a book that you fish for sharks from canoes on Ontong Java," I said. "The book said you fish with bone hooks the same way that your ancestors did hundreds of years ago. Is that true?"

"Get shark, same Grandfather."

Irene, Paula holding Paula Joy, Paula Joy's mother, and many friends

Visitors from Ontong Java

"If I went to Ontong Java, could I see you catch a shark?"

"Yes, catch shark."

"Could I be in a canoe next to the fishing canoe taking pictures?"

"No, same canoe."

We didn't commit to going to Ontong Java. I wanted to go, but we hadn't forgotten that David Chetwynd five-day trip had lasted over a month.

We received an invitation from the governor general to a reception aboard the Auki, a new patrol boat donated by Australia. I wore my ramo necklace and Paula wore her Peace Corps princess necklace.

Eric Mason told us that the governor general was his assistant for several years when Solomon Islands was a protectorate. Eric thought he was very capable and arranged for him travel to England and study for a master's degree.

When he graduated, he returned to the Solomon Islands as a highly educated native. He was soon appointed governor general thereby depriving Eric of his highly trained employee. We had lots to eat and drink. Eric's status with the governor general enabled him to arrange for us to accompany him and the captain on a private showing of the ship.

There was a police band seated on an accompanying ship. We danced to one of the fast numbers and got

Charlie, Paula, and Eric
got a private tour of the patrol boat

quite an ovation from people in canoes surrounding the ship. Paula took lots of pictures of me with the "Big Men."

Chief Isaac came to our office the next Monday. Paula was at home working on her application for sewing machines for Dala village. I took the opportunity to talk to him about what I had learned when I visited the Begau village. "I saw a ceremony that was ordered by the paramount chief's *debil*," I said. "Does your tribe have a ceremony like this?"

Isaac smiled and raised his brow to signify an affirmative answer. We continued discussing the Ano Naki Naki tribe's ceremony and I learned the practices were similar. He told me that he held a position like that of the Begau paramount chief. He confirmed that only he and his *debil* knew the secret ceremony. Like the Begau, the *debil* would give the secret ceremony to someone in the tribe when Isaac died.

We talked about Begau customs for cannibalism and I heard differences and similarities. He answered my questions candidly about the butchering process. "When your tribe ate a man, did you use fingers or a fork to handle the meat?" I asked.

"Use fork," Isaac answered.

"Do you have any of the forks?"

Isaac smiled and raised his brow to signify an affirmative answer. He turned the conversation to questions about Paula's and my associations with Japanese. "You friends with Japanese?" he asked.

"Yes, Yasuo and Masako Isozaki are our good friends. Paula and I are also friends with several J.O.C.V.s."

"Why friends with Japanese? Japan and America fight big war. Japan kill Americans."

I thought a bit before answering knowing about the continuing animosity among Malitian tribes. "The war is over. Japanese and Americans are not killing each other now. It's better to be friends. Paula and I are friends with many Japanese people. Japan and American are also friends now."

"American fight Japan in Solomons, Solomon man help America. After war, America help Japan, not Solomons. Why America no help Solomons?"

That question was harder to answer. I pretended to ponder until Isaac tired and made a request. "I want see Buma project," he said. "Want see sawmill."

"I would be happy to take you to Buma, Isaac," I said. "They have a great project. If you can go tomorrow, it would be a good time. Tomorrow is a work day for them."

"Tomorrow good."

Isaac came to our office the next day for our trip to Buma. We took a market truck as far as we could then began walking. We had to walk slowly because of his damaged ankle. There were about thirty men working diligently. I asked for Simon and was pointed toward five men. Isaac walked closer and closer to me as we approached Simon and his group of four. I introduced Isaac and explained that he was interested in seeing their project.

Isaac crowded so close to me that our bodies literally touched. Simon and I talked about the project, but Isaac didn't speak. He was trembling and made no attempt to move away from me. I understood the accuracy of expatriates' assertions that Malitian tribes didn't mix. Isaac was Kwara'ae-Kwaio.

We were standing in the middle of about thirty Kwara'ae. Isaac was afraid of being physically harmed or killed.

Isaac was soon satisfied with what he had learned. We walked to the main road and waited for a market truck. It was not a long wait. We climbed onto the truck bed and situated ourselves among market goods and bags of copra. We returned to Auki without speaking of what had occurred in Buma.

Buma tree nursery

We got a call from Farmer-to-Farmer officials. They said their best forester had a conflict and couldn't come on the date they originally scheduled. They asked if we wanted to wait or would accept a lesser qualified person. We told them that we would like the best, but we might still be in New Zealand on the new arrival date.

We finally received a letter from World Wise Schools that Friday. We wrote a reply letter and sent a calendar, pictures, and information about the Solomons. Gus Comstock arrived unexpectedly in our office late in the afternoon. "I just came from Atori," Gus said. "I went up to see how Glen and Katharine were getting along."

"It's good to see you," I answered. "Welcome to Auki! Do you want to spend the night with us? We have an extra bedroom."

"Thanks, but I have reservations at the Auki Lodge. However, I would like a ride to the airport tomorrow if you can make arrangements."

"I'll call Alison and Colin and ask if I can borrow their car. Anyway, please come to our house for supper."

Gus agreed to have supper with us. I made a call and Colin answered the phone. "Peace Corps Country Director Gus Comstock is visiting us," I said. "He'll fly back to Honiara tomorrow afternoon. May I borrow your car to give him a ride to the airport?"

"Of course," Colin replied. "Come and get it when you need it. Do you want to come for supper sometime this weekend?"

"We would love to come Sunday. We're having Dr. Graham and Sheila over for supper tomorrow to talk about our trip to New Zealand. Please join us. We're going to Saenaua to pick strawberries tomorrow. We'll bring the strawberries for dessert on Sunday."

Gus came back Saturday morning and ate breakfast with us. "Would you like to go to Saenaua and pick strawberries with us?" Paula asked. "Your flight doesn't leave until the afternoon. You can also see the Saenaua S.P.A. project."

"A trip to Saenaua sounds like fun," Gus answered. "It'll give us a chance to catch up on things."

We toured the Saenaua reforestation project with Jim and Salamai. Gus was impressed. We left the Misuka family and traveled to their garden to pick strawberries. "You're really making things happen in your job," Gus observed. "Paula, if we get to the point where I nominate you for that Peace Corps program for women and minorities, your accomplishments will really impress the reviewers."

"I'm really interested," Paula said. "What would happen if I were to be selected?"

"You would go to Washington, D.C. for up to a year for training. After completing the training, you would be assigned to a Peace Corps position. Jimmie Wilkerson got her job in the Solomons by that system."

"Jimmie did talk about the program, so I know a little about it. Charlie and I will talk about it when we think about what we will do when our Peace Corps time is up."

"It's a good program. The Peace Corps is a good organization. It does a lot to benefit the United States."

"We agree," I said. "Just having a few volunteers in developing counties results in positive impacts that couldn't be achieved any other way."

"I should tell you that the Peace Corps hierarchy is structured differently from most organizations. I'm the Solomon Islands' country director. I report to staff in Washington, D.C. with authorities over country directors. Larry is the administration officer, so he reports to a D.C. group with authorities over admin officers. How do you think that system would work in the army, Charlie?"

"I don't think it would work very well," I answered. "The only way that system would work in any organization is if everyone liked each other and cooperated. John Mark told us in orientation that medical issues are private. He said that situation sometimes makes a lot of problems."

"John Mark was right. Mary reports to D.C. nursing authorities, but I don't have any problems with her. She keeps me informed of any issues that might cause problems.

Jimmie reported directly to training authorities. That structure allowed for problems to develop when I came."

"How did that make problems?" Paula asked.

"Jimmie was made acting director when John Mark left. She had ideas and goals different from John Mark and was implementing them. When I came, I had my own ideas and Jimmie didn't accept me, my ideas, or my position. She used the organizational structure to try to undercut me."

"We heard rumors about that," I said. "We're in Auki, so don't know much about what happens in Honiara. Anyway, we didn't want to get involved."

"Jimmie tried to get everyone else in the office to reject me including the Solomon Islands' staff. One thing I did to tick off everyone was to send two *Newsweek* magazines to married couples. The Peace Corps sends a magazine for every volunteer. Up to the time I came, the office was only sending one to married couples. They were giving the extra copies to their Solomon friends."

"We noticed we started getting two magazines soon after you arrived. We didn't ever question why. We give them to our Solomon friends after we've read them. The Solomon Islanders love them."

"Another change I made was to suspend the volunteer welcoming party. Previous directors had a party at the Mendana Hotel for each group of new volunteers at the end of their training. Volunteers from Honiara were invited, and they loved the great food and drinks. Did you ever attend one of the parties?"

"We knew about the parties, but we didn't ever attend one. It was too much trouble and expense to get to Honiara for a party."

"I know the Honiara volunteers are upset with me over canceling the parties," Gus continued. "But fair is fair. Volunteers outside Honiara couldn't attend, and the parties cost a great deal of money. Jimmie also tried to get volunteers to dislike me. I think she had varying degrees of success."

"Jimmie didn't ever say anything negative about you to us," Paula said. "She did say she was ready to resign before she was informed that she was being transferred."

We moved to a new spot where we thought there might be more berries. We picked the small berries and put them into our basket. "I knew everything she was doing because Larry kept me informed," Gus eventually continued. "Soon after I arrived, Larry went scuba diving after a night of hard drinking. He got the bends and had to leave the Solomon Islands for treatment. I didn't report all the details to Washington, D.C., so Larry felt he owed me. Jimmie had enough successes with her reports to Washington that the Peace Corps inspector general came to the Solomons."

"We spent several hours with the I.G., but he didn't ask us any direct questions," I said. "We didn't say anything negative about anyone or anything."

"Every organization has its share of politics. Peace Corps is no different."

"Who will replace Jimmie?" Paula asked, as she put strawberries into our basket.

"A former Peace Corps Volunteer named Amy Newcomber has been assigned here. Amy had one of the Peace Corps training appointments for women and minorities. I know her from the time I was in D.C. preparing for this job. I think you'll like her."

We finished picking strawberries and returned to Auki. I borrowed Colin's car and gave Gus a ride to the airport. "It doesn't seem like Gus wants to enforce the rule about Peace Corps Volunteers not driving," I said, as we were returning to Auki.

"I was thinking the same thing when we were on our way to the airport," Paula said. "Maybe you won't need to wear your life jacket anymore when we ride in a canoe."

"I'll continue to wear my life jacket when I'm riding in canoes. Rules are rules!"

Isaac came to our office with a huge basket of leaf lettuce that week. He had grown the lettuce from seeds that we had given him. There was enough lettuce for every expatriate in Auki. "Come Ano Naki Naki?" Isaac asked.

"I can come to Ano Naki Naki," I said. "When would you like me to come?"

We exchanged ideas and decided that I would go with him at that time. When we arrived at the village, I had a big surprise. Isaac had purchased portable sawmill equipment like we had for Buma. He had never asked for a grant or any help for his village. I was truly impressed.

Colin, Alison, Dr. Graham, and Sheila ate supper with us that evening. Dr. Graham and Sheila went over arrangements for us to use their car when we arrived in Auckland. We were to call Sheila's daughter, Fiona, when we arrived in Auckland. We played Dingbats and Pictionary to end the evening.

The time before our trip to New Zealand passed quickly. We were getting our minds ready for our vacation. Dr. Graham and Sheila came over and finalized arrangements for us to use their car when we in New Zealand. They gave us a ride to the airport the next morning and we flew to Honiara.

# CHAPTER 20

# *North Island N.Z.*

When Paula and I arrived in Honiara, we paid for our tickets to New Zealand and bought traveler's checks. We did other necessary things to prepare for our month-long vacation. We also went to the Peace Corps office to get our Peace Corps passports.

We were introduced to the new training officer, Amy Newcomber, when we were in the office. I knew several Newcombers from Russell, but I didn't bring up the issue. I didn't want to sound as naive as the Malitians who told me they had known a Peace Corps Volunteer several years before then asked if I knew them. As Gus predicted, we did like Amy.

We went to Tom Scherer's house to spend a couple of days. Tom had told us that he would be in Isabel, so we had his house to ourselves. We laid around, sunbathed, and basically did nothing. I watched the ocean to ensure that the tides kept their proper schedules. On our departure day, we woke without the benefit of the alarm clock that sat nearby. "Today is our big day," Paula said. "It's time we get started on our trip."

Amy Newcomber at work

We dressed and made our way to the Honiara International Airport. The flight was uneventful, and we arrived in Auckland at 11:00 p.m. We called Sheila's daughter, Fiona, and let her know we had arrived. We spent the night at Travelers International Motor Inn, but neither of us slept well.

Fiona came to the Motor Inn the next morning, picked us up, and took us to Takapuna to get Dr. Graham's and Sheila's car. Takapuna is a central, coastal suburb of the North Shore. It had a population of around 2,200 when we were there. There were several shopping and entertainment facilities. "Do you think you can find your way back to the Motor Inn by yourselves?" Fiona asked.

"I really don't feel comfortable driving back alone, Fiona," I answered. "We're leery of the motor ways and roundabouts. We officially drive on the left in the Solomons, and we manage without any trouble. But driving in New Zealand will be much different than driving in the Solomon Islands. Our Peace Corps friends, Jim and Clair Miller, were in a bad accident in New Zealand."

"No problem. Just follow me. I'll go slowly. I'll make a stop on the way to introduce you to my brother, Aidan."

We enjoyed meeting Aidan. Talking with him was very interesting. He was an actor, and had performed in the movie, *Chess*. We promised to try to see *Chess* while we were in Christchurch. We followed Fiona back to the motel. Jim and Clair Miller's accident was constantly on our minds. We ventured out to the shopping mall where I bought a new pair of shoes. There was a repair shop in the mall, so I left my old shoes to be re-soled. That was enough activity for one day. We found our way back to the Motor Inn and retired for the evening.

We slept late and made coffee when we woke. It seemed a little strange to not have a mosquito net covering us. "Do you know what day it is?" Paula asked.

"I think it's Thursday or Friday," I answered. "Is it a special day?"

"It's Friday, February 14, 1992, Valentine's Day! Happy Valentine's day."

"Happy Valentine's Day, Lover," I responded, with a hug and kiss. "What do you think we should do today to celebrate?"

"I think we should get on the road. We didn't come to New Zealand to sit in a motel room for a month. This map shows Rotorua would be a place to go next. It's in the middle of the North Island. There are several tourist things to do there."

"How far do you think it is?"

"It must be around 225 kilometers. How far is 225 kilometers in miles?"

"Humm, 225 kilometers? That must be around 140 miles. We can make it in a few hours. If we're lucky, we'll have time to check into a youth hostel to save some money."

We loaded up the Stuart-McBride car and began our trip to Rotorua. We stopped at the Cowboy Café on the way and ate a bite of lunch. It was raining by the time we arrived at our destination. Rotorua was a beautiful city, situated on the southern shores of Lake Rotorua.

When we arrived in Rotorua, we went to a Pack and Save store and bought a few groceries. We asked the clerk for a youth hostel recommendation and was told the Rotorua Youth Hostel Association (Y.H.A.) was the best. The Rotorua Y.H.A. was full, so we spent the night at a motel. After several months in the Solomons, our supper at McDonalds was special fare. We picked up several brochures to provide information on tourist activities.

We slept late again and woke to a light rain. "What do you want to do today?" I asked. "It looks like it might rain all day."

"I looked at that brochure on the Rotorua Agradome," Paula answered. "It's only ten minutes from the city center and it's mostly covered."

"We also have a brochure about the Maori Cultural Center that sounds interesting," I added. "We could go the Agradome today and the Maori Cultural Center tomorrow or the next day."

The Agradome was in the center of 350 acres of farmland and included a farm show featuring trained animals. After the show, we went to the farmyard nursery and watched children play with baby animals in a petting zoo. There was a guided tour on the Acrodrome 350 acre working farm. We were told that if we went, we would get to hand-feed friendly animals. We would also get to sample kiwi fruit juice and honey that were produced on the farm. "Do you want to go on the tour?" Paula asked.

"It sounds interesting, but I don't want to battle the rain," I said. "We get more than enough walking in the rain in the Solomons."

"I don't want to go either. The Woolen Mill and Shearing Museum sounds like more fun."

There was a sheep shearing demonstration at the museum. A guide told about early New Zealand pioneers, the Bowen brothers. After the show, we drove to Pack and Save where we bought roasting ears, steaks, and wine. We returned to our motel for a wonderful meal. It had been

Sheep shearing demonstration

several months since we had seen a television show, so we quickly found something to watch. We even thought the advertisements were interesting.

We slept late and looked at brochures while we watched television. I enjoyed just being with my best friend, Paula. We eventually decided to go to Wai-O-Tapu Thermal Wonderland. Wai-O-Tapu Thermal Wonderland was one of Rotorua's many geothermal attractions. We had a picnic lunch of fruit, yogurt, and wine topped with a cup of coffee at Wai-O-Tapu. We picked up more groceries at Pack and Save on our way back to our motel.

Our motel utilized the geothermal properties to create natural hot tubs for their guests. Paula disrobed and climbed into our hot tub. "It's really hot," she said. "If you're going to get in with me, you'll have to do it quickly. I can't stand this hot water too long."

I quickly joined her. "You did say it's hot," I agreed. "It has a strong smell of sulfur. It must be healthy."

We soon left the hot tub then showered to rid ourselves of the sulfur. We made reservations to go to the Maori Cultural Center the next evening. "What does the brochure say about the program we're going to see?" Paula asked.

"It says we'll learn about the history of the Maoris in New Zealand," I said. "There will be Maori dancing as part of a show."

We started our day with a visit to a nearby museum and art gallery that had been

Elderly playing lawn games

converted from a bath house known as Tudor Towers. "What do you want to do next?" I asked.

"Let's just wander around until we get tired," Paula said. "Everything we see will be new to us. We have a lot of time before the Maori Review. I don't want to spend it sitting in a motel room."

As we wandered about, we were surprised to see dozens of older men and women playing croquet and lawn bowling. They were all dressed in white and seemed to be quite serious about trying to win.

We strolled through flower gardens and then went to a special orchid garden where we saw a musician play a water organ. "I want to go shopping," Paula said, while we were eating at McDonalds. "Do you want to go?"

"Shopping doesn't sound very interesting to me," I said. "I'll fill the car with gas then go back to our room."

Paula soon joined me in the motel room with her only purchase, ice cream. We soaked in the geothermal hot tub until we could no longer stand the hot water. We watched television until it was time to get dressed for the Maori Review.

The Maori Culture Center had a Maori guide that provided an interesting history of the Maoris. He told us that the Maori had migrated to New Zealand using canoes. They came in waves beginning about 1,200 years ago. Our guide talked about Maori culture and tried to explain Maori's thought processes. There were interesting displays and Maori artisans working on custom projects.

Paula and I were selected to be part of the Dances of Life Show. The audience was told that dances and songs have been used for hundreds of years to tell the Maori's origins, journeys, struggles, and their very existence. We danced and sang until it was time for the men's warrior dance.

Paula and the other women begin leaving the stage. As they were departing, I got a quick lesson on how to do the Haka. We stomped our feet and beat our chests. The Polynesians chanted in Maori and I chanted in Kwara'ae. We ended by striking macho poses, tongues extended to their maximum, fierce faces, while emitting our most frightening screams. I was very satisfied with my warrior performance. "I think I understand Solomon Islands' culture better," I said, as I sat down beside Paula.

"What do you understand about Solomon Islands that you didn't know before?" Paula asked.

"I think that the reason we Solomon men scream when the electricity goes off is to make a mini war chant. We're telling potential adversaries that this home is well protected."

"Well, you're not a Solomon man! If you can find that theory in one of the books you've been reading in Honiara, you can scream all you want, day or night, with or without electricity. Until that time, what you learn in New Zealand can stay in New Zealand!"

We loved Rotorua and could have stayed longer, but we wanted to see more of New Zealand. We traveled to the city of Taupo that sat beside Lake Taupo. Lake Taupo was formed by a huge volcano that last erupted in 181 A.D. According to Maori legend, the lake was the beating heart of New Zealand's North Island.

Taupo was a great place for tourists who loved to fish, ski on nearby Mount Ruapehu, and explore geothermal phenomena. Visitors could also enjoy

Charlie prepares for his
Flying Fox zip line ride

year-round mountain biking, traditional cycling, hiking, and golfing. "What shall we do first?" I asked.

"I saw advertising signs for the Taupo Flying Fox when we came in," Paula said. "It's supposed to be a long, exciting zip line."

"Sounds adventuresome and won't take too long. We can go zip lining then find a place to stay."

We both rode on the Taupo Flying Fox and got some good pictures. As we expected, it was fast, beautiful, and exciting.

We soon moved on to find a place to stay. We found a unique place with the appearance of a Swiss chalet. It was an individual structure with a kitchen and a spa, hot tub.

I wanted to buy Paula something special for our twenty-fifth wedding anniversary, so we went shopping in Huka Village. I found a jewelry store that had a sterling silver ring that I liked. I wanted to surprise Paula, but I had to have her try it to get the right size. I wanted it engraved, so we had to leave it. We paid for it and told the clerk we would return the next day to get it.

We went to New World grocery store to get groceries for our stay in Taupo. I bought a magic trick for the van den Bosch children before we returned to our Swiss chalet. "This cool weather makes me feel great," I announced. "I think I'll go jogging."

When I returned from jogging, Paula was watching television. "It's so long since we've watched a television show, I nearly forgot what it's like," she said. "It's some kind of soap opera, but I think it's interesting."

Paula enjoyed a bubble bath

Paula found a bubble bath liquid and added to our spa. We enjoyed sitting in our bubble bath before preparing our dinner of spaghetti. Afterwards, we went to the Spa Bar for beer and pool where Paula won two out of three games.

We started our next day by writing post cards to send to family and friends in the U.S. We toured a replica Maori meeting house then went back to Huka Village to pick up Paula's ring. The ring wasn't ready, so we decided to go horseback riding.

It was our first time to ride with English style saddles. We were required to follow a guide, single file. Our guide led our horses at a walk along a well-traveled path. It was nothing like the wild ride we enjoyed in Australia. "How did you like the ride?" our guide asked, when we returned to our starting point.

"It was really slow," I answered. "I expected to have a real horse ride."

"You can take your horse out and run him in the paddock. Most of our guests are novices, so we put their safety first."

I did take my horse to the paddock where he and I both enjoyed more spirited riding. After the ride, Paula and I went to the store and picked up her ring. It turned out very pretty. Afterwards, I went to the library, and Paula went shopping. I found a book that told more about Scotsman John Renton's prolonged stay in the Solomons.

I learned that Renton and four American sailors stole a whale boat and deserted the guano ship *Renard* in 1868. Two sailors died on the way, but Renton and two others drifted 1,250 miles to Malaita. The two other sailors were soon killed, but Renton survived on Sulufou under the protection of Kabbou, a chief and son of a chief.

Crew member from the blackbirding ship *Bobtail Nag* rescued Renton in 1875. Renton's return to Scotland, via Australia, created a news sensation. He acknowledged joining Sulufou warriors in headhunting raids, but he denied Sulufou Islanders participated in cannibalism, asserting they had fish to eat.

Renton used language skills that he acquired in his seven-year stay in the Lau Lagoon to get employment as an interpreter on blackbirding ships. He returned to Lau Lagoon in 1875 with generous gifts for Kabbou. A well-known ramo, Kwaisulia, was among those recruited for labor in Australia.

Renton's life on Malaita and the logs from his voyages on blackbirding ships were published in *The Adventures of John Renton*. He was killed by natives in 1878 on Aoba Island in Vanuatu working from the ship *Mystery*.

I met up with Paula. We bought a few groceries and went back to our room. "I found a really neat book at the library that has a summation of the life of John Renton," I said. "I copied some of it. I can use it to give real accuracy to the book I'm writing on Renton. There was a book published on his life in Malaita titled *The Adventures of John Renton*. I would like to get a copy someday."

"Good luck with your book search," Paula said. "Anyway, let's sit in the spa tub. My bum is sore from the horseback ride! I want to turn in early. We're heading toward Wellington tomorrow."

We went out, played pool, and enjoyed a good time with new friends in the bar. We came back to the room where we watched television with cokes and popcorn.

We left Taupo the next day with a goal of reaching Palmerton North. We stopped at Queen Elizabeth II Army Memorial Museum on the way. It was a great museum! We ate a picnic lunch on the museum grounds then continued our drive toward Palmerton North. We stopped at a small town where they were having an antique car rally. Nearly all of them were American cars in excellent condition. Traveling down the road made us feel like we were in a time warp. Antique cars were in front and back of us and some were passing us!

All the motels in Palmerton North were full because of the antique car rally. We learned there were over 1,000 cars registered for the rally. We went on to Leirn, but we could only stay Friday night at the Redwood Motel. All the motels were booked for Saturday and Sunday because of a scheduled surfing event.

It was raining when we got up, but we managed to load the car. We tried to find a place that served pancakes, but we had to settle for bacon and eggs. We decided we wanted to find a place to stay and relax for a few days. We stopped in several towns, but everyone was booked due to a golf tournament.

We stopped at the Southward Museum and looked at antique cars. We continued seeing many antique cars on the road. We stopped at the Lindale Agriculture Farm, but we didn't take a tour because of the rain. We headed South again in hopes of finding a motel.

Paula admires an antique car

We eventually found a room at the Marina Motel not too far from Wellington. Rooms were getting more expensive as we were getting closer to Wellington. We decided that this would be a good place to relax and rest for a few days. We spent one day relaxing and doing nothing. "This isn't as much fun as I thought it would be," Paula said. "I want to do something."

"I'm glad you feel that way," I said. "We can lay around and do nothing when we're old. Let's move on to Wellington tomorrow."

We arrived in Wellington and found a cheap motel at $100.00 a week. It had communal toilet facilities, but we were resigned to getting what we paid for. Wellington is New Zealand's capital city and had 412,500 residents. Wellington features a temperate climate with a claim to be the world's windiest city.

We started our first day in Wellington by seeking a restaurant to serve pancakes or waffles. We found a place that served waffles for lunch and dinner but never pancakes. We had a roll and coffee then went to a museum. We met an anthropologist who was interested in our lives in the Solomon Islands. We made an appointment to meet him the next day.

It was raining, blustery, and cold when we got up. "Wellington is known as the windiest city in the world," Paula said. "It's definitely windy, but I've had it much worse in Lakin."

"I remember some of the wind we had when we were living in Garden City," I said. "Maybe we're here on a calm day."

"If this in calm, I don't want to be here when it's windy."

I went to the museum and visited with the anthropologist we had met the day before. He was very intelligent and offered opinions about what I had observed when I visited the pagan Begau. He told me that I should go to the Turnbull Library to find more about the history of the Solomons. We made another appointment to meet the next day. We found a restaurant that evening that served waffles. "What do you think of the waffles?" I asked, while we were eating.

"They were worth the wait," Paula answered. "But the American hot dog I had for lunch was terrible."

We ended our day with a movie. The theater was old, very stately, and beautiful. After drinking a beer, we went back to our room, played canasta, and wrote post cards.

We got up at 7:00 a.m. to get ready for our 9:30 appointment with the anthropologist. I invited him to come to Malaita where I would introduce him to the pagan Begau. We went walking and walking and walking after we left the museum! We found the Botanical Gardens, but we didn't see much of it. "I'm tired of walking up hill," I complained. "Do you want to see if we can find the Turnbull Library?"

"I'm tired too," Paula said. "Let's go to the library. It can't be too far from here."

We eventually found the Turnbull Library. As soon as we got in, they made everyone leave. A water main had broken and there was no water. "It seems like Auki isn't the only place that has problems with water," Paula observed.

We returned to the Alexander Turnbull Library the next day. The library was impressive. We learned that the library provides world-class research services. Turnbull Library employees are experts in all kinds of topic areas and research in general. Staff members were very helpful in directing me to books and articles on the Solomons. Many books included anecdotes of their old customs of headhunting and cannibalism. Paula was less interested in Solomon culture and went to another section.

I found many old pictures of the Solomons at the museum. I ordered some duplicates made. I found Paula and interrupted her reading. "I had them make duplicate pictures from the Solomon Islands," I said. "Would you like to see them?"

Paula raised her brow to signify an affirmative answer. I handed her the pictures. "What is this one?" she asked. "It looks like an artificial island in Langa Langa Lagoon."

Artificial Island in Langa Langa Lagoon Courtesy Alexander Turnbull Library

"That's what it is. It was taken in 1906. The islands haven't changed much in the last eighty-five years."

"You have several pictures of villages. When were they taken?"

"They were also taken in 1906. The descriptions didn't say what island they were on, but they are of the cannibal village of Foate in the Solomon Islands."

"Who is this old man?"

"That's Soga. He was a famous ramo from Isabel Island. The picture description said he commanded over 200 warriors. They were feared as headhunters and cannibals. Soga led raids that destroyed many coastal villages. They killed everyone on San George Island."

Cannibals in Foate Courtesy Alexander Turnbull Library

"He doesn't look so fierce in the picture. When was it taken?"

"It was taken in 1892. He eventually converted to Christianity and used his influence to get everyone on Isabel to convert."

"Where was this picture of the women taken?"

"The island wasn't identified, but it was in group of pictures featuring the Solomon Islands. It was also taken in 1906."

We met a photo journalist named Paula Palmer. She had a photo display called "Palestinian Images of Oppression." She told us about her experiences in Palestine while taking her photos. I stayed at the library while Paula went window shopping. She returned at closing time. "There are many interesting books on the Solomons here," I said. "I enjoy reading about the old customs. It helps me understand what we are experiencing in the Solomon Islands. What did you do this afternoon?"

"I rode on a cable car and took a stroll through the Botanical Gardens," she said. "I met a retired gentleman by the name of Burt who told me a lot of the history of the gardens and Wellington. I've had enough for one day. I did a lot of walking and my feet are sore."

"I didn't walk very much, but my feet are sore too. It'll take some time to break in these new shoes."

Soga of Isabel
Courtesy Alexander Turnbull Library

We ate at the American Cafe then went back to our room and played cards until we went to bed. We were lulled to sleep by a soft rain.

I went to the library after we ate bite of breakfast. Paula said she would go window shopping. She met me at the library, then we went to see the movie *Highlander II*. "There are so many books about the Solomon Islands," I said. "They're all very interesting. How was your morning?"

"I had a facial done and did some more window shopping," Paula said. "I would love to have some new makeup and Estee Lauer's Private Collection or Lancôme Maggie Moiré. I decided to wait until we leave the Solomons."

We went back to the room and played three games of canasta. We had coffee and rolls and later went to a near-by pub. We drank a few beers and danced. "I'm really having fun on our vacation," I said. "I'm very happy to have you for my wife!"

"I'm happy to have you for my husband," she answered. "I'm really enjoying the holiday with my best friend."

We slept late the next morning then went on our separate ways. I went to the library and Paula left for unannounced destinations. We met back at our room at 5:00 p.m. "I didn't have much happen at the library," I said. "What did you do?"

Solomon Women
Courtesy Alexander Turnbull Library

"The first thing I did was go to the laundromat," she said. "After that, I went shopping. I froze my tail off, so I ate a bite at Kinney's Café and came back to the room to warm up. I called Mom and Dad to see how everything was in Kansas."

"Well, you do have some news then. What did you learn?"

"Everyone is all right. Linda hasn't had her baby yet. Mom has my social worker's license. The Lakin Independent printed another one of the stories you sent them. Other papers in Western Kansas reprinted them."

"I'm glad they printed the articles. We are really having unique experiences. Did your mother say anything about Chuck and Jason?"

"The boys are fine. Chuck had a job interview in Russell. He didn't get hired, so he's going to Manhattan. They told me the laundry would be done at 3:00 p.m., so I picked it up and came back here."

We went to Kentucky Fried Chicken to eat then came back to our room. We played cards until it was time to go to bed. Things started to liven up in a near-by bar, so it was a little hard to sleep.

We discussed going to Dunedin while we were eating breakfast. We decided to check on flight tickets and started down town. When we got to the airline office to check on tickets, the place was closed.

We ate lunch at Flannigans Bar, played more canasta, then went to see about a movie. We thought the tickets were too expensive, so we bought a cake and candy bar and went back to the room. We went to the Youth Hostel Association and bought a membership. We made reservations to go to the South Island the next day on the Interisland ferry at 10:00 a.m.

We repacked and then went out that evening. We went to a pub and was introduced to the Karaoke video shows. Paula sang "Sleeping Single in a Double Bed." We met people from Germany and New Zealand. Peter from New Zealand gave Paula a Harley Davidson tee-shirt. We were to call him and his friend, Grant, when we got back from the South Island. The plan was to celebrate Grant's twenty-fifth birthday.

The unemployment rate in New Zealand was at sixteen percent when we were there. Despite severe economic conditions, the New Zealanders were very cheerful about their situations. Grant worked for a radio station. He asked Paula to get him an album that her parents made to play on the radio. We had a wonderful time.

We got up at 7:00 a.m. to get ready to take the Interislander to Picton. We made reservations to stay at the motel when we returned. "Can we leave our car in the parking lot while we visit the South Island?" I asked.

"You can leave the car," the clerk answered. "But we won't be responsible for any damages."

"I understand. I'll park the car out of the way."

The North Island portion of our New Zealand vacation was wonderful. We were looking forward to visiting the South Island. We were especially anxious to get to see Dr. Arun and Elaine Menon again.

# CHAPTER 21

# *South Island N.Z.*

We got up early and made it to the wharf for our ferry ride to Picton. Our travel to Picton was very pleasant. We bought bus tickets at Picton for the next leg of our trip to Christchurch. We stopped for a short coffee break and watched wild seals playing near the shore. We arrived in Christchurch around 7:00 p.m.

Christchurch had a population over 350,000 when we were there. The Avon River flows through the center of the city. Archaeologists believe that Polynesians settled the Christchurch area about 1250.

We took a shuttle bus to Cora Wilding Youth Hostel where we were assigned to share a room with a Japanese couple. We weren't totally prepared for our living arrangements, but we were in a youth hostel. We bought a can of beans and sausages and four slices of bread for supper. We didn't try to visit with our roommates. We read tourist brochures and played Chinese checkers. We managed to settle in while the Japanese couple was out of the room.

We slept late then showered before eating our breakfast of eggs and toast. We started washing our dirty clothes and played chess while we were waiting. We were getting ready to go downtown when we met another U.S. couple who was also staying at the youth hostel. They introduced themselves as Bob and Gloria Willis. "We're going to the Botanical Garden to see the Wizard," Gloria said. "Would you like to go with us?"

"We're going to go downtown and would love to go with you," Paula said. "We don't know who the Wizard is, but everything we see will be new and interesting."

"We read about the Wizard in our tourist book," Bob said. "He's famous in New Zealand. The Prime Minister of New Zealand appointed him the official Wizard of New Zealand in 1990."

As we walked toward Cathedral Square, the Willis told us that the Wizard was an Englishman born in 1932. He served in the Royal Air Force and was highly educated. In 1974, the Wizard migrated to Christchurch and began performing in Cathedral Square. He always spoke from a step ladder that he carried with him.

Paula with Bob and Gloria Willis

When he first started speaking on a regular basis, the city council had him arrested as a public nuisance. By that time, tourists and locals had grown to love him. There were organized demands that he be allowed to continue performing. The city council reversed its decision and made the square a public speaking area.

The Wizard was climbing onto his step ladder as we approached. His costume included an oversized, black cloak and a large, black, pointy hat. His cloak and hat were covered with colored stars. When he had climbed to about four feet, he stopped and majestically waited for an audience to assemble.

The Wizard's speech included political messages. He claimed that he had founded the Imperial British Conservative Party to provide a counterbalance to international Capitalism and various forms of Nazism. He told us that he was in university in England during the Viet Nam War. He opposed the student Pacifist Society sending money to the Viet Cong. He claimed that he founded Alf's Imperial Army devoted to sensational, non-violent, campus opposition to the Pacifist Society.

We continued our afternoon with Bob and Gloria by touring a museum, looking at arts and crafts, and eating Greek food. We all went back to the youth hostel where the Willis replaced the Japanese couple as our roommates. Over our evening meal, the Willis told us that they had earned their trip to New Zealand by transporting cargo for a company. The company bought their plane tickets and gave the Willis the cargo they wanted to go to Christchurch. They were only allowed to bring what was in their carry-on baggage.

We got up early and ate breakfast with the Willis. We said our good-byes then took the train to Dunedin to see the Menons. Dunedin was the forth-largest city in New Zealand with a population of around 100,000 when we visited. The harbor and hills around Dunedin were formed by a then extinct volcano. Dunedin's economy included manufacturing, publishing, technology-based industries, education, research, and tourism.

We were served a New Zealand special Devonshire tea on the train. We arrived in Dunedin around 2:40 p.m. Elaine and the kids met us and took us to the hospital to see Dr. Arun. "I'm so happy to see you," Dr. Arun said, with a mischievous grin. "I won't be home tonight because it's Tuesday. On Tuesday's, I have to stay here at the psychiatric hospital. You can stay if you like, Charlie, but I don't know what I can do for you in one night."

"I'm not that desperate," I responded. "More importantly, it would be hard for you to analyze me when I was busy analyzing you. By the way, what do you do during the night? Aren't the patients sleeping?"

Dr. Arun, Elaine, Neil, and Sumitra

"It's usually pretty slow. I'm taking courses to further my public health credentials. I use some of the time to study."

Elaine and Dr. Arun's house was very cozy. Elaine was due with their third child in about five weeks.

We had picked up tourist brochures before we went to the South Island. We studied them to decide what we would do the next day. We visited a bit, had a glass of wine, then went to bed.

"What do you want to do today?" Elaine asked, as we were eating breakfast. "There are many interesting things to see and do in and around Dunedin."

"We looked at several tourist brochures before we arrived," Paula said. "Everything looked interesting, but we didn't decide what we wanted to do first."

"Let's pack a picnic lunch and go view albatross," Elaine suggested. "They're worth the trip."

Elaine did take us to see albatross and we also saw seals. The albatrosses were fascinating. She next took us to historic Fort Taiaroa where we got to see an Armstrong disappearing gun. The gun was an obsolete type of artillery that was mounted on a carriage that lowered the gun when it was not being fired. This enabled the gun and its operators to hide from direct fire and observation.

We ate our picnic lunch and took a scenic route back to Dunedin. We picked up Dr. Arun from the hospital and went to their house. The four of us got two bottles of wine and went to a Thai restaurant while the children stayed with a sitter. We had a lovely time with our friends.

We woke late and learned that Dr. Arun had gone to work. We ate breakfast and talked about what to do. "I want to start my day by doing a load of laundry," Paula said. "We seem to need to do that even if we're on vacation."

"I want to split some of that firewood that you have in back," I said. "I haven't swung an ax for a long time. It will be good exercise."

I started my wood splitting while Neil watched from the doorway. I would swing the ax once, then look back to assure myself that Neil was keeping his distance. I believed that Neil was capable of running toward the swinging ax to learn if I was capable of preventing him from being hit.

Elaine eventually put the kids down for a morning nap. Elaine and Paula went to the supermarket while I continued making big pieces of wood into smaller pieces. I found Neil very easy to manage when he was asleep. Paula and Elaine returned before the kids woke. We ate a bite of lunch then took the kids to Creshe Day Care before going to Larnach Castle.

Bill Larnach began construction of what was to be his private family residence in 1870. The home was designed and constructed in the style of a Gothic Revival mansion. It took around 200 workers several months to build the main structure.

Larnach had materials imported from around the world for his majestic home. Larnach quickly learned that the family couldn't use the verandahs during the cold winters. To solve this

Larnach Castle

problem, he imported twenty tons of glass from Italy in 1875 to enclose them.

Larnach added a 3,000 square foot ballroom in 1887 as a birthday present for his oldest daughter, Kate. The mansion eventually contained forty-three rooms. The Larnach family employed forty-six servants to manage the home. We had tea in the ballroom, returned to pick up the kids, and met Dr. Arun at the public library. We stopped and bought fish and chips on the way home.

After supper, Dr. Arun took Paula, the kids and me for a scenic drive. Elaine stayed home as she wasn't feeling well. She had a cold and sore throat. Her unborn was being very active making her even more uncomfortable. Dr. Arun stopped at a large grassy area that had a deep, concrete drainage ditch running through the area. We walked about while Dr. Arun and I exchange good-natured insults. Suddenly, Neil made a dash toward the drainage ditch.

The ditch was about seventy yards from us. Neil had run about twenty yards and was showing no signs of stopping. I believed that Neil was running toward the ditch to learn if anyone was capable of saving him from disaster. "He'll probably stop soon," Dr. Arun said.

I looked at Dr. Arun. He looked concerned. I looked at Paula. She looked concerned. I looked back at Dr. Arun. He looked worried. Suddenly, he dashed off in pursuit of Neil. He overtook Neil and brought him back. Dr. Arun decided we had sufficiently toured the area and returned to the car.

When we arrived back at the house, Elaine got the kids ready for bed. When her task was finished, we adults sat down and reminisced about our lives in the Solomon Islands over wine. "How do you like living in Dunedin, Dr. Arun?" I asked.

"I like living here," he said. "But, I find it difficult to study. I don't like sitting still."

We eventually said our goodnights and headed to our room. "Sumitra is really growing," Paula said as we were getting ready for bed. "She chatters up a storm. She's a little doll."

"What do you think of Neil?" I asked.

"Neil is still Neil. He has a lot of influence over Sumitra. I don't know how Elaine will manage three of them."

"We leave tomorrow, but I want to stay in touch with the Menons. I would like to know what Neil will be doing in twenty-five years. I love that little kid. If he survives childhood, he'll probably be a brain surgeon or a nuclear scientist."

Elaine took us to the ticket station after breakfast. We bought our tickets for the train to Christchurch that was leaving at 1:10 p.m. I went to a museum while Paula went window shopping. We met Elaine and went to the train station. We had a sandwich in the Octagon Restaurant then boarded the train for Christchurch.

We checked into the Ambassador Hotel when we arrived in Christchurch. "Where are you folks from?" the clerk asked. "I can't tell from your accents."

"We're Americans," I answered. "But we've lived in the Solomon Islands as Peace Corps Volunteers for the past several months."

We visited with the motel staff about the Peace Corps and the Solomons. Paula called the movie theater to try to get tickets for *Chess*. They were sold out all the days we would be in Christchurch. We walked down town and ate in a Greek restaurant. We watched a chess game that was played on an outdoor, twenty by twenty feet, concrete pad with two-foot tall chess pieces. There were stadium benches for spectators to watch the players.

We stopped at Pack and Save and got some groceries. We later went to the train station, but it was closed. We went back to the motel and was able to make train ticket reservations by phone.

We got up early to get ready to go to Wellington. We boarded the 8:10 a.m. train to Picton then took the Interislander to Wellington. The ferry was crowded and the weather lousy, so we were forced to stay inside. There was no room to sit on benches, so we sat on the floor all the way.

I went to the library the next day while Paula called the travel agent about return tickets to Honiara. "What did you learn about our plane tickets?" I asked, when we met.

"There are flights to Honiara on Tuesdays and Thursdays," she said. "We have to decide which day to go."

We chatted a bit and decided to leave on Tuesday. "We'll need to call the airline tomorrow and confirm that we want tickets for March 17," I said. "We should also call Peace Corps and see what is happening with our Farmer-to-Farmer application. What else did you do?"

"I called Mother to let her know where we are and to see if Linda had her baby. She had a baby boy March third. He weighed a little over nine pounds and had a head circumference of fourteen inches. He's a big boy! I don't know his length,"

"He is a big baby," I agreed. "What did they name him?" Linda and Steve named him Dylan Roy. I also talked with Bill, Brenda, Jack, Lisa, and Dad. It was good to talk to them. I called Linda later and visited with her as well."

I spent the rest of the day at the library and Paula went window shopping. We met back at the motel at 6:00 p.m. "You're really spending a lot of time in libraries," Paula said. "I don't remember you being so studious when we were in college."

"Not when I was working on my undergraduate degree," I said. "But I practically lived in the university library when I was working on my M.P.A. at K-State."

"That seems like a long time ago."

"Did you buy any windows?" I asked, with intention of changing the subject.

"Very funny," Paula said. "I didn't buy anything. The next time I go shopping, I'm going to max out our credit card!"

"I don't think it would take too much more charging to max out our card."

"That's true. Let's stay in tonight. We need to get on the road early tomorrow."

Morning came too early. We showered, had coffee and muffins, then loaded the car. Our first attempt to leave for Palmerston North quickly failed. We went around in circles on a roundabout, but we couldn't find our way out. We stopped and walked to locate our correct turns. It was much easier than we originally thought. We had a leisurely drive to Palmerston North.

Palmerston North had a population of over 70,000 making it the seventh largest city in New Zealand. The city's location was once just a clearing in a forest occupied by small communities of Maori. The Maori called the area Papa-i-Oea. Papa-i-Oea translates as: "How beautiful it is." Paula and I agreed that it was beautiful. British and Scandinavian immigrants settled there in the mid-19th century. Massey University was established in 1927.

We found a room at the Masonic Lodge then went to Massey University. Paula talked to the department head about working on a master's degree in women's development. I talked to instructors in the anthropology department about studying for a PhD. The head of the anthropology department was very encouraging. "We have a seminar coming up in June," he said. "If you're available, I would like for you to attend and present a paper. Unfortunately, I wouldn't be able to offer any funding."

We went back into town to our motel and did a load of laundry. We walked to a take-away and bought fish and chips. We walked to the town square and ate. It was a little chilly, but it was fun. "Do you know what I would like to do tomorrow?" Paula asked.

"No," I answered. "What would you like to do?"

"I want to go to a ballet."

"Then we'll go to a ballet."

We slept well and woke early. We met a young woman named Serina at breakfast. She was interested in moving to the States. Paula thought she might talk to her later about going into business together. After we ate breakfast, we went to buy tickets for the ballet. We were lucky and got them at half price. I went to Massey University and Paula did another load of laundry. We met back at the room in time to dress up and get to the ballet for our first time.

The performance was *Orpheus the Ballet*. It was a neoclassical that only lasted thirty-minutes. It was composed by Igor Stravinsky from Hollywood, California in 1947. It was interesting entertainment and pretty. We ate supper at McFles afterwards.

We saw Serina again and initiated a conversation. Serina thought she knew of a better and cheaper place to stay. She took us to look at a motel that was $30.00 a night more expensive and didn't take American Express. She wanted to take us to some other places, but we told her we'd look the next day. When we were alone, we decided we would travel on in the morning.

We ate breakfast at McFus, said goodbye to Serina, loaded up the car, and left. We drove from Palmerston North back to Taupo. We checked into the same hotel where we stayed when we arrived in Taupo. We unloaded the car then went to buy a few groceries. On the way back to the hotel, we stopped and watched bungy jumping.

Taupo Bungy is likely the most beautiful place in the world to go bungy jumping. The scenery was spectacular with a platform type structure extending about fifty feet over Waikato River. The platform base was firmly attached to a sheer cliff. Jumpers could buy a video of their jump for an additional fee.

Bungy jumpers got to choose how close they would get to the river. Some jumpers chose to be immersed into the river before being snapped back by the extended bungy rope. They bobbed up and down like a yo-yo. There was a small boat in the river to pick up the jumpers at the end of their jump.

I bought a tee-shirt that said: "I watched and was amazed." We went back to the room, fixed lamb steaks and delicious roasting ears. We watched television while we ate. We discussed what new adventure we could find the next day until we went to sleep.

We got up late, showered, dressed, and ate. "What shall we do for excitement today?" I asked, as I munched on my toast.

"I think we should go to Huka Falls and do the jet boating," Paula said.

"I'm game. The car has plenty of gas, so I'm ready to go."

As we drove by Lake Taupo, we saw people parasailing. We stopped to better see how they were doing it. It was a popular event, so people had to make reservations. A small boat with an outboard motor picked people up from the wharf and took them to a 400 square foot raft floating some distance from the shore.

People donned a harness that attached to the parasail. When the rider was ready, the boat sped off lifting the rider into the air. The boat towed the rider around for a time then maneuvered him or her back to land on the raft. "That looks like fun!" Paula exclaimed. "Let's do that instead of going jet boating!"

"It does look like fun," I agreed. "We're here and we don't know if we could even get jet boating tickets if we were at Huka Falls."

We made reservations for 3:00 p.m. and were there for the boat to pick us up. We donned life jackets and took a short ride to the raft. An attendant began hooking me into the harness while the boat operator was fastening the parasail tow line to the boat. "I saw people parasailing from a distance," I said. "But what do I have to do?"

"Don't worry about it," he answered. "We know what we're doing. We've done these many times."

The tow line was soon attached to the boat and the operator somehow determined I was ready. I didn't doubt that they had done it hundreds of times, but I hadn't. I couldn't help but thinking that I was deeply involved in wanting success for this adventure. The boat operator took off without further instructions and I was promptly lifted into the air. The ride was exhilarating! I felt so alive and free. It was a real adrenaline rush.

After several minutes of my bird's eye view, the operator slowed the boat until I slowly drifted toward the water. When my feet touched, he accelerated lifting me again into the air. When he thought I had my money's worth, the operator maneuvered the boat, so that I was successfully deposited onto the raft.

The attendant helped me get out of the harness and began strapping it on Paula. She had a huge smile as the boat operator accelerated and lifted her into the air. "Look how properly she's sitting," the attendant said. "You were in a more upright position. That wasn't right."

"I didn't feel comfortable in that semi-standing position," I said. "But I didn't know I was supposed to sit."

The operator gave me a look of pity as we continued to watch Paula. I could see

Paula getting ready for takeoff

her alternate pulling on the right then the left lines that attached the harness to the parasail. Her line tugging caused her veer to the right then the left. "Look how well she is managing the lines to make her ride more interesting," the attendant said. "You didn't do that."

"I wish I had thought to ask you what I was to do before I was lifted into the air," I sarcastically asserted. "It would have made my ride more enjoyable."

The operator gave me another look of pity as if to cause me think to that I should have intuitively known proper parasailing techniques. I considered innocently asking him if he was Australian. Fortunately, I remembered Bishop Loft's threat to throw me off his porch for the same question. I held my tongue.

Paula coming in for landing

Paula was safely delivered back to the raft. We were soon returned to the shore and our car. We exchanged our thoughts about our successful parasailing adventure. "I think I'm ready to try bungee jumping," she said. "We have ten percent discount coupons."

I didn't share her enthusiasm for this latest challenge to living to be old people. "I don't know about bungee jumping," I cautioned.

"We've already been on the Flying Fox and just finished parasailing. Anyway, we're short of money."

"We could use our American Express card," she argued. "We could get videos of this adventure to show everyone back home."

I continued to voice my opposition to her latest proposal. She continued to voice her opposition to my opposition. "You don't have to do it if you don't want to," was her final argument. "I'm going to do it. We have plenty of time today, and we can put the charges on our credit card."

I was defeated. I would have to jump. The thought of returning to the Solomon Islands, and later to the States, to tell of our adventures was foremost in my mind. Paula would be gushing about how much fun she had bungee jumping and showing the video. I would be relegated to showing my tee-shirt that read: "I watched and was amazed."

We drove to the bungee jumping area and made our way to ticket counter. I presented our American Express card and said we wanted to jump and have videos taken. "Sorry, we don't take American Express," the clerk said. "Do you have another card?"

"We don't have another card and we're short of cash," I said. "We'll have to do this the next time we're in Taupo."

Paula looked disappointed. I feigned looking disappointed. We went back to our room, ate a bite, then went to play pool and have a beer. We finished our day by setting in our indoor spa and watching television.

We woke without definite plans for the day. "How much more time do we have in New Zealand?" I asked.

It's Friday the thirteenth," Paula answered. "We leave from Auckland on March 18. That give us five more days."

"I wonder if our Farmer-to-Farmer Volunteer has arrived in Honiara."

"We could call and find out. It seems like a long time since we left the Solomons."

We did call the Peace Corps office and learned that the volunteer and his wife were in Honiara. We were told the couple's names were Larry and Marion Christiansen. "I'm glad they've arrived," I said. "I'm sure the logger will be a tremendous help with our projects. What else do you want to do today?"

"I really don't care," Paula said. "As long as I'm with my best friend, I'll have a wonderful day."

"I feel the same. I'm really enjoying our time in New Zealand. And you are my best friend."

We got up early the next morning and started to town. I went to the library and Paula went shopping. Paula bought a present for our granddaughter, Ashley. We picked up a few groceries on the way back to the motel. We decided to go for a ride on a jet boat to Huka Falls. We drove to the area, paid for our tickets, and stood in line to get on the boat.

Our operator explained what our ride would be like. "You're about to experience the exhilarating power of the Hukafalls Jet," he claimed. "You'll experience an incredible water-level views of the spectacular Huka Falls."

"How fast will we be going?" a young woman setting toward the front asked.

"We'll be traveling up to eighty kilometers per hour," he answered. "That's about fifty miles per hour for those of you from the States. You'll get a real thrill as I perform my trademark, 360-degree spin. Hang on and let's go!"

It was an exciting ride as promised. We were splashed by spray from the white water of the Huka Falls. We passed by clouds of steam rising where a hot stream joined the river. Our pilot zipped within a few feet of sheer rock cliffs. We returned to our starting place a little wet and happy. We went back to the motel and settled in. "Which did you like better, the jet boat ride or parasailing?" Paula asked.

"I liked them both," I said. "I wish we could have gone bungee jumping, though. That would have been an experience."

"You didn't want to go bungee jumping, you coward! Anyway, I liked parasailing better."

"We should get to bed early," I said, changing the subject. "We have to travel to Auckland tomorrow."

The thought of traveling to Auckland stopped Paula from any more critiquing of my reluctance to go bungee jumping. We spent an hour in the spa, then ate and watched television. We exchanged our customary hugs and kisses before turning in for the night.

We ate breakfast, packed our things, and drove straight through to Auckland. Paula drove most of the way. We stopped at the Manukau Mall where Paula bought Ashley and Dylan baby outfits. She planned on mailing them when we returned to Auki.

We checked in at the Gateway Motel and I made reservations for a tour of Auckland the next day. I washed Sheila's car, filled it with gas, and returned to the motel. "Let's watch television," Paula suggested. "We won't have television shows when we get back to Auki."

We went on a tour of Auckland that lasted until 12:30 p.m. We stopped at the museum then took a quick tour of Auckland including traveling to the top of One Tree Hill to view all of Auckland. After a brief rest, we went to the mall for a bite to eat. We bought chocolate bars for our friends in Auki. Paula also bought Ashley and Dylan each a pair of socks to go with their outfits and some pocket packets for Masako Isozaki. I went to the library while Paula continued shopping.

We changed clothes and went to Fiona and Paul's for supper. Sheila Stuart-McBride had arrived the night before, so she filled us in on the latest happenings in and around Auki. After supper and coffee, Sheila took us back to our room. We went down for a beer and then hit the sack. We had to get up at 4:15 a.m. to be at the airport by 5:30 a.m.

We got our 4:15 a.m. wake-up call with a knock on the door. The power was off, so we started to make our way around in the dark. It had rained during the night which may have been the cause of the power loss. The electricity came on soon and we made it to the airport without trouble.

Our flight to the Solomon Islands was uneventful. We arrived in Honiara at 2:00 p.m. We took a cab to the Peace Corps office where we expected to meet our Farmer-to-Farmer Volunteer and his wife.

# CHAPTER 22

# *Farmer to Farmer Arrival*

We took a cab to the Peace Corps office where we met Larry Christiansen and his wife, Marion. "How long have you been in Honiara?" I asked.

"Today is March 17," Larry said. "We've been here a week. I had a meeting with Robert Ramo a couple of days after I got here."

"Robert Ramo? The name doesn't ring a bell. Who is Robert Ramo?"

"Robert Ramo is the permanent secretary for natural resources for the Solomon Islands. I had a conference with him. I informed him I was here and told him what I wanted to accomplish during the three months that I'll be in the Solomon Islands."

"Interesting. It sounds like you've been busy."

"Anyway, I'm glad you're back. I need to get things done. I have a meeting scheduled tomorrow with someone from Iumi Together Holdings and Anthony Carmon from Sol-Trust. Those meetings will complete my preliminary research. We can get on to Malaita after that. I've got a lot of things I want to accomplishment before I leave on June 1."

Paula and I picked up our mail then went to Amy Newcomber's house to spend the night. "Have you met your Farmer-to-Farmer Volunteer?" Amy asked.

"Yes, we have," I said. "We met Larry and Marion Christiansen at the Peace Corps office."

"What do you think of them?"

"Marion didn't say much, but Larry seems to be a take-charge guy," I said. "I don't know how his aggressive personality will fit into Solomon Islands' laid-back way of doing things."

"I don't know how Larry's aggressive personality will fit into Charlie's way of doing things either." Paula said, with a laugh.

"You know where the shower is," Amy said. "Why don't you two get cleaned up while I go pick up the Christiansens. They're staying at the Honiara Hotel. We can have a spaghetti supper and you can get to know them better."

Amy soon returned with Larry and Marion. Larry talked about himself and his work history in the logging industry while the ladies fixed supper. The spaghetti was soon ready. We enjoyed it with a green salad and a bottle of wine. Amy returned the Christensens to the Honiara Hotel at the appropriate time. Paula and I were tired, so we went to bed while Amy was gone.

Paula and I met Larry and Marion at the office of Iumi Together Holdings early the next morning. Officials from Iumi Holdings were there as was Anthony Carmon from

Sol-Trust. Larry kept the conversations focused on himself, his work history, his previous jobs, and what he wanted to accomplish in the Solomon Islands.

Our meeting started early in the morning. Paula and Marion left during our first break to go to the Peace Corps office. Our meeting finished at 12:30 p.m. Larry went back to the Honiara Hotel to meet Marion and I met Paula for lunch at the Mendana Hotel. "I thought our meeting was productive," I said. "I also learned more about Larry Christiansen than I really wanted to know. Modesty is the only virtue that he didn't claim to possess in abundance. What did you do at the Peace Corps office?"

"Marion and I met with David and Leigh Lally," she said. "We worked on the cookbook that we're putting together. Everything was normal there. The cookbook is coming along nicely."

We left by ship the next morning and arrived at Auki early in the afternoon. We left our own luggage at our office to make it easier to get Larry and Marion's belongings to their house. It was the house that Jim and Clair Miller had recently vacated. Paula had convinced Mary Alisha that our foresters should be allowed to use it for three months because they would provide valuable assistance to Malaita.

I unlocked the front door and walked in. I flipped the light switch and the electricity was on. I opened a faucet and the water was working. I was relieved because I wanted Larry and Marion to feel comfortable. I knew there would be many occasions in which they would be without water or electricity. "This house is terrible!" Marion asserted. "We're simply going to have to get a better place! How do you expect me to live here? And it's so hot. How do you expect me to live in this miserable house in this hot weather?"

"This was the only house available," Paula said. "I was only able to get it because I'm friends with Mary Alisha."

"I would've liked to have a house as good as this when I was in Russia," Larry said. "I was there for three weeks on a Farmer-to-Farmer project. I learned to speak Russian while I was there. I won't have any trouble learning to speak pidgin English."

Christiansen at an early party

The expatriate community welcomed Larry and Marion by inviting them to their events. Marion was meek, yet took every opportunity to complain about the heat, insects, food, and housing. Larry dominated every event, regaling them with his life history and many accomplishments. I was glad that Dr. Arun Menon was in New Zealand. Had he been there, he would have let me know that he immensely enjoyed the discomfort Larry was causing me.

We kept our copies of the U.S. Constitution in a box in the spare bedroom. When I gave Chief Isaac one, he asked for more to give to men in his village. When I got four more for Isaac, I noticed that there were only about a dozen left. Paula and I decided to ask for another fifty copies. We sent a letter explaining how popular they were with our request for an additional fifty copies.

Our next few days passed quickly. Paula wanted tuna fish sandwiches for supper, but we needed tuna. I went to Margaret's Chinese Store for chili tuna, rice, and cokes. The clerk sat my order on the counter. I started reaching for my wallet, then paused. "Two rolls," I said.

The clerk retrieved two cigarettes from a pack and placed them with my order. I paid and walked home with my supplies. "Did you buy cigarettes?" Paula asked, as I was putting my purchases on the table.

"Why would I buy cigarettes?" I asked, rather than answer directly. "I don't smoke, and you don't smoke."

"You sometimes buy cigarettes because you can buy them as singles. You and that silly, old Australian."

"He really doesn't seem so silly now. It really seems logical to buy single cigarettes even though we don't smoke. Where will we ever be able to buy cigarettes one at a time when we leave the Solomons?"

"You didn't answer my question. Did you buy cigarettes?"

I smiled and raised my brow to signify an affirmative answer. We sat on the screened porch that evening and enjoyed our cokes and cigarettes.

Paula and I took the Christiansens to interesting sites in Malaita and introduced them to influential people. Among them were Matthew Kiri, the district forester for Malaita Province and Henry Doro, minister of lands for Malaita Province. I was surprised that the Malitian officials seemed very accepting of Larry and his aggressive personality.

Jim, Irene, & Paula view growing trees

Paula and I went to Misuka's garden to see if the strawberries were ready to pick.

There were not very many berries, but Paula helped Salamai pull weeds while I talked to Jim. "Jim, would you check with Chief Walasina again?" I asked. "He said that I might get to go see the pagan Kwara'ae at Siele sometime."

Jim nodded to express agreement. "I ask," he said.

Masako came to tea one Saturday afternoon. She brought us some nice cookies to enjoy with our conversations. "How do you like the new Americans?" she asked Paula.

"They're not what I expected," Paula answered. "Marion is constantly whining about the unsuitability of housing. Larry must continually stroke his own ego which is as big as the all out-of-doors."

"He thinks he knows everything," I added. "People like him that think they know everything are very annoying to people like me who really do know everything."

"Very funny," Paula said, with a laugh.

Masako joined Paula in laughing. I maintained my stoic face. "I do my best," I said.

"Is Larry helping with your sawmill projects?" Masako asked.

"We haven't been out to any of our project sites yet," Paula said. "We've talked to Simon Ruarafi about having a workshop at Buma. I don't know how Larry will be accepted. His constant story telling is becoming a real bore. He's the biggest know-it-all I've ever seen! It's obvious he's come here with his own agenda. The reasons why we asked for him to come is secondary."

Paula and I continued teaching English to J.O.C.V. nurses. They were quite sincere about improving their English skills.

Paula and I appreciated the help they gave us on our nutrition program and were always happy to help them. The J.O.C.V.s told us that their Pisin language skills created confusion for them when they spoke English.

English lessons

Our plans for having the logging workshop with the Buma community eventually resulted in a confirmed date. Larry came to our office to discuss our upcoming trip. "Who owns the land where I'm going to have my seminar?" he asked.

"It's custom land," I said. "It's not owned in the way we think of property being owned. It's communally owned with different individuals and groups asserting competing rights."

"It has to be owned by someone," Larry argued. "That's the way every country operates. There're always land deeds and titles."

"Solomon Islands is different from other countries. There are no titles or deeds on the land where we're going."

"If you don't know, you should just say you don't know! You should just admit it when you don't know something!"

The day for our workshop at Buma Village arrived. I had arranged with Eric Mason for his driver to give us a ride to Buma. "I'm glad you have a ride for us," Larry mused. "You're too fat to walk that far."

"I know that I could walk that far," I said. "I've walked farther than that many times. But I don't want to take that much time."

We arrived at the Buma project and found many Buma men waiting for us. Simon and I had previously agreed that Larry would demonstrate proper chain saw use, safety procedures, and proper tree felling techniques. We gathered at a hundred-foot tall tree that was to be cut. Larry assembled one of the chainsaws and installed the chain. "Chain on backwards," one of the Buma men observed.

"I know; I know," Larry said, as he reversed the chain. "I know; I know."

As Larry was reversing the chain, Simon told me that the man's name was Johnathon. He had worked for a logging company in Western Province for several years. When Larry had the chain saw properly assembled and filled with gas and chainsaw oil, he took an ax and strode within about twenty feet of the selected tree.

He extended his arm and held the ax in his left hand by one finger and his thumb. By doing so, he created a functional plum-bob and aligned it to the tree to determine which way it might be leaning. In due time, Larry majestically turned toward the assembly. "It should fall that way," Larry announced, as he grandiosely pointed.

"Fall that way," Johnathon immediately replied, pointing fifteen degrees left of Larry's chosen direction.

Larry glanced towards Johnathon's chosen direction. "We will fall it that way," Larry said, pointing in Johnathon's direction. "Who's going to run the chainsaw?"

I was not impressed with Larry's knowledge, skills, and abilities. This lesson helped

Johnathon cuts a tree

solidify my opinion that Larry was more likely an administrative official in the logging industry. He lacked the basic, technical skills that we needed.

Johnathon stepped forward and picked up the chainsaw without speaking. He cut the huge tree without incident. We rigged up the frame and began making lumber. Larry and I began our return to Auki. He was unusually quiet on our trip back.

Larry and I soon had a meeting with Jim Misuka, Thomas Misuka, Benjamín Kiki, and others in the Saenaua Association. Larry spent considerable time informing them of his many wonderful accomplishments and the wonderful development projects he envisioned for them. Jim told me that he had talked to Chief Walasina again about my request to visit the pagan Kwara'ae. "Walasina said no go," Jim said. "Walasina say Ben Burt go. Timi Ko'oliu die. Can't go."

Later in the week, Larry and I met with Matthew Kiri, the District Forester for Malaita Province. "I've done considerable research on the Saenaua Custom Associations Reforestation project," Larry said. "This project is being funded by the New Zealand Government. New Zealand has them planting teak and mahogany."

Matthew Kiri listened attentively. He raised his eyebrows to signify understanding or approval. "They're planting on overgrown garden areas to reclaim tropical forests that have been destroyed by slash and burn gardening," Larry continued. "Don't you think that tree species indigenous to the island could be grown?"

I didn't interrupt to state that Jim Misuka had told me they were planting pencil cedar. I didn't mention that the species being planted were designated New Zealand officials for their own reasons. Nor did I say that the New Zealand initiative included many areas where they were cutting down native species to make room for new trees. Matthew agreed that indigenous tree species could be replanted. Larry seemed pleased.

I went to the bakery after work to get a loaf of bread. I set the bread on the table when I returned home. I got a glass of iced tea and sat down to rest. "I got a telephone call from Amy Newcomber while you were gone," Paula said.

"What did Amy have to say?" I asked.

"She was calling to remind us that we have a non-formal education workshop the sixth through the tenth in Honiara."

We traveled to Honiara for the non-formal education workshop. Marla Handy was the coordinator. Marla's program was interesting, but it was largely a repeat of what we had in our initial training. Paula and I agreed that the highlight of our trip was being away from Larry.

We returned to Auki and went back to our normal routines. Needs assessments, making reports, writing articles, making action plans, and going to villages with Larry were activities that filled our days. Larry and I were walking back to Auki from one of our village visits when I noticed his arm. "How did you get that cut on your arm, Larry?" I asked.

"I did it a couple of days ago," Larry said. "It's nothing. I heal very quickly."

"Any open cut in the Solomons can be very dangerous. That small cut could quickly turn into a bad infection. I think you should get something from Dr. Graham or Dr. Paul."

"That won't be necessary. I never put anything on a simple scratch like this."

We were always happy to get home after a day's work. We finished our supper and washed the dishes on the last day in March. We were discussing playing canasta when the phone rang. Paula had a brief conversation with me being privy to what she was saying. "They're coming April first?" she asked. "That tomorrow!"

She paused a bit while the other party spoke. "Tell me again who's coming and why," she said.

"What was that all about?" I asked, when she hung up.

"That was Amy Newcomer," Paula said. "Dan Vernon, the Solomon Islands' charge de' affaires, is coming tomorrow afternoon. He wants to give the Buma Community a mock check. He's flying in at 11:00 am. He wants to get pictures to send to Washington D.C. to show a successful, S.P.A. funded project."

"They aren't giving us much notice."

"He wants to get a picture showing him giving a Buma representative a check. Amy and Marla Handy, the non-formal education workshop coordinator we met in Honiara, are coming with Dan."

"It would be nice if they were coming on a work day, so Dan could better document the project success. I'll ask Colin if I can borrow his car tomorrow. I'll go talk to Simon about Dan coming."

"Maybe you could also use Cameron's car to pick them up at the airport. We could have lunch at our house then go to the project."

"That sounds like a promising idea. If we give Simon enough time, he might be able to get some of the villagers to the project."

Dan Vernon views Buma nursery

"I think I'll also invite David Oeta and his wife, Seneth, to lunch. It will be nice for David and Dan to get to meet."

Colin let me borrow his car and I made an early trip to Buma to see Simon. I explained who Dan Vernon was and said that the Buma project was recognized as Solomon Islands' success story. Simon seemed pleased that Dan wanted to tell officials in Washington about it. "The Big Man wants a picture of him and you," I said. "He'll be giving you a piece of paper."

Simon raised his brow and nodded to show his understanding. "He'll send the picture to Washington," I continued. "Dan will tell the big man in Washington that he is giving you a check for the project. It will only be a piece of paper. You already have the money. There won't be any more money."

Everything went extremely well despite the short notice. I used Colin's car and picked up the entourage at the Auki airport. I brought them to our house where Paula was preparing lunch. Premier Oeta arrived on time with a surprise. We were expecting him to bring Seneth, his second wife, but he brought Agnes, his first wife!

We went to the Buma project for the picture taking ceremony. We were gratified that Simon had managed to have about seventy men there working on the project. I was impressed even though I had seen it several times before. Dan Vernon was also impressed. I used Colin's car and took Dan, Amy, and Marla back to the Auki Airport.

Paul Kennioriana came into our office later that week. He was accompanied by three men in their early thirties. All of the young men were neatly dressed in khaki shorts that came to their knees and button-up, collared shirts. Their faces, arms, and legs had been vigorously scrubbed and their short crew-cut haircuts allowed their heads to shine. "Kwaio Chiefs," Paul said. "Want you live with them."

I stood and shook each of their hands. Each smiled broadly but didn't speak. "I would be honored to visit your village," I said. "I have heard a lot about the Kwaio people."

Paul blushed deeply. "Want Charles and Paula live with Kwaio forever.

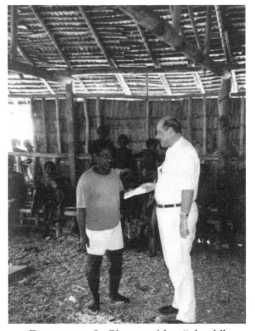

Dan present0s Simon with a "check"

Keesing lived with them, went away. David and Kate lived with them, went away. Want you live with them forever."

I looked at Paul inquisitively. I thought this might be a Robert Dettka moment. His look said that he and the Kwaio were very serious. "It's great honor," Paul said.

I knew we didn't want to live them with the rest of our lives, but it was not an offer to be summarily rejected. I told them it would be difficult. I told them we had many things to consider with our families in the U.S. I thanked them profusely without refusing or accepting their invitation.

We talked about our invitation to spend the rest of our lives with the Kwaio over supper. "Do you remember what is happening tomorrow?" Paula asked, changing the subject.

"All I can think of us the van den Bosch and Isozaki anniversary party," I said. "But that's not tomorrow. The only other thing I can think of is we have an appointment with J.O.C.V. Coordinator Yasuo Kasai," I said. "Yasuo and Masako made arrangements for us to discuss the possibility of getting jobs teaching jobs in Japan. He's coming to Auki to meet us and see the Buma project."

"Tomorrow is April 12th. It's Katie van den Bosch's sixth birthday. We said we would go to her birthday party."

We went to van den Bosch's the next day for Katie's party. We later met with J.O.C.V. Coordinator Kasai and escorted him to the Buma project. We thought our meeting with Mr. Kasai was positive. He asked us to each write a resume' that

Isozaki and van den Bosch anniversary party

he would forward to Japanese officials with letters of recommendation.

We had joint parties for Yasuo and Masako's thirty-third wedding anniversary and Dr. Paul and Dr. Teresa's twelfth wedding anniversary. Paula baked a cake for the event. The party was well attended. Everyone gave them small gifts and cards. It was a nice party, and everyone left around midnight.

Paula and I were working on articles for the *Malaita Nius* when we had a visitor. He introduced himself as a chief and asked us to travel to Manna'oba and Basakana for needs assessment. I was very interested in going because Manna'oba was the island where John Renton had lived for a few weeks when he first landed in the Solomons. I began planning for the trip.

Larry and I accepted an invitation to travel to Bina. Larry was very interested in Bina because it was a likely spot for a deep-water port. He knew there was currently a proposal and study to develop a deep-water port. Larry saw Bina offering the opportunity for shipping. He mentioned Bina was in an area that had more virgin forest in the surrounding areas than other parts of Malaita.

There was an established, commercial sawmill at Bina. The equipment was old, but most was functioning. One of the sawmill employees insisted that we look at a piece of equipment that wasn't working.

Larry and I didn't think we were there to repair logging equipment, but we gave it a cursory look. We then announced we didn't know what was wrong.

"Most volunteers that come to the Solomons islands are teachers," I observed. "There are also volunteers like Paula and me that work in community development. What they need more of are volunteers with practical

Bina's sawmill

skills. Volunteers that can repair equipment and teach the younger generation those skills. I have been asked to fix five typewriters since I've been here. I'm not a typewriter repairman and I didn't have tools or parts, but I was able to get all five of them to work."

Irene & Paula plant an avocado

Paula thought her avocado sprouts were getting large enough to transplant. We took the plants and made a trip to see the Misuka family.

I visited with Jim while Paula and Irene planted the three avocado trees. "How long do you think it will take them to bear fruit?" Paula asked, on our way back to Auki.

"I can't guess," I said. "However long it takes, we won't be here to see it. I do wonder what we will do next. I'm really not ready to go back to Kansas. Maybe you will get a Peace Corps minority appointment."

"I think about that possibility a lot. It would really be exciting."

"Whatever happens, we'll be ready for it. But for now, we have our Peace Corps projects to complete."

# CHAPTER 23

# *Farmer to Farmer Departure*

I was preparing breakfast a few days later while Paula was getting dressed. "I'm going to go to Busurata today to visit with their women's group," she said. "Larry said he wanted to go with us and talk to the men. You didn't answer when Larry asked if you were going to go."

"I'm not going to go," I said. "I have some things I need to catch up on."

"I think that you don't want to go because you're aggravated with the whole bunch of them. You're upset about being refused to see the pagan Kwara'ae for the second time. You're also aggravated because Larry seems to have convinced Kwara'ae tribe members that he can walk on water."

I was a little miffed because she was really accusing me of acting childish. I was not acting childish! I didn't argue with her because I was much too busy thinking of things that I had to catch up on. We walked to the office to wait for Larry. "What are you going to do while I'm gone?" she asked.

"I'm going to catch up on things," I answered. "I have many important things to do. I haven't decided on what I'll do first."

Larry soon came, and they left for Busurata. I busied myself looking for things to catch up on. I remembered that I had a typewriter to fix and set it on the desk. I started pushing keys one at a time to see why the thing wouldn't work. They all seemed to function well. I put in a sheet of paper and started typing. I was stopped by the "r" and "y" keys sticking when I tried typing: "Larry is a jerk."

I thought it likely that I could spring each key in turn until they could pass freely. However, I thought it would be best if I took

Larry and Paula view Malitians practicing traditional lumber manufacturing

more time to consider my options. I considered my options for some time then went to an early lunch. After a long lunch, I thought I should consult with George Toritelia in case he had something important to tell me. "Hello George," I greeted him. "How are you today?"

George smiled and raised his brow in way of a greeting. His white teeth were striking. I chatted with him and learned that he didn't have anything important to tell me. I then went to see Fred Fono, Malaita's financial officer. Fred didn't have anything to tell me. I went in turn to see Premier Oeta, Paul Kennioriana, Albert Nori, and Colin Cameron. All of the men seemed pleased to see me, but none had anything important to tell me. I returned to my office to catch up on things. I continued studying the typewriter until Paula and Larry returned.

We received a package from Bob and Des Renner that week. They had sent candy, a calendar, Kool-aid, taco seasoning, and a sewing repair kit. Paula wrote letters to Bob and Des and her folks. Paula, David Dwayne, and I joined Father Jon for supper and canasta. Father Jon and I were partners and we won both games we played. David Dwayne left, so Paula took the opportunity talk to Father Jon privately. "I've decided that I definitely want to be baptized," Paula said. "I asked Sheila and Dr. Graham to stand in for my parents and they said they would."

"This will be very special event," Father Jon said. "You might want to have Bishop Loft perform the baptism. I already asked him, and he said he would."

"That's very nice of Bishop Loft, but I don't want him to baptize me. I want you."

"Then that's what I'll plan. I'll let you know when I have arrangements finalized."

I got up the next morning feeling refreshed from my good sleep accentuated by paludrine dreams. "I think I'll stay home today." I announced. "I don't feel very well."

"I don't think you're sick," Paula answered. "I think you want to stay home to write your John Renton book and stay away from Larry!"

"That's not true," I protested. "I really don't feel well. I probably have malaria."

"Well, if you think you might have malaria, you better take a blood sample for checking."

Paula went to the office while I worked on my book about John Renton. I decided I didn't have malaria, so I didn't bother to make a blood slide. Paula brought a letter from Jim and Sherry when she came home for lunch. I went to the office in the afternoon. We wrote an article on our Farmer-to-Farmer program for the *Malaita Nius* and sent a copy to Amy Newcomber. Alison, Colin, and David came for supper that evening.

We went to Dr. Graham's and Sheila's home for the Jewish Passover meal then went to morning mass. Dr. Graham and Sheila invited us over for dinner. We were late, so Sheila called and told us that Dr. Graham was coming to pick us up. We really enjoyed the evening.

Yasuo and Masako came by that Friday and asked if we wanted to go to the falls. We asked them if David could go with us. Of course, they said he could come. We had a picnic lunch then we guys climbed the river to get to the falls. Paula swam in the pool while Masako watched. We all got bitten by insects, especially me. Paula and I took showers with buckets of hot water when we got home.

Masako, Yasuo, Paula,
and Charlie at the falls

David and Monique came that evening and we played canasta. David left to spend the night at Monique's house and Monique spent the night with us.

I walked to the Saturday market to buy vegetables for the upcoming week. I was disappointed because few venders were there due to a holiday. Larry-the-Logger stopped in and Dean, David, and Toby soon arrived. Paula fixed pancakes for everyone for breakfast. Monique went home, and Paula and I wrote letters and worked on resume's. Paula fixed supper and we went to bed early.

It was Chloroquine Sunday and Paula was getting ready to go to church. "Are you going to go to mass?" she asked.

"No, I'm going to stay home," I said. "I need to work on my resume' and you should work on yours too. We have to get them finished and sent to Mr. Kasai."

Easter dinner party
Katie didn't let a fractured
wrist slow her down

Dr. Paul, Dr. Teresa, and the van den Bosch children came over for coffee after church. Katie had her wrist in a cast. "What happened to Katie?" I asked.

"She fell off our water tower and fractured her wrist last Wednesday," Dr. Paul said. "She's much better today."

Paula baked a cake, cooked a pot of lima beans, and made guacamole dip for Easter dinner at Dr. Graham's and Sheila's. We ate dinner at 2:00 p.m. then played Pictionary and Dingbats. Larry didn't want to play the games, so he and Marion left. Paula watched Sheila's video on daycare. "I have a little song you might be interested in," Dr. Graham said. "Would you like to hear it?"

This was first time that Dr. Graham or Sheila had offered to play a song, but I didn't think anything of it. "Sure," I answered. "Let's listen to the song."

The song began with a somber tune. The lyrics were sung slowly by a man with a deep, base voice. The lyrics described a macho lumber jack who could fall a tree with one powerful swing of his ax. He was a tall man with wide shoulders and narrow hips. He had black, wavy hair, a square jaw, and pearly, white teeth. I had an image of Paul Bunyan. It was definitely the image that Larry-the-Logger had for himself.

The song progressed with the singer's voice getting faster and higher. The macho lumber jack was being transformed into a much less manly figure. The song continued with quicker and quicker tempo. The singer's voice was eventually elevated to a soprano. It ended on a happy note with the lumber jack wearing a pink, classical tutu performing minuets in a gay bar. Everyone seemed very pleased with the song. None more than me.

We came home in time to go to Father Jon's for canasta. Father Jon and I were partners and Monique and Paula were partners. We played from 7:00 p.m. to mid-night. Father Jon and I won four out of five games. Monique spent the night with us.

We had left-over cake for breakfast. When Monique went home, Alison came over and had Paula blow-dry her hair. It looked very nice. Paula and I made Katie a get-well card. Paula took it to her and had coffee and cake with the van den Boshes. When Paula came home, we went to see Larry and Marion. "Larry, we came to talk to you about a trip to Basakana and Maana'oba," I said. "We have a request to look at their forests and make recommendations."

"That's what I'm here for," Larry answered. "When do you think we can go?"

"I don't think Paul Kennioriana will arrange transportation because Basakana and Maana'oba are out of the area where Paula and I are assigned. I can talk to Eric Mason about renting his truck to get us there. Can you pay for the truck rental?"

"I have enough funds to pay for the trip. How long do you think we should plan on being gone?"

"We should plan on two or three days. I'll let you know when we can get transportation."

We stopped by to see Eric Mason on our way to work. Eric agreed to provide transportation. We also talked to Mathew Kuri later in the morning about going to Basakana and Maana'oba with us. He said he would go. I asked a woman in the premier's office, Bernadette, if she would type our resume's for SI$ 1.00 per page. Bernadette agreed to do our typing. Paula wrote a letter to her sister, Brenda, and completed her quarterly report on Saenaua.

Rocky came to see us in the afternoon. He was drunk on his butt. I recognized that my efforts to be culturally sensitive by having George ensure that Rocky didn't come in drunk hadn't been successful. I remembered that Paula was annoyed when Rocky told her to shut-up because she was only my child. I sent him away with an admonition not to come back when he was drinking.

I felt a little guilty for being strict with Rocky. However, since it seemed likely that I would have to choose between Rocky or Paula being mad at me, I made the right choice. Paula didn't comment about the incident, but she seemed pleased. Larry stopped in and we talked about about our upcoming trip.

Our weekend was uneventful. We went shopping at the Auki market Saturday morning. Father Jon and Monique came over in the evening for canasta. We went to church on Sunday, and Colin and Alison came over in the evening and ate supper with us.

The sun was shining when we walked to work Monday morning. Colin soon stopped in our office with some news. "Do you know a young Kwaio man named Jacob?" he asked. "He only has one arm"

"Yes, I know Jacob," I said. "He has talked to me a couple of times about developing a project. I told him it might be possible if a chief would make a request."

Colin and Jacob with
human teeth jewelry

"Well, Jacob is in my office with a human teeth necklace. I thought you might like to see it. He also has a human teeth headband."

"I would definitely like to see it! I read about them in books. They said that old ramos used to wear then as trophies. They wove them into jewelry to displaying how many enemies they had killed. I thought souvenir hunters had taken all of them out of the Solomons."

I accompanied Colin to his office where Jacob was waiting. Jacob showed us a large necklace and a headband that had been woven into traditional pieces displaying human teeth. Colin tried them on for my photo opportunity.

April 22, 1992 was the day we had scheduled to go to Maana'oba and Basakana. We left Auki around 9:00 a.m. via Samson's truck. No one from forestry went with us. We stopped at Kwaisulunu to pick up Peter Ufa. Peter had broken his hand and his wife had just came home with their fifth baby. He sent his brother, Phillip, instead.

We arrived at a staging area where a canoe was waiting to take us to Basakana Island. Phillip insisted that our driver go with us. He was concerned that the driver would leave without us. Marion and Paula stayed on the mainland because the canoe was full. Two Solomon women from Basakana paddled across the channel in a dugout canoe to get Paula and Marion.

It was soon approaching darkness when Paula and Marion arrived. Our evening meal was soon ready, and we were seated on the ground. We were served fresh fish for the main course. Our fish had been prepared by throwing them on a small cooking fire. They were whole, had not been gutted, and still had their scales. When they were deemed properly cooked, our chef removed them from the fire with bamboo tongs. We brushed away the dirt and ash and managed to eat them with kumara.

Larry and Charlie view
Basakana Island forest

Paula and I were assigned a private home for the evening. "How was your canoe trip with the women?" I asked.

"Marion was scared out of her wits," Paula said. "She was shrieking constantly and rocking the canoe. We were lucky to make it without sinking."

Morning arrived, and we walked to the forested area. Marion made a real effort but couldn't go on. Paula turned around and went back to the village with Marion. We viewed the forest with Larry promoting sophisticated logging and marketing techniques.

We returned to the mainland in a large dugout canoe late in the afternoon. The

Charlie helps paddle the canoe

natives teased me about my poor paddling skills by calling me a bush man. Larry made a comment that the canoe might sink because I was so fat.

Eric's driver took us on to Takwa where we visited with Father Sebo while Phillip arranged for a canoe to take us to Maana'oba. We spent the night on Maana'oba in a young men's house that was under construction. We went to bed early. "How was your day with Marion?" I asked.

"About what you would expect," Paula said. "She fell three times going back to Basakana. We visited with village women until you came back."

The night was cool, but we didn't sleep well because the villagers were singing and dancing most of the night. We learned in the morning they were preparing for a bride-price ceremony. Their preparation was why they were awake all night. Marion waited on us in Maana'oba while we trekked through the forest.

We returned to Maana'oba, ate lunch, then returned to the mainland in a larger dugout. Marion had another big scare of the day. By the time we reached the mainland, Paula and Marion were soaking wet from the waist down. We returned to Auki and went to Masako and Yasuo's for supper. They gave us Japanese mayo for our anniversary.

We received fifty more copies of the U.S. Constitution that week. We had given away all that were in our first shipment. We opened the box, and each took a few to give to Solomon friends who had asked for one. We talked a little about life and privileges of being U.S. citizens with each present.

Ros Angs and her friend Leslie were visiting the van den Bosch family. Ros was accompanied by her daughters, Louise Angs and Cicely Angs. In the morning, Paula and Dr. Teresa took Leslie, Ros, Louise, and Cicely to Salamai's garden. Ros and Leslie took lots of pictures and they all bought vegetables.

Paula had a cool drink at the van den Bosch home then came home for lunch. She joined me in the afternoon at the office. Tai came by to talk about us doing a nutrition talk on May 5 at Malu. Anthony came by and borrowed the key board when we got home.

Paula fixed a stir fry and we took it over to Larry and Marion's house. We planned on eating then playing canasta afterwards. We talked about the logging workshops over the stir fry. Larry showed me his lap-top computer on which he was making notes. He read what he was writing for his report to his V.O.C.A. Farmer-to-Farmer sponsors.

I was surprised to learn that he had documented what I had told him about the Solomons. He had disagreed with me on every critical issue, but what he had written in his report was accurate. "This was the most fun time that I've had with Larry," I said, when we were walking home.

"I agree," Paula said. "We had an enjoyable time once Larry finally shut his yap!"

Paula went shopping at the market early in the morning then judged girl's netball uniforms. Paula and I stopped by van den Bosch's house for a cold drink. I fried a pumpkin for lunch. Everyone congregated at our house. We decided to go to the Fiu River to listen to water music.

Malaita women made unique music by singing while slapping the water to provide rhythm. The music was lovely.

We continued on to Dukwasi to see the Riba Cave. Riba Cave was dark and only Colin had a flashlight. Hundreds of swallows nested in the cave making the floor slippery with their excrement. Riba Cave featured a

Women making water music

sinkhole, several subterranean chambers, an underground river and huge stalagmites and stalactites. I expected the cave to end, but it led to an open basin. The basin was circular

Charlie with stalagmites

with the basin area being about two acres. It was covered with trees and grass. It would have made a wonderful place for a picnic. We talked about a future excursion and returned to Auki through the swallow excrement.

Larry and I made a trip to Buma for an update on the forestry project. We took care of business and began our walk back to Auki. "I could walk forever," Larry bragged. "I can outwalk any white man in Malaita. I want to get Matthew Kiri in a situation like this, so I can show him up. I know I can outwalk Matthew. You could walk farther if you weren't so fat."

We continued our jaunt in silence. I wondered if anyone would notice if I returned to Auki without Larry. I wondered if I returned without him, if anyone would care enough to ask where he was. I stopped and removed my belt. I showed Larry the worn place on my belt that marked the current size of my waist.

I then wrapped the belt around Larry's waist and held the hole that indicated the size of Larry's waist. "It seems my waist is two inches larger than yours," I said. "I don't think that two inches difference is waist sizes is important enough for us to have any more conversations about it. Don't you agree?"

Larry stood slack-jawed. I was gratified to learn that he was capable of having his mouth open without spewing stupidity. I aggressively stepped toward him. "I don't think we're going to have any further discussions about me being fat!" I asserted. "Don't you agree that this topic has been exhausted of any benefit that it might have ever had?"

Larry didn't respond which was also gratifying. I stepped back and replaced my belt. We continued our walk toward Auki. I thoroughly enjoyed Larry's silence. The wind made a melodious sound as it passed through the trees. Birds called out to attract our attention. I noticed the unique odor of wet, decaying plants. I definitely enjoyed Larry's silence.

Larry seemed to be walking slower. I quickened my pace to see how he would react. I didn't think he could outwalk Matthew Kiri. I didn't think he could walk on water. However, I thought he should have been capable of walking back to Auki without difficulty. He started falling behind and I noticed him sweating profusely. I slowed to his pace. He went even slower. "I don't feel very good," he said. "I don't know what's wrong."

I thought it unlikely that my mild rebuke could be causing him any physical problems, but he did look sick. The farther we went, the worse he looked. "Larry, you really don't look well," I said. "I don't think we should go all the way to Auki. I think we should stop by Kilu'ufi Hospital and see a doctor."

"O.K. I'm sure I can make it to Kilu'ufi."

I knew Larry was sick. He had been in the Solomon Islands for nearly two months. This was the first time I said something that he didn't offer a contrary opinion. We made it to Kilu'ufi where Larry was admitted. I continued walking home where I found Paula. I explained that Larry was sick and had been admitted into Kilu'ufi. We went to Christianson's home and told Marion.

Dr. Graham stopped by that evening and told us that Larry had an acute infection throughout his system. He also told us that he had stopped by and told Marion before he came to our house. "I offered to take her to Kilu'ufi to see him," Dr. Graham said. "She didn't seem concerned about Larry and she didn't indicate that she wanted to go to see him."

Charlie and Paula celebrate their 25th wedding anniversary Dr. Teresa, Katie, Peter, and Elisabeth also pictured

Paula and I celebrated our twenty-fifth wedding anniversary on May 7 by having supper with Dr. Paul and Dr. Teresa. On May 9, Masako and Yasuo had a big party for us. Alison had crocheted bride and groom dolls. They had the number 25 setting upright on the cake.

We were given a nice plaque of Malaita that everyone had signed. Marion was there and chatted with everyone. She was cheerful and engaged in conversations on many topics. "How is Larry getting along?" Paula asked her, during the party.

"Dr. Graham says he's getting along fine," Marion answered. "I haven't been out to see him."

Paula and I had been selected to provide technical assistance for incoming Peace Corps Group 44. We went to Honiara on May 10 to attend a three-day workshop on the training of trainers. We worked in the Peace Corps office preparing for the May 17 arrival of the new trainees. We helped with logistics planning and made and critiqued lesson plans.

We stayed with Amy Newcomber during the three days. David and Leigh were also going to help at Group 44 training and were at Amy's most of the time. We had another interview with Yasuo Kasai about teaching English as a Second Language in Japan for J.O.C.V.s. Kasai San asked us to prepare a paper on a Peace Corps/J.O.C.V. integrated team approach.

We talked to Amy about our job possibilities in Japan and said we might need to leave around August 13. She told us we needed to write a letter to Gus explaining our situation and asking for early termination authority. We had supper with Bill Wise and Tom Scherer while we were in Honiara. We flew back to Auki May 18. Sheila and Vincent picked us up at the airport and took us home.

Larry was released from the hospital soon after we returned to Auki. He looked pale and weak, but his spirts were good. He insisted that he was going to continue working. Gus Comstock finally told him that he must leave the Solomon Islands immediately. Larry reluctantly made flight arrangements. "When are they leaving?" Paula asked.

"Next Thursday," I said. "They're scheduled to go to Honiara on the *Compass Rose* at 9:00 a.m. They will stay in the Madonna Hotel then fly to the U.S. Friday."

We helped Marion and Larry pack their things. Marion was more assertive during the process. Missionaries Graham and Glenda had a going away tea for Larry and Marion. It was well attended by Auki's expatriates. On their departure date, we helped Larry and Marion get their things to the *Compass Rose*. "That part of our Solomon Islands' adventurer is over," I said, as the ship pulled away from the dock. "How do you feel now that they're gone?"

"It feels like the weight of the world has been lifted off my shoulders," Paula answered. "I wonder if Marion will revert to being subservient to Larry."

"I wonder what Larry will say about us in his report. I would really like to get a copy of it. But now, we have to get ready to travel to Makira to help train Group 44."

# CHAPTER 24

# *Training in Makira*

Paula was thoughtfully making an entry into her diary. "We've accomplished a lot in the time we've been here," she said. "It makes me wonder why the group that we replaced had trouble getting things started."

"I credit Paul Kennioriana for a lot of our successes," I said. "He established guidance for us then allowed us freedom to develop projects that would benefit the villages and people we were working with. Dr. Graham got us off to a good start with the Nutrition program and appointment to the Malaita Province Primary Health Care Committee."

"I hope that our projects are continued after we leave."

"I'm concerned about that too. I really like the Solomon Islanders we're working with. I want them to be successful."

"Maybe we can get some of the governments officials or aid donors

Paul Kennioriana and family

that have ongoing programs to add some of ours to the existing programs."

We asked Paul Kennioriana and his family to come to dinner to talk about ideas. Paul showed enthusiasm and encouraged us to pursue our initiative. We first talked to District Forester Matthew Kiri and Minister of Land Henry Doro. Both men supported our goals of seeing the projects continued.

We talked to New Zealand officials who were funding Saenaua Association's reforestation program. Paula talked to the women and I talked to the men. The officials agreed to include the Buma Sawmill project into the Solomon Islands reforestation program.

We also talked to officials with European Economic Community. The European Economic Community officials were implementing a $23 million grant. After discussion, research, and consideration, the Buma Sawmill project was cited as the model for small scale timber production's reforestation systems that wish to be funded by the European Economic Community's $23 Million grant.

We began working on drafts of our Peace Corps Descriptions of Service. We used our quarterly reports for information that we included in our descriptions. "This is really getting big," Paula said. "I'm up to nine pages already."

"Mine is just a large," I agreed. "But we did those things. I don't know how we will ever use our descriptions of service, but I think we should make a record of our accomplishments."

The Peace Corps organized a trip for Paula and me to travel to Makira. We were expected to familiarize ourselves with the villages and learn if the villagers were ready for the Group 44 training. I could foresee a problem with water seal toilets not being completed as promised. Paula and I celebrated my forty-eighth birthday in Manabina Village, Makira on Sunday, June 14, 1992.

We flew back to Honiara and made a report to Gus and Amy. We returned to Auki by ship. I picked up the mail at the Auki Post Office on the way to our house. The mail included a large envelope from Oregon. I opened it when we got home. "Paula, do you remember me telling you that I wished we could get a copy of Larry Christenson's final report?"

"I remember you saying that," she said. "We didn't think there was much chance of that happening."

"I didn't think we would get a copy either. But here it is!"

I began reading Larry's final report for his Solomon Islands' V.O.C.A. forestry assignment. It was immediately apparent that the report was well written. "Paula, your first impressions of Larry were spot on," I said.

"What first impressions are you talking about?" Paula asked.

"You told Masako that it was obvious that Larry came here with his own agenda. You said the reasons for us requesting him were secondary."

"What specifically did he write?"

"He begins his report by correctly stating the reasons why we asked for a forester. He wrote the objectives were to improve sawmill operations, improve quality of processed timber, improve reforestation skills, and introduce timber marketing skills. But then he wrote that in achieving these objectives, the focus became more complex and enlarged."

"It sounds like he was saying he knew what we wanted, but that he came with his own agenda."

"It sounds exactly like that. You had him pegged right from the beginning."

"Did he say anything about us?"

"I haven't read the entire document. I'm impressed with what I've read. It's well written and accurate."

Larry correctly noted that our sawmill projects would not create problems to the eco-systems. He scribed that our projects should be recognized as a first step in developing a forest industry. "Paula, look at this comment that Larry made," I said. "He thinks that investment and venture capital is needed to develop forest and resources as a viable element for progress."

"Do you think that he had a goal of developing a plan for American timber interests to invest in the Solomons?" Paula asked.

"I think it's possible. But you were right when you said he came here with his own agenda. If he did have potential investors, he should have told us. We could have worked together to make something positive and permanent for Solomon Islands."

Paula took Larry's document and continued reading. "Look at these great ideas," she said. "He's developed a sound economic development plan that he proposes be implemented in phases. He begins with a proposal to develop a sawed timber receiving station and air-drying facility at Auki."

"That does sound very practical. What's your opinion of his next phase?"

"He advocates chain saw operations like we started at Buma and Saenaua evolve to break down logs into cants for remanufacturing at a central location."

"He didn't say anything like that when he was here. Again, it's very practical. What do you think about the next phase?"

"In phase three, he proposes that sawmilling and veneer manufacturing facilities be established. It assumes that a deep-water port would be developed. His phase four proposal includes developing a wood chipping facility."

"Larry didn't say anything about those things while he was here. He spent most of his time talking about how important and smart he was."

Paula went to the refrigerator to get us glasses of iced tea. She handed me the report on her way back. I continued reading where she left off. "Larry recognizes the high quality and beauty of hardwoods indigenous to Malaita," I said. "He thinks that a fine furniture manufacturing enterprise would be practical. He sees the availability of material and recognizes the carving and craft skill of native populations. He writes that this should be an attractive way to add value to the forest output and provide jobs for Malaita citizens."

I eventually read the report in its entirety. Larry had complementary things to say about Paula and me in his conclusion. He wrote:

> The assignment was rewarding. As most first-time volunteers, I was generally disappointed in what appears to be progress in inches rather than feet. What successes I did enjoy were the result of the foundation the Peace Corps team of Charles and Paula Sellens established in their community development mission.

> The two forestry programs they had initiated prior to my arrival were the centerpiece of my effort. Because of the high esteem in which the Sellens were held by the villager and provincial leadership of Malaita, my assimilation and acceptance was rapid and gratifying.

"I want to get a copy of his report to our replacements," I said. "If Larry's trip was financed by investors as a fact-finding mission, our replacements could do more for the Solomon Islands that we could have ever imagined."

Jim and Salamai Misuka organized a going-away feast for us at one of the forestry sites. It was raining softly, so we met under an open shelter. Benjamín Kiki drove up in a pick-up to join the ceremonies. They had a small fire going to dry us off. Thomas Misuka spoke briefly and thanked us for what we had done for them. Others added brief remarks and thanks.

Several young members of the Saenaua tribe were present. "The Saenaua people have a big project with New Zealand," I told them, when I was asked to speak. "Your fathers and mothers are planting trees and taking care of the trees to help them grow."

I pointed to the young, growing, project saplings. Both the children and adults listened attentively. "When trees are big, New Zealand people will buy them," I continued. "Most of the old people that are doing this work will be gone when the trees are sold. They're working so you will benefit in the years to come. When your mothers and fathers are old, you must take care of them. You must take care of them to thank them for the work they are doing today to take care of you in the future."

I didn't expect either the adults or children to respond. None did, either verbally or with body language. Paula and I exchanged thanks and hand-shakes with the Saenaua tribe members then we returned to Auki.

Father Jon baptized Paula on Sunday June 23. She was then confirmed and took her first communion in the Catholic Church. Dr. Graham and Sheila stood in for her parents. Father John from Papua New Guinea made a video of the baptism, so we could share it with people we knew.

We had a champagne brunch afterwards then celebrated with Monique, Sheila, and Dr. Graham at Father Jon's house. Of course, supper and games of canasta were part of the celebration. Father Jon gave Paula a rosary and a plaque. The rosary was very special because the Pope had given it to Father Jon.

We had our first in a series of expatriate, going away parties on Sunday, June 24. It was a lovely event hosted by Dr. Tereasa and Dr. Paul. "Time has gone by so fast," Paula said. "It doesn't seem possible that we've been here for two years."

Yasuo and Masako organized our next going away party on June 26. Many people came to wish us well. What we would do next was a frequent topic of conversation. "Have you heard anything about job possibilities in Japan?" Masako asked.

"We haven't heard anything yet," I said. "We continue to hope that we will get job offers."

We learned that Group 44's new trainees had arrived in Honiara. Nan, Mark, and Connie arrived for their walkabout a few days later on an afternoon flight. I used Colin's and Alison's car and met the trio at the airport. We introduced ourselves and gave them a ride to Auki. Mark and I took their luggage to the Auki Lodge while Paula finished supper and visited with Nan and Connie.

Nan and Mark were a married couple who were replacing us. Connie was a sixty-nine-year old man who was to work in the provincial transportation department. He was to supervise and train the Malitian mechanics in performing their duties. During our supper, I told Connie about the incident I had with Tire Man wanting to borrow money using a transportation department tire as collateral.

Paula and I took Mark and Nan to see the Buma and the Saenaua projects. We told them we were hopeful the projects continued. We also gave Mark and Nan a copy of Larry's V.O.C.A. report and talked about the possibilities. The trio completed their walkabout and returned to Honiara. They soon transferred to Makira for Group 44 training in Manakuki Village and Manabina Village on Makira Island.

Simon Buarafi organized a feast for us in Buma. Virtually every villager was there. The feast featured pork baked in umus, kumaras, bananas, pineapples, popos, other fruits, fish, megapode eggs, green coconuts, and taro pudding. The food was served on banana leaves, Solomon style.

We were seated together and ate with our fingers. When our meal was finished, we went to Simon to say good-bye. A small girl stood beside Simon. "My granddaughter," Simon said. "Name Patricia."

Buma Village preparing our feast

We told Patricia we were happy to meet her and shook her hand. We moved about thanking other villagers and saying our good-byes. Simon gave us pork wrapped in banana leaves to take with us. We gave the pork to our driver when we got out of the vehicle in Auki.

Paul Kennioriana organized a debriefing meeting in his office. Albert Nori made remarks about our work with literacy and reporters for *Malaita Nius.* He didn't say anything about the G.E.D. program. We didn't say anything about the G.E.D. program effort. We made only positive comments.

Dr. Graham made brief comments about the successes we had with various projects. I responded by thanking him for our first assignment with the nutrition program and later appointment to the Malaita Province Primary Health Care Committee. Paula informed everyone how he and Sheila contributed to our project successes by loaning us their cars.

Colin added comments about our projects and successes. Paula responded with appreciation for his help in making our projects successful. She told everyone that he and Alison were always willing to loan us their car.

Paul ended the debriefing by complementing us for our tenacity to continue projects when confronted with obstacles. He specifically recognized difficulties created by land conflicts that we had to overcome when we were applying for Buma's grants.

He told everyone that I had learned to speak Kwara'ae. He related the incident in which I had called to Mange in Kwara'ae telling him to come here quickly. I was surprised that the word had spread. His praise was far too lavish, but I didn't disagree with him by stating that my Kwara'ae skill were very limited.

Paula and I flew to Makira on June 30 to begin our parts in Group 44 training. There were eleven trainees in Group 44. They had been in Manakuki four days when we arrived. Liz, a licensed attorney, was the training officer. She and her husband had been Peace Corps Volunteers in Papua New Guinea. David, Leigh, Rick, and Carrie were also volunteer trainers.

Paula described one of the trainees, Nikki, as a real sweetie. Nikki was tall, pretty, and intelligent. Her long, blond hair fit well with her cheerful personality. I told her that if I could choose a wife for our son, Chuck, I would choose her.

Roger was a single man. He was tall, slender, and athletic. He showed me a picture of his girlfriend. She was a beautiful German woman. Roger was a U.S. Army veteran who was assigned to Small Malaita. When other trainees went on their walkabouts, he wasn't sent to his job assignment because of transportation difficulties.

We learned that Roger didn't want to serve in Small Malaita. When his fellow trainees went on walkabouts, he used the time to approach Honiara officials to ask for an assignment. Honiara officials would have been happy to have him. He told Gus and Amy that he wouldn't serve in Small Malaita, but he would serve in Honiara. They were not pleased with his initiative and sent him to Small Malaita on walkabout. Their goal was to try to convince him he would be satisfied with the assignment.

There was a young, single man who was scheduled to replace Tom at the clam farm. He was another tall, blond trainee. When he told us that his mother was German, I spoke to him in German. However, he couldn't understand or speak the language of his mother.

Stephanie and Joel were a married couple. Joel was African-American, and Stephanie was a self-proclaimed feminist. They were newly-weds and spent most of their time together.

The trainees were well settled into their host family homes when we arrived. We were assigned a room with our own host family. I put up a sleeping net to ward off mosquitoes then sprayed the area where we were to spread our sleeping mats with an insecticide. This practice had proven successful on previous occasions in detouring mites from sharing our bed and blood.

Group 44 training was similar to our own. They worked on Pisin language, culture, government issues, needs assessments and health issues. There were tea breaks around 10:00 a.m. and 3:00 p.m. Peace Corps provided our lunch. Our breakfasts and suppers were furnished by our host families.

Most of the trainees attended church with their host families. Paula organized a picture taking event with everyone posing with member of our host family. Two of our host family's daughters, Joyce and Sherri posed with us.

Sherri was sixteen years old and took an immediate liking to Paula. She was very helpful in making us comfortable in our new accommodations. Both Paula and I liked her, "I think I'll take you home with me," Paula told her.

Joyce, Charlie, Paula and Sherri

Two days later, Sherri's father approached me "Decided Sherrie go with you," he said.

I understood the misunderstanding. What Paula had said as a light-hearted compliment, Sherri and her family had taken literally. They were willing to allow their daughter to go with us on what they might have thought was a permanent arrangement. I used my best culturally acquired skills to gently tell him that it would not be possible.

Liz had concerns about Connie, the 69-year-old. He refused to try to learn or speak Pisin. Most of the other trainees were adjusting better. I enjoyed learning about their lives before they joined the Peace Corps.

I also enjoyed listening to the trainees discussing their reasons for joining the Peace Corps. Joel filtered his opinions through his African-American ideology. Stephanie channeled her opinions through her feminist ideology. Most trainees were very respectful of others' opinions, but not always. "I hate that women's liberation junk!" Connie exclaimed, in response to one of Stephanie's positive comments about the feminist movement.

Everyone was silent in anticipation of how Stephanie might respond. "I was happily married for decades," Connie continued. "My wife and I got along just fine. Then that women's lib business came along. My wife bought into those stupid ideas. She ended up divorcing me."

Charlie and Paula
at the U.S. Embassy in Honiara

David broke a tooth during the training. There was no dentist in Solomon Islands, so he had to go to Vanuatu for treatment. Naturally, Leigh wanted to go with him, but Gus wouldn't have Peace Corps pay for her trip. David brought me back a chocolate bar from Vanuatu.

Paula, and I flew back to Honiara on July 4 to see Mr. Kasai. We talked to him about creating a plan for a joint Peace Corps/J.O.C.V. project. We attended an Independence Day celebration at the U.S. Embassy.

Dan Vernon was a very gracious host. We stayed with Amy waiting for our close of service conference that was to begin on the July 8.

Rick and Carrie flew in on July 6 for the close of service conference. Our first day of the conference was in the Peace Corps office. We had a Tuesday session with Nurse Mary then went to Vulelua for the rest of our conference.

While we were in a meeting at Vulelua, Amy left to take a telephone call. She promptly returned. "It's for you, Charlie," she said.

I moved to the phone. "Hello," I said. "This is Charlie Sellens."

"This is Kasai," he said. "I'm calling to tell you that you can probably have a job with J.I.C.A. in Komagane. K.T.I. Director Takashli Nagakura wants you go to Komagane to meet him for his final decision. Can you go to Japan?"

"Thank you very much, Kasai San! Of course, I'll be able to travel to Japan to meet Nagakura San!"

"I know you're at your end-of-service conference in Vulelua. Can you meet me in Honiara when your conference is over? I have a contract for you to look at and sign."

"Yes sir. Where can we meet?"

I met with Kasai San in his office that Friday afternoon. I read the contract and was happy to sign it. He told me that my job would likely start in September 1992 in Komagane, Nagano Prefecture. He told me that I definitely would have to go to Japan to meet Director Nagakura for final decision.

On July 12, we all ate supper at Bill Wise's house. We started to leave with Tom and had a flat tire. We jacked up the car and removed

Amy, Paula, Margaret, Carrie, Charles,
Matt, Bill, and Rick at Vulelua

the lug nuts. We tried to remove the tire, but it was stuck. "That's strange," Tom said. "I've never seen anything like that."

"I suspect the tire is rusted to the hub," Matt said. "Do you think we could pry it off?"

We discussed prying it off but rejected that idea. We worried that any prying might result in knocking the car off the jack. Someone suggested that we put the lug nuts on loosely then drive forward a couple of feet. The idea was that this action would break the rust seal. We did it, jacked up the car, and removed the tire easily.

Our close-of-service included extensive medical checks. Rick, Carrie, Paula and I spent over a week on the activities then prepared to return to Makira. We went to the airport Saturday morning at 6:15 a.m. to be ready to leave at 7:00. We were bumped and had to take the 10:00 o'clock flight. We returned to Rick and Carrie's house to fill the time. On the way back to the airport, we stopped at Foodtown to pick up a few groceries.

We landed on the grass runway in Manakuki and debarked the plane. David, Leigh, and most of the trainees were there. "Why is everyone here?" I asked David, when we were alone.

"Stephanie came down with malaria while you were gone," David said. "She and Joel are going to leave when the plane returns to Honiara."

"That's too bad. I really liked them. They've only been here less than two months. She must have gotten infected soon after she arrived in country."

"There was another trainee that left yesterday. He was under a lot of stress. Two days ago, he wandered out into the ocean. He was up to his waist when I saw him and got him back on land."

When Roger returned from his walkabout, he maintained his position that he would serve in Honiara but not Small Malaita. Gus eventually got the word to Roger that he had to serve in Small Malaita or terminate. I liked Roger and thought he would be successful in either location. I once asked him about his military service. "What was the focus of your Army job?" I asked.

Manakuki men build a bat tower

"I was an armor officer," he said. "I was trained in operation, tactics, and maintenance of armor forces and equipment. I trained on the M1 Abrams tank, the Bradley Fighting Vehicle, and various other equipment. I bet there won't be many Americans that served in the Peace Corps and served as an Army officer."

I understood the distinction he was making between officers and enlisted. I accepted the distinction when I was on active duty, but I didn't see a carry-over status to Peace Corps service. "It's not all that uncommon," I said. "Gus Comstock and Tom Scherer both served in the Navy. I served in the Army, same as you."

Paula and I saw a few men working on a project outside the village. We walked closer to see what they were building. They had lashed light poles together to begin constructing a small tower. "What are you building," I asked an old man who was supervising.

"Bat tower," he answered.

"What is a bat tower? What do you do with a bat tower?"

The old man went on to explain that the tower would be build higher. They would then drape spider webs among the highest extensions. The bats "sonar systems" would not detect the spider webs and small ones would be entangled. The bats were considered a delicacy. "That's something we haven't seen before," I said. "I bet if we stayed here for years, we would learn something new every day."

"These kinds of things seem normal now," Paula said. "I wonder how I will think about things like this in twenty-five or thirty years. I'm going back to our house and get our camera. No one will believe us without a picture."

I left on July 17 to attend an environmental of meeting with Kasai San and several J.O.C.V.s in his office. The nurses that were so helpful in our nutrition program were there. I traveled to Auki after the meeting and went to my own office. I was going through papers when Isaac arrived. "Come to talk," he said, earnestly. "Know you leave soon."

"Yes, Paula and I will leave soon, Isaac," I said. "I'll never forget you and my other Solomon friends."

Isaac paused and handed me two wooden picks. They were each about seven inches long with the last inch tapering to a point. They were about the same diameter as a cigar. "What are these used for?" I asked.

"Fork for eating man," Isaac answered, while demonstrating a movement to simulate how the picks were used.

"These are very special. Do you want me to have them?"

Isaac nodded and raised his brow to indicate a positive answer. I reached for my wallet to give him a present. He stopped me. "No money," he said. "This to remember me. When village convert Christians, Christians destroy these."

I thanked Isaac profusely and pledged to keep them forever. Isaac nodded and waited. He was obviously thinking deeply. I could see he was struggling to put his thoughts into words. "Send *debil* with you," he finally said. "He take care of you."

It was time for me to pause in deep thought. Isaac could see I was struggling to put my thoughts into words. I questioned Isaac to ensure that he was saying what I was hearing. I understood him to say he was offering to assign his paramount ancestor to be my personal guardian. He assured me that my understanding was correct.

I didn't dismiss the possibility that his paramount ancestor did exist and could be assigned to me. I thanked Isaac profusely, but explained that Paula and I were going to live in Japan. I opined that his paramount ancestor might not like living in Japan and harm me for taking him there. I believed that my responses and answers satisfied him.

I returned to Makira July 20. We were in a training session when we were interrupted by Nurse Mary bursting into the area. "Come see the whales!" she excitedly said. "There are three whales near land! You'll have to come quickly because they are moving away."

We all followed her outside. There were indeed three whales swimming in the bay. They were all adults and were moving away from land. These were the only whales I saw during my two years in the Solomon Islands. I felt lucky to have seen them. Connie sought me out for a private discussion later in the day. "I think I'll go home," he told me. "This isn't what I expected. I don't fit in."

2 YEARS, 2 SHELLBACKS

"Connie, I don't want to see you leave," I said. "Training was the hardest part of Peace Corps service for me. When you're finished with training, you'll go to Auki. You'll have freedom to influence how you live and interact with Solomon Islanders."

"I just turned seventy years old. I'm too old for this life."

"There are other older people serving in the Peace Corps. John and Lottie are retired and must be in their late sixties. They're functioning very well in Small Malaita. Anyway, think of the precedent you might set. There might be other seventy-year old people that want to volunteer. If you quit, maybe others might be judged by you quitting."

Roger left on July 24 because he didn't like his assignment on Small Malaita. He wouldn't agree to serve in Small Malaita, but he wouldn't voluntarily terminate. Gus Comstock eventually made the decision to send him back.

Paula and I flew back to Honiara on July 28. Kasai San had asked us to do some work on a proposal which Japan was keen to sponsor. He envisioned a joint project between J.O.C.V.s and Peace Corps Volunteers. The volunteers were to teach math in a primary school. I thought that a community development project would be more useful, but Paula and I worked diligently on the project Kasai San envisioned.

We returned to Auki and enjoyed more going away parties. Father Jon and Bishop Loft had a party for us on July 29. Father Jon joked about the primary skills needed by our replacements was the ability to play canasta. Bishop Loft had a more serious thought. "I'm glad someone like you comes along every few years," he said. "We need someone to shake us up occasionally."

Missionaries Graham and Glenda had had another party on July 30. Eric Mason had a going away party for us on July 31. Yasuo and Masako had a going away party for us. We thanked Yasuo and Masako for their efforts in getting to go to Japan. We exchanged promises to see each other when they returned to Japan.

Group 44 training had run smoothly for the most part. I wasn't very productive, because I had spent considerable time in Honiara with our end-of-service conference and meetings with J.O.C.V. officials.

Paula had arranged for us to stay with Dr. Paul and Dr. Teresa when we came back from Makira. Her idea was to allow Mark and Nan to have our house. Paula returned to Makira on August 4 to attend the swearing-in ceremony. She had an idea of giving trainees the pictures she took of them and their host family on arrival day. Her idea was well received. Peace Corps officials had the film developed and presentations were made during the trainees' graduation ceremonies.

When Paula returned, it was near the time to leave, so we didn't stay with the van den Bosch family. We packed our things and went to Honiara. We had several books that belonged to Peace Corps that we packed into a box. We left the others for Mark and Nan to continue as Auki librarians. David Duane was also traveling on our ship. He helped us load our luggage and the box of books. He put the box of books under a bench and I set the luggage in front of the books.

We arrived in Honiara without incident. We took a taxi to Amy Newcomer's house. Paula and Amy began preparing our supper while I organized our luggage. "Oh wow," I said. "I left a box of Peace Corps books on our ship."

"Take the Peace Corps pick-up and go get them," Amy said. "We'll have supper ready by the time you get back."

I drove the pick-up to the wharf, but I couldn't find the ship. When I asked, a dock worker told me that the ship had been moved into the bay for security reasons. I could see it anchored about 200 yards away. The worker told me that it would come back early in the morning to get ready for passengers. I returned to Amy's home. We enjoyed our supper and Paula and I enjoyed hot showers.

I woke early and asked Amy if I could use the pick-up to go to the wharf. When I arrived, the ship was not there. It was too early for the ship to have docked, loaded cargo and passengers, and left. "Where is the ship?" I asked a dock worker.

"Ship sunk," he answered, pointing toward the bay.

The ship's sinking somehow seemed to be a fitting end to our Peace Corps service. I returned to Amy's house and explained that the ship and the Peace Corps books were gone. Amy was neither surprised by the ship sinking nor the loss of the books. "When I was a volunteer, I lost a lot more than a box of books," she said. "Forget about it."

Dan Vernon had organized several events to pay tribute to Americans who served during the Guadalcanal Champaign. Paula and I attended the Guadalcanal American Memorial dedication on August 7, 1992. The memorial was established as a tribute to the Americans who lost their lives. The date was chosen to honor the 50th anniversary of the August 7, 1942 Red Beach landings by U.S. Marines. An account of events was inscribed on red marble tablets erected inside the monument compound.

We showed Amy our draft description of Peace Corps services. They were about ninety percent the same. "These are really big," Paula said. "They're both eleven pages long."

"Have you used to much verbiage in describing each accomplishment?" Amy asked.

"Not really," Paula explained. "For example, our Farmer-to-Farmer project was a big effort. We spent over two months with it. All I said was: 'Initiated a request for, and received, a volunteer through Volunteers in Overseas Cooperative Assistance (V.O.C.A.). The V.O.C.A. volunteer provide technical assistance in sawmilling, reforestation, and marketing of timber projects.' That's as brief as I can get it."

"Let me look at them," Amy said.

Amy reviewed the drafts. "You two really accomplished a lot in your two years," she said. "But I agree that they're too long. I checked many that you could just make into one sentence rather than your one or two paragraphs."

We followed Amy's advice and managed to reduce four pages into two paragraphs that read:

Collaborated with relevant government, nongovernment and community agencies, and groups involved in volunteer work and/or community development. Agencies include: Save The Children, UNICEF, South Pacific Commission, National Council of Women, Non-government organizations, European Economic Commission, New Zealand High Commission, and Japanese International Cooperation Agency.

Collaborated with many Solomon Islands' governmental departments including: The Office of The Prime Minister, Ministries of Home Affairs, Education, Human Resources, Health and Medical Services, Natural Resources, Police and Justice, Provincial Government, Tourism, Aviation and Transport, Works and Utilities, and the National Parliament to solicit input for programs and to establish collaborative relationships.

We spent our last few days in the Solomon Islands relaxing. We said our good-byes to our friends and made plans to travel to Japan to meet with the K.T.I. director. We flew to Japan via Hawaii and were in Komagane on August 12. This entry completes a circle that began with our Chapter 1 meeting with Nagakura San in Komagane.

Paula and I had considerable excitement and many adventures in the Solomon Islands. We made many life-long friends with Solomon Islanders and expatriates. We participated in filming a documentary about shark callers in Laulasi. We achieved a better understanding of Solomon Islands' tribal medicines. We learned Melanesian customs and had a memorable trip to Ngongosila Island.

I participated in a unique ancestor worship ceremony to a pagan Begau village. We traveled to Australia, New Zealand, and many islands in the Solomons. We visited Kennedy Island in Western Province. We received an invitation from three Kwaio chiefs to live the rest of our lives with the fierce tribe.

I thought about the goals that had prompted me to apply to the Peace Corps. I had accomplished many of my trivial objectives. I traveled south of the equator and achieved shellback status. I saw many scantily clad women in primitive villages. Some of the women danced and some of them were young and beautiful. I saw water whirling as it drained from a sink and learned that that water can whirl clock-wise and counter-clock-wise in both the northern and southern hemispheres.

I had also enjoyed success in my more consequential goals. My patriotic sense of duty to country had been fulfilled. I am as proud of my Peace Corps service as I am of my military service. I understood that learning more than I taught was not a platitude. I enjoyed adventure, excitement, and more than my share of danger. My new job with the Japanese Foreign Service exceeded my goal of obtaining international employment.

I recognize that some of my earlier goals might be considered trivial. Thus, I have developed new and more acceptable objectives. A new goal for this publication is to create interest in Peace Corps returning to the Solomon Islands. Other goals include motivating readers to consider joining the Peace Corps or organizing a travel adventure to the Solomon Islands.

Yet another objective is to encourage private timber investments based on Larry Christiansen's report for developing timber production in the Solomons. These goals are enumerated for others to accomplish. If someone does accomplish one or more of them, please acknowledge Paula and me and remember us fondly.

# *Epilogue*

**Paula Sellens and Charles Sellens.** We spent one day in Komagane then flew to Los Angeles and spent a day with our younger son, Jason. We next traveled to Las Vegas to see our older son, Chuck. We flew to Kansas City Aug 16, 2014 for visa applications with plans to travel to Russell to see other family and friends.

My mother, Josie Sellens, had an open house in Russell for our friends to come and renew acquaintances. One of the first visitors was Lelia Newcomber. "My niece, Amy Newcomber, is in the Peace Corps in the Solomon Islands," she said. "Did you happen to know Amy?"

I was flabbergasted. Of course, we knew Amy. I chided myself for failing to ask Amy if she might have relatives in Russell County, Kansas. I had thought about it, but I had resisted. I didn't want to sound as naive as the Solomon Islanders who asked if I knew a Peace Corps Volunteer from Chicago, New York, or Boston whom they knew years before.

We lived in Komagane, Nagano Prefecture for thirteen years. My job with Japan International Cooperation Agency (J.I.C.A.) was very rewarding. I enjoyed paid vacations for over three months each year. We used the opportunities to travel in the U.S. and internationally. Paula developed a successful English language school in Komagane.

We returned to the U.S. in 2005. Paula took a job teaching Family and Consumer Science at Dodge City Middle School. I taught E.S.L. at Dodge City Community College for several years. I later managed Maverick Enterprises in Greensburg. I traveled to Germany, Switzerland, Estonia, and Latvia on a fact-finding mission for Maverick Enterprises. We are retired and are both very active in the American Legion.

**Charles S. Sellens.** Chuck, now prefers to be called Charlie, joined the Army and served four years as a Ranger. He met Rhonda Brown while both were in sergeant's training school. Charlie and Rhonda married in a Shinto ceremony in Komagane, Japan in 1998. Rhonda retired after serving twenty years in the Army. She had served in the military police, criminal investigation division. After Army service, Charlie did three tours as a private contractor in Iraq. He next had a position as a security officer for the president of the World Bank. He worked in this capacity for seven years, rising to the position of head of security. He was the senior security advisor for Global Guardian at the time of this publication. Charlie and Rhonda live in Woodbridge, Virginia.

**Jason D. Sellens.** Jason moved to Japan in 1995 with Mary and Ashley. Jason taught E.S.L. in a private school for two years. Ashley attended kindergarten and began speaking Japanese. After returning to the United States, Jason and Mary divorced. Jason later married Kori who had a son, Tavin, by a previous marriage. Jason and Kori have one son, Jacob. Jason, Kori, Ashley, Tavin, and Jacob all live in Russell, Kansas. Ashley is married to Kenny Hull. They have a son, Kenny Hull Jr. Jason makes his living as an independent contractor.

**Yasuo and Masako Isozaki.** Yasuo and Masako returned to Yokohama, Japan when Yasuo's job in the Solomons was completed. Yasuo continued to work part-time for the Japanese government. We visited them several times in their home. They visited us several times in Komagane. We met their son, daughter-in-law, and grandson in Yokohama.

Yasuo and Masako's daughter, Haruko, is now Haruko "Sunny" Nishikawa. Sunny has served as a translator for many English-speaking dignitaries who were making official visits to Japan. She works under confidentiality agreements thus client names are omitted. We edited an English document for Haruko that she had translated from French to English.

I was interviewed by J.I.C.A. Magazine in 1996 for an article being written about the Peace Corps. This interview gave me an opportunity to document how much we valued Yasuo's and Masako's long-term friendship.

**Yasuo Kasai.** Paula and I met Kasai San in Tokyo when he returned from the Solomon Islands. We bought him lunch and thanked him for recommending me for employment with J.I.C.A. Kasai San continued employment with the Japanese government.

**Dr. Paul and Dr. Teresa van den Bosch.** Paula and I visited Dr. Paul and Dr. Teresa in London in November 2015. Both were working as family physicians near Guildford, about 40 miles southwest of London. Dr. Paul was a member of the steering committee of *Give a Kidney – one's enough*. He donated a kidney in 2008. Dr. Teresa donated a kidney in 2013.

Dr. Paul worked for *Médecins Sans Frontières* (Doctors Without Borders) in Jordan in 2016. He helped provide medical care to Syrian refugees and vulnerable Jordanians. Dr. Paul and Dr. Teresa were V.S.O. doctors in Sierra Leone at the time of this publication. Dr. Paul was working in the hospital and training local clinic staff. Dr. Teresa was teaching in the School of Midwifery. They were scheduled to be in Sierra Leone until April 2019.

**Katie van den Bosch.** Katie preferred to be called Kate when she reached her teens. She is now married with a corresponding name change to Kate Adams. She trained as a teacher and has lived and worked in Austin, Texas with her husband since 2014.

**Peter van den Bosch.** Peter was a junior doctor in 2015 and has now completed dental school. He had started the long, arduous training to become a maxillo-facial surgeon at the time of this publication.

**Libby van den Bosch.** Libby had returned from Amsterdam in 2015 where she had spent a postgrad year. She was working in London as the Digital Communications Officer for a U.K. charity at the time of this publication.

**Alice van den Bosch.** Alice was born at Kilu'ufi Hospital in 1993. She had to be medevacked to Australia with a respiratory problem. Alice was studying ancient history at university in 2015. She completed a master's degree in Copenhagen and was working at Exeter University at the time of this publication. She was in the process of applying to join a doctoral program.

**Joy Wells and Peter Wells.** Dr. Teresa van den Bosch's parents returned to England after their vacation in Auki. Joy passed away in 2010 and her father, Peter, slipped away peacefully in 2018 at the age of ninety-three.

**Alison Cameron and Colin Cameron.** Paula and I traveled from Japan to Bulgaria in 2004 to visit friends with whom I had taught in Japan. During our stop in England, Alison traveled from Scotland to London to see us. We stayed at the home of Cameron's son in London at that time.

Colin was active in Scotland's effort to become independent from the United Kingdom. He twice ran unsuccessfully for the national parliament. He participated in a round-table discussion concerning the Scottish Government's proposals for an independent Scotland in 2014. Paula and I traveled to London in November 2015 to see the Kansas City Chiefs play at Wimberley Stadium. We traveled to Scotland and spent several days with Colin and Alison after the Chiefs' game.

**David Chetwynd and Stephany Chetwynd.** David was appointed to the position of Solomon Islands chief magistrate and registrar of the High Court in 1991. The couple returned to England in 1993, but they came back to Honiara in 1998. David served as registrar and trained a local magistrate for the position. They left the Solomons during the period of civil unrest, but they returned after the coup.

The Chetwynds moved to Sierra Leone where David assumed the position of master and registrar of the Supreme Court. He held the position in Sierra Leone until 2008. He returned to England and took a position in the Royal Borough of Windsor and Maidenhead.

In 2010, the Chetwynds returned to Solomon Islands for David's position as a judge of the High Court. David assumed a position of registrar of the Supreme Court of Turks and Caicos in 2012. They lived in the capital of Grand Turk until 2014. He was appointed to the Supreme Court of Vanuatu in 2015. He and Stephanie lived in Port Vila at the time of this publication.

**Roger Keesing.** Roger Keesing died suddenly of a heart attack at the Canadian Anthropology Society dance and reception in 1993. He was cremated, and ashes were transferred to the Solomon Islands. The families of his Kwaio associates reportedly accord him the status of an *andalo* or ancestral spirit.

**Ben Burt**, Ben Burt continued working for the British Museum as an anthropologist, educator, and curator in what is now the department of Africa, Oceania, and Americas. He has published museum educational materials and studies of the culture and history of Solomon Islands.

**Dr. Graham and Sheila MacBride-Stewart**. Dr. Graham and Sheila moved to New Zealand in 1996 after their service in the Solomon Islands. Dr. Graham did an M.B.A. in health and population, then retrained in general practice. He taught in the Fiji School of Medicine for three years. They were in Fiji at the time of a military coup, but they never felt threatened. They returned to New Zealand to work in public health. After retiring, they lived as companions to a Cistercian Monastery for six years.

Sheila returns to the Solomons every few years to support Catholic women's groups. The groups and a program for young women were still active after 28 years. She completed her Master of Philosophy degree at Massey University on the movement. She is currently writing a less academic version of her thesis with less text and more pictures. This publication will enable the present generation of Solomon women to read about the heroics of their mothers and grandmothers in breaking down some of the shackles of custom.

Dr. Graham and Sheila are now living in Takapuna, Auckland. They are active in the parish with support from two Christian meditation groups. They organize Holy communion for the sick in one of the local rest homes. They travel back to the United Kingdom every few years to see family and friends including some from their time in the Solomon Islands.

Vincent lives in Auckland and works for Salesforce. Fiona lives in Helensville and has an on-line business focusing on yarns. Aidan lives and teaches in the United Kingdom.

**Bishop Gerry Loft.** Bishop Loft reached retirement age and returned to Auckland, New Zealand to do some parish work. Bishop Loft, Dr. Graham, and Sheila had great plans for their time together in New Zealand, but it was never to be. Bishop Loft passed away unexpectedly in 2007.

**Father Jon Volkers.** Father Jon returned to Holland in 1993 for a hip operation. He returned to work in the Solomons for three more years. When he returned to the Netherlands, he was assigned duties as mission procurator of the Marist Fathers in the Solomons and Bougainville. He also assisted with priestly duties in various parishes around Nijmegen. He was planning on a pilgrimage with the sick in Belgium and a reunion with old students at the time of this publication.

**Father Chris Kamphuis.** Father Chris continued his work in the Solomons until his retirement. He returned to Holland and spent his last years pleasantly reminiscing with Father Jon on their lives in the Solomons. Father Chris died on Easter day in 2006.

**John Roughan.** John continued his position of director of the Solomon Island Development Trust. He passed away October 24, 2013.

**Dr. Arun Menon.** Dr. Arun continued living in Dunedin, New Zealand for some years. When the sexual health doctor in Dunedin retired, Dr. Arun assumed the position. Dr. Arun's service expanded to work in the P.N.G. Highlands where he established sexual health clinics to diagnose and treat HIV/AIDS.

Dr. Arun was appointed director of sexual health for the Townsville Hospital in Townsville, Australia. He won a prestigious national award for innovation in the delivery of sexual health services in Australia and overseas. The Royal Australasian College of Physicians presented Dr. Arun the *Dr. Menonits 2013 Sexual Health Medicine Award for Innovation in Service Delivery in Sexual Health.*

**Paul Hartman.** completed his two-year commitment in Vanuatu and extended for another year. Monique Incitti transferred to Vanuatu during Paul's additional year of service. Paul has taught high school in Colorado Springs for over twenty years.

**Monique Incitti.** Monique completed her two-year assignment in the Solomon Islands. She then extended to serve for a year in Vanuatu. Paul Hartman and Monique married and live in Colorado Springs, Colorado. They have three children, Maggie, Domenic, and Ellie. Monique earned a master's in education – E.S.L. at Regis University in Denver. Paula and I visited Paul and Monique at their home in 2016.

**Bill Wise.** Bill returned to the U.S. after Peace Corps and continued work in accounting. He is married and has converted to Catholicism. Bill is a finance leader and business partner. He demonstrates a passion for operation excellence that informs comprehensive financial management in his business. Bill and his wife have a daughter that was in college and a son that was in high school at the time of this publication.

**Rick Treleaven and Carrie Hooton.** Rick and Carrie returned to the U.S. after Peace Corps service. They divorced in 1994. Paula and I were unable to locate Carrie to get updated information. The last Rick knew, Carrie was a high school French teacher in Portland.

Rick married Kelly in 1996. Kelly lived in Portugal during the years our group was in the Solomons. Kelly and Rick moved to Bend, Oregon in 1999. They travelled extensively. Rick took up climbing mountains for many years and climbed on four continents.

Their lives changed when Kelly had a spontaneous carotid artery dissection in 2010. She can no longer work or do serious traveling. However, she and Rick have gotten to know their local area in greater detail. Rick continues to work long hours. The agency he manages has grown tremendously since he assumed management.

**Margaret and Matt Ottinger.** After leaving the Solomons, Margaret and Matt spent four months backpacking through Asia. When they returned to the U.S., Margaret was hired by the University of Minnesota to work in disability services. Matt started a catering business serving members and guests at the St. Paul Curling Club. Their son, Harvey, was born in 1995. Their daughter, Lila, was born in 1999.

Matt still had the travel bug, but Margaret didn't share his wanderlust. To keep peace in their marriage, Margaret sanctioned Matt leading adventure camping tours in the Canadian Rockies and Alaska for fifteen years. After eight years in Minnesota, Matt returned to university to get his master's in education and a teacher's license. In 2001, they moved to Vermont where Margaret went to work for the University of Vermont and Matt started teaching at Middlebury Union High School.

In 2006, Margaret found her real love and started working with teenagers. She worked at Vergennes High School and Middle School for the next ten years. Unfortunately, Margaret was diagnosed with brain cancer in 2015 and passed away in 2017. Her passing had a profound effect on the Ottinger family.

Matt left the teaching profession after seventeen years and was on a new journey with an unknown destination. During the many trips Margaret and Matt made to Boston for her cancer treatment, they often relived their time in the Solomon Islands. Their Peace Corps service was a true highlight in their lives. Harvey received his Bachelor of Science degree in 2017 from Macalester College in Minnesota. Lila was a sophomore at Simmons College in Boston at the time of this publication.

**Tom Scherer.** Tom took six months traveling home after his Peace Corps service. He obtained employment with the National Marine Fisheries Service (N.M.F.S.) He worked for the N.M.F.S. from 1993 to 1998. He served in Oregon, Hawaii, and Massachusetts.

He earned a master's degree, then transferred to the U.S. Fish and Wildlife Service (F.W.S.) in Corpus Christi, Texas on the campus of Texas A&M. Tom's primary responsibility was as the Texas F.W.S. liaison for the recover team of the endangered Kemp's Ridley sea turtle. Tom retired in 2017, after twenty-nine years of federal service.

Tom's significant other, Kendal, is a natural resource planner with the Texas Parks and Wildlife Department. Tom and Kendal have been a couple for many years. They have a home in Rockport, Texas and a small rancho in the country. They have a bee hive, lots of plants, oak trees, and a nature trail in the country. They enjoy traveling and have seen three total eclipses.

**Patricia Maelado.** We wrote to many of our friends in the Solomon Islands over the years. None of them responded. We sent checks that were never cashed. Simon Buarafi's granddaughter, Patricia, is the only Solomon Islander with whom we are still in contact. Patricia grew to adulthood and moved to Honiara. She is married and works for BLK Investment Co. LTD. BLK Investment Co. is a shipping company whose business includes ownership of a fast ferry that travels to Malaita three times per week.

**Simon Buarafi.** continued to live in Buma. One of my J.O.C.V. students, Yoshi, was assigned to Malaita. Yoshi traveled to Buma and had a picture taken with himself, Simon, and the Buma chief. Simon lived with his son, John, in Buma in his later years. Paula and I sent Simon a letter in 2015. We told him we wanted to visit Malaita soon and asked if we could stay with him. Simon had Patricia Maelado respond by email inviting us to stay at his house. Unfortunately, we were unable to make the trip. Simon passed away in 2016.

**Greg Grainger**. Greg Grainger continued making travel and adventure documentaries. He has numerous distinctions including being a Logie Award winner for "Best News Coverage" and 2011 IAB Awards "Best of Show". He produced the *Making Tracks* campaign for DDB Sydney & Tourism Australia, which won 1st prize for Best of Show during the 2011 IAB Australia Day. Grainger has been being appointed one of Tourism Australia's cultural ambassadors, as part of the "Friends of Australia" program.

**Solomon Islands coup.** Many Malitians continued to migrate to Honiara to secure jobs. Native Guadalcanal residents became increasingly resentful of what they considered intruders. In 1999, a militia group made up of indigenous Isatabus from Guadalcanal formed the Isatabu Freedom Movement. They began terrorizing immigrants from Malaita. The Malaita Eagle Force was formed to defend their interests.

**Andrew Nori.** Albert Nori's brother, Andrew Nori, was quickly recognized as Eagle Force's leader. In June 2000, the Malaita Eagle Force stole police weapons, forced Prime Minister Bartholomew Ulufa'alu to resign, and seized control of Honiara. The rival groups soon agreed to a cease-fire, barely averting a civil war. Although a peace agreement had been signed, warring factions continued to do battle.

The Australian Defense Department organized an expatriate evacuation. Australia also dispatched Special Air Services units to Honiara to secure the country's airport. The evacuation was successful, and hundreds of expatriates left on Australian ships.

Five of my former K.T.I. students were among those expatriates evacuated from the Solomon Islands. These five J.O.C.V.s returned to K.T.I. to see me. They thanked me and attributed my instruction on Solomon Islands' culture as helping them survive their ordeals. I didn't think I deserved such praise, but I could only tell them that I was very happy that they got out alive.

In July 2003, at the request of the prime minister, a 2,250-strong international peacekeeping force led by Australia arrived on the island to restore order. Australia's intervention was highly successful. More than 50 people were killed during the months of fighting. An estimated 20,000 Malitians fled from Guadalcanal to their own island. Andrew Nori died in Honiara in 2013.

**Bougainville Civil War.** The mining operations and income distribution conflicts that were paramount when Paula and I served in Solomon Island, continue to this day. Bougainville Revolutionary Army (B.R.A.) secessionists frequently invaded the Solomon Islands in the 1990s.

In mid-1997, talks were held in Honiara and Burnham, New Zealand resulting in a truce. Monitors from New Zealand, Australia, Fiji, and Vanuatu were subsequently deployed. They reported frequent truce violations. In 2006, the United Nations responded to complaints that mercenaries were still being employed to fight in the conflicts.

The Bougainville government was given control of mining following the March 2015 signing of the *Bougainville Mining Act*. However, the Panguna mine remains closed. As part of the current peace settlement, a referendum on Bougainville independence is scheduled to be held sometime before 2020.

The civil war is recognized as the largest conflict in Oceania since the end of W.W. II. Australian government officials have estimated that between 15,000 and 20,000 people died in the conflict. There were over 60,000 Bougainvilleans living in internally displaced persons' camps by the mid-1990s. Thousands more had fled into the Solomon Islands.

Made in the USA
Middletown, DE
05 January 2023

18989799R00154